PORSCHE
– THE RACING 914s –

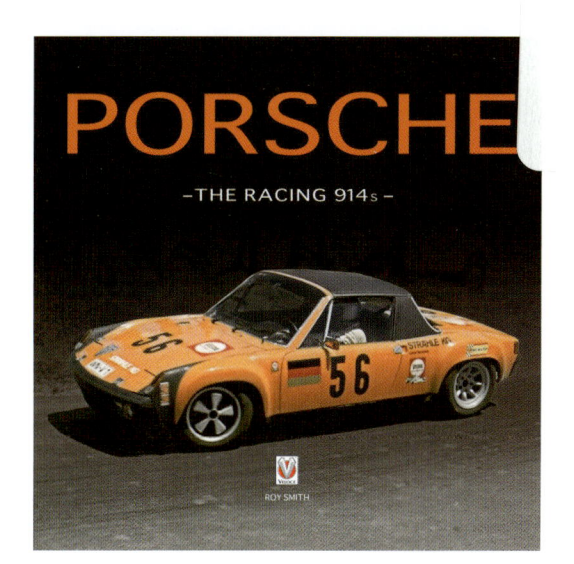

Roy Smith

Other great books and ebooks from Veloce –

General Porsche

Porsche Boxster (Long)
Porsche 356 (2nd Edition) (Long)
Porsche 908 (Födisch, Neßhöver, Roßbach, Schwarz & Roßbach)
Porsche 911 Carrera – The Last of the Evolution (Corlett)
Porsche 911R, RS & RSR, 4th Edition (Starkey)
Porsche 911 – The Definitive History 1963-1971 (Long)
Porsche 911 – The Definitive History 1971-1977 (Long)
Porsche 911 – The Definitive History 1977-1987 (Long)
Porsche 911 – The Definitive History 1987-1997 (Long)
Porsche 911 – The Definitive History 1997-2004 (Long)
Porsche 911 – The Definitive History 2004-2012 (Long)
Porsche 911, The Book of the Air-Cooled – Limited Edition (Long)
Porsche 911SC 'Super Carrera' – The Essential Companion (Streather)
Porsche 914 & 914-6: The Definitive History of the Road & Competition Cars (Long)
Porsche – The Racing 914s – (Smith)
Porsche 924 Carrera, The (Smith)
Porsche 924 (Long)
Porsche 928 (Long)
Porsche 944 (Long)
Porsche 964, 993 & 996 Data Plate Code Breaker (Streather)
Porsche 993 'King Of Porsche' – The Essential Companion (Streather)
Porsche 996 'Supreme Porsche' – The Essential Companion (Streather)
Porsche 997 'Porsche Excellence' – The Essential Companion (Streather)
Porsche Racing Cars – 1953 to 1975 (Long)
Porsche Racing Cars – 1976 to 2005 (Long)
Porsche – The Rally Story (Meredith)

Essential Buyer's Guide Series

Porsche 911SC (Streather)
Porsche 911 Carrera 3.2 (Streather)
Porsche 911 (993) (Streather)
Porsche 911 (964) (Streather)
Porsche 911 (996) (Streather)
Porsche 924 – All models 1976 to 1988 (Hodgkins)
Porsche 928 (Hemmings)
Porsche 930 Turbo & 911 (930) Turbo (Streather)
Porsche 944 (Higgins)
Porsche 986 Boxster (Streather)
Porsche 987 Boxster & Cayman (Streather)

www.veloce.co.uk

First published in 2024 by Veloce, an imprint of David and Charles Limited. Tel +44 (0)1305 260068 / e-mail info@veloce.co.uk / web www.veloce.co.uk
ISBN 978-1-787119-34-5 UPC6-36847-01934-1 © 2024 Roy Smith and David and Charles Limited. All rights reserved. With the exception of quoting brief passages for the purpose of review, no part of this publication may be recorded, reproduced or transmitted by any means, including photocopying, without the written permission of David and Charles Limited. Throughout this book logos, model names and designations, etc, have been used for the purposes of identification, illustration and decoration. Such names are the property of the trademark holder as this is not an official publication. Readers with ideas for automotive books, or books on other transport or related hobby subjects, are invited to write to the editorial director of Veloce at the above address. British Library Cataloguing in Publication Data – A catalogue record for this book is available from the British Library. Design and DTP by Veloce. Printed in India by Parksons Graphics.

PORSCHE

—THE RACING 914s—

ROY SMITH

Contents

Introduction and acknowledgements 5

Forewords by Hurley Haywood and Günter Steckkönig 9

1. Centre of attention The mid-engine idea 11

2. 1967-1976: The road cars Concept – design – politics and production 32

3. The competition begins Racing in Europe 1970 54

4. Good times Racing in Europe 1971 103

5. Rescue: 914/6 GT The first racing fire/safety quick response vehicle 138

6. Privateer time Racing in Europe 1972-1976 155

7. Tarmac and dust The 914 rally story 178

8. Big country Racing in the USA 1970-1975 216

9. What came next USA and Europe 1976-present 254

10. Race records Europe – North America – rallying – hillclimbs 281

Index 319

Introduction and acknowledgements

The first hard cover limited edition book, *Porsche – The Racing 914s*, was found to be more popular than the publisher and author ever imagined. A complete sell-out has meant that there are a lot of fans of this remarkable, and perhaps unlikely racing car that missed out. It was also noted that the chapter on race records could benefit from a revision, contributing to the decision to create this revised soft-cover edition.

To its critics back in 1970, the 914 Porsche was, at best, a mish-mash of ideas and definitely not a proper Porsche. After all, it had Volkswagen parts! But maybe they had forgotten that the iconic Porsche 356 had many VW parts, as well as the 911/912. It is recorded that, in the USA and UK, the idea that the VW Porsche 914 could race alongside the 911 on track was definitely out of order. Thankfully, it would be given a chance.

This is a story that is not just about the works team, which had significant funds to play with, but, as the reader will see, it also features the 'little guys'; the privateers and dealer teams who eventually did most of the development, moulding the 914 into the great little racer it turned out to be. Granted, in its day, the professional rally drivers were not keen; in fact they were downright nervous about driving it at the limit. Yet the records show that 914s were driven to at least 41 class wins and at least 71 positions on the other two steps of the podium, in regional, national and international rallies. On racing circuits, 914s came home first in their class (up-to 2L in Europe – 2.5L in the USA) on more than 120 occasions. In the USA, where they are still to be seen racing regularly, the 914 became the starter race car for many who would later become legendary drivers. Of course, the public's favourite, the Porsche 911, is the champion race winner compared with the 914, but when I interviewed circuit racing drivers, not a bad word was said about the handling or general performance of the 914, except that because its engine was in the middle, it was easy to drive it at 9/10ths, but to drive at 10/10ths you really needed to know what you were doing. The race engines were always powerful, due to the almost limitless tuning possibilities: even a 4-cylinder 2L version could be pushed to produce 250+ bhp. With the 6-cylinder cars, 250bhp was perfectly do-able, but the engine was heavier. The secret for circuit racing the 914, though, was its mid-engine configuration.

In the 1970s, Porsche was setting out to build outright race winners, and this it achieved under the great Norbert Singer, winning 16 times at Le Mans alone! Meanwhile, the little unloved (even within the company) 914 was not to be given the development effort afforded to other models. The only memories most race-following enthusiasts have of significant victories, or that are openly recorded, are the 1-2-3 at the 1970 Marathon de la Route (86 Hours of the Nürburgring), the equal third place on the 1971 Monte Carlo Rally, and the class-winning performances at the 1970 Le Mans 24 Hours and the 1971 Daytona 24 Hours. However, in 1971, the first year of the IMSA GT (GTU) class of racing in the USA, the 914/6 GT of Peter Gregg and Hurley Haywood won the GTU Championship. Then, in 1977, Walter Maas won that year's IMSA GTU Championship in a 914/6 GT, as a private entry, beating all the factory teams who were fielding their latest machinery.

The 914 raised eyebrows because it was different: it had a joint-venture life, part Volkswagen, part Porsche, and it had a mid engine. It was an unusual shape, and initially the VW 1.7L engine did nothing for its performance, though the 6-cylinder 2L Porsche-engined examples and the later Porsche-improved 4-cylinder 2L would make their mark. The 914's development was dogged by inter-company politics and changes in top management in both companies, as well as resistance by the engineers and existing Porsche 911 fans – all things that could have been a recipe for disaster on the sales front. However, again the records are there to see. Between 1969 and 1976, around 119,000 914s were built and sold, though when the 6-cylinder model was killed off in 1972, due to a lack-lustre reception, one might have thought: 'End of story.'

Be prepared to be surprised. Today, originals and variations of the 914 can still be seen racing and rallying in Europe and the USA, just like its better-known sibling. In recent times, the 6-cylinder versions have seen values rocket, and even those 4-cylinder cars that have survived in good condition from a pre-galvanized era are being snapped up: who knows where demand will take us? However, this work is not about the market or values; it's about a car that, in its short life, was controversial; forgotten by many. Now we see interest is booming, its mid-engine configuration used by so many racing sports cars, and leading to the Boxster and Cayman from Porsche. I invite the reader to sit back, settle-in behind the steering wheel, and take to the track, for this study is about all the *racing 914s*.

Acknowledgements

A book like this does not get written by guesswork. It involves the help of many people, a lot of travel, interviews, visiting, and researching in various archives. This means there are also a lot of people to thank, and this is where we will start.

A huge thank you to Porsche Headquarters in Stuttgart: Jens Torner and his colleagues in the Stuttgart Public Relations Historical Archive Department. My grateful thanks, too, for the permission of the company Dr Ing hc F Porsche to print this revised edition and use the images supplied by the Historical Archives for this work. A personal thank you to Günter Steckkönig and Hurley Haywood, who both wrote forewords for the first edition, and are as much a part of the Porsche history now as they were in the heyday of our subject. Thank you to the following, too, for sparing the time and patience to answer my many questions for the first edition, and still valid here: to Rainer Bratenstein, the late Walter Näher, Jürgen Barth, Günter Steckkönig and Roland Kussmaul. Also, and very importantly, Herbert Linge, a man who has been at Porsche from the beginning and seen it all.

Thank you to all who shared their stories and, in many cases, advice about driving the 914 in anger: Gérard Larrousse (France), again Günter Steckkönig and Roland Kussmaul (Germany), James Calvert (UK), Guillermo Rojas and Héctor Rebaque (Mexico), José-María Fernández (Spain), and Ralph Meaney, Wayne Baker, Hurley Haywood, Doc Bundy and Alan Johnson in the USA. Many of these were the young race drivers starting out on their path to success. I also thank Porsche North America for their assistance in pointing me in the right direction for certain facts from the period. Finally, if he is up there somewhere, thank you to the late, great – in fact one of the best rally drivers of them all – Björn Waldegård, whom the author had the pleasure of interviewing just a few weeks before his passing.

Several websites now offer good access for race details; stand-out examples to mention are:

>   www.ultimateracinghistory.com
>   www.racingsportscars.com
>   www.914world.com
>   www.ddk-online.com
>   www.pbase.com/9146gt – Armando Serrano
>   www.stazak.com/914 – Glenn Stazak

To all those who remember, know and knew the Porsche 914, and who had something to contribute, no matter how much or how little, thank you: Porsche fan extraordinaire and great enthusiast John Sanson (whose collection of Porsche archives rivals that of Stuttgart!); Porsche Club Great Britain and 914 Registrar Kevin Clarke; Martin Holmes Rallying; Kremer Porsche; Maxted-Page and Prill in the UK; and the Seiler family; Dave Finch of Raetech; Bill Oursler; János Wimpffen; François-René Alexandre; Brent Martin; Michael Keyser; Dennis Aase; Wayne Baker; Jacques Duval; Vic Elford; José-María Fernández; Filip Fischlein; Elliott Forbes-Robinson; Chris Frank; Oriol Vilanova; Fred Gallagher (for the supply of all the ONS records); Louis Galanos; Jack Gazlay; Wilfried Geerts; Wolfgang 'Gustl' Scheicher; Hurley Haywood; Martin Holmes; Ron Kielbiski; Dave Klym; Paul Kooyman; Jürgen Lasser; Fred Lewis; Brian Long; Enzo Manzo; Ralph Meaney; Derek and Don Meluzio; Noël Messersi; Frans Oestlandt; Tim O'Leary;

Introduction and acknowledgements

Dave Pateman; Joseph Reip; Paul Rogers; Guillermo Rojas; Steve Screaton; Ted Walker; Tom Seabolt; Bill Siegfriedt; Simon Bowrey; Patti Tantillo; Colin Taylor; Christian Vignon; Vincent Vincent; Dan Wildhurt; Tom Winters; Paul Woodbury; Dug Wright; Ron Zitza; Martin Spetz; Daniel Muñiz; Ian McMath; Richard Morgan; and Manuel Medina.

My grateful thanks to Ole-Petter Refslund in Norway and Dominic Smith of Mercedes F1 for helping with translation of many documents in German. Also to car design guru Peter Stevens, who kindly advised about the raison d'être behind mid-engine thinking. Also to Chris Horton and Keith Seume of 911 Porsche World.

Most importantly, I thank Helen, my long-suffering partner, for her unstinting attention to spelling, grammatical correctness and initial proof reading, and for carrying out a considerable amount of translation and research on my behalf into yet another racing car. Following the writing, of course, comes the publishing and that enormous task should never be underestimated; therefore my grateful thanks are due to Rod Grainger and his team at Veloce, for once more having had faith in my work.

Bibliography

16 Porsches – Un piloto: Julio Gargallo by Fernando de la Hoz
Juan Fernández: Cuatro décadas de competición de un deportista ejemplar by Pablo Gimeno and Enrique Coma-Cros
Jägermeister Racing by Eckhard Schimpf
Escudería Montjuich: Afición sin límite by Enrique Coma-Cros and Pablo Gimeno
Die Sportwagenlegende 914 VW-Porsche by Thomas Lang
Herbert Linge: Pionier in Pole-Position by Frank Wiesner
Das Grosse VW-Porsche-Buch by Michael von Klodt
Porsche: Excellence was Expected by Karl Ludvigsen
Professor Porsche's Wars by Karl Ludvigsen
The Porsche Book by Jürgen Barth and Gustav Büsing
Porsche 914 914-6 by Brian Long
Targa Florio – 20th Century Epic by Pino Fondi
Porsche: Engineering for Excellence by Tony Dron
24 Hours Le Mans (official yearbook) by Jean-Marc Teissèdre, Christian Moity and Alain Bienvenu
Time and Two Seats by János Wimpffen

Magazines (period and current):

Christophorus Magazine, Porsche Panorama, Excellence, 911 and Porsche World, GT Porsche, Classic Porsche, Motor Sport, Autosport, Motoring News, Mundo Deportivo

Images:

All image sources are identified by the following codes, in no particular order. Again, my personal thank you to all those credited and whose permission was given to publish, especially permission from Porsche Archives to use any images held by them. The ownership of image rights is to be respected, please. Please note there are images taken by different photographers from the same position within this work. In those instances, selection has been made according to which has the best historical significance for publication. Apologies to those who think an image might be theirs, and another's work is credited. It's just the selection process.

Historical Archive Dr Ing hc F Porsche . . . . (©P)
Historical Porsche images from various sources . . . (P)
Porsche North America . . . . (PNA)
Historical Archive Mercedes Benz . . . . (©M)
Maxted-Page & Prill Archives . . . . (MaxPP)
Simon Bowrey . . . . (SB)
Martin Spetz . . . . (Sp)
Michael Keyser/Bill Oursler . . . . (MK BO)
Michael Keyser . . . . (MK)
Brent Martin . . . . (BM)
Brumos Porsche . . . . (Brumos)
Christian Vignon . . . . (CV)
Christian Descombes . . . . (CD)
Alain Jourdain/François-René Alexandre . . . . . (AJFR)
Alan Johnson . . . . (AJ)
Kremer Porsche . . . . (K)
Norbert Vogel . . . . (NV)
Jürgen Barth . . . . (JB)
Paul Kooyman . . . . (PK)
John Sanson Collection . . . . (JS)
Ron Kielbiski . . . . (RK)
Martin Holmes Rallying . . . . (MH)
Wilfried Geerts . . . . (WG)
David Finch . . . . (DF)
Pete Austin . . . . (PA)
Noël Messersi . . . . (NM)
Vincent Vincent . . . . (Vin)
Archive Targapedia.com
   (Vittorio Giordano, Piergiorgio Ferreri, Enzo Manzo) . (EM)
LAT Photographic archive . . . . (LAT)
Fred Lewis . . . . (FL)
Filip Fischlein . . . . (FF)
Ferret Photographic (Ted Walker) . . . . (Ferret)

Flavien Marçais . . . . (FM)
Jürgen Lasser . . . . (JL)
Nicke Nilsson and RaceFoto . . . . (NN)
Simon Puttick . . . . (SP)
Fred Gallagher . . . . (FG)
José-María Fernández collection . . . . (JMF)
Steve Screaton Collection . . . . (SS)
Luis Reverter . . . . (LR)
Chris Frank . . . . (CF)
Louis Galanos . . . . (LG)
Dave Pateman . . . . (DP)
Jack Gazlay . . . . (JG)
Guillermo Rojas . . . . (Rojas)
Paul Rogers . . . . (PR)
Glenn Stazak . . . . (GS)
James Calvert . . . . (JC)
Richard Morgan . . . . (RM)
Angie Rose . . . . (AR)
Conceptcarz . . . . (CC)
Peter Collins . . . . (PC)
Eckhard Schimpf . . . . (ES)
Roy Smith . . . . (RS)
Unknown . . . . (U)

To all of those who helped me and any whom I may have – horror of horrors – inadvertently missed out, thank you!

Notes
The cars
Several of the 914/6 GTs are in private ownership, where strict confidentiality and privacy have been observed. We have used chassis numbers only where we can be reasonably sure of accuracy; speculation is not entered into.

Horsepower
Throughout this work we will be using the terms hp and bhp as general terms unless otherwise stated; this is because listing and figures were observed to vary in documents in several cases. It is advisable to read the figures quoted as a guide only.

Archive documents
During research for this work the author was given access to the full archives of the 914 projects at Dr Ing hc F Porsche in Stuttgart. Most of the documents are in German, of course, and therefore not practical to reproduce within an English language work. However, with diligent study and careful translation, considerable unpublished information is referred to. Where possible the documents are named and dates given in verification of the event being described.

Important notice
Even in a work where every attempt has been made to obtain permissions and verify comments, statements, data and information, there may still be omissions, miscredits and/or some differences of opinion. I hope the errors are few; everything contained within this work is published in good faith and strictly in the spirit of bringing the history to the reader and to preserve the story of the 914 race cars in the period for future generations, above all other considerations. I apologize here for any unintentional errors or omissions in technical or photographic acknowledgements.

Forewords

By Hurley Haywood and Günter Steckkönig

Hurley Haywood, three-time winner of the Le Mans 24 Hours, twice IMSA GT Champion:

I had won a race with Peter Gregg (Brumos Racing) in a 911, my first big international race at Watkins Glen, in 1969, before duty called and I went off to Vietnam. When I returned from Vietnam in the early part of 1971, I was ready to get back to racing. Peter Gregg had kept me up to speed with racing developments and I had agreed to buy a 914/6 to race in IMSA. I was still processing out of the Army when I first saw and raced the 914/6 at Virginia International Raceway. Peter Gregg was alongside, and together we soon got the label of having the car that was a giant killer. We never qualified very well, but were always a threat for the overall win. The first 914s that I saw were regular ones and I knew what the 914 line-up looked like, but then when I saw the 914/6GT, that was it: this was a real race car. Driving it was great fun, in both rain and dry conditions. All Brumos cars were painted orange in 1971 and 1972 with Brumos Porsche/Audi painted on the side.

Although I had started my racing in 1969 with a 911S, which I loved driving, getting used to a mid-engine car was no problem. It had no bad habits. The racing fans, though, were not so keen on the 914. Too much VW influence, but the bottom line was it started to win races. Both Peter and I were IMSA GTU (under 2.5L) co-champions in '71 with this brilliant little car, well prepared at Brumos, chassis 0315. Right from our first race in the championship at Danville, Virginia, Peter and I were always battling like crazy with the Corvettes and Camaros, and we beat them all. Danville saw our first win in the successful hunt for the championship. We realized then we now had a great car; that mid-engine concept was something really important for Porsche. We started to sell a lot of them because of the racing at this higher level.

However, as was always the case in those days, the 914/6 GT was sold off at the end of the season like all old race cars. It went off to Mexico to Hector Rebaque, whom Peter had loaned another 914/6 on a few occasions in 1971. Both Peter and I lost touch with that car. There were a lot of improvements going into the 911 models for 1972, as Porsche has always had the 911 as the benchmark for their efforts, so it was not hard to understand that they wanted us to return to race a 911 in 1972. We went on to win the IMSA championship again that year.

One day, many years later, a friend called and said I think your 914 is sitting in a field with a tree growing through the floorboards! We sent our crew chief down and he confirmed it was the car. So we bought it and trailered it back home, put it through a complete restoration and it now sits alongside the 1972 championship 911 in our Brumos showrooms in Jacksonville. I often get to race it in historic races, and these days the 914 is looked upon with as much passion as the 911s of that period. I was very pleased when Roy

Porsche The Racing 914s

Hurley Haywood – three-time winner of the Le Mans 24 Hours, twice IMSA GT Champion.

Günter Steckkönig – test driver and multiple GT class winner with the 914/6 in Europe in the 1970s.

asked me to write a foreword for this book – the first time anyone has made the effort to record the racing history of the car that really started my driving career, which continues to this day.

Hurley Haywood
Jacksonville, Florida, USA

Günter Steckkönig, test driver and multiple GT class winner with the 914/6 in Europe in the 1970s:

During 1969/70 a small team was set up at Porsche to build a bespoke race and rally version of the 914/6. Step-by-step improvements were conceived and realised, specifically resolving problems with the type of engine, transmission, cooling, reinforcements of suspension and reduction of weight, especially in the body. Testing was intensive, and all the mechanics and drivers involved took turns to drive them. I was in the middle of it all, but then just as 'young Steckkönig.' It was a very difficult time because the name Porsche meant the 911 and now we had got a new car; a completely different car. I think maybe it was Strähle who said OK, let's try this new car. He bought a series production 914 and built a race car step-by-step in his workshop in Schorndorf, with a kit of special parts from Porsche. Linge (Herbert) drove a 911 for Strähle during 1970. Then in the latter part of the year he decided it was time to stop racing and brought me into the Strähle team. That's how I started my driving with Strähle, and it started with the 914. I can say that was a fantastic time, because the 914 was being developed more and more. Success had been achieved even from the earliest races in 1970. In June at the 1970 Le Mans the French-entered Sonauto car achieved victory in the GT class and 6th overall, driven by Chasseuil/Ballot-Léna. Then, in August, Porsche took the top three places at the Nürburgring on the Marathon de la Route with the 914. I was in the driving team in the Group 4 car No 2 with Claude Ballot-Léna and Nicolas Koob; we finished 3rd overall after the 86-hour race. In October 1970 at the Österreichring 1000km, I took victory with Prince Ferfried von Hohenzollern in the GT category, driving the Strähle-entered 914/6. I remember Mr Strähle, who was a rally driver, often used to tell us to drive the car on the road if we were going to a race at Hockenheim which is not far from Schorndorf. A lot of people then used to have small trailers, but he used to say it was normal for us to drive with the race car. Be careful if you see a police car, though! Then when we got to the track everyone would ask where our trailer was; they were quite surprised when I told them I drove it there. The 914/6 was then quite competitive and we did a lot of testing and races with it, including some fun at the Targa Florio, which you can read about in this book.

Many victories also came in the States, and I think with some more development time the successes could have been much more widespread, because the foundations were in place. I'm glad Roy has now written a book which documents the racing 914/6 story in great detail. It's a forgotten car in the general history of motorsport.

Günter Steckkönig
Stuttgart

1

Centre of attention
The mid-engine idea

When one comes to analyse mid-engine racing cars over the years, it is with some surprise that one finds only a few examples before the 1950s, whereas just ten years later the mid-engine concept was taken to be the only real way for race cars to gain the best of all worlds in terms of aerodynamics, weight distribution, centre of gravity, polar moment of inertia and, that all-important criterion for a racing car, balance. We can add to the list power-to-weight ratio, because it is the management of that ratio that affects acceleration, braking and cornering characteristics. Perhaps the thing that impacts most is the position of the centre of gravity; the famous balance point well known to car designers that varies from one car to another, depending on where the weight is put. It may well, as in all early race cars, not be near the ideal – that is, the middle of the car. It is not by whim that all successful race cars would switch to the concept of mid-engine; it is still the favoured solution today, not only in the top Formula, F1, but also in the highest category of sports racing cars, LMP 1 (Le Mans Prototype 1).

Whilst it may seem obvious today, we need to consider how Porsche arrived at the creation of a mid-engined road car in the 1960s, the 914, returning again to the mid-engine concept in recent times with the Boxster and Cayman production cars.

What is the raison d'être of a mid-engine configuration? The reader may already know about a thing known as the polar moment of inertia. For the uninitiated, it is not an Antarctic earthquake, but something crucial to the performance of a racing car. It brings into play the considerations of weight and its distribution at the various points between the wheels and around the car. The further a heavy part of the car is from the centre of gravity, the greater the polar moment of inertia. The greater the polar moment of inertia, the higher resistance there is to a change of direction. The lower the polar moment of inertia, the less resistance there is. Ever driven a Kart (Go-Kart)? That is the epitome of a perfect low-resistance fast-reacting chassis, because it has a low polar moment of inertia. However, a Kart is so reaction-sensitive that its polar moment of inertia is too low for a normal road or race car. In a racing car, we are looking for the optimum, not only in straight-line and directional stability, but also in fast direction changes. With modern high-downforce race cars, aerodynamics are also involved, of course, but in this work we are concerned first with the placement of weight, meaning the engine, gearbox and driver/co-driver – the heavy bits. It stands to reason that the best solution is to place them between the front and rear wheels, ideally equidistant front to rear. We do not know when Dr Ferdinand Porsche first realized this, but someone else had certainly thought of it in the early years of the 1920s: one Dr Edmund Rumpler, who designed and built a car named the Tropfenwagen. But let us go back to the dawn of motoring: though

Porsche The Racing 914s

The 2014 championship-winning Formula 1 Mercedes, regarded by many technical pundits as the most effective F1 car ever. Mid-engine, of course. (The green dye at the rear is for aerodynamic analysis.) Silverstone, 2014. (RS)

Also 2014: the state-of-the-art Porsche mid-engined hybrid LMP1 sports racing car going out on track for the first time under racing conditions. Porsche returned to sports car racing in 2014 after a break of nearly 15 years. (RS)

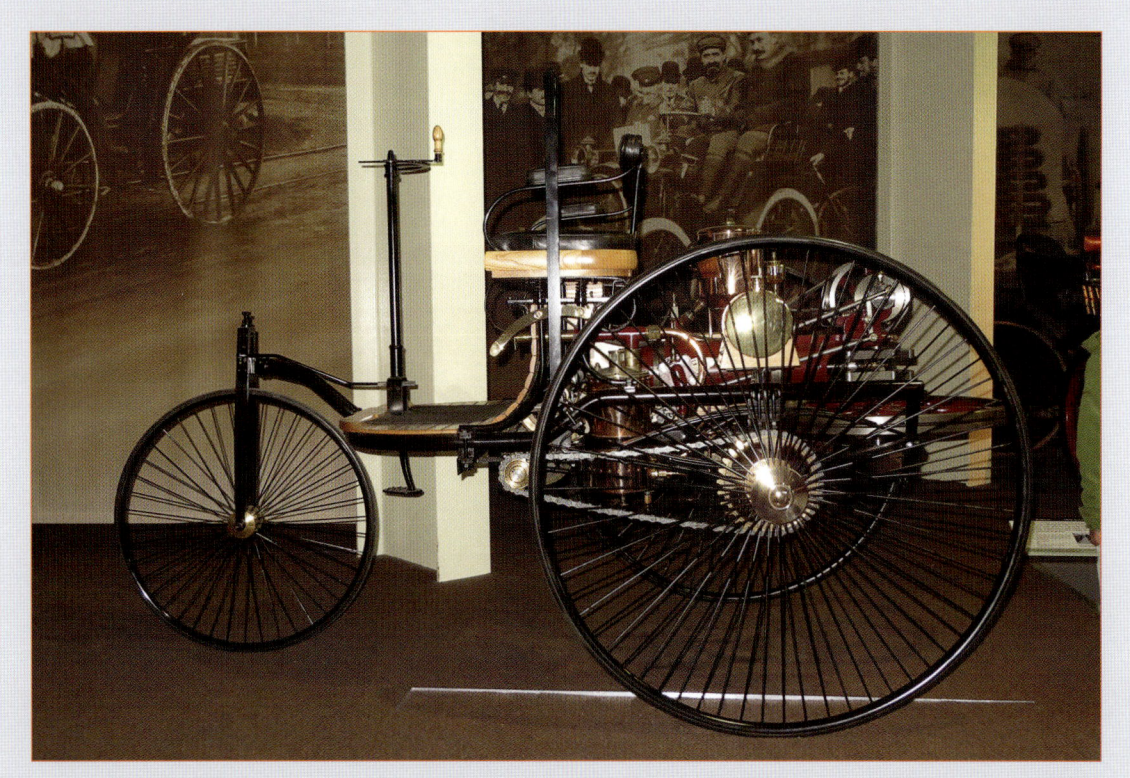

First Benz engine. (RS)

it is a rather tenuous link, it is here that we see the first recognized petrol-engined motor vehicle, the Benz Patent Motorwagen, which appeared in 1885. Its motive drive was in the back of the vehicle, behind the structure supporting the seat. Liquid fuel was the combustible propellant for the engine, which was started by turning a huge flywheel.

Karl Benz himself, credited as originator of the petrol-engined vehicle, wasn't so keen on going fast, but others were, and we see the names of De Dion-Bouton, Peugeot, Panhard, Levasseur, for example, begin to emerge. And along with those names came a new competition – a proper race, over several hundred miles at speed. The overall victor for the fastest time in the first race of its kind, held in 1895, Paris-Bordeaux, with the requisite passengers on board, was the No 16 car of a Monsieur Koechlin in a time of 59h 48min. His Peugeot had its engine in the back. So we see mid/rear engines feature right from the start of motoring. Indeed, in the Paris-Amsterdam-Paris race held 7-13 July 1898, a 6hp Mors driven by a Mr Levegh had a rear-mounted V-shaped in-line engine that drove through belts to change gears, and in the 1899 Tour de France Automobile, Monsieur Gabriel, driving a rear-engine four-cylinder Decauville, took victory in the voiturette class, ahead of two more Decauvilles in the same class in 2nd and 3rd, after 2175km of incredible terrain! It is also known that the company Nesselsdorfer Wagenbau-Fabriks-Gesellschaft AG built a car called the Rennzweier, a 12hp race car, in 1900. (This company would later morph into Tatra; a young Hans Ledwinka, later to become famous as a designer, was then in the workshops.) Its engine was in what could be called a mid-chassis location, behind the driver. Most of the competition in the new world of motorsport, though, with a few notable exceptions, would turn to front engine in the coming years for the obvious reasons of cooling and accessibility.

In this book we will not be covering the complete history of the cars of Ferdinand Porsche, which is adequately covered by many other eminent works. Instead, we turn immediately to the mid-engine Porsche story.

Dr Ferdinand Porsche had left the Austro Daimler Company where he had been technical director, creating aero engines, motorized military equipment, boat engines and, after his time first as an apprentice then as a designer with the Lohner Company, showing his incredible ability to design and develop at a prolific rate. He had met and worked throughout the war with one Karl Rabe, and it was he who took over from Porsche at Austro Daimler. Already famous throughout the motor industry, and well known in Austria, Porsche's path following the First World War led to Daimler-Motoren-Gesellschaft in Stuttgart. It was here that he bumped into the aforementioned Dr Edmund Rumpler and his Tropfenwagen: they had been acquainted already during Porsche's time at Austro Daimler. Rumpler was now working with the Benz Company.

It could be that this was the point when Dr Ferdinand had a eureka moment. (The Tropfenwagen is worth a story in itself, but not here. If readers would like to know more, I would refer them to Karl Ludvigsen's works about the history of Mercedes-Benz, and, indeed, his equally enlightening story *Professor Porsche's Wars*.) Rumpler was ahead of his time, and had gone to the Benz Company in Mannheim with his ideas to enlist its help with development. Daimler had connections with Benz, and Ferdinand Porsche, as the new technical director and a member of the Board of Daimler-Motoren-Gesellschaft, we can assume in view of what comes later, is likely to have seen the car and been impressed.

Dr Ferdinand had joined Daimler-Motoren-Gesellschaft at a time when economic conditions in Germany were becoming desperate. Rampant inflation had driven the economy to ruin, and his appointment was not popular amongst Daimler employees. The Benz Rumpler car, the Tropfenwagen, would drift off the scene, although perhaps not entirely as, in 1926 Daimler-Motoren-Gesellschaft united with the Benz Company to create Daimler-Benz-AG, and Dr Ferdinand Porsche would lead the company's design team to a new range of Mercedes-Benz cars. However, the idea of an engine in the back of the car was not featured in any of his creations at that time – everyone in the motor industry was producing front-engine designs.

Even in a period of severe austerity, there were still those who could afford the best, and Dr Ferdinand's models met their needs. However, in spite of greatly influencing the development of Daimler-Benz in that period, he was to fall out with other members of the Board in 1928, and left to join the Austrian company Steyr-Werke AG as technical director, although he stayed there for only a short period. A merger took place between Austro Daimler, his old company, and Steyr-Werke. It was now a case of too much top management, and with the world going deeper into depression, he was asked to relinquish his highly paid position.

It was at this point in his life that Porsche was considering forming his own independent design company, and he chose Stuttgart as the most likely location to provide the work he was looking for. The establishment 'Dr Ing hc F Porsche GmbH, Design and Consulting Services for Engines and Vehicles' was born in 1930 and officially inaugurated in Stuttgart on 25 April 1931. Ferdinand's son, 'Ferry' (christened Ferdinand Anton), then 22 years old, also joined him as one of the first employees, at the same time as the very talented Karl Rabe. On 31 October 1931 Erwin Komenda,

Porsche The Racing 914s

Almost a sports car: by 1922/23 the mid-engined Rumpler Tropfenwagen was racing. Rumpler's car, now known as a Benz, carried a riding mechanic! (©M)

European Grand Prix Monza, 9 September 1923. Three Benz Tropfenwagens were racing; this one, driven by Ferdinando Minoia, would come home 4th overall; a second, driven by Franz Horner, would finish but not classify, whilst the third, driven by Willy Walb, did not finish. (©M)

previously at Steyr, but who had moved to Daimler-Benz, also took a leap of faith and joined the fledgling company. In August the same year, Porsche Design had filed its first patents for a torsion bar suspension system, a development that would influence generations of automobiles to come.

Disturbances in world order, ongoing since the First World War, were to affect what was also a period of great division within the motor industry. Arising out of a number of the many changes was the establishment of the Auto Union Company, created in 1932 by the amalgamation of Horch, Audi, Wanderer and DKW. Auto Union became a client of Porsche Design, and in 1933 Auto Union's management would employ the Porsche Design Bureau to take responsibility for monitoring, developing and coordinating the activities of their designers for a new racing car project. It would be headed up by Dr Ferdinand's son, Ferry.

There is an interesting little story as to how this came about. It seems that in 1925 the famous racing driver Hans Stuck (Sr) met up with an old friend who had invited him out for a day's shooting. During that day, Stuck was introduced to one Adolf Hitler. Daimler-Benz had stopped racing, but Stuck wanted to continue, and it seems he told Hitler this. Many years later (exact date uncertain), when Adolf Hitler was setting his sights on becoming President (Chancellor) of the German nation, he remembered the earlier meeting with Stuck and what he had said, and gave him a call. Hitler told Stuck he wanted to bring motor racing back to life in Germany for propaganda purposes; Stuck pricked up his ears. As history records, in January 1933 Adolf Hitler became the new German Chancellor in a somewhat dubious election. The reign of the Third Reich had begun, and at the February Berlin Motor Show it was announced that 500,000 reichmarks would be made available to the manufacturer that could build an all-German racing car to the then-new 540kg formula – a Grand Prix car.

Stuck was asked to make a list of requirements for a suitable car. Having been closely involved with Daimler-Benz whilst Ferdinand Porsche was in residence, he knew that Porsche had opened up his new design company, and made contact. The two put their heads together and called on Baron Klaus von Oertzen, Managing Director of the Auto Union Company. Ferdinand Porsche already had a design for a mid-engine racing car on the shelf at his home that he had been involved with privately for a wealthy and enthusiastic amateur driver. Begun in 1926, the project had been put on hold due to costs. (As it happened, Ferdinand Porsche had also been acquainted with Hitler at the time of the German Grand Prix held at the Avus Ring that same year (1926), where Mercedes-Benz took victory. The meeting was brief, but it had been Hitler who had sought out his Austrian compatriot, so influential to the Austrian motor industry when Hitler was a young man – Hitler was a big fan of motorsports.) Now, in 1933, Porsche saw a chance that the well-funded Third Reich might be able to put some business his way. With the Porsche design office having Auto Union amongst its clients, Dr Ferdinand now offered his mid-engine design idea to Hitler. The Daimler-Benz company had hoped to get a sole contract for the new racing car with their Mercedes marque, but it is said that Ferdinand Porsche persuaded Hitler at a meeting in May 1933, with von Oertzen and Stuck present, that two German teams would bring even greater publicity/propaganda. Hitler, who saw Porsche as an Austrian hero, agreed.

It was decided: Auto Union would build the Porsche-designed mid-engine racing car. They would build it at the Horch works in Zwickau, where Auto Union's business manager was Adolf Rosenberger. Rosenberger also had some experience of a mid-engined car, because in the 1920s, coincidentally, he had occasionally raced the Benz (Rumpler) Tropfenwagen. Porsche's so-called P-Wagen had found a home! It became the Auto Union Type A. Adolf Rosenberger, from a Jewish family, did not see it come to fruition, choosing to leave Germany soon after Hitler rose to Chancellor.

The mid-engine concept in a race car was here to stay, and entered a new phase of development. Of course, as is well known, from 1934 through to the last-ever race for that era of Grand Prix cars, the Yugoslavian Grand Prix, the Auto Unions were the main competitors to Mercedes-Benz, although it must be said that there were few other challengers! That last race was held on a fateful date, 3 September 1939, remembered as the official commencement of World War II. Adolf Hitler's Third Reich had wasted no time in developing its aims during the 1930s, which included many new ministries – among them the Reichsverband der Automobilindustrie (the German Reich Automobile Industry Association). As well as the Auto Union work, Porsche, meanwhile, had continued to seek contracts for car and component design, and in 1933 the NSU Vereinigte Fahrzeugwerke AG visited Porsche with an idea to create a small, 'working man's' car. Porsche Design was given a free hand, and what came out was the all-new Porsche Type 32, its air-cooled engine placed in the back.

The design, a platform chassis mounted on a central tube, featured torsion bar suspension with trailing arms and swing axle at the rear. But most recognisable was the body shape, for here we see the first ideas of the car that would also become an icon. This design was presented to NSU on 10 November 1933. Two prototypes in wood and steel were built by the Heilbronn-based

Porsche The Racing 914s

Dr Ferdinand Porsche surveys his design company's new creation, the Auto Union mid-engined racing car. (©P)

Here we see a later, but in principle the same design, Type C Auto Union (Porsche Type 22). Mid-engine, 16 cylinders, V format at 45˚, 6L. The first units produced 295hp from 4.4L. It was first driven in 1934 by Willy Walb, who had also been involved with the Tropfenwagen when at Mercedes. (©P)

Centre of attention The mid-engine idea

Drauz organisation. From these came a third prototype with an all-steel body, made by Reutter; based, like Porsche, in Stuttgart. Developments continued, though NSU lacked enthusiasm. Via a mutual acquaintance, Jakob Werlin, Ferdinand Porsche came into contact with Hitler again when the new State organisation, the Reichsverband der Automobilindustrie, was created. The Reichsverband der Automobilindustrie signed a contract with Dr Porsche's design company in 1934 to develop a small car – a people's car. With the contract in hand, the latent NSU project became what was to be the first Volkswagen. The prototypes were driven to Munich in Bavaria by Ferry Porsche and Ferdinand's lawyer, son-in-law Anton Piëch, to be demonstrated in front of Hitler. This direct approach upset the people from the Reichsverband der Automobilindustrie, as they wanted Porsche to go through them, and the prototypes received intensive criticism from the organisation. Porsche, though, pressed on, and in 1936-37, after a lot of minor adjustments and extensive testing, the famous shape that we know today was ready for the market. A company was set up to handle the design and production of Hitler's 'Volkswagen' (people's car): the Gesellschaft zur Vorbereitung des Deutschen Volkswagens. Ferdinand Porsche himself was to receive a one mark royalty on every car made.

Since its inception in 1931, the Porsche Design Bureau had been extremely successful and profitable: so much so that a new establishment was set up, not only to design but also to build and test vehicles. The site chosen was in Zuffenhausen, to the north of the centre of Stuttgart. The date: June 1938. Karl Rabe would manage the creation of the new car, its body shape created by Erwin Komenda, and under the guidance of Porsche a new engine was designed by employee Franz Reimspiess. It was a flat, 'boxer' four-cylinder air-cooled unit: the engine that would go into the millions of VWs that came after.

As World War II loomed and Hitler's ambitions eventually forced the world into what was arguably the darkest period of the 20th century, all German industry was compulsorily taken over by the demands of the Third Reich. This included the fledgling Volkswagen Company, otherwise known as Volkswagenwerk. There is a long and detailed history concerning the finance of the project for a people's car using a government-instigated 'crowd-funding' idea (author's note: there is nothing new!), but as we are concerned

The beginnings of the Porsche Type 32: a platform chassis mounted on a central tube featured torsion bar suspension. (©P)

Testing the prototypes in the Alps in September 1936. (©P)

primarily with mid-engine concepts, the reader might like to look up the KDF Wagen story via the web or in print. Volkswagenwerk and the Porsche Design Company operated throughout the war period, mainly designing or producing military vehicles. Dr Porsche's designs and ideas were to feed the Third Reich's war machine with engines for aircraft, tanks, amphibious vehicles, and were even ordered to construct rocketry components through to the end of the war in 1945. (Again, the author draws the reader's attention to the aforementioned works by Karl Ludvigsen for the full story of this military period. We are concerned here with racing cars.) Interestingly, one project that had to be shelved when the Third Reich entered the scene was an exhaust-driven turbocharger for the VW air-cooled engine. As the reader may know, the turbo would not arrive at Porsche in the 911 model until 1964.

The Porsche Design Company in Stuttgart and its offices, which had been hastily moved to Gmund, Austria, in 1944 to escape the infernos caused by Allied bombing, had started to find its feet by 1948, and we see the first signs of a car about which so many books have been written: the legendary Porsche 356. One man, who will appear frequently in our story, remembers the period – Herbert Linge:

"I first started at Porsche, training to be a mechanic, in 1943, during the War. But at that time I was not making anything serious; it was a school, an apprenticeship. When I left normal school, I was not good enough to go straight to engineering college so I had to do two years Ausbildung (training) to be ready for the next stage; normally I was supposed to finish in 1945. Porsche as a company was even then a very 'social' place to work, but when the war ended before I had finished my training, the plan to take my exams never worked out because of the war and its aftermath. During '45 and '46 many people came back from the war and it became a case of too many people and not enough jobs. Sometimes, because of these newcomers, there was only work for a short period at a time. We guys, about 20 of us in Stuttgart, were put to work for the American army, repairing jeeps.

"Luckily, because I had been at Porsche for a while, I was known to a man by the name of Hans Klauser, who was a link man with Porsche in Gmünd, Austria, where Porsche was to build the first cars. After the war, Klauser asked me and four other guys to go to Baden-Baden, in the French sector, where the old Professor Dr Ferdinand Porsche had been requested to go to design and build a car for the French government." Germany was split into sectors directly after the war: Stuttgart was under the control of the American army, while Baden-Baden was controlled by the French Occupation Forces. Herbert Linge continues: "When we got there, we found he had been arrested by the French! We didn't know what to do, so we went to the French officials and told them why we were there, and they gave us a big garage, saying, 'We own about 20-25

Volkswagens. You will be our service mechanics.' So we started to work on these and looked after them until 1948, when we heard that the Porsche family and many of the workers in Austria were planning to come back to Stuttgart."

In the meantime, Herbert Linge had gone to work with the Hahn Company, one of the largest Volkswagen dealers – more of them later. Hoping he could get back into Porsche when the company regrouped in Stuttgart, Herbert Linge continues: "I was able to rejoin Porsche in 1949. They were already very close to the Reutter body manufacturing company, and there I was, sent to work with Erwin Komenda." Reutter is another company we will hear more of as our story progresses. Herbert Linge: "It was a small office and workshop; we had no tools, just a small place to start work, nothing else. I had to bring my own tools from home and we started to design and make the foot pedals for a new Porsche: the first new car, foreseen as what we now call a mid-engine design."

The mid-engine concept had been in planning at Porsche in Austria. However, finances were extremely tight in the days directly after the war and little could be done to move the project forward. Then a fairy godmother came their way – although she brought mixed blessings. The Porsche design office had received a request to build a racing car (eventually identified as the Type 360) for a gentleman by the name of Piero Dusio, who had funded and founded the newly formed Cisitalia Company. The design work would provide the financial input to help the cash-strapped Porsche Design Company make the progress it needed and distance itself from utility vehicles in favour of car development.

At that time, as already mentioned, the Porsche family faced a major problem when Dr Ferdinand and his son-in-law Dr Anton Piëch were arrested in Baden-Baden by the French authorities in December 1945, when they went there to discuss the design of a new car. Now the family faced serious financial problems when they were asked to pay a huge bail fee to get Dr Ferdinand out of prison.

It must be remembered that, during the war, Porsche had been part of the manufacturing effort of the Third Reich and its requirement for military vehicles. This alone would have made the company and its directors a target following the cessation of hostilities. It was then some months since the war had ended. Ferry Porsche, in Gmund, had also been arrested, held for a shorter time and released in July 1946. The complete story of this period can also be read in several other works, and, again, it is not within the scope of this book to go any deeper.

The family decided that part of the money from Dusio for the new design should be used to obtain the release of both Dr Ferdinand and Dr Anton Piëch, and they eventually returned to the company. Karl Rabe and Erwin Komenda had continued with design work. The Dusio Cisitalia single-seater story is shrouded in dramas, but suffice to say here it was a mid-engine Grand Prix car that unfortunately never raced. This was hardly down to the design of Porsche, but more attributable to the up-and-down nature of Cisitalia's financial situation, a company in Buenos Aires named Auto-ar, and, especially, the aforementioned Mr Dusio, who was to liquidate the company and give the one and only Grand Prix car to Argentina's President Perón, a racing fan, who put it in his private museum.

By December 1946, at Porsche Konstructionen GmbH in Gmund, work was continuing on component designs for other people. Cars were never far from Porsche's attention, though, and by the middle of 1947, with the Cisitalia project in full swing, Karl Rabe and Ferry Porsche were pondering the design of a two-seater sports car based on Volkswagen parts. The first drawings of the new car, called the Type 356, are dated 17 July 1947. The drawing on page 21 demonstrates that the engine was originally planned to be ahead of the rear axle.

The 356.001 was built in Austria, and this mid-engined car received its Carinthian state (the area in which Gmund was situated) roadworthiness approval certificate on 8 June 1948. The design drew upon the ideas of a car known as the Type 114 that had been drawn up just before the start of World War II. The 114 was seen as a sports version of the people's car –the Volkswagen Beetle – the design being drafted by Karl Frölich. A wooden model had been made in 1938, designated a study for a competition car. In the sketches the engine was shown as being ahead of the gearbox and differential. Interestingly, the thinking was to install a V10 1.5L engine.

The famous 356.001 had that important feature for the future: it was a 'Porsche' car, designed with a mid-engine configuration.

However the Volkswagen components on which the new Porsche was relying did not lend themselves to regular series production with this engine layout. The engineers were obliged to turn the whole engine/gearbox/differential unit round the other way for ease of manufacture, putting the engine at the back. With this layout, the required items from the VW suspension fitted perfectly, and 356.002 was created in this format. Whilst Ferry Porsche was keen to go racing, in the years that followed the Porsche family management in general preferred to concentrate on 356 production rather than create anything new for competition.

There is an interesting hint of what might have been the future and even the not-yet-dreamed-of 914 model when Dr Ferdinand 'Ferry' Porsche is recorded as saying in an interview to *Porsche*

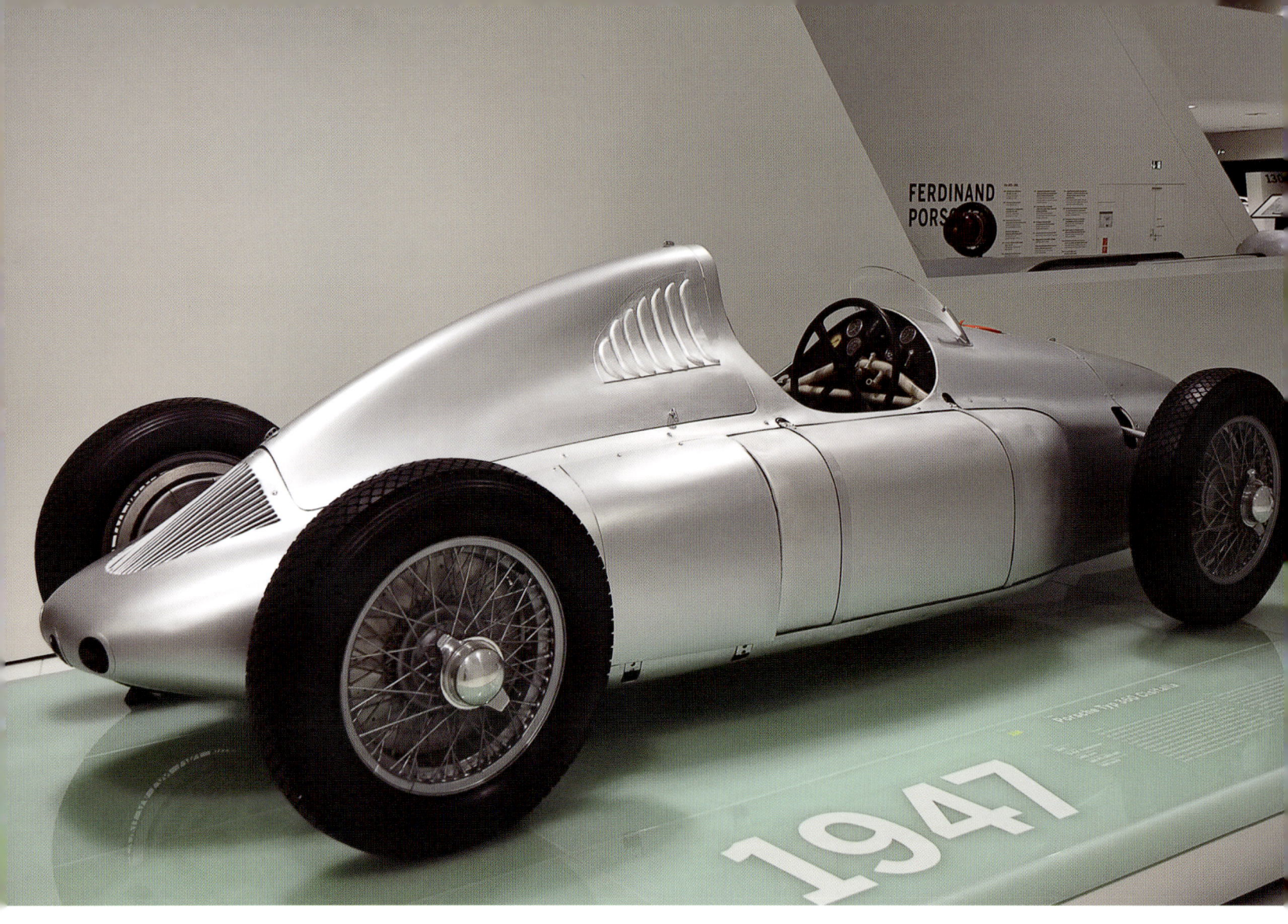

The mid-engined Cisitalia can be seen today at the Porsche Museum in Stuttgart. (©RS)

Panorama magazine in 1979: "It was an old dream of mine. In the last years before war broke out, in 1938 and 1939, we wanted to develop a small sports car based on the Volkswagen. But we were told then that a state-owned firm couldn't deliver parts for private business use. So we developed our own 1.5L sports car along the lines of the Auto Union racer. This had a mid-mounted engine, an in-line five, such as Auto Union uses in today's Audi. Ours, however, featured dual overhead camshafts and hemispherical combustion chambers. The gearbox was behind the rear axle and three (people) could sit abreast in the front, with the driver and steering wheel in the middle or on the left. When war came, we had to set aside all such plans and drawings."

The first Porsches to race were the aluminium coupé versions of the 356 built at Gmund, to save the cost of developing something new. Except for that first 356.001, the 356 competition cars were all rear-engined. All the road cars prevailed with rear engines favoured over the mid-engine design, and along with the Gmund coupés received many updates in engine development and chassis tuning,

Centre of attention The mid-engine idea

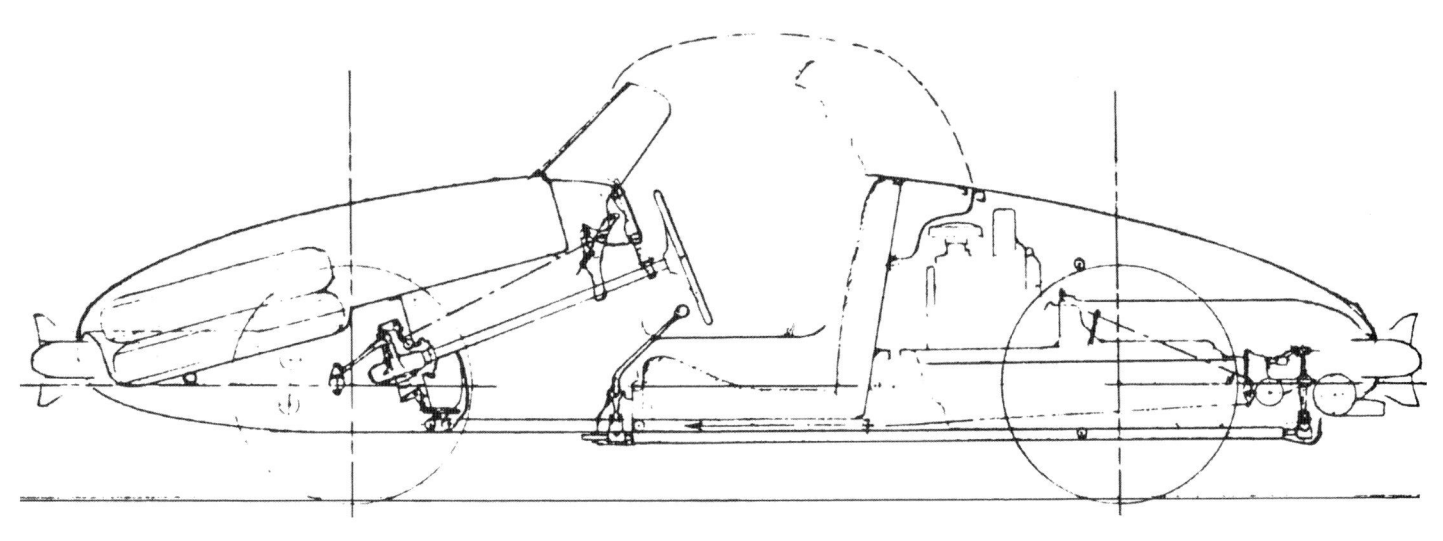

The 1947 sketch, clearly showing the mid-engine concept. (©P)

becoming extremely successful on the race track, and leading to a significant demand from many private racing teams for Porsche sports cars to race.

The first postwar Le Mans 24 Hours took place in 1949. Since the start of this type of racing in 1923, all entries had carried their motive units in the front – pulling rather than pushing power, so to speak. But in 1949 the arrival of a new type of car saw the rear-engine 4 CV Renault, driven by Camille Hardy and Maurice Roger, break the mould with its little 759cc engine; unfortunately they were obliged to retire seven hours into the race. In 1950 Jean Sandt and Hervé Coatalen took their 759cc 4 CV Renault to 24th place overall and first in the up-to-1100cc class, covering 2314.41km at an average speed of 96.433km/h. By comparison, the overall winner of the 1950 race, a mighty front-engined 4.5L Talbot Lago T26 GS, covered 3465.12km at an average speed of 144.38km/h. So what, you might think: big car beats little car, no surprise. However, there were already signs of a change in engine layout for racing cars, which gained ground when that same year at Le Mans a car was seen which signalled revolutionary thinking. First, it was diesel powered, and second, it had a mid-engine installation – a layout that followed the ideas of the Dr Ing hc F Porsche GmbH Company. The Le Mans mid-engined car, though, driven by Pierre Veyron and François Lacour, had nothing to do with Porsche: it was in fact the creation of MAP (Manufacture d'Armes de Paris). The four-cylinder, horizontally

The early signs, 1938: a wooden model study Type 114, a sports car based on the VW. The project was shelved in September 1938 as hostilities loomed. (©P)

21

Porsche The Racing 914s

356.001: its first version had a mid-engine layout. (©P)

The Type 114 would rise from the drawing board with a streamlined aluminium body, the whole being described as the Type 64. Here we see Austrian Otto Mathé with the only surviving example on the Coppa d'Oro in the Dolomites in July 1952. (©P)

The original mid-engine installation, the first Porsche-created road car with this concept. (©P)

Centre of attention The mid-engine idea

opposed, water-cooled diesel engine of nearly 10L didn't last very long: it gave up the ghost, coincidentally, also at seven hours, as had the first rear-engine car at the great race.

Porsche, having progressed sufficiently in the years since the war, decided it would enter the Le Mans race in 1951 for the first time with its trademark rear-located air-cooled 1086cc flat-4 unit in the new design, the Type 356. The Le Mans-entered car was in fact one of the rear-engined Gmund coupés. Auguste Veuillet (later to run the French importer team Sonauto) and Edmond Mouche took the new car to 20th overall and 1st in the up-to-1100cc class. A first victory had been chalked up, just as Renault had done in 1949. It was the start of a mighty adventure, though mid-engine cars from Porsche at Le Mans were still a few years off.

Since his father had created the torsion bar suspension system in 1931 and put it on the new Auto Union Grand Prix car a few years later, the die had been cast. Porsche would forever more go racing – it was in the Porsche family blood. The 356 engine behind the rear axle line was fine for road cars and gave easy access for mechanical attention, but in the mind of Ferry Porsche and Karl Rabe, his long-time faithful colleague and expert chassis designer, there was a better engine/axle configuration for racing. Over the years, Ferry Porsche had become acquainted with one of his

The 10L flat mid-engine four-cylinder water-cooled diesel MAP (Manufacture d'Armes de Paris) of Pierre Veyron and François Lacour. (FM)

future key players, who had become a good friend. This was Baron Huschke von Hanstein, already by that time a well-known and very capable motorsport competitor. After WWII he had been brought into Volkswagen at Wolfsburg and then relocated to Porsche. Von Hanstein would play an important role, being on good terms with a newly appointed (1950) Volkswagen agent, Walter Glöckler. Glöckler was a racer; he knew what Porsche was doing, but he felt he could do better on the racing scene with a better-balanced car. He believed in and turned to the mid-engine concept. Herbert Linge again: "He [Glöckler] started in 1948, using VW parts to make his own racing car. Glöckler was in very close contact with Porsche and he actually made the first Porsche Glöckler, a good car; it had the engine in front of the gearbox and differential. I know the car very well, because Max Hoffman later bought it, taking it to America, and I was sent there to take care of it. He ended up winning many races against much bigger cars; the Jaguar XK 120s, etc."

At the same time others, one of whom was Petermax Müller, another VW dealer, also chose to turn round a VW engine/gearbox/diff unit to place the engine directly behind the driver. Müller had also acquired some special hemispherical chamber cylinder heads from Porsche, left over from prewar and wartime experiments. He used these 'Vogelsang heads' to help him win the 1100cc class championships in 1948 and 1949. These two people – Glöckler and Müller – can be cited as the forerunners to the introduction by Porsche of the mid-engine concept for its race cars in the years ahead. The Walter Glöckler VW dealership became very successful.

One of the early Glöckler Porsches was acquired by Max Hoffman, seen here in 1951. (©P)

Centre of attention The mid-engine idea

Glöckler, along with his workshop manager Hermann Ramelow, had created the new car, its engine ahead of the transmission. The engine would be a Porsche Type 369 unit.

In 1951, Ramelow drove the car to victory in a race at Hockenheim. It went on to be successful for other drivers, too, after Glöckler sold it on. As Glöckler grew even closer to Porsche, his cars started carrying the Porsche badge and Porsche as a company began to assist him. The first official Glöckler Porsche mid-engined sports car ran at the Freiburg-Schauinsland hillclimb in August 1951, winning its class and establishing a class record. Glöckler's trademark was quality: the cars were immaculate, beautifully put together, whilst remaining very light, and therefore, with the power available, very racy. This particular car was fitted with a new Porsche Type 502 engine, a 1500cc unit that was to become the staple for the 356. It made extensive use of aluminium components.

For 1952, the early part of the season saw Helm Glöckler,

Baron Huschke von Hanstein in the Petermax Müller Volkswagen car. (©P)

Helm Glöckler, Walter's cousin, in an early Glöckler Porsche at the Nürburgring in 1952. (©P)

Glöckler Porsche at the start of the Freiburg-Schauinsland hillclimb, August 1951. (©P)

An early covered version in late 1951 – an experimental car which would lead to the Glöckler coupé for 1952. (©P)

Walter Glöckler's cousin, dominate many races, culminating in him winning the German Sports Car Championship. A full coupé-style roof was installed during the year. During this period, at a time when Porsche was running its own early Gmund 356 coupés in rallies (and that first attempt at Le Mans in 1951), Glöckler and Porsche became synonymous. As Porsche production moved forward, with orders coming in from many parts of the world, Ferry Porsche decided to go racing as the Porsche Company rather than as Glöckler Porsches. With Huschke von Hanstein, Porsche had the man to take the racing fortunes of the company into the future. By 1953, competition in racing from the Italian, British and French manufacturers demonstrated to Porsche that their early cars, the 356 and Gmund coupés, were getting long in the tooth. Ferry Porsche and von Hanstein, along with their long-time colleague Karl Rabe, designed a new car, using the ideas and installation layout of the Glöckler models. First came the mid-engined Type 547, then the much-revered Type 550 – a car that Porsche would enter racing as a factory team. The power unit began as a 1500cc Super, a pushrod-type flat-four-cylinder. The 1953 Le Mans saw Helm Glöckler joined by a young Hans Herrmann in the mid-engined 550-01, with a second car, the 550-02, driven by Richard von Frankenberg and rising Belgian star Paul Frère, a journalist who was no slouch behind the wheel.

The Frankenberg-Frère car took the 1101-to-1500cc class victory, finishing a credible 15th overall at the 1953 Le Mans 24 Hours, the race which, above all others, captured the regular public's imagination, because the cars that ran at Le Mans in this period could also be seen on the roads, and even bought to use personally. For Porsche, competition was to be their mantra for many years to come, as they raced in the GT classes – and still do – with the type that is the most famous of the marque's range: the model 911. Then, as now, what was learned racing was carried forward to the road cars.

Let's hear again for a few moments from Herbert Linge, who has a few interesting stories to tell: "When Porsche came back from Austria they first started with space at the Reutter works, but it was very small. I began working in the engineering shop and, because of my training, and, by now, great deal of knowledge about the VW and Porsche engines, I started to work on experimental projects. That led to me doing the testing of the parts in the cars. Then one day I was asked to act as co-driver to Count von Berckheim on the 1952 Carrera Panamericana. We started okay, but during the third stage,

Centre of attention The mid-engine idea

The all-Porsche Type 550 mid-engine prototype of 1953. (©P)

The Type 550 Porsche prototype also gained a hood to become a coupé. (©P)

from Puebla to Mexico City, the gearbox failed. Von Berckheim told the press it was a stone that broke the gearbox, but in fact it was more like a stone inside the gearbox! The transmission was a secret experimental racing one that we were testing – no stone, it just broke! Then in 1954 Hans Herrmann, one of Germany's greatest drivers, was asked to do the Mille Miglia in the new 550 Spyder 1500. He knew nothing about the technical side of cars, so he said:

'I need somebody who knows the car well enough and is able to do some work, and it must also be a regular driver in case something happens – you never know in a race like this.' And so I was chosen to be his co-driver. Now, for this race as co-driver I decided to create a road book to record the route, because at that time you could not see the road clearly because of the crowds – you didn't have to know the way in the Mille Miglia – there were people standing there and you couldn't go anywhere else. But we needed to know what speed we could drive, how the corners went, etc. So I started writing a road book. Hans and I would go out every morning during the week before the race at 4 or 5am and I wrote down all of the route, like today's pace notes; it was the first time I think anyone had done that properly in great detail. When we got back to the hotel later in the day, I would write the day's work in my road book. Denis Jenkinson got to hear about this from Alfred Neubauer, who was then at Mercedes, having even worked with the old Dr Porsche back in the Auto Daimler days. He was staying in the same hotel, knew me and had asked what I was doing. Later Jenkinson asked me if he could borrow some of our notes to prepare for the 1955 Mille Miglia. He borrowed my book and then made his own notes and put it in a roll like a toilet roll in a little machine, which has become famous for the drive with Stirling Moss in 1955.

"In August 1954 after the Mille Miglia, where I used the road book, I did the Liège-Rome-Liège with Helmut Polensky, who had been European champion the year before. We used one of the early aluminium cars, but we put one of the first overhead-cam engines in it. The same question had cropped up concerning who was going to be the co-driver, because with all this new equipment somebody had to know about it. Of course, I had been responsible for putting it together. Polensky said his co-driver should be a technical guy and a capable driver, because it was a race of five days and four nights without any stops. I had done the testing, so that's why they chose me. On some of the stages Polensky let me drive, and then he said: 'I think you should be a driver rather than a co-driver!' He told Professor Porsche: 'If you need a driver, I know somebody.' He was the first one who got me into the driving seat.

The next big race was with the first 550 for the 1954 Tour de France with French distributor Storez, who at that time was French champion for sports cars. Same situation again: who would co-drive? Everything was new on the car, so I drove it from Stuttgart to Paris, and then we did the whole week in the Tour de France, a fantastic rally: nine race circuits, 6041km. We won all seven hillclimbs and finished 2nd overall. Storez told me to drive the hillclimbs. Professor [Ferry] Porsche then said I must be one of their drivers. Actually, I never wanted to be a professional driver. Because I was so involved with the development and testing of the car, for me racing was the summit, the end of our work. That's why I always drove the test cars. From then on – 1954 to 1970 – I drove many times, whilst always doing the testing of new things. Then in the mid 1960s I took charge of the development workshops, and that is how, in 1968, I was given the job for my department to build the first 914."

We will return to Herbert Linge's part in our story later on. For now, we return to the year 1955. The Type 550/1500RS had been made available to the public, and the developments of this car also fed into the Type 356A/356B programme and to the new model, designated the 356 Carrera.

The 356 model range comprised all rear-engined cars, whereas all the racing developments continued to be mid-engined cars, the models 550 on to the Type 718, the 904 and by 1966 the 906.

As we have seen, the progress of the mid-engined cars for racing was relentless. As we arrive in 1965, we see a new model to replace the 356 road car. Originally the Type 901, it was eventually named the Type 911. For much of the car world, this would be the car that defined Porsche, though in spite of the success of the racing cars, the new road car was still rear-engined, as was the 356, and of course always utilising the now highly developed air-cooled principle, but going from a flat-four-cylinder power unit (essentially a development of the original Volkswagen engine that Porsche had created before the war) to a new flat-six-cylinder unit incorporating all the lessons learned to date. However, as our study here does not really concern the 911, we will return to the Volkswagen company and delve behind the scenes to see what transpired to bring us to the creation of the 914 VW-Porsche.

At the outbreak of the Second World War, Heinrich 'Heinz' Nordhoff had been on the senior management team of Opel, and in 1936 he was responsible for introducing the first Opel Kadett. Opel, of course, like all other industries in Germany during World War II, had had to do as it was told by the government of the Third Reich, though Nordhoff himself carried no affection for the Nazis, or their regime. Like Volkswagen, the Opel works were a target for the allies and suffered heavy bombardment. When war ended, Nordhoff, although a senior director of the Opel Company, like so many others found himself unemployed. However, luck of a sort was on his side, and he found a job working in an Opel garage in Hamburg, where he was tracked down by British intelligence. Volkswagen as a manufacturing plant, having survived (if somewhat battered), was now under the control of the British, and one Major Ivan Hirst was in charge. Nordhoff was installed at Volkswagen to take over and lead the recovery of this once-efficient organisation. Nordhoff took up the role on 1 January 1948 – the day before his 50th birthday. Just ten years after the Volkswagenwerk Company had been opened to a huge fanfare of optimism, he inherited a factory of which 80 per cent had been destroyed.

Recovery would be on the basis of building cars to the specification of the existing or previous models for those that could restart commercial business post-war. In Volkswagen's case it was, of course, the Beetle. Volkswagenwerk AG came

The mid-engined 550A Spyder of Heinz Schiller at the start of the 1956 Mille Miglia. (©P)

The next development: the Porsche mid-engine RSK 718 at the 1957 Le Mans. (©P)

The Porsche Type 718 WS mid-engined Spyder at the Nürburgring 1000km, 1962. (©P)

Mid-engine 718 GTR red coupé of 1962. (©P)

into being in May 1949, still under British control, though it was subsequently returned to full German management later in the year, with production rapidly recovering and new models in planning. During this period the Karmann Karosserie Company, another fast-recovering organisation, brought to the private car market a cabriolet Volkswagen Beetle; this was in July 1949. Most importantly, as we already know, there was ongoing communication between the Porsche design organisation and Heinz Nordhoff. Volkswagen was, of course, developed with the input of Ferdinand Porsche. Porsche had employed many parts from the Volkswagen Company before the war and after. Ferdinand, father of the Porsche Design Bureau, had also registered the design of the prewar

In 1964 the Porsche 904 Carrera GTS coupé mid-engine came along; it was the first glass-fibre-bodied Porsche car. This one, along with car 29 at Le Mans that year, had, in place of its original four-cylinder, a flat-8 unit of 1984cc. This one was driven by Colin Davis/Gerhard Mitter. (©P)

Beetle in his name, thus ensuring that it was officially listed as a Porsche design development, with Volkswagen's administrative offices being set up in Salzburg as Volkswagen Austria, and acting as the central office for all administrative purposes. Ferry Porsche and Nordhoff officially finalised an agreement after the war, and a contract was signed for the Volkswagenwerk to cooperate in production with Porsche on 17 September 1948, a year before VW was handed back to the German nation. Within this agreement was a clause whereby VW agreed to pay Porsche five deutschmarks for every Beetle it built. They also agreed to supply the new fledgling Porsche manufacturing company with parts to create the Porsche sports cars. Just over a year later, at the end of 1949, Porsche Konstructionen was officially set up in Stuttgart, moving back to the city all the equipment and paraphernalia from the site it had occupied in Gmund, Austria, since 1944. The Gmund production facility finally closed its operation on 20 March 1951. On returning to Stuttgart, Porsche initially started by renting space – 600m² – in a building owned by the aforementioned Reutter Coachbuilding Company.

The four companies (Porsche, Volkswagen, Karmann and Reutter) developed through the 1950s, and as Porsche especially developed its racing department, so the Karmann company and the Reutter company became involved in both the prototype and production work of the road cars. By 1956 Porsche sales were soaring, mainly on the back of over 400 victories since the start of competition in 1951. Unfortunately, Professor Ferdinand Porsche (Sr) did not live to see this success, passing away on 30 January 1951 following a stroke in the later months of 1950. Ferry and other members of the family, though, had been running the business efficiently, and by the early years of the 1960s Porsche was preparing to bring to the market the replacement for the now ageing 356 model: the Type 901/911.

Volkswagen, too, had what it perceived to be an ageing model, the evergreen Beetle. Its components had been used to power the Karmann Ghia sports model first announced in 1955, the year that VW sold its one millionth Beetle. Numerous Porsche 356 variants and many of the racing cars still received VW parts. By the time Porsche was ready to bring out the 911 in the early/mid 1960s, Volkswagen thought it was time for a change in its own line-up. Naturally, it turned to Ferry Porsche and the Porsche design group.

VW had given the design offices of Porsche many projects. During the late 1950s the automobile industry was suffering from too many producers making similar products all aimed at the same markets; there would inevitably have to be changes. Amalgamations became almost mandatory if a company was to survive, and several designs were put on hold. Until this point Auto Union, NSU, Volkswagen, Daimler-Benz and Porsche were all independent. Then, in 1959, Daimler-Benz acquired Auto Union, and in 1964 created Audi AG. This company's ideas would offer a new challenge to Volkswagen and Porsche. At Porsche, the costs of creating the new 911 were escalating; it was not an easy beginning for this soon-to-be-famous model. Costs had risen to such an extent that the potential buying market was expected to be limited, and there was talk of a 'starter' Porsche for those who could not afford the new 911. At the same time, Heinz Nordhoff at Volkswagen wanted a fresh model – something sporty. VW already had in plan a new model, the Type 728 family car, which had been undergoing experimental work with Porsche in Zuffenhausen since the late 1950s. This would develop into the VW Type 411 of the late 1960s.

Porsche and Volkswagen both had Porsche family members involved in their companies, although they worked together and produced cars separately for different markets. An idea for a joint cooperation on a new car was suggested, with sales being made through the use of both companies' worldwide agencies. Volkswagen's sales were suffering against not only the new competition from their home market, but also Ford and Fiat. Affordability of the 911 was, as mentioned, causing Porsche concern, and as the production of the 356 model was drawing to a close, they decided to launch alongside the 911 a new version, the 912, in 1965. It would utilize the 1582cc four-cylinder Volkswagen-based engine. It was hoped that the 912 would meet the demands for a 'people's' Porsche 911 – a lower-cost version.

The mid 1960s proved to be the time when mid-engined cars started winning all the major races. Ferry Porsche had not wavered in his conviction that maybe mid-engine was the way to go for road cars, too, in spite of the risk of loss of luggage or passenger space. Ferrari had brought out the Dino 246 GT with a body by Pininfarina; De Tomaso had the mid-engine Mangusta; Lamborghini had the Miura; from the UK came the mid-engined Lotus Europa coupé, which used a Renault engine, and from France came the Matra 530. Mid-engine thinking was becoming the trend. In short, it worked: the roadholding capabilities of this format were outstanding because of the considerations mentioned at the very beginning of this chapter: the balance of a mid-engine car was superior to that of any other layout.

The first outright racing victory for the mid-engine sports car at Le Mans had been taken by Ferrari in 1963, and by now all Grand Prix Formula 1 cars were mid-engined – even the Americans became convinced in 1965 when the Lotus Ford-engined car won the Indianapolis 500. Porsche had been building mid-engine race cars since the number one in Gmund. The Glöckler Porsches were a revelation; the Porsche 550, 718 and recently the 904 road racer all proved the point. Porsche had form in this area: it was only a question of time. But one thing was on everyone's mind in the mid 1960s: the cost of production. Porsche needed sales, and it decided that cooperation was the way to go. Heinz Nordhoff was still at the head of the now extremely successful Volkswagen Company, which had investments throughout the world. Nordhoff needed little persuasion: with his market share shrinking, VW and Porsche knew they needed something new to compete with the lower-cost sports models that were coming out of Fiat, BMW, Ford and Opel. Karmann, too, was thinking about a new car, closely linked to Volkswagen due to the body production line that was building Karmann Ghia cars based on Volkswagen components. Not only this, but since 1961 they had been supplying Porsche with 356 bodies; there was a potential joint venture here that could work. Heinz Nordhoff and Ferry Porsche came to an agreement that Porsche would design and develop a new mid-engine sports car for Volkswagen to sell, using the new engine that Volkswagen was developing for the new saloon car, the VW 411, due out in 1968 – a 1679cc unit. The idea was to create two new sports models: a four-cylinder-powered item carrying a VW badge, and a six-cylinder Porsche 911-engined example carrying the Porsche badge. The Type number would be 914.

2

1967-1976:
The road cars
Concept – design – politics and production

In this chapter we take in the road cars, but only briefly. As the full history has been well written by others, we do not need to go into much detail. We also want to get onto the main subject of this work – racing. That said, we do need to check out how the 914 got to that stage. Ferry Porsche gave a clue as to what was in his mind in the aforementioned interview given to *Porsche Panorama* in 1979, where he went on to say: "We already had considerable experience with performance engines. During the war, I (more or less secretly) drove my VW cabriolet with an engine producing 50hp, thanks to the use of a Rootes supercharger. As early as 1950, the year production actually began in Stuttgart, Dr Ernst Fuhrmann began designing a high-performance engine with two camshafts on each cylinder bank. It was intended for racing at first – we only put it into production five years later."

Racing was clearly the target, and although we have seen how Porsche and others arrived at the mid-engine for racing, it is here that we will look at the concept of our subject, the Type 914 sports car. As a new road car, not only did it have to suit the aspirations of Volkswagen; for Porsche it had to look completely different from the 911. By 1967, in spite of its cost, the 911 was enjoying huge success competition-wise and, whilst not selling in large numbers to the general public, was a favourite amongst those who aspired to own a truly great sports car. The proposed new car, therefore, must not upset sales of the 911, but add to the Porsche experience.

There were those in Porsche who were worried: it was essentially a Volkswagen project, and whilst Porsche was the contracted designer, it was still looking for that 'people's' Porsche, which had to be at a 'people's' price, because the 912 wasn't exactly setting the world on fire. Also, Porsche didn't have overall control of the 914 project, even though the family was closely linked. And the fact was that, if the new car was successful, it might even take the shine off plans for future 911s.

The first thoughts for the design came out of an idea of Heinrich Klie in the Porsche design studio, coupled with a drawing Ferdinand Alexander Porsche ('Butzi'), eldest son of Ferry, had seen elsewhere. The 'elsewhere' had been the Gugelot Design Company. Gugelot Design had wanted to expand into vehicles in the early 1960s. Gugelot's thinking was to bring BMW on board to provide the power unit. It foresaw a car made out of plastics, or maybe glass fibre; the Bayer Chemical Company had the technology. Butzi Porsche had been deeply involved with bringing the 911 to the market, so was only mildly interested, until discussions began between Ferry Porsche and Heinz Nordhoff, and the decision to go ahead came into focus. By then, Butzi and Klie knew that the Type 914 project had to be different, and they understood the concept and advantages of a mid-mounted engine on the racing scene where, as we have seen, mid-engine was rapidly becoming king. There had also been an interesting design by Pininfarina in Italy, created on the

1967-1976: The road cars Concept – design – politics and production

The area that defines the 914 VW-Porsche design. (©P)

Finally, after much deliberation, a design is decided upon. This later drawing is dated 25 November 1968. (©P)

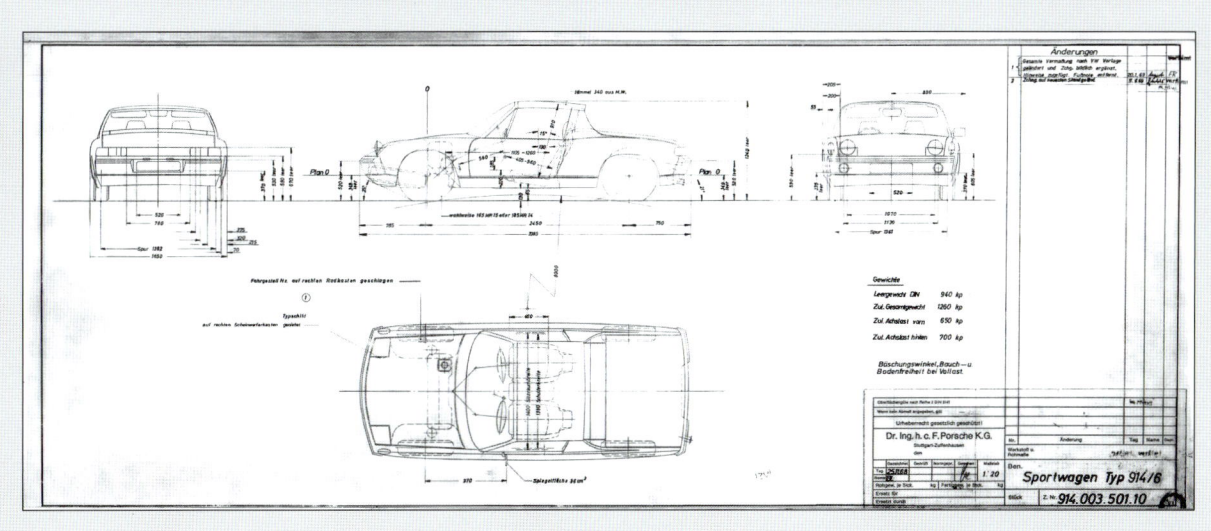

chassis of a Fiat 2300 in 1963 – the cabin area being of particular interest. Ferry Porsche became deeply involved, as did Ferdinand Piëch, who had been responsible for the mid-engined 904. The Porsche design team set to work and came up with the shape that specifically defines the 914.

From the very beginning it was controversial: some liked the new square shape while others detested it, thinking it did not have the smooth lines of the 911, but they were missing the point: it must not look anything like the 911. There were, however, more for than against at that time, and for good reason. Its engine bay, directly behind a spacious cabin, was big enough to take both the Volkswagen engine and the Porsche flat-six.

As we arrive from concept to design, we see a car whose mid-engine layout looked on paper to be the perfect solution – its logically perfect balance (driver and engine in the middle, power train out the back) offering perfect traction. Because the cockpit area had no driveshaft tunnel occupying a chunk of space in the middle, the habitable compartment could be set low in the car, offering perfect balance and making the car agile, its low centre of gravity reducing roll and giving superior grip when cornering. With no engine sticking up under a front bonnet, the frontal area was small and aerodynamics would benefit. The enthusiastic design engineers even pointed out that the driver and passenger were better protected without the risk of the engine mass coming through the front bulkhead in the event of an accident, the free space acting as a progressive crumple zone. (Today, of course, there are different standards of car construction requirements to prevent the eventuality of engine movement.) Likewise, with the engine in the rear, ahead of the transaxle, the rear also offered a crumple zone. The low-mounted gearbox allowed the boot to be effectively a large luggage space, with a second luggage space in the front.

However, with the engine in the middle, access for servicing could be difficult and heat and engine noise in the cockpit might be an issue for the driver and passenger. No problem in a racing car, but such things are important in a road car, where the comfort of driver and passenger is paramount. Radiators were not a problem because of the choice of an air-cooled engine. A suitable support frame would be required for the engine and gearbox, and mounting of the independent suspension would be critical. That said, Porsche was the expert of mid-engined race cars and rear-engined models for both road and racing. With its competitors all offering mid-engine sports cars, it was inevitable that the new model 914 would be state of the art. It was decided that Volkswagen would place an order on Porsche, with the Karmann Company making the bodies and Volkswagen supplying the engine in a VW-badged version, and

Spacious in the back, it met the requirements for luggage space, even when the central targa top was removed and stored in the upper part of the rear boot space, offering roof-off motoring for customers who wanted an open-top car, but not a full cabriolet. (RS)

Very spacious in the front, and there was even a spare wheel located low down, almost below the car's floor level. (RS)

the six-cylinder Porsche engine for those cars to be sold and badged by Porsche. Karmann was a company that dated from the early days of car development (1874, to be precise), making car bodies since 1902. They had joined with the Ghia Design Company in the 1950s to produce a shapely sports car powered by a Volkswagen

1967-1976: The road cars Concept – design – politics and production

engine. This was available as a coupé and a cabriolet, and in addition Karmann had, as already mentioned, produced the VW Beetle cabriolet, as well as supplying Porsche with various coupé bodies since 1961. Karmann was the natural partner when Ferry Porsche and Heinz Nordhoff shook hands on the deal.

However, it was not to be a smooth gestation: politics and illness would dominate the early period as development and testing began. Unfortunately, the man who had made Volkswagen what it was since the post-war recovery, Heinz Nordhoff, was now in poor health, and in 1967 plans were agreed to seek a successor for the day that Heinz Nordhoff decided to retire. Kurt Lotz would join VW, having been personally selected by Nordhoff from his chief executive position at the Swiss company Brown Boveri. However, Heinz Nordhoff's health began deteriorating fast, giving Kurt Lotz little time to get to grips with how the business ran, and especially how the relationship and business with the Porsche family was conducted. Nordhoff had to spend many hours away from the business in hospital. This went on through all of 1967 and into 1968, when on 12 April Heinz Nordhoff passed away in the Wolfsburg Hospital. The effect on the development of the 914 was catastrophic, as Lotz set to work with a completely different mindset to that of Nordhoff. We now know that the main problem arose because very little – in fact practically nothing – had been written down concerning the agreements between the Porsche family and its design group and the Nordhoff-led VW people. Having worked together in business and as a family so successfully since the war, they perceived that there was no need for formal agreements. This relaxed attitude was also reflected in the fact that Porsche assumed it would have an equal right to produce its version of the 914 in its own way.

Lotz assumed nothing; he studied the financial books and the basis of the project's working practices and determined that, because it was VW who had formally requested Porsche Design to create a car, all the rights to the product were Volkswagen's alone. Oops, one might say! But there was another factor involved: it was a sports car – did he really want it in the range of Volkswagens that he saw primarily as family cars? He wanted to progress the company's main production along those bread-and-butter family car lines. His intention, it is said, was at some point to pass the whole project over to Porsche, who would be requested to do as VW asked, with an official contract. It would be a Porsche car, but VW would take the profits. In supporting this view, he was instrumental in assisting Porsche in expanding its Research and Development Department at Weissach, where an investment was to be made of around 20 million US$ in the comparisons of the day. Paul Hensler, one of Porsche's leading design engineers, was given the task under Ferdinand Piëch to expand the then (relatively) secret facility to include test tracks, skid pans and off-road development areas. Dipl Ing Paul Hensler had joined Porsche in 1958, starting in the Porsche tractor engine design office. He had progressed over the years and was to become head of the engine department in Zuffenhausen, where eventually a team of 100 looked after all the 911 road and racing engines. The Weissach project began construction in 1969. Four test areas were created with engine dynos and other development technology to hand. The facility would take three years to complete and was kept pretty secret from the outside world until May 1972, when certain invited journalists were allowed in. Below is what they saw.

The extensive track system within the test facility. The test buildings and offices can be seen bottom right. (©P)

Along with the finance to develop this facility, Lotz also gave Porsche a formal contract to design a new passenger family car. Known then as Project EA266, it was intended to feature a mid engine under the rear seats; they foresaw a sports coupé, a roadster and a vehicle that resembled the VW Campervan. However, Lotz knew that Porsche needed a new vehicle to help their market share and sell a lower-cost sports car; here he saw, as already suggested, a chance to partake of a financial input to Volkswagen, but without the need to take the car into the VW range. But there was another set of circumstances that would occupy his attention. Audi and NSU had been acquired by the Volkswagen Company and this acquisition gave Lotz a different perspective on sales agencies around the world. It is said that some heated discussions took place between VW and Porsche management, which was, of course, at that time mostly family. There was a lot of to-ing and fro-ing.

Herbert Linge remembers: "Here in Stuttgart, we were originally all together – design, prototype, build, everything. But already some things were being done in different places. I came in very much at the beginning of the 914. Here in Stuttgart, I was in charge of the complete shop – experimental mechanics, racing, etc – and so I had a big group here.

"We made the first 914 in our workshop. I tell you frankly, the old Porsche people were not very happy. Our idea was to have something stronger and bigger than this lightweight Volkswagen; we didn't want to step back. It was a bit of a mess, because various people kept coming with different ideas. Then the marketing men wanted to create a competition model, six-cylinders. We had started with just a four-cylinder engine, initially 1.7 – too small to do anything." Testing of the first six-cylinder car, though, began to take place and results of the first wind tunnel test can be seen in internal document H67, dated 22 May 1968. The 914 design displayed interesting results compared with the 911. The test forces were done at a reference speed of 150km/h with a vehicle in primer. Here is an interesting comparison:

	914	911
Drag coefficient absolute	0.377	0.376

The results, too numerous and complex to display here, indicate that the 914 had slightly more lift at the rear and less lift on the front than the 911. The tests, carried out by engineer Helmut Flegl, indicate that aerodynamically the two cars, although completely different in design, were in fact quite close in terms of overall aerodynamic efficiency, which may come as a surprise as the brick-like shape of the 914 differs considerably from that of the sleek 911. The tests had begun on 914-001 on 18 April 1968. Work continued with both the four- and six-cylinder powered models.

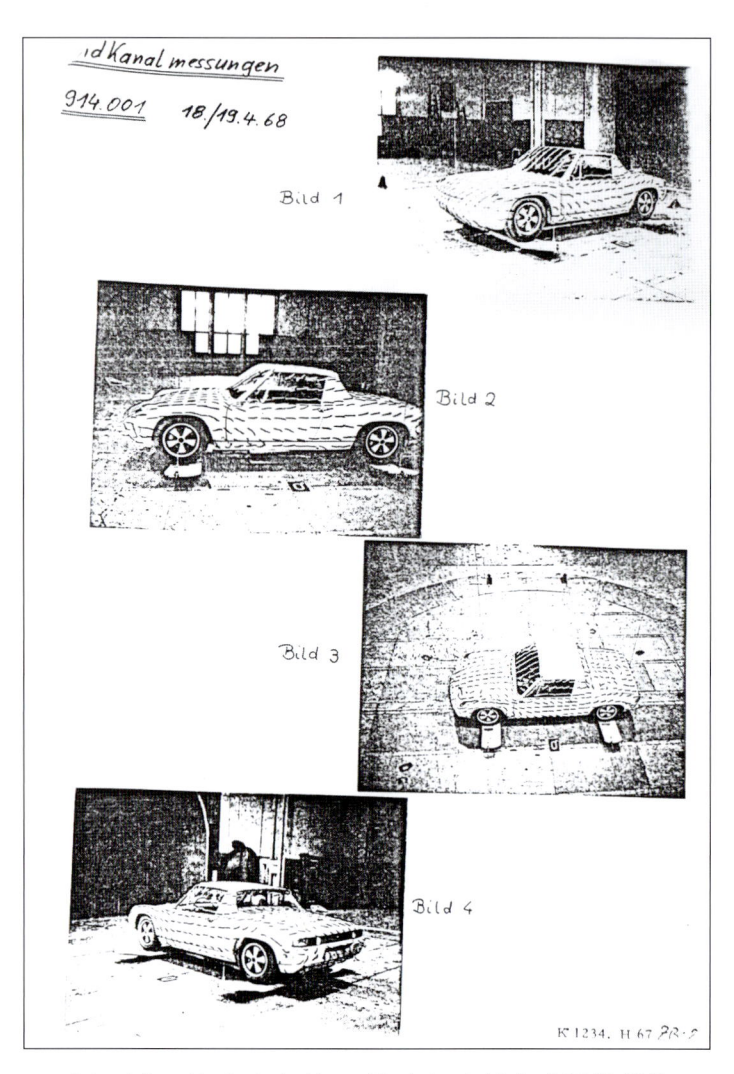

Extract from the first wind tunnel test sheet, 18 April 1968. (©P)

Throughout 1968, whilst the engineers carried out their work, the business of marketing and how to sell the car was in limbo following the Nordhoff situation. However, after much discussion it was decided in January 1969 that the two organizations would create a new company, jointly owned by both Porsche and VW, to sell the 914s built by both companies in Germany. Porsche would then create a separate company to the existing Volkswagen

1967-1976: The road cars Concept – design – politics and production

The 914-001 1968 prototype, having completed wind tunnel trials, appeared painted green and with plain wheels. Note that the badge on the back states '914/6 VW Porsche.' (©P)

organization in the USA, called Porsche+Audi, and the new company would have the distribution rights. An undisclosed financial agreement was reached between the two companies regarding the sales income. The German distribution company would be named as VW-Porsche Vertriebsgesellschaft GmbH, commonly known as VG, and owned 50/50 by Volkswagen and Porsche. To the outside world, this development looked as if VW was making a move to acquire Porsche, and the press interpreted it as such. This was strongly refuted. Ferry Porsche said at the time: "Porsche remains Porsche! The two families, Porsche and Piëch, who are exclusive owners of the firm, have no intention of taking up outside funds or joining any other group. We are a private enterprise; we want to remain as such and are able to do so." He also said: "We have built a car [the 914] in common with Volkswagenwerk because our partner wanted to gain a more sporting image." In reality it was a compromise, due to the circumstances of Lotz 'wants' and Porsche 'desires.' Karmann

Porsche The Racing 914s

The Volkswagen-powered Karmann Ghia Type 34 of the mid 1960s. (RS)

In the agreement between Porsche and VW was the requirement that all the six-cylinder cars should be badged 'VW Porsche.' (©P)

38

1967-1976: The road cars Concept – design – politics and production

in Osnabruck would build all the bodies and finished chassis and, in the case of the four-cylinder cars, would also install the engine and complete the cars. For the Porsche version of the 914, the six-cylinder model, Karmann would do all the body and chassis work, including painting, but not the mechanical and engine installation. Up to this point, Karmann had been producing the Type 34 Ghia, in some respects a similarly boxy creation.

Incidentally, at that time Karmann was also building bodies for the 911 at the same plant, so the 914s that were destined to have the six-cylinder engine would be taken to Stuttgart for engine installation and Porsche style finishing along with 911 shells. However, due to an accounting procedure (so it was said), Lotz at VW ended up having Karmann charge Porsche more for the 914/6 chassis than for the 911 chassis. He also initially insisted that identification should show VW as well as Porsche on the rear of the car.

This caused problems in the USA, where buyers perceived Porsche to stand for an upmarket image, whereas VW was seen as just a regular car. The 914, they said, was not a proper Porsche. A huge campaign was started to convince potential buyers that it was an all-Porsche design, citing the history, development and pedigree of the first Porsche. Eventually, the VW identity would be dropped in the USA: only the Porsche name would be on display. Despite all the wrangling and disputes, the 914 made its public debut at the 1969 Frankfurt Motor Show, with both Porsche and VW logos boldly displayed.

On paper, all aspects of the car pointed

Two colours popular in the period were displayed. (©P)

The Frankfurt Motor Show 1969, a joint initiative on view: VW Porsche. Note the Mahle wheels; these would be an option for the Fuchs or plain steel items. (©P)

39

Porsche The Racing 914s

The six-cylinder 914 exploded. (JS)

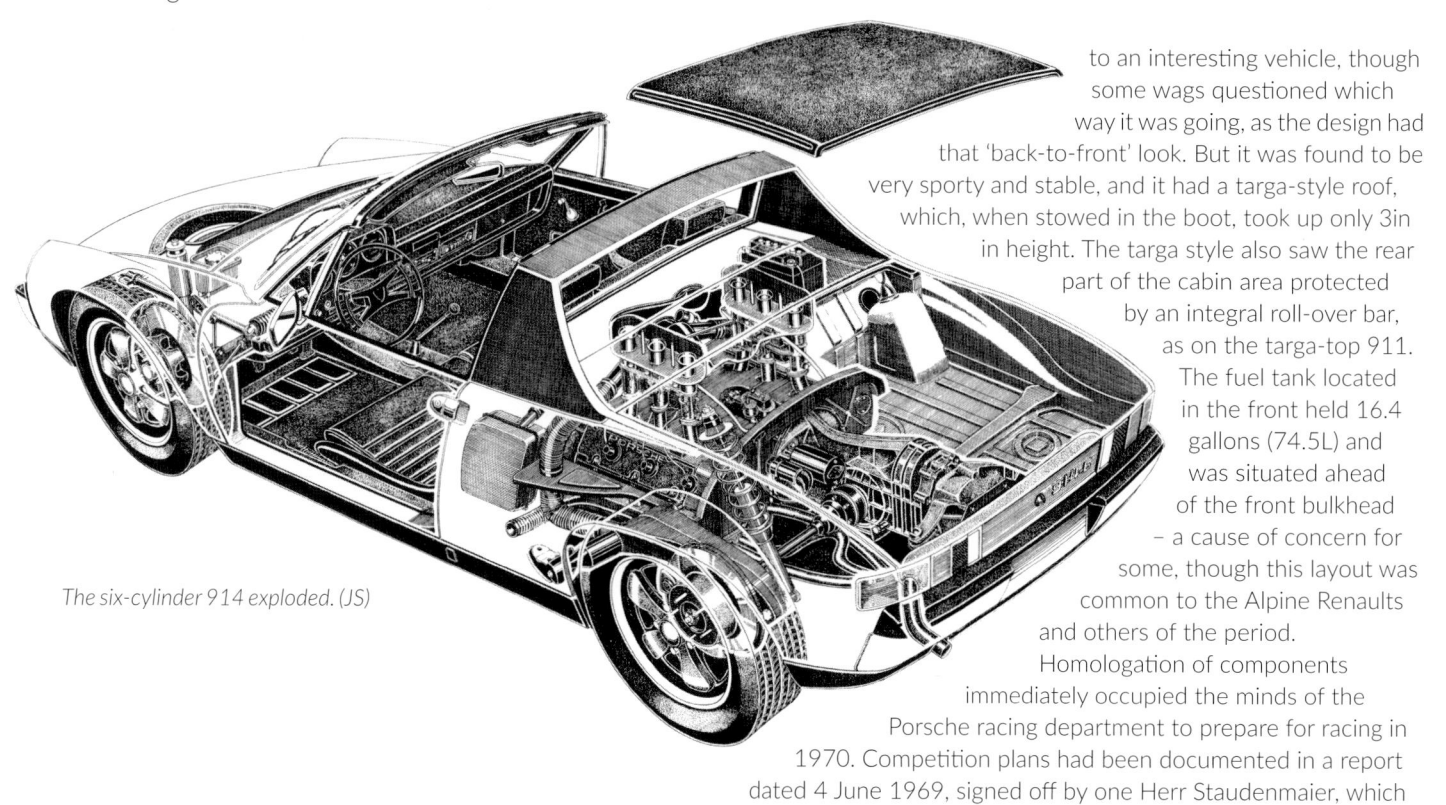

Porsche was keen to demonstrate the car's luggage capacity. (©P)

to an interesting vehicle, though some wags questioned which way it was going, as the design had that 'back-to-front' look. But it was found to be very sporty and stable, and it had a targa-style roof, which, when stowed in the boot, took up only 3in in height. The targa style also saw the rear part of the cabin area protected by an integral roll-over bar, as on the targa-top 911. The fuel tank located in the front held 16.4 gallons (74.5L) and was situated ahead of the front bulkhead – a cause of concern for some, though this layout was common to the Alpine Renaults and others of the period.

Homologation of components immediately occupied the minds of the Porsche racing department to prepare for racing in 1970. Competition plans had been documented in a report dated 4 June 1969, signed off by one Herr Staudenmaier, which mentions the use of the 911S engine and the fitting of 7in and 9in wheels, together with numerous other modifications.

1967-1976: The road cars Concept – design – politics and production

Homologation – the front suspension was almost a compete lift from the 911: MacPherson struts, torsion bars and rack-and-pinion steering. (©P)

Hubs, discs and callipers would be the 5-stud 911 for the six-cylinder cars. (©P)

The VW hub of the four-cylinder cars was also homologated. (©P)

The homologated 5-speed gearbox/differential transaxle would be basically the same as that employed in the Porsche 904 and 906 cars, but designated 914/11. Interestingly, the unit in this image is marked 914/01 – possibly one from the prototype car. (©P)

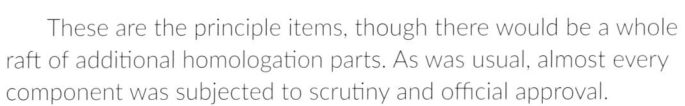

These are the principle items, though there would be a whole raft of additional homologation parts. As was usual, almost every component was subjected to scrutiny and official approval.

Competition was initially seen to mean rallying. Rainer Bratenstein had joined Porsche to be in charge of the development of the competition cars and numerous memos in the archives carry instructions specifying the use of lightweight panels and stronger anti-roll bars (sway bars), along with the required preparation for building a rally car. Jürgen Barth was in charge of the homologation of all the 914s for competition.

The engine for the homologation 914/6 road car was to be the same as that in the 1968 911T: 110bhp, dry-sumped 2L. For competition, the 911S power unit was identified in June 1969 as the likely unit to provide more horsepower. (©P)

In the first cars and the road 914/6 cars the cylinder head was a conventional one-plug unit. (©P)

For homologation for racing, the twin-plug competition item was installed in the 914 GT, along with dual ignition. (©P)

Porsche was following known practice, suspension-wise, keeping close to the 911 specification. The layout at the front for the 914/6 and for the 914/4 would be the same, with only the hubs changed to take Volkswagen parts on the four-cylinder versions. The rear was slightly different due to the requirement to use either VW or Porsche engines, though the geometry was almost the same as the 911's. The shock absorbers at the rear sported a coilover unit attached to the familiar trailing arm system that gave a slight camber change under compression. In fact, it turned out to have a little more camber than the same-period 911. For the four-cylinder 'Volkswagen' cars, VW 4-stud hubs were used, whilst the six-cylinder Porsche-badged cars would have the regular 5-stud hubs.

When the VW 411 was displayed at the 1968 Paris Motor Show, its engine was on carburettors. Then in 1969 Volkswagen fitted

1967-1976: The road cars Concept – design – politics and production

Twin triple-choke Webers provided the fuelling delivery. (©P)

A 914/6 single-plug 110hp (DIN) engine. (©P)

Even at this early stage, homologation also involved the fitting of wider wheelarches. These images are dated late 1968. (©P)

43

Porsche The Racing 914s

Front wing in prototype development stage. (©P)

the 411 engine with Bosch/Volkswagen-developed electronic fuel-injection of a type already in use in the USA. Created by Bendix and licensed to Bosch, it used an early computer design to control the process. When introduced, the 914 also benefited from that 1969 upgrade. As it turned out, the engine in the VW 411E was of a design that lent itself ideally to use in a sports car. Its 1679cc had a larger bore than the Porsche production engine fitted in the 912 1582cc unit. Later, the 914 VW-powered cars would use a Volkswagen 1.8L unit from the VW 412LS. In fact, the standard 914 six-cylinder engine fitted in the Porsche versions of the 914 didn't set the world on fire with 110hp (DIN). However, the 914 was a lighter car than the 911. The 914/6 had the same dry-sump lubrication, but its fuelling system, by twin triple-choke Weber carburettors, made wonderful noises! The

Note the cut-out in the front bumper for the oil cooler installation. (©P)

1967-1976: The road cars Concept – design – politics and production

907: the first Porsche to use injection at Le Mans, 1967. The Jo Siffert/Hans Herrmann mount finished in 5th place overall. (©P)

USA got the same type but a different version of this engine, due to emission controls and depending on whether it was a Sportmatic or not.

Following tests in the mid 1960s, Porsche mechanical injection followed the early Bosch principle. By 1966, the Carrera 906 was using that injection system, the factory cars first using it on hillclimbs and then at the 1967 Le Mans 24 Hours in the 907 of Siffert and Herrmann.

The 914/6 road cars were produced in relatively small numbers: 2657 in 1970, 432 in 1971 and 249 in 1972.

Unfortunately, due to the underwhelming early interest, production of the six-cylinder 1991cc production model was brought to an end in 1972. Further development of these cars in Europe and the build of more cars for the market ceased at this point. The public's response demonstrated that it wasn't keen on the shape and that the 911 with its six-cylinders was still the preferred Porsche model. It would be a struggle to get the 914 off the ground. However, as we will see, in fact the 914/6 was to receive a lot of attention amongst the dealer teams and privateers racing in Europe through 1970 and '71, and once the

45

Porsche The Racing 914s

Americans got their hands on it, it was to be the staple learner race car for several future famous drivers in the States. Porsche was questioned by the press as to future developments. How much power could the chassis take? What was on the cards? Sales in the USA of the four-cylinder started to pick up, and Porsche was already looking forward, planning to bring out a new version. The question of emissions in the USA had brought the performance of the VW 1700cc and 1800cc engines into focus as their power was reduced, and this was not what the sales teams in the USA wanted. The 914/6 was okay, but it was the more expensive option and no more were being produced after 1972; the sales team wanted a car with more power, but at a lower price. Porsche came up with a new plan for 1973. The buying public suddenly took interest. Whilst the 1679cc unit was efficient and in most cases had initially been sufficient, it was a bit wheezy at the top end of its range. A new engine would bring a revelation to the road testers.

Porsche Design took the 1679cc unit in-house and enlarged it to 2L (1971cc, in fact). The engine would look the same externally as the earlier item, and in fact internally it used the same crank, though it had some Porsche modifications. Now Porsche had increased its stroke from 66mm to 71mm, new connecting rods were used, and overall the new-specification engine was not far off the spec of the 4-cam Carrera race engine of the late 1950s, producing 100hp (DIN) at 5000rpm and 116lb of torque at 3200, compared with the 80hp (DIN) of the earlier unit. With the electric fuel-injection, this offered lively performance. This engine, known as the 2L and produced in numbers by VW, found a strong following in the USA. It brought the performance of the 914/4 2L close to that of the heavier standard 914/6, with the single-plug 110hp of the 2L 911-engined car.

The four-cylinder 2L engine and updated models of the 914 four-cylinder car would see production through to 1976 and a production run of over 70,000 cars – more than double the total of all the other 914 models built from 1969 to 1976. According to a press release from the time, it was offered on the UK market as the VW-Porsche 914SC. In fact, there are some who are of the opinion that this model, when well tuned and with a blueprinted engine, was the best of the bunch. To support this, none other than Vic Elford told the author in 2014 that "I just did not like the 914/6 and didn't think it was a very good car. The 914/4 2L, on the other hand, was a great little car – especially for a young driver wanting sporting performance. It was well balanced (much better than the 914/6), handled well, with nice power-to-weight ratio, though not too much for a novice." He was not alone in this thinking.

The 914/6 220 hp (DIN) unit with two banks of Webers and, in this case, the twin-plug dual-ignition circuit. Note the two ignition coils located alongside the battery. (©P)

1967-1976: The road cars Concept – design – politics and production

Introduction of the proto 914/6 GT at Hockenheim in autumn 1969. Note aforementioned pre-GT kit-style wings. (©P)

Before we move into the racing era, let's take a look at a few specials – perhaps 'what might have been' from Porsche, had it decided to develop them. These ideas came from quite early on, and Ferry Porsche was heavily involved. First came the idea to use a limited-slip differential, which could be supplied on request. As mentioned already, the 911 of that period had a dry-sump engine. This engine leant itself to significant tuning, and, with competition in mind, a special version of the 914/6 was created, listed as the 914/6 GT, of which Jürgen Barth's *The Porsche Book* lists 14 cars, each with the type 911/25 six-cylinder of 1991cc and giving 220hp (DIN) at 7000rpm. Eleven 914/6 GTs are listed as produced in 1970 and three in 1971. (Two chassis were not, in fact, made.) As we will see in future chapters, these cars were the competition items that made an impact.

The new GT car was introduced to the press at the Hockenheim circuit in the autumn of 1969.

Ever adventurous, by 1969 Porsche had also built two very special cars. One would be given to Ferry Porsche, and one to Ferdinand Piëch.

Porsche The Racing 914s

Freshly finished: one of the two eight-cylinder specials. (©P)

One of the two flat eight-cylinder versions (this one 914006) presented to Ferdinand Piëch and Ferry Porsche. These were the 'what might have been' cars and were known as the coupé 914/8, both having the Porsche Type 908 flat-8 2997cc engine, one with 300hp (DIN) and one 250hp (DIN). The latter car became a favourite of Ferdinand Piëch, whilst Ferry Porsche loved his car, and racked up some 10,000km in it. (©P)

The 914-8 was a spectacular car; its engine rev limit was 8400 and in first gear would reach 50mph, 80 in second, 105 in third and 130 in fourth. Ferdinand Piëch's car had a full-on 908 race engine with open inlet chokes and unsilenced exhaust and racing injection system; it was limited to use on the Weissach test track, though it did venture onto the road occasionally when duly silenced. Quite a sight and sound! In addition to those two cars from 1969, 11 916 Porsches were created in 1972, first identified as project 916 on 13 July 1971 in a memo to Rainer Bratenstein. These cars did not have the targa top of the 914 but were fixed-top coupés and had high-performance 2.4L engines. It is said that, officially, to the world outside of Porsche, they never existed. It was one of those brushed-under-the-carpet-models, developed, presented to the marketing guys and then thrown out due to the price. So why were 11 built? That remains a mystery, but when the project was abandoned with 11 so-called prototypes built, five of them would find their way

The Ferdinand Piëch eight-cylinder prototype had numerous additions for testing. Most visual here are the wider headlamp covers: underneath as they opened up were two sets of twin headlights. Production 914/6s only had one set. (©P)

Tight squeeze: the 908 flat-8 2997cc engine with Bosch mechanical fuel-injection just fits. (Sp)

The interior of the eight-cylinder. (Sp)

50

1967-1976: The road cars Concept – design – politics and production

The 916 2.4L coupé, fitted with the 911S engine, providing 190bhp, whilst a prototype 2.6L, modified to 2.7L, would put out 210bhp. (©P)

Crayford Auto Developments: a strip-out and refit would be required to convert to right-hand drive. (JS)

within the Porsche family, one would go to the USA and the other five, it is said, were sold under the counter in Germany!

The 916 also received strengthening treatment in the floor of the cabin. The bodywork likewise saw changes, as can be seen in the image above. It was quick and could go from 0-100km/h in less than six seconds and test drivers reported its handling as being quite exceptional. With this information from within the Porsche organization, one wonders again what might have been.

These special cars were somewhat at a distance in terms of performance from the 914/4s, heavily restricted with emission controls, where the installed power was down to 75hp (DIN) on the smaller engine, 95hp (DIN) on the larger unit used in the USA, and 100hp (DIN) on European unrestricted cars. All the 914s had been left-hand-drive cars, though there were experiments with right-hand drive, and eventually a few left-hand-drive cars would be converted to right-hand drive by the Crayford Auto Development Company, at that time in Westerham, Kent, in the UK. It is to be noted that the manufacturer's warranty was invalidated by this modification.

The interior trim was restyled and the handbrake moved to the right-hand side, and interestingly the sales documentation notes: "The floor carpeting in the 914 is changed to a superior-quality English Wilton"! A new fascia was of course required, as were new pedal units. A replacement rear bulkhead was installed, the driver's seat being adjustable as opposed to the fixed one on the passenger side. It is thought about 40 or so cars were converted by Crayford, according to Karl Ludvigsen's work *Excellence was Expected*.

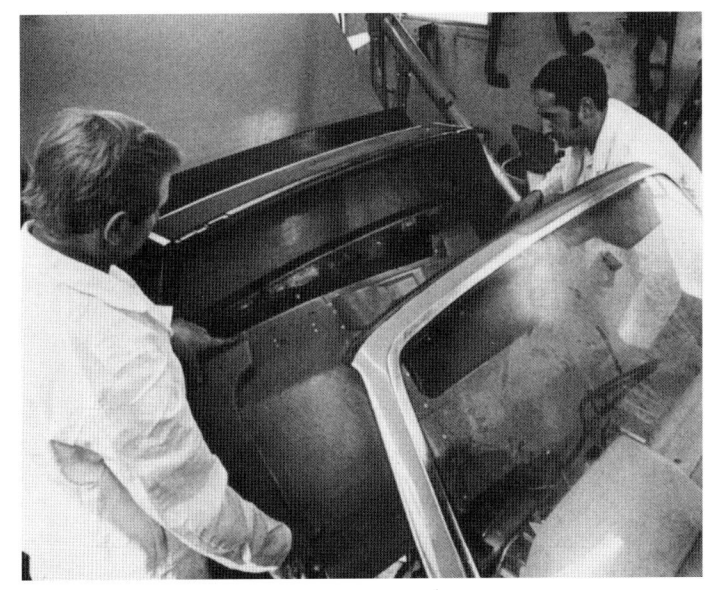

A new dashboard and changes in instrument clusters, let alone alterations to the pedals and steering and moving the handbrake to the right, would make this no easy job. (JS)

The floor carpeting in the 914 was changed to a superior-quality English Wilton in the RHD conversions. Around 40 cars were converted in this way. (JS)

Owners of the 914 would find that it could carry a lot of luggage at quite high speed; in fact you had to be going over the limits to spin off the road or turn it over, the roadholding being so impressive because of the layout. This, coupled with the all-disc brake set-up, made for a car that was a delight to drive. All in all, it had been well engineered, with neutral handling and superb steering lock. Steering correction when cornering hard was barely necessary, and in a test comparison with the 911S on a slalom course the 914 out-manoeuvred the 911, the latter requiring racing tyres to achieve better results. Only in a straight line was the 911 faster. It is recorded that the 914/6 had a six to eight per cent advantage in cornering power over a comparably powered 911. With normal radial tyres it was able to develop up to 0.9 lateral G on a skid pan against the maximum of 0.82 to 0.85 achieved by the 911. Even with those racing tyres on the 911, the 914 performed better overall, at 1.0 G compared with the 911's best of 0.93. It was noted that the impressive result of this test was that the 914 chassis handled in exactly the same way, be it in the wet or in the dry. In short, it was in a class of its own. With a comparable-powered engine in both cars, the 914 held the road and handled better. The mid-engine layout, the flat ride, the near 50/50 balance – all added up to give the driver a positive feel and provide a fun drive, whilst for the passenger the low centre of gravity made for a comfortable, low-roll ride. Tests showed that in fact all round it was an excellent car, with hard cornering bringing out small percentages of understeer and oversteer alike, its recovery from understeer being so gentle as to make it most forgiving. Everyone commented on the firm ride, and not everyone was happy with the power available. Then again, they were all expecting a performance equivalent to the favourite 911. In fact, each of the testers from Europe and the USA came up with differing reports. Several hadn't liked the styling; it was alien to the jaundiced eye of the regular motoring journalist. The American magazines, especially *Road and Track* and *Car and Driver*, were scathing. They said it was a good replacement for a Volkswagen but not a replacement for a Porsche 911. In fact, the 911 had set such a high standard it would be difficult to beat. But then they were testing the early 914/4. However, the comments continued to apply when the 914/6 was tested: the only good thing they had to say was that it was quick and the engine delivered a wonderful sound!

Initial sales were slow, not helped by the terse reviews. However, once the man in the street started to try the car the mood began to change, with a significant number of sales between the launch and 1976. So, would it make a good racer? We will soon find out, because as ever within Porsche, there was competition in the blood and if successful in racing, the cars would sell. Hurley Haywood, former Vice-President of Brumos Porsche in Jacksonville, USA, and a former champion racing driver who won his first title in a 914, says: "The 914 model very quickly had a cult following and owners would return for second and third cars to trade in to buy the next one, right through to when production finished, and today these are seen racing on a regular basis." That was the secret: once more, Porsche had, in the end, followed its racing strategy to sell cars and raise its profile. In May 1974 Porsche announced the building of the 100,000th model, and with that came the information that 60,000 had already gone to the USA. It had, then, not been the failure that the press expected: in fact the total run size for a sports car was very respectable. But Porsche had other things on its mind. The 914 had been a success, but not at the level it would have liked, and it still needed a cheaper entry-level car because the 914 had eventually worked out more expensive than originally planned. After a remarkable series of circumstances, it found its people's Porsche in the first front-engined water-cooled Porsche: the 924. Again, this story is well recorded elsewhere (including the author's work *Porsche - The 924 Carrera, Evolution to Excellence*, published by

1967-1976: The road cars Concept – design – politics and production

Deliveries by the transporter-load: testing, training and a race car off to do the business of motorsport. (JS)

Veloce). Kurt Lotz, who had followed Heinz Nordhoff at Volkswagen, suddenly left Volkswagen-Audi in September 1971; his departure would make things tricky for Porsche, which had been working on a new saloon for Volkswagen, the earlier-mentioned Project EA 266. Rudolf Leiding, Lotz's replacement, decided against that project and ordered immediate cancellation of EA 266. Leiding, though, was to encourage the development of another new project which was given to Porsche Design in 1972. Listed as EA 425, it was to become the early beginnings of the Porsche 924. Leiding left Volkswagen in 1974, to be replaced by one Toni Schmücker early in 1975, who neither liked nor wanted to continue with the 914 or the new 924. Porsche meanwhile were thinking about a water-cooled six-cylinder engine, but the project was not developed. VW at this time was also about to launch a future gem of the fast hatchbacks, the Golf. Porsche stepped up to the plate as 914 production was drawing to a close, and bought back project EA 425, on which VW had already paid for work up to date.

However that's another story; for you, the reader, we are about to go racing with the 914. The concept was about to become reality.

The mighty 917 model, purely for racing and a development tool, shook the motor racing world on its first appearance in the late 1960s; eventually in 1970 it would bring Porsche its first outright victory at Le Mans. Could the 914/6 GT bring victory in the GT classes? We will see.

3

The competition begins
Racing in Europe 1970

In the previous two chapters we have taken a brief look at the mid-engine principle and the concept and creation of the 914. Now we come to the focus of our story.

The Porsche ideal in that period – and still in many areas today, although models have deviated of late – was to provide a born-to-compete sports car for the discerning buyer. Ferry Porsche and most of the family-owned company were, and are, enthusiasts. Racing was in the blood, right from the early days of Dr Ferdinand Porsche at the start of the 20th century. Competition falls into several categories, two of which we can roughly define as racing and rallying. Note: to save constant switching of disciplines, we will continue our story first with racing on the tracks. We will then turn to rallying in chapter 7. The European Hillclimb Championships, so much a major feature in the 1970s, are not forgotten and in chapter 10 the results of the 914s in this discipline show just how many events there were – so many, in fact, that we cannot possibly go into detail on all of them, although we will mention a few in the following racing section chapters. Sprints and slaloms in mainland Europe, principally in Germany, were also an area much frequented by the 914, but they are so numerous and mostly regional, and therefore likely to be of little interest worldwide, that we don't go into detail. 914s were used in all forms of motorsport – much more so than many may realize, so whilst we concentrate on the

Mid-engine racing style of the early 1950s. A recent restoration. (©P)

54

The competition begins Racing in Europe 1970

international and national events, we occasionally dip into smaller events to give the depth of flavour.

In the 1950s, mid-engine was fast becoming the way to go racing. We have already seen that Walter Glöckler in Frankfurt, an acquaintance of Ferry Porsche, had started racing early on with the mid-engined concept; Porsche engines powered those early Glöcklers. Ferrari, always a major competitor to Porsche, was late in the game – it stuck with front-engined cars, winning at Le Mans as late as 1962. the first mid-engine sports car from the prancing horse stable only arriving in 1963, with the 250P making a sensational debut at the Sebring 12 Hours. It also came away with a first mid-engined car overall victory at Le Mans, with the 250P of Ludovico Scarfiotti and Lorenzo Bandini. Ferry Porsche was close to the scene: the penny had dropped long ago, but although he had always been convinced of the mid-engine concept, it was only in 1953, with the model 550 Porsche, that factory-entered cars with mid-engines first hit the track. From then on there was no stopping Porsche, although it took many others some time to realize that the mid-engine layout was the best solution to roadholding in racing cars. All the time, though, whilst Ferrari was winning overall using its big engines, Porsche, with its 1500cc 550 model, won its class in 1953, '54, '55, '56 and '57, and with the development of the 550 the RSK won the up-to-2L class with a 1587cc car in 1958, and the same class with the 1600GS in 1960, '61 and '62; in 1963 with the 1962cc model 718/8; in 1964 with the Porsche 904; in 1965 with the 1967cc 904/6; in 1966 with the 906/6, and in 1967 with the 907/6. In 1968, with the engine now up to 2196cc and eight cylinders, the Porsche 907/8 finished 2nd overall and won its class (up to 2500cc). In 1969, the year that the Porsche 914 was first introduced to the public, Porsche again finished 2nd overall with the 3L 908, winning the up-to-3L class, of course! The following year, 1970, was the breakthrough into the top spot at Le Mans, with the now-famous victory of the mighty 917 of Richard Attwood and Hans Herrmann. All these Porsche entries were mid-engined. Surely by now it was logical to go for a mid-engined road car? As we have seen in the previous chapters, the 914 was on a path of destiny. But would it make a good racing car? It had all the requirements. Motor *Sport* magazine's highly respected Bill Boddy said: "Driving the 914 on dry roads, I was quite unable to reach optimum breakaway; you corner faster and faster in disbelief that the car will get round. But it always did." That pretty much sums it up, as most of the road testers said the same thing. However, as we will see, such roadholding capability, whilst fine for road use, did not endear itself to the top racing and rallying professionals of the period.

Porsche, of course, was keen to promote the 914 in the racing scenario, for not only was it in the genes, it also had a lot of cars to sell to the public. Work was already beginning before the paint had dried on the show models to create a Group 4 class 914, to be called a GT, in the famous Werk 1 building in Zuffenhausen. A prototype car was ready by 3 October 1969.

Testing began. Porsche was considering an entry in the 1970 Monte Carlo Rally as early as September 1969. Proof of this can be seen in documentation from Herr Piëch to Herr Bott, dated 25 September that year, where Piëch sets out his desire to prepare three 914/6s and three 911Ss; the 914s were to be powered by the 911S 2.2L engines. Many Carrera 906 parts would be used, including a twin-plug system. However, whilst the racing department was under pressure to produce, management eventually decided to hold back and not play its hand with a new car too quickly. Questions were being asked, and the answers from the development team, led by

Chassis 9140430019 prototype 914/6 GT: the template for 12 special 914/6 GTs that would be created for competition. (©P)

Porsche The Racing 914s

Rainer Bratenstein, deemed it too early to expose an untried car. In fact, today he says: "We were more or less against the 914 as far as the rally business was concerned, because we thought the 911 was the better basis, but the sales and marketing departments started pushing us." Walter Näher, in the same interview with the author, says: "It was Huschke von Hanstein who was pushing us; then instead of the 2.2L S we wanted to use, we had to use the 2L engine for homologation reasons. The 911T."

With the decision to cancel plans for an early entry in the 1970 Monte Carlo Rally, further development was set in the planning programme and a confirmed final specification decided upon for a competition car that would serve the factory team when it was ready and could also be supplied to customers. In the records, we find that several versions were initially foreseen. Version 1 was a street version, Version 2 would be for racing and version 3 would be for rallying. Each version offered three options:

1: A version 1 car (street): a sporty version powered by the 911T engine, fitted with suspension mods but not a full competition spec.

2: A version 2 car (racing): powered by a 1991cc 210bhp engine, to be homologated to Group 4 Special GT up-to-2L.

3: A version 3 car (rally): powered by the 2L 911S engine from 1968 with 160bhp.

The specification of a competition-prepared car as foreseen in 1969 was as follows:

Chassis	
Frame	Welded assembly, sheet-metal box section, unitized with body
Suspension	Front independent suspension with shock absorber struts (system MacPherson), installed with an anti-roll bar
	Rear independent suspension with longitudinal trailing arms
Springs and shock absorbers	Front: torsion bars and Bilstein shock absorbers
	Rear: shock absorber struts with coil springs
Steering:	Rack and pinion
Brakes:	4-pot hydraulic operated ventilated disc brakes, Carrera S, dual circuit
Wheels	Forged alloy, front 6in (7in, 8in), rear 7in (8in, 9in) x 15 Fuchs and Minilite
Engine	
Engine	Carrera 6 Type 901/25, six-cylinder, 1991cc with two triple Weber 46 carburettors, four-stroke boxer, air-cooled
Transmission	5-speed, limited-slip diff, race clutch
Crankcase	Magnesium, pressure casting
Cylinder head	Light alloy
Ignition	Dual circuit, Bosch BHKZ ignition
Dimensions	
Length	3985mm
Width	1700mm
Height	1205mm
Wheelbase	2450mm
Track	Front 1377mm Rear 1427mm
Fuel tank	100L
Oil tank	11L
Transmission	2.5L
Brake fluid	0.3L

For motorsport, everything needed to be lightweight. The interior fitted in the road car was the first thing to be changed: out went the regular carpeting, the radio, parts of the dashboard, many 'comfort' fittings, and on several of the GT factory cars the handbrake was located between the seats, as opposed to its position by the driver's door as on the road cars.

Steering wheels were changed, the door cards were replaced with a thin cardboard panel covered with black vinyl, and a plastic door-release lever replaced the metal item used in the road cars. The steel-framed seats were replaced by vinyl-covered glass-fibre ones with a corduroy-covered foam seat pad.

Externally, boot and bonnet lids became glass-fibre items

100L fuel tank with through-the-bonnet filler. (RS)

The competition begins Racing in Europe 1970

The very recognizable Porsche filler cap tops off the large tank. (RS)

Access panels cut in the floor of the boot – seen here on one of the 914 GTs. (RS)

On racing versions the handbrake consisted of a simple, small lever placed between the seats, which activated the brakes by hydraulics. (RS)

Glass-fibre bonnet and boot with balsa wood cross-pieces for strengthening. (RS)

with cross-supports of balsa wood. The engine cover received a replacement external release mechanism to aid speed of entry, compared with the internally mounted pull lever on the road cars.

America was always going to be a prime target for sales – a country where it was customary for manufacturers to show off their wares by racing, utilising a form of promotion familiar to all – the mantra of 'Race on Sunday, sell them on Monday.' In an effort to develop their public persona, much work was done to prepare a number of 914/6s, straight off the production line, for an assault on the US racing scene and other major events. As such, the USA warrants a detailed section of its own to avoid confusion and constant switching between the USA and Europe. The story of 914 racing in the USA begins in chapter 8. For now, and in the next few chapters, we will concentrate on the 914's motor racing in Europe.

Porsche The Racing 914s

The oil cooler was moved to the front and protected inside by a cover. (RS)

One of the original 914-6 racing GTs as it is today, fully restored – formerly the Walter Simonis car. (RS)

Chassis 914 043 0709 would be used extensively for testing and driver training. Here in Sweden it's tyre testing. (©P)

Björn Waldegård would be the main driver during the tests. (©P)

The competition begins Racing in Europe 1970

welded into place where the suspension pick-up points were located. Under-body protection was different for the rally cars, as we will see later. In Germany, ONS and FIA rules called for driver protection by a separate roll bar in addition to the integral one included in the car's design.

It was decided that once the 914/6 had been homologated by the FIA, a series of special 914/6s would be built with the FIA touring car regulations in mind – specifically Special Grand Touring. 500 examples of the production six-cylinder road-going 914 were required to comply. This would be easily achieved in the early part of the year, and over 2600 of the six-cylinder production 914s were built by the end of 1970. Following the initial tests by various drivers, including Björn Waldegård, who did a lot of work for the team, Porsche decided on the special series to be built with the reference M471, a general term for a sport version. "The M471 designation," says a Porsche insider, "is a legendary number. M471 changes sometimes, but has existed since the start of Porsche competition. Normally it is the 'sport' version of a car. The even hotter designation was M491 (like the '73 RSRs). For example, with the 911 Carrera RS 2.7, the sport version carried the M471 designation whilst M472 was the touring version."

For racing purposes the standard ride height would be reduced to allow only 4in (101mm) of ground clearance. Various makes and types of shock absorbers were tried, including those frequently seen today: Bilstein and Koni. The brakes on the 914/6 GT were those

Björn Waldegård (left) shared the driving with Åke Andersson. (©P)

Testing had continued through the winter and in all conditions, as we see above in the early part of 1970 in Austria and Sweden, where Björn Waldegård and Åke Andersson would be the drivers for a series of tyre tests.

Early track competition was thought to have appeared first in Germany in late 1969. However, ONS (Oberste National SportKomission) records, which contain details of every event held under their jurisdiction as the governing body for motorsport in Germany at the time, show no early competition. The first time we see a 914 in competition is on 4-6 February 1970 at the Bayerische Winter-Rallye Marktredwitz, where Weinberger/Trübsbach took a 914/4 to 5th overall in the unlimited GT class.

Later that February, a series of distance tests was carried out with a six-cylinder car at the new Weissach track, where a 914/6 fitted with a 220bhp six-cylinder engine covered a distance of 7922km. Wheels, tyres, shock absorbers, brakes – everything breakable – was tested to near destruction. Weaknesses were found. The suspension mountings would not, in standard form, be strong enough for the rigours of motorsport, so in the limited-production factory GT model (12 cars) extra steel plates were

FIA requirements allowed Porsche to install a cage design, which also stiffened what was deemed a rather flexible chassis floor. (©P)

59

Porsche The Racing 914s

New and stronger front lower wishbones were installed, along with different thicknesses of anti-roll bar being made available, depending on the intended use. (©P)

Domed pistons and twin-plug heads assist in boosting the power output. (©P)

from the racing 911S, fitted with lightweight alloy callipers and ventilated discs. Where the regulations allowed, the steel bonnets at the front and rear were replaced by glass-fibre items, as were the rear and front bumper units. For those cars destined for circuit racing, the heavy flip-up mechanisms for the headlights were also removed. In the engine department, the 914/6 GT used Weber carburettors at this stage rather than mechanical fuel-injection, which would come later. The cylinder heads had bigger valves and the compression ratio was raised by utilising domed pistons.

Steel rods and a counterweighted crankshaft with fully balanced components saw an engine with 210hp (DIN) available at 8000rpm. In addition, the racing engines could be tuned to give 220hp (DIN). For racing, the car weighed in at 1900lb (861.8 kg), some 200lb (90.72kg) less than the standard 914/6 production model. Even so, this allowed plenty of scope for further lightening, being still some 60lb (27.22kg) above the required homologation weight.

At the factory, according to internal documents, plans were being made in early February (6/2/70) to prepare and send a 914/6 to that year's Sebring 12 Hours in the USA, and also to take two cars to Sicily for Targa Florio training in March. On 20 February there appears a documentary internal notice of consideration being given to an upgrade kit of special parts, which could be supplied to customers to create their own racing GTs. This kit was called a Sportpaket, widely known as the sport kit. The parts list (ref number 6024.14) to turn a production 914/6 into a race car ran to 45 pages, covering everything from engine to handbrake lever. In this same memo, we also see mention of competing in the Tour de Corse later in the year, and plans to compete on the Tour de France Auto, and the Marathon de la Route also crops up for the first time.

But first there was more testing to be done. Porsche combined the testing of two 914s used earlier for tyre testing with training for that year's Targa Florio. The factory racing team, headed by Rico Steinemann at that time, headed off to Sicily with the two special factory cars, chassis 914 043 0705 and 0709. The two 914/6 GTs, in rally specification, would join three 911s for training on the Targa Florio circuit, along with two of the new 908-3s and a road-registered 917 race car. The 917 and the 908s, normally in the pale blue livery of Gulf, had to be painted red on the instructions of the Sicilian Police Department, because testing was being carried out on roads open to traffic. By painting the cars red, they reasoned,

The competition begins Racing in Europe 1970

Chassis 914 043 0705, one of the original factory 914/6 GTs registered as S-U 3908, would have a hard life before being refurbished and sold to Peter Gregg of Brumos Porsche to race in 1971. (©P)

Handwritten notes by Günter Steckkönig, regarding the cars involved at the Targa Florio test, confirm the two 914s in use. (©P)

oncoming traffic would see them more readily, and thus safety would be less compromised!

The 914/6 GTs and 911s were used by the drivers to learn the course and note any changes that had taken place since the year before. Drivers were Björn Waldegård, Leo Kinnunen, Pedro Rodríguez, Brian Redman, Jo Siffert, Vic Elford and Richard Attwood. I think the reader will agree, that is some line-up!

The 908 was the favoured car for the high-speed multi-cornered Targa course; while the 917 was, of course, incredibly fast, it suffered under-body damage during testing and was heavy on its tyres. The 908-3s would be chosen for the race in May. The 917 suffered further damage while it was being driven by one of the Porsche engineers back to the garage in Cefalù: it was involved in an incident with a local Sicilian truck, and although moving at relatively low speed, the 917 was shunted hard into a tree and broke in half. Fortunately both drivers escaped with only superficial injuries. Both the 914 GTs were in the familiar orange colour that Porsche was utilising at that time, as confirmed in the author's interview with Rainer Bratenstein, Günter Steckkönig and Walter Näher in 2015.

These were two of the eventual 12 special 914/6 GTs built at the competition department under the charge of Rainer Bratenstein. (Data indicated that two more numbers were allocated. In his official record, Jürgen Barth states that 11 914/6 GTs were built as special factory cars in 1970, and three more in 1971, which of course makes 14. However, although the numbers for the other two were allocated, it seems the cars were never built.)

Porsche The Racing 914s

Chassis 914 043 0709, last used in Sweden for tyre testing, would go on to be one of the practice cars for the Monte Carlo Rally. (©P)

Following the introduction of the 914 at the Frankfurt Show in 1969, the idea of racing the cars had been in the mind of the Porsche factory team, which was at the time heavily involved with the 917 developments. There was also the potential of the dealer teams which, with factory support, could do more privately to promote sales of the 914/6. Amongst these were the Strähle Company, Hahn Motor Sports and the very active Reutlingen-based Autohaus Max Moritz. Moritz had set up a Zündapp motorcycle agency in Reutlingen, launching his first car sales in 1936 alongside his motorcycles. After World War II, Moritz became a VW main agent

The competition begins Racing in Europe 1970

The Max Moritz team was among the first to try an off-the-production-line 914/6 in 1969. In this photo from 1971, we see (l-r) race engineers Johann Malle, Norbert Schwander, Dieter Schweizer, team boss Erwin Bock and race engineer Waldemar Ulbich, with their famous Gerd Quist/Dieter Krumm 914/6 GT. (©P)

First race in 1970 at the Hockenheimring: Rudolf Sauter in the Autohaus Max Moritz entry finished 9th in the up-to-2L class. (Ferret)

63

Porsche The Racing 914s

and extended the buildings as the business grew into a modern car dealership. In 1962 he opened a second workshop in the Max-Planck-Strasse in Reutlingen, forming a racing team with a series of 911s and, over the next few years, the 914/6 GT. Several of the factory kits would eventually appear on its menu.

These teams will get plenty of mentions as we progress with the story. Let's start with the aforementioned Autohaus Max Moritz team, which put its first 914/6 GT on track in anger for the first time at a round of the German National GT Championship at Hockenheim on 12 April 1970. This entry is also generally thought to be the first competitive outing for a 914/6 GT on a race circuit, and the ONS records show that Rudolf Sauter in the AvD-WAC-Jim Clark Memorial race finished 9th in up-to-2L.

Two other 914/6 models were entered: race No 137 for Gerhard Denu, entered by Porsche dealer Autohaus Rolf Götz, and car 138 for Ingo Hopp; unfortunately their participation has eluded us. Just a week later, the respected Nürburgring 300km race (DARM Int ADAC-300-km-Rennen Nürburgring um den Goodyear Pokal) saw Ingo Hopp involved again (car 27) and two more entries: Gerhard Denu in the Autohaus Rolf Götz No 26 car and Willi Nolte in a privately-entered car. Unfortunately it was dnf for Denu and Hopp, but a 7th in GT 2L for Nolte.

In France on 26 April the annual Coupes de Vitesse, a round of the French National Championship, would see one Fritz Leinenweber compete with a 914/6 and finish 4th overall at the Montlhéry circuit. Leinenweber was a well-known competitor in Porsches, having started with a 356 in the early 1950s, and had run in the 1969 season under the Gepard racing name in a fine-looking Porsche 910. It is not known if the Porsche Racing Team Pirmasens entry was a

ADAC 300km Nürburgring, 19 April 1970. Gerhard Denu, driving the Autohaus Rolf Götz entry – a kit-equipped GT. Unfortunately, it was a dnf on this occasion. (©P)

Ingo Hopp in his privately-entered 914/6 GT in the ADAC Nürburgring 300km. (©P)

The competition begins Racing in Europe 1970

Early days: Willi Nolte in the car noted as chassis 914 043 0462. Originally sold to Hülpert Porsche in Dortmund, it would be one of the production 914/6s converted to a GT by the use of a factory-supplied kit. At the Nürburgring 300km it was listed as a privately-entered vehicle. (©P)

GT or a regular 914/6. Up against tough competition, he was able to finish just behind the 3rd placed Lola T70, 2nd placed GT40 and the victor, Guy Ligier, in his Ligier JS1.

The day before had seen the sixth running of the Monza 1000km in Italy. Claude Haldi had entered in a 914/6 acquired by Porsche Club Romand, however it failed to qualify for round 4 of the International Championship for Manufacturers. On 3 May in Germany, at the DARM event at Kaufbeuren airfield (one of many airfield circuits in use in that period), Götz and Hopp were out again, with Hopp claiming a podium placing for a 914/6, taking 3rd in GT2 in this German National round. This is probably the first top-three finish for the 914/6.

On the same weekend in Sicily, Brian Redman, destined to win the Targa Florio of 1970 with Jo Siffert, was using one of the 914/6 GTs from the March test in a pre-race practice session before stepping into the 908 on 3 May to tackle the great race. Brian Redman is recorded as saying: "It's often trickier during practice because the roads are open; there is a lot of traffic and you have 900 corners to remember in the 43 mile circuit. You hardly ever learn it. For instance, at the Nürburgring, with 170 corners over around 14 miles, you can learn that in about 60 laps. But at the Targa it's an impossible task." Ingo Hopp was out again on 17 May with his all-yellow 914/6 GT in a round of the German National Championship in Belgium, on the border with Germany at Zolder: he was to come home 6th overall.

Porsche 914s, of course, would soon find their way to Spain, like France, a traditional hotbed of motorsport. The first car we see racing there is actually the German entry of Joseph 'Sepp' Greger, a hillclimb racer who was running in the European Hillclimb Championship. Hillclimbing was, and is, a favourite sector of motorsports in mainland Europe, particularly in Germany and Switzerland. In 1969 Sepp Greger became the German champion in a Porsche 911, and now in 1970 he was part of the 914 promotional programme. Porsche had even put out a press release (numbered PRP 17a), dated 19 May 1970 on the occasion of the International ADAC-Nibelungen-Bergrennen, held on 17 May, round 1 of the European Hillclimb Championship. The press release stated that Greger had finished 1st in the GT up-to-2L class up the 3.3km climb on a very slippery track. A footnote says that Sepp was also driving another car, a Porsche 910, in the unlimited class, and set fastest time of the day. Now he would run a 914 in the 7th Montseny hillclimb, the second round of the European Hillclimb Championship, near Barcelona in Catalonia, Spain, on 24 May. His car, believed to be chassis 914 043 0674, finished 9th overall and 2nd in Group 4. The 1991cc 914/6 was a customer GT-kitted car. The 1970 event was won overall by the famous Georgian royal family member, Jorge de Bagration, in a Porsche 908.

Continuing for a moment with hillclimbing, as mentioned, the European Bergmeister Championship was a big deal on the competition calendar, and the factory teams in the 1950s and '60s regularly sent cars. From 1968, Porsche built special, super-light cars like the 909 Bergspyder.

On 31 May, whilst Gerhard Denu was finishing 3rd in the over-1300 GT class at the Bremgarten GT race in the Autohaus Rolf Götz car, one of the season's big events was taking place at the Nürburgring: the 1970 edition of the Nürburgring 1000km. This

Porsche The Racing 914s

The competition begins Racing in Europe 1970

would see the opening full-blooded assault in a major race for the 914/6 GT. By this time, a lot of testing had been done at Weissach by drivers, mechanics and various members of the competition department. Quite a few of the 914/6 production cars had gone to the dealer agencies, where they were built into racing cars utilising the special kit of parts which Porsche was supplying to its special customers at that period of development. This saw the introduction of the already mentioned sport kit, more of which in a moment. Racing driver Günter Steckkönig, then at the start of his illustrious career, told the author: "I think the dealers liked the 914 because it was a bit cheaper than the 911 race car. But it was a very difficult area at this time for Porsche to go racing with the 914, because to everyone Porsche was the 911, and now we had got a new, completely different car. Strähle, Hahn, Max Moritz and others were up for the challenge and said okay, let's try this new car. The car we had did not come from Porsche ready to race. The dealers had to decide to build a 914 race car, and they built a GT racer from a production car with a kit supplied by Porsche. Step-by-step they built the car in their workshops. Strähle was in Schorndorf. We had good help from Porsche, of course. At the time I was a private driver, not a factory driver, and the Nürburgring 1000km would be an important step for me."

The entries were:

#	Drivers	Chassis	Team
88	Robert F Huhn/Günther Schwarz	043 1415	Lufthansa
93	Paul Kaiser/Günter Steckkönig	043 0258	Hahn Motorfahrzeuge
101	Alexander Nolte/Werner Christmann	043 0462	Hülpert Porsche
96	Gerd Quist/Dietrich Krumm	043 0691	Max Moritz

It was the international race debut for each of the teams, and a major turnout of Porsche personnel was present. Practice went well and the specially prepared cars of Hahn Motorfahrzeuge and Autohaus Max Moritz were placed 42nd and 41st respectively on the grid. The experienced private driver pairing of Günter Steckkönig and Paul Kaiser performed even better, with a 36th grid place. Nolte and Christmann were on 45th. All were entered in the GT up-to-2L class. 84 cars in total had entered the race; 58 qualified and 54 started – huge numbers for a grid, but remember, this was to run on the full 14.189 mile (22.835km) circuit. The race covered 624.3 miles (1004.740km).

It was cold and rain was in the air for the whole event. Jo Siffert had set the pole time with a 7min 43.3sec lap – an average speed of 110.254mph (177.436km/h), in the No 20 Porsche 908/3, the fastest of the 914/6 GTs being the car of Kaiser/Steckkönig with

The very special mid-engine 909 Bergspyder, driven in 1968 by Rolf Stommelen. It weighed just 430kg (948lb). Hillclimbing continued to be a major sporting attraction in the 1960s and '70s. 914s were used extensively in this discipline, as can be seen in the statistics in chapter 10. (©P)

67

Porsche The Racing 914s

Nolte/Christmann in the Hülpert Porsche-entered 914/6 race spec kit customer car – a racing debut in the Nürburgring 1000km for chassis 0430462. (©P)

a time of 9min 58.9sec. At the start, the Porsche 908 of the John Wyer Gulf team, driven by Pedro Rodríguez/Leo Kinnunen, shot into an early lead; they would have a gap of 14sec at the end of the first lap.

As the laps went by, Siffert in the sister car closed in, but both got bogged down in pit stops and then Rodríguez went off the road. The Siffert/Redman car stopped on lap 22 with oil pressure problems. The race was won by Vic Elford and Kurt Ahrens in a Porsche Salzburg 908/3. Meanwhile, in the intermittent mist and rain, the 914/6s were running like clockwork, and at the finish were only pipped for GT class victory by a rapid 911L of the Porsche Salzburg team in 18th overall.

Second in the 2L GT class was the No 88 car of Huhn/Schwarz, coming 19th overall and finishing just five seconds down on the

The competition begins Racing in Europe 1970

043 0258: a 914/6 built up into GT. Entered by Hahn Motorfahrzeuge for Paul Kaiser/Günter Steckkönig, this car would eventually find its way to Porsche+Audi in the USA for 1971. (©P)

Loos/Pesch 911. Along the way, the 914 set fastest lap in the class with 9min 42sec, an average speed of 77.7mph (125.04km/h). Third in class and 20th overall would be the 93 car of Kaiser/Steckkönig; 4th in class and 21st overall were Nolte/Christmann.

The 5th place in the class was taken by the Quist/Krumm 914/6. For the international debut of the 914/6 it had been a creditable performance all round in exalted company. The car had proved to be reliable and consistent – vital in this, its first real competition test in the big league.

Just how reliable it was can be seen from a detailed study of the records (though not all the races are listed in our chart in chapter 10). Chassis 914 043 0462, for example, entered by Hülpert

69

Porsche The Racing 914s

1000km at the Nürburgring Huhn/Schwarz, 043 1415 GT: in this race-kitted car, sponsored and entered by Lufthansa, they would get fastest lap in the 2L category. (©P)

The competition begins Racing in Europe 1970

Quist/Krumm in the Max Moritz 914/6: 5th in the GT 2L class. (©P)
Inset: Leif Hansen (in the car), about to be accompanied by the future King of Sweden for a few laps of experience on the Anderstorp circuit. (NN)

Porsche Dortmund during 1970, raced on ten occasions, then a further 16 times in the hands of EFG racing team Dortmund, before going to Kamei Racing Team Wolfsburg to race another 14 times, and then another 18 times in the hands of Franz Konrad by the time 1976 arrived!

In Sweden on 7 June, round 4 of the European 2L Sports Prototype Championship took place, where another GT car built up with one of the official factory sport kits supplied by Porsche was entered as a 914/6 GT, thought to be chassis 043 0071. Leif Hansen was the entrant and driver.

The overall result was decided over two races on the circuit at Anderstorp, each comprising 40 laps of the 4km (6.43 mile) circuit. At the end of the day Hansen and his 914/6 GT finished 7th overall and 1st in Group 4. It is thought that this may have been the chassis also driven occasionally in circuit racing by Björn Waldegård in 1970.

The big race of any year for the sports car racing fraternity was – and still is – the Le Mans 24 Hours. This iconic race, which was first run in 1923, is the ultimate test of endurance. The 1970 version, the 38th edition of the great race, was to see the first overall victory at Le Mans for Porsche; it would be the start of its legendary dominance for many years to come. (Author's note: I was privileged

71

Come qualifying day, the car covered the 8.369 mile (13.469km) distance of the La Sarthe circuit in 3min 19.8sec, an average of over 150mph. No one had seen anything like it! (©P)

May 1970: the 917 long-tail, straight out of the factory at Werk 1, Zuffenhausen. In this frighteningly fast projectile, Vic Elford and Kurt Ahrens took pole at the 1970 Le Mans. (©P)

Willy Kauhsen, seen here in the second 917 long-tail, was 12th on the grid. The Larrousse/Kauhsen car finished 2nd overall. (©P)

The competition begins Racing in Europe 1970

Leaving the pits for practice, the 914/6 GT factory special (chassis 043 1020), built for the Sonauto team at Porsche and to be driven by Claude Ballot-Léna/ Guy Chasseuil, passes the eventual race winner, the No 23 917K. (FRA/AJ)

to be there to see it, so can report here from experience.) All eyes were on the incredible 917 Langheck (long-tail), one of the most spectacular cars to grace the La Sarthe circuit.

There was not only one of these cars but two, the result of a lot of wind-tunnel work. Car 3 was also a 917 Langheck. Gérard Larrousse/Willy Kauhsen had the pleasure of driving the spectacular Technicolor green and blue example.

In the all-white Langheck of Vic Elford/Kurt Ahrens, Ahrens took pole at an average speed of 150.798mph (242.685km/h) around the 8.369 mile (13.469km) La Sarthe circuit in a time of 3min 19.8sec! No one had seen anything like it before. As well as these two super-fast cars, there were also six 5L Porsche 917K super-cars to take the start. The performance of the 917s is legendary, and whilst the long-tails were the fastest, it was the 917K of the Porsche Salzburg team, driven by Richard Attwood and Hans Herrmann, that took the victory that year.

Whilst the 917s were taking all the limelight, there on the entry list were Claude Ballot-Léna and Guy Chasseuil in the 914/6 GT chassis 043 1020, both having been well acquainted with the products from Stuttgart in the previous years. They were, however, the only entry to turn up out of four originally on the list for qualifying, the missing entries being the André Wicky and Tartaruga team cars and the Nicolas Koob car. Porsche France importer Auguste Veuillet's Sonauto team would run the lone car of Ballot-Léna/Chasseuil. (Auguste Veuillet, incidentally, was one of the drivers in the first Porsche to be raced at Le Mans in

Porsche France importer Sonauto would eventually run a team of cars, building four for competition of all types. (P)

1951.) Scrutineering began on the Monday before the race in the traditional way in front of Le Mans Cathedral, finishing at midday on Wednesday, ready for the first practice session that started at 6pm on the Wednesday evening. Practice brought no problems on either the Wednesday or the Thursday night sessions, the big Porsches at the front of the provisional grid dominating proceedings. The factory-prepared 914/6 GT chassis 043 1020 was ready to race, qualifying 45th on the grid of 51 starters.

The cars were set diagonally, as per all the previous Le Mans starts, but this year, following John Woolf's tragic death (the result of a horrendous accident on the opening lap whilst driving his own privately-entered 917 Porsche in 1969), the drivers were seated in their cars in qualifying order, and with the mandatory (for the first time) seatbelts done up, and the start would not involve the traditional scenario of drivers running across the road to their cars. It was the only time this start was to be used, but it was truly dramatic, as the author can recall.

The buzz of the crowds and the sounds of the pre-race festivities started to quieten, and then silence fell over the multitude. It was a bit chilly, with a cool breeze and dampness in the air after a very hot week. The excitement rose as the tension increased. No personnel were on the track, just 51 cars all lined up. At 4pm the French tricolour flag was dropped by none other than Ferry Porsche. The cars were all set to start on the button, and so it was that all 51 fired up together. The sound of thousands of horsepower going from silence to near maximum in a fraction of a second is something never to be forgotten. Elford, in the rumbling, white long-tail 917, shot off up the road. The race had begun.

Rain and violent thunderstorms came and went day and night, with vivid lightning making the action on track seem like a scene from a Wagner Opera or Shakespearian drama. Through the night they ran, a night interspersed with rain and enforced slow driving periods due to accidents.

As several of the faster front runners in the GT class dropped out, so the reliable Porsche flat-six in the No 40 purred away, gradually climbing its way up the field, until by 8am on Sunday, as daylight came, the little 914/6 GT was up to 10th from 45th on the grid.

At this stage it is time for the teams, and certainly the team managers of those cars still running, to start biting their nails. Could they make the finish? With just a few hours to go, amazingly, the ultra-reliable 914/6 GT had moved up to the front end of the field, untroubled by the problems of others. Soon after midday, the Sonauto car was in 7th place overall and 5th in index of performance, with the Greder/Rouget Corvette ahead, though not quite in sight. The more powerful Corvette in the 5L+ GT class pressed on, though its drivers found that they could not shake off the smaller, but more manoeuvrable, Porsche. Already Ballot-Léna and Chasseuil had got ahead of several of the prototypes and seven of the 911s that were still running. After 22 hours, this was excellent news for the PR people. Suddenly the heavens opened again, and the 914 nearly went off near the top end of the pits, aquaplaning in the cloudburst. Fortunately it recovered and gingerly pressed on. As the 24 hours came up and the chequered flag came down, it looked like Sonauto would be proclaiming a top-ten finish, 7th overall. However, at Le Mans, as at all events, there are rules, and one of those rules is that to be classified as a finisher you have to complete

The competition begins Racing in Europe 1970

The start, with the super-quick front runners well on their way; the 914/6 GT of the Sonauto team begins the long 24-hour haul. (©P)

A dry track would soon change to an intermittently wet one. For the slower cars, the object of the game was to make fast and steady progress, while keeping out of the way of the flying 917s and Ferrari 512s. In fact, the 911s and the 914 were lapped after only three circuits of La Sarthe by the lead 917s! (©WG)

In the half-light under darkening skies and heavy rain, the 914/6 kept going, whilst the two following cars (No 20, the Gulf Porsche 917 of Siffert/Redman, and No 63, the 911S of Chenevière/Rey) went out at the 12- and 13-hour marks respectively. (©P)

Still raining: Sunday morning, dicing with the Wicky Racing entry 911T of Guy Verrier/Sylvain Garant. (©WG)

not only enough laps to put you ahead of the next competitor, but also cover a minimum distance set out by the organizers for that particular car. The Henri Greder/Jean-Paul Rouget Corvette had suffered maladies during the night, a night of attrition in the pouring rain for many competitors, but it had survived and come to the finish, having completed 286 laps when they crossed the line in 6th place (according to official records), having led the GT class overall for 16 hours. But the little 914/6 GT had been catching the mighty Corvette by a few seconds a lap, hour after hour, and eventually crossed the line on 285 laps, having covered a greater distance than it was required to do to be classified, according to its allotted target, whilst the Corvette had failed to cover its own distance requirement. The ACO (Automobile Club de l'Ouest), organizers and rule setters of the event, applied the letter of their laws, and the Corvette was officially not classified, promoting the very happy Sonauto team to 6th place, and to victory in the GT class.

The competition begins Racing in Europe 1970

Attwood/Herrmann, first outright victory for Porsche at Le Mans, 19 years after the first running of a Porsche at the Le Mans 24 Hours. (©P)

The despair in the Corvette camp was palpable, whilst the joyful Porsche team was blessing their good fortune. Porsche's marketing department now had a good story to tell.

Remarkably, in 9th across the line but also unclassified, came the Steve McQueen-entered Solar Productions Porsche 908 of Herbert Linge/Jonathan Williams. McQueen had wanted to drive, but his management and insurers would not agree, for this was the year that the filmmakers came to Le Mans – and what a story that was! You may well have seen the film Le Mans; if not, I recommend you get a copy now – it's one of the few great motor racing films. Dated, but apart from the lightweight story, superb.

Whilst excitement in sports car racing was mainly being concentrated on Le Mans, there was racing still to be done in the various national series in each of the motor sporting countries of

Porsche The Racing 914s

Solar Productions Porsche 908 of Herbert Linge/Jonathan Williams. (RS)

The PR machine went into action to promote the virtues of the new 914 Porsche for all prospective customers to see. (©P)

No slouch behind the wheel himself: actor Steve McQueen with a line-up of Porsche 917s and Ferrari 512s, filming after the Le Mans weekend. (©P)

The competition begins Racing in Europe 1970

Europe. It is to Hockenheim that we now turn, the same weekend as Le Mans (13-14 June), for a round of the German Championship. Four 914s were entered. Hart Ski Racing had entered a 914/6 GT for Ernst Seiler, carrying No 53. This was chassis 043 0181, a customer-supplied 914/6 fitted with a GT kit by Porsche. This car would go on to live a long life, and is still in existence in private hands today.

Ingo Hopp brought his 914 out and came home 6th in GT 2L, with Paul Kaiser hot on his heels in the No 60 car in 7th, thought to be the chassis 043 0258 supplied to Hahn Motorfahrzeuge and built into a GT utilising the official kit and entered by Hahn. The final 914 was that of Günther Schwarz, 8th overall in the Scuderia Lufthansa car, chassis 043 1415.

As previously mentioned, the European Hillclimb Championship was an important competition from the 1950s to the 1970s, and this year there were seven rounds:

24 May Montseny, Barcelona Spain
21 June: Mont Ventoux, France
5 July: Trento-Bondone, Italy
12 July: Cesana-Sestriere, Italy
26 July: Freiburg-Schauinsland, Germany
9 August: Mont-Dore, Clermont-Ferrand, France
29 September: Dobratsch-Klagenfurt, Austria

On 21 June at the French Hillclimb and European Championship round on the mighty Mont Ventoux, Sepp Greger would finish 9th overall and 1st in Group 4, with fellow 914/6 GT competitor Henri Balas 5th in Group 4. The next European Hillclimb Championship round was on 5 July: the Trento-Bondone in Italy. At this one, Greger would come home 3rd in Group 4. In Germany on 5 July it was back to Hockenheim for six of the 914/6 GT racers for the European Sports Car Championship and rounds of the German National Championships.

Ernst Seiler and Gustav Schlup would run in this race. Seiler took 9th overall in the second of the two 30-lap qualifying races (aggregate to count), but a dnf in the first of those two races led to non-classification overall. Schlup finished 13th overall. In the GT national race, Gerd Quist took 4th overall and won the 2L class in his 043 0691 Autohaus Max Moritz-entered car. Paul Kaiser

Ernst Seiler. (MaxPP)

Ernst Seiler en-route to 5th overall and 2nd in GT 2L in the Hart Ski-entered 914/6 GT sport-kit car built at Porsche. (MaxPP)

79

Porsche The Racing 914s

put in a good performance to finish 8th overall and 2nd in the GT 2L class to Quist, with Günther Schwarz in the Scuderia Lufthansa entry finishing 24th overall, and Gerhard Denu in the Autohaus Rolf Götz car finishing 15th overall.

The European Hillclimb Championships had moved on to the Cesana-Sestrieres hillclimb, Italy, for the fourth round of 1970. Sepp Greger would again compete and finish 3rd in Group 4. The championship moved on to Freiburg-Schauinsland on 26 July, and here Greger again finished 3rd in Group 4.

Hockenheim, home to literally dozens of races each year. On 5 July it would be the European Sports Prototype Championship races. (Vin)

Ernst Seiler (chassis 043 0181) working hard, but he would not classify in the 5th round of the European Sports Car Championship at Hockenheim. (©P)

The competition begins Racing in Europe 1970

Returning to Italy, on 19 July, the next round of the European Sports Car Championship took place at Mugello, where three 914/6 GTs would take part, two of them new ones – those of Carlo Fabri, of whom we will hear more later, and Elvio Maria Zanini. Fabri came home 9th in the 2L GT Class, with Zanini four places ahead in 5th, both completing just four laps of the huge 66.2km circuit. Over 70 starters lined up; 41 finished. This was an event of attrition, with many famous names going out, including Vic Elford and the Italian favourite from the Targa Florio, Nino Vaccarella. The exhausting race was won by Arturo Merzario ahead of Leo Kinnunen, both in Abarth 2000 SPs.

The German GT Championships were taking place at Ulm Laupheim the same weekend as Mugello, and here Dieter Krumm took victory in the Max Moritz 914/6 GT car, chassis 043 0691. Second was Paul Kaiser in the Hahn Motorfahrzeuge entry, followed by Hart Ski-entered Ernst Seiler in 3rd.

At the non-championship National GT race at Niederstetten, Germany, on 26 July, we see Paul Kaiser finish 1st overall, this time beating Dieter Krumm (chassis 043 0691) to 2nd place. Racing at the airfield circuit of Sembach came next, and here the Special GT up-to-2L race was dominated by the 914/6s: 1st Hermann Dorner, 2nd Ingo Hopp, 3rd Willi Nolte.

On 9 August, six 914/6 GTs headed up the Group 4 non-championship race at the Hockenheim Motodrom; yet again the little cars took control in the up-to-2L class, with Krumm 1st, Huhn 2nd, followed by Kaiser 4th, Hopp 6th, and the Pirmasens Porsche Racing Team, a new 914 entrant to this series, with American Bob Stoddard driving, finishing 10th in the class.

By August 1970 the 914/6 had demonstrated that, in spite of the negative

Ernst Seiler lifts a wheel en route to 3rd place at the Ulm Laupheim German National GT Championship race, chassis 0430 0181. (MaxPP)

Hockenheim, 16 August 1970: a front-row start for Ernst Seiler in the Swiss Rennsport regional non-championship race. (MaxPP)

vibes from the general Porsche-loving public, and, in fact, some of the professional rally drivers who had been conducting tests, it was no lemon amongst the semi-professional and amateur racing drivers. Here was a car that could get results in competitive conditions. It had also proven successful on regional and even international rallies, as we will see when we reach chapter 7.

So far we have looked at the start made by the dealer teams and private entries. At this point it is worth considering where the factory was in terms of development. The Porsche competition department had built up a number of 'works' cars. The chassis built so far were:

914 043 0019: According to Rainer Bratenstein and Walter Näher, this was the first prototype test car; it was dark green.
914 043 0705: A test and training car used at the Targa Florio test days in March.
914 043 0709: A test car that had been used for tyre assessments earlier in the spring, and in Sicily with 0705.
914 043 1640: A test car that was used to develop the cars for the planned attempt on the Marathon de la Route. Registered as S-04732, it had taken a heck of a pounding and was destined to be broken up.

In addition to these four, also in-build or nearly completed were:
914 043 0983: Also said to have been a test car, and may have been a factory GT kit-built car. It was eventually sold to Gotthard Egerland.
914 043 2541: Built into a Group 6 spec car for the Marathon de la Route.
914 043 2542: Built into a Group 4 spec car for the Marathon de la Route.
914 043 2543: Built into a Group 6 spec car for the Marathon de la Route.

There were plans, too, to tackle the British RAC Rally in the autumn, and it is said that chassis 914 043 1732 would be used first for training and then on the RAC rally, but at this stage in 1970 nothing had been finalized. As the reader will have noted, three cars were to be prepared for the Marathon de la Route, held on the Nürburgring race track.

Before we take in this event, let's take a brief look at its history. The Marathon de la Route started life in 1931, though it traces its roots back to the 1920s as a randonnée d'endurance, with a run from Liège to Paris and back. In 1927, the endurance event ran Liège-Biarritz-Liège (2300km). Then followed the 1930 edition: Liège-Madrid-Liège (3300km), taking 83 hours to complete. In 1931, it became Liège-Rome-Liège for cars. (Motorcycles played a part too. In the 1920s, a Liège-Sheffield event took place, and in the 1930s Liège-Milan-Liège, all run by the Motor Union of Liège.)

The challenge remained as the Liège-Rome-Liège throughout the 1930s. War intervened, of course, but the event restarted as the Liège-Rome-Liège in 1950. In 1951, 138 cars started what had pretty much become a race rather than an endurance trial: only 57 were classified as finishers! In 1961, the race changed to Liège-Sofia-Liège until 1965, when it first ran at the Nürburgring as the 82 Hours of the Nürburgring. The change was deemed necessary, as the increasing volume of traffic meant racing on public roads offered too great a risk to drivers and other road users alike. The mighty Nürburgring, with all its twists and turns, was ideal: road-like conditions, but on a track where everybody was at least going in the same direction (usually, anyway!). They kept extending the distance, with the 1966 event becoming the Marathon de la Route 84 Hours at the Nürburgring. In 1967 Porsche took its first victory, with Vic Elford/Hans Herrmann/Jochen Neerpasch driving a 911. In 1968 the Porsche victory was repeated with the 911 of Herbert Linge/Dieter Glemser/Willi Kauhsen. The 1969 Marathon went to Lancia, but we arrive now to 1970, which was to be the penultimate race.

Renamed again to 86 Hours, the Marathon de la Route was a style of race from a bygone era, and its days were numbered. The logistics and planning that went into this event are legendary. Imagine it today: all the mechanics, drivers, spare parts, fuels and lubricants, catering for 86 hours of racing, plus teams of personnel to support the racing element. If the Le Mans 24 Hours was big, this was indeed a mammoth event in every respect. It commanded a lot of publicity and to win here again would be a big deal for the team, the marketing men and the name of Porsche itself, because, as we have seen, Porsche had won it twice already with the famous 911. They had form; they knew how to race in this event and win. If the 914 model could do the same as the 911, then the publicity gained would be extremely useful.

The factory test cars had undergone continuous trials at Weissach. Walter Näher told the author: "All the guys had driven during the tests, because it was such a huge job. A lot of the engineers were conscripted, too, including us. Day and night we ran the test cars continuously for days on end, only interrupted by mechanical problems. We tested everything, because the race would be non-stop over 86 hours."

The rules were complex regarding pit stops, and a lot of time could be lost over the simplest of problems. The Le Mans race held in June runs over 24 hours; we are talking here about a race the

The competition begins Racing in Europe 1970

The programme for the 1970 Marathon de la Route. (RK)

equivalent of three Le Mans 24 Hours races and then some, and it was into this cauldron that the Porsche factory team was flung on 18 August 1970. In fact, the decision to do the Marathon had been taken quite early on, and an order placed on the Karmann company (the makers of the bodies – see previous chapters) to create three body shells with the factory 'sport kit' fitted. The order on Karmann is dated 25 February 1970; the cars were scheduled to be delivered on 19 June, with construction scheduled to be completed by 1 July 1970. A further memo in the archives, dated 2 June 1970, and bearing the signature of Ferdinand Piëch, confirms the last two dates. Three cars were prepared – see the pictures overleaf.

Arriving at the Nürburgring a few days before, the by now well-used chassis 043 0705, SU-3908, was again put into service as a training car. Following this training, as already mentioned, this car would eventually go back to the factory to be prepared as a pure race car and sent over to Brumos Porsche in the USA for Peter Gregg to use in 1971. There is an interesting story attached to this and the Jacques Duval car, which can be read in chapter 8.

Two of the cars, Nos 1 and 3, would be prepared to Group 6 prototype regulations, which allowed the interiors to be stripped out to reduce weight. Prototypes also had wider wheel rims that were not homologated; mechanically, they were fitted with some experimental parts. Car 2 was a Group 4 GT, built to the regulations of Group 4, and thus a little bit heavier. This car, it was assumed, would be the really reliable car should the other two, more experimental cars, fail. The cars were, of course, three of the twelve special GT factory-built models. Each car had a limited-slip differential, a 26.4gall (118.8L) fuel tank, 908 brake callipers fitted to the front with extra-thick pads, uprated front shock absorbers with anti-roll bars front and rear, an additional oil cooler in the front, open air intakes to the carbs, and modified cams to allow 7200rpm. These racing versions could go to 220hp (DIN), but for this race, where absolute reliability was paramount, the maximum possible was reduced. Lightweight panels were added to the mix on the prototypes. More powerful lights also aided the drivers at night.

Interestingly, even then there was a regulation that restricted the exhaust sound to 85db! A spare wheel, brace and jack were also to be carried, as well as a fire extinguisher.

The race cars were:
043 2541, reg S-W 1947: 1 Gérard Larrousse/Claude Haldi/Helmut Marko, Group 6 spec.
043 2542, reg S-W 1948: 2 Claude Ballot-Léna/Günter Steckkönig/Nicolas Koob, Group 4 GT spec.
043 2543, reg S-W 1949: 3 Björn Waldegård/Åke Andersson/Guy Chasseuil, Group 6 spec.

Team logistics were vital, and here Jürgen Barth had a role to play behind the scenes supporting the team manager at the time, Rico Steinemann. Long-time Porsche engineering genius Roland Kussmaul told the author: "You know, for such an event you have to have one complete team per car to allow for changes of personnel during the race; each team was of 12 men. But unlike today, we

Three factory 914/6 GTs: fully equipped race cars for the 86 Hours of the Nürburgring. Chassis 2541, 2542 and 2543 would race, while chassis 1732 was available as a spare for training, as was one of the original 914/6 GTs, chassis 0705. (©P)

The men of the work's shop that made the cars: (r-l) Herren Kleisch, Kleinbeck, Mayer, Ristl, rally manager Rainer Bratenstein, Mönnich, Kaiser, Steckkönig and Bauerk. Unfortunately the name of the last man has eluded us. (©P)

The competition begins Racing in Europe 1970

A young Werner Hillburger, destined to become an ace Porsche engineer, prepares the 0705 used as a practice car in the Nürburgring outer paddock, which still looks very similar at the time of writing. (©P)

Marathon: careful preparation would be imperative for this feat of endurance. The more standard Group 4 car in the foreground. Porsche was determined: it needed a victory to help sales of the car. (©P)

85

For this race, a spare tyre had to be carried: it just fitted under the enlarged 118.8L fuel tank on the Group 6 cars. (©P)

The Marathon car cockpit of one of the stripped-out Group 6 versions. (©P)

did not have any teams of catering personnel. Somebody would be delegated to make some sandwiches, get drinks in, maybe make some spaghetti or something, but nothing was properly organized on the catering side, even though it was Porsche and you think it was all perfect! In those days all the racing teams did the same. It was like this for years. Even when I went the first time to Paris-Dakar, for instance, we never had a doctor in our team. I went for three days to Freiburg University and a doctor from the university taught me what to do when you have a broken leg and what to give for snake bites: I learned it all from him. So I was the doctor – oh, and also on that team, boss of the kitchen! We had to take care not to mix up the instructions, from doctor to chef to mechanic, whether it was at the Nürburgring or on the Safari!"

The race began for the 64 participating teams (72 had entered) at 1am on Wednesday 19 August 1970. In one long line past the pits and grandstands came the racing snake of assorted vehicles, including several not normally regarded as long-distance racers: an NSU Ro 80; Datsun 1600; VW 1600; Citroën DS21; a Mini Cooper; numerous more appropriate BMWs, and one extraordinary Rover P6 with a V8 4.3L engine, driven by Roy Pierpoint, Roger Enever and Clive Baker – an official factory entry by the then British Leyland Competitions Department in Abingdon.

As the cars swept left to enter the southern loop of the Nürburgring just after 1am, in the darkness the Rover charged into

The chart for planning the team and its working timetable during the Marathon de la Route. (©P)

The competition begins Racing in Europe 1970

The amazing Rover P6 with a V8 4.3L engine, driven by Roy Pierpoint as it appeared at the Nürburgring, but seen here at a later in-period race at Brands Hatch. (PA)

Fuel-up, refuelling and service was done in a special area of the pits at the end of a designated lap; there were penalties for entering the pits during the race, so the distance a car could go between fill-ups was an important factor. (©P)

Still dark: a pit stop for the No 2 GT of Claude Ballot-Léna/Günter Steckkönig/Nicolas Koob. (©P)

A nice drive in the country: a dry track – what more could you wish for? The No 2 Group 4 class 914/6 of Ballot-Léna/Steckkönig/Koob. (©P)

the lead as if it was a sprint race rather than a marathon with 86 hours of endurance ahead. At the end of the first lap of both the South and Nordschleife of Nürburgring, one of the greatest race tracks ever, the Rover held a huge lead over the second-placed car, a roaring 1300cc Mini Cooper!

At the Porsche pits there was no panic. Steinemann and his team of mechanics, timekeepers and spotters had carefully calculated a pace to suit the cars and the distance of the race. Even so, at the start, for the opening laps and for the next 12 hours, the target lap time was found by the organizers to be some 4min faster than that set down as a guide for safety at the drivers' pre-race briefing.

As mentioned, the rules for this race were complex, and one of these dictated that a car must complete as many or more laps during the final 12 hours of racing (if they were still running, that is) as they had in the first 12 hours! This could be a game-changer, because one has to consider the extremely variable weather conditions at the Nürburgring. Steinemann did just that, and, as the first 12 hours passed, he set a lap time for each of the three cars at between 13min 30sec and 14min. At the front, the Rover was still charging along. The three 914/6s, in 22nd, 25th and 26th places at the end of the first lap, were gradually moving up the field. By 1pm on the first day, up front that pesky Rover was putting in a tour de force, still pounding round. Holding 2nd place at the first 12-hour mark was the Erwin Kremer/Franz-Josef Rieder/Heinz Degen Porsche 911 2L of the Porsche Kremer Racing Team. Behind that came a pair of Porsche 911s and a Triumph TR6.

The competition begins Racing in Europe 1970

Driver change: Gérard Larrousse looks in whilst Herbert Linge, doyen of Porsche drivers in the 1960s, looks on, standing, hands in pockets, right. Well into the race now. (©WG)

Ten cars would go out by 4pm on that first day, and still the Rover held the lead until 5pm, when it suddenly appeared in the pits – its race was over. The Marathon was now led by the Kremer Porsche. As they entered the first night period it started to rain, gently at first, until a thunderstorm broke and it started pouring down. A few competitors had started on dry-weather tyres, so this caught a number of teams out, and the field lost several participants due to aquaplaning. This included the No 61 entry of privateers Simonis/Hoier/Kayser in their 914/6 GT; they crashed just after the Adenau Bridge. It was their first race – what an event to choose as your first!

As the night wore on, the rain thankfully stopped and, as luck would have it, the track dried and stayed that way for the rest of the race. As night turned to day on Thursday 20 August, with the race entering its second day (already well past the time taken to complete the Le Mans 24 Hours), pit stops came and went like clockwork at Porsche and at the refuelling stations.

There was drama, though, in the Kremer garage at 10.45am: the 911, reliable up to that point, came in with crankshaft failure and did not go back out. The Belgian Automobile Club Mayen Porsche 911S of Babendenderde/Königshofer/Theissen inherited the lead. With 38 hours of the race gone, the planned shift changes for the mechanics in the Porsche pit were working well so far. For now, in 2nd, 3rd and 4th places overall was the trio of 914/6 GT factory

89

Porsche The Racing 914s

Not able to go as quickly, being slightly heavier, the Group 4-spec No 2 car of Ballot-Léna/Steckkönig/Koob was obeying the rules of team manager Steinemann, its drivers wondering why the Larrousse team car seemed to be going quicker! (©P)

Porsche racers. Pit-stops were becoming more frequent for the lead car, and it proved only a matter of time before the Belgian 911 failed.

Just after the 39th hour had passed, the three factory 914s went into the lead in team number order. This all sounds pretty boring – pounding round hour after hour – even if it was on the most challenging track in the business, and it was, especially for the top drivers like Larrousse and Waldegård. But they in fact were indulging in their own little game. Gérard Larrousse told the author: "Because we were in the factory car, one of the stripped-out ones, it was very well prepared; every pit-stop, every driver change, oil, fuel, etc – everything was organized perfectly. The only problem for us was who would win the race! We were sure we could, but which one of us? I was with Helmut Marko and Claude Haldi. We knew what to expect, we knew it would be boring, but also we wanted to win. So we met together and said okay, we have to keep to management orders, because they had, of course, a lap chart; they had given us times, so we were obliged to do each lap no faster and no slower. But the three of us wanted to win and also to have some fun together, so we all decided to go very fast on each of our out-laps and each of our in-laps. Because the Porsche people were only writing 'Start/Stop lap' on the lap chart, we knew those two laps were not timed. At first, no one noticed except the official time keepers, who had recorded all the times. Our team management was only concentrating on consistent race laps. Of course, after a while as the race progressed, we took the lead!"

In an interview shortly before he died, Björn Waldegård told the author: "You know, we thought it was strange that the Larrousse car seemed faster. I asked Steinemann about the cars: 'They are all the same!' he said. Then Günter Steckkönig spoke to me about the same thing, and suddenly we realized they were playing games and having some fun. So we decided to do the same! It was a long time into the race before our management identified the games we were playing! But by then our friends/'foxes' in the No 1 car were two laps ahead!" Indeed that was the case, because after 43 hours the positions were:

Larrousse/Haldi/Marko: 176 laps
Ballot-Léna/Steckkönig/Koob: 174 laps
Waldegård/Andersson/Chasseuil: 174 laps
Gaban/van Butsele/Braillard: 174 laps (Porsche 911S)
Babendenderde/Königshofer/Theissen: 170 laps (Porsche 911S)
Barbara/Duvauchelle/Mordacq: 169 laps (Triumph 2.5L)

During the race, the organizers issued bulletins at the end of each day, giving information about the race and notices of instructions if there were rule adjustments, etc. These bulletins, of course, showed the overall positions and results.

The competition begins Racing in Europe 1970

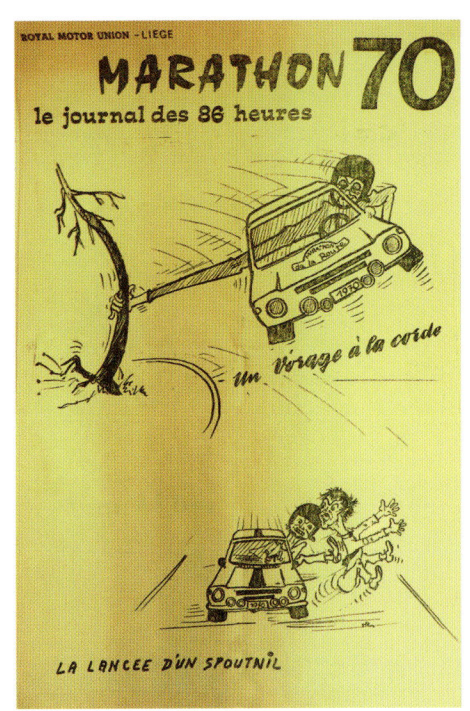

The front covers of the Marathon de la Route daily bulletins, issued to teams and available to the press and public. (RK)

A two-lap lead at the Nürburgring full circuit in those days was significant: even with 28 teams still in the race, the 914s looked to be in a strong position with half the race run. Pit-stop timings were vital, as a harsh rule stated that a lap would be deducted from your total distance for each minute your car spent in the pits – harsh indeed! Refuelling took place away from the team pit, but tyre stops were a critical phase. A contemporary report says: 'No lap in the race could take more than 24min; with an in-lap of, say, 16min, the car comes in; the driver has to do the changes along with two allowed mechanics; he jumps out, jack and wheel brace in hand, and proceeds to change the wheels; the clock is ticking; he changes only two wheels; the clock is now at 21min of the 24 allowed for that lap.'

Roland Kussmaul says: "When you went over 1min in the pits you lost one lap, so in our case, when we changed the tyres, the mechanics put only two nuts on the car and then the driver went out from the pit, and 300m later there was a place where he would stop, jump out and fix the rest of the nuts. The driver had the nuts in his pocket and a wheel brace was in the car. Also, on arrival at a pit-stop, before going into the pit, he stopped and loosened three nuts, so that it was faster in the pit and you didn't lose a lap. Normally the fuel station was outside of the pit for this race. It did not count in the time penalty programme."

Back to the contemporary report: "With the wheels changed, the tools are thrown back in; the two tyres taken from onboard and carried in the race are replaced with new ones; the bonnet goes down and out he goes with only two nuts holding the new wheels on, but he must go to be within the 24min allowed. Some teams would go through the nut procedure again, one lap later, so that by the third lap the other nuts were fitted and tightened!"

Several of the teams were doing this, or the Porsche version, and frankly it was dangerous. The organizers spotted the situation, but it was not until the 60th lap that a ruling was made to cease the practice. At Porsche, though, with such a commanding lead, it was on the pit-stops that the training and practising for this part of the race paid off when the 'nut ruling' was enforced. Jürgen Barth says: "The two mechanics alone would then change all four wheels and tighten all the nuts in 1min 45sec. In fact, on the 914s they were only changed after 60 hours – 4600 miles of Nürburgring racing! No slicks, of course: the Porsches were on road-legal tyres. The brake pads would not be changed throughout the race. Frequently the

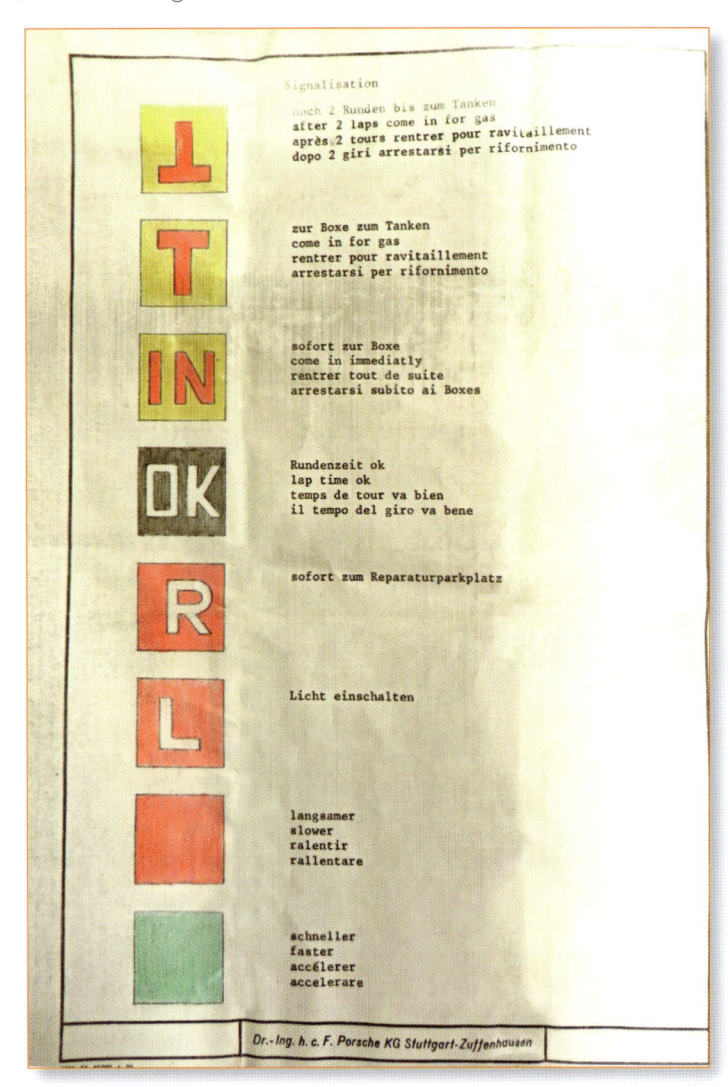

During the race, a team had to have pit-signal boards, using a code known to the team and drivers. Here we see a copy of that instruction from the personal files of Roland Kussmaul.

At night the service is the same as in the daytime. "Stay calm!" Andersson is told. Note the huge film camera – remember, this is 1970! (©P)

Two days in and still going strong: the Group 6 version of Waldegård/Andersson/Chasseuil, ready for a driver change. (©P)

drivers would change small items on the cars themselves in a special area, not in the pits, but of course it counted for lap time."

All through Thursday and Friday the cars ran faultlessly, relentlessly piling up the lead distance ahead of the others, the only change being that Waldegård and his team moved into 2nd place. By Saturday morning, with 80 hours run, the three 914/6 Porsches led the field by 30 laps. Come the 3pm finish, that total lead had grown by three more laps as the victorious team set about organising a formation finish. The 1970 Marathon de la Route 86 Hours at the Nürburgring saw the following top six results:
1st Larrousse/Haldi/Marko, 914/6 358 laps (6300 miles)
2nd Waldegård/Andersson/Chasseuil, 914/6 357 laps
3rd Ballot-Léna/Steckkönig/Koob, 914/6 354 laps
4th Eisenschenk/Stoffel/Wendel, BMW 2002 327 laps

The competition begins Racing in Europe 1970

A 1-2-3 demonstrated dominance for the new 914 model. The press was impressed by their reliability, and the success of the new car would change a few minds. Here was a proper Porsche, winning in the style they were accustomed to. (©P)

Porsche The Racing 914s

Never backward in coming forward: several poster advertisements were created, some featuring VW-Porsche, others just Porsche. (©P)

Robert Huhn: 45th overall at the Nürburgring 500km in the No 62 Scuderia Lufthansa car. (©P)

A good result for the Ernst Seiler 914/6 GT in the Monza Coppa Intereuropa: 3rd overall, 2nd in class. (MaxPP)

A busy field of Porsches, BMWs and other makes in the Coppa Intereuropa GT race, with Ernst Seiler in the 61 car. (MaxPP)

5th Babendenderde/Königshofer/Theissen, 911 Porsche 323 laps
6th Gellert/Huhn/Bialas, Opel Rallye 1900 319 laps

Here was proof that the 914/6 GT was indeed a car of exceptional ability, reliability and performance. The result would boost sales and bring more respect from those who, until that time, doubted its capabilities. Even so, quite a few private owners of racing Porsches, having tried the 914, decided to stick to the 911, because it had half a litre more capacity and more horsepower than the 914/6 GT. Soon the 911S would boast 250hp+.

With the Marathon de la Route over and the trophies packed

The competition begins Racing in Europe 1970

Proof of the action: the Monza 1970 pass. (MaxPP)

away, it was down to the marketing departments to make the best of the victorious efforts of the Porsche team and several privateers who were having success with the 914/6 in the GT classes. Mindful, though, of the aforementioned scepticism towards the model, and with sales needing another boost, the engineering department was put under pressure to bring home another publicity coup, and so would begin to turn its thoughts to the next major target: the 1971 Monte Carlo Rally (see chapter 7).

After the August holidays, the privateers and Porsche dealer racing teams adjusted their thoughts towards the Nürburgring 500km race – round 6 of the 2L European Sports Car Championship – on 5 September. With the fast cars being out-and-out sports prototypes, the 914s would find their challenge down in the smaller classes. Although fairly quick in their own right, 22 laps of the 22.853km version of the circuit proved a challenge, and Gotthard Egerland was the highest placed 914 Porsche finisher in 27th place, driving the Gotthard Engineering and former factory test car entry No 61, chassis 043 0983. The 914/6 came some four laps down on the outright winner, Vic Elford in a Chevron B16. Georg Loos is recorded as the 35th-place finisher in his GELO 914/6 GT racing entry, and Robert Huhn 45th in the No 62 Scuderia Lufthansa car.

7 September was the date of the Italian Grand Prix, where a support race saw Ernst Seiler take a fine 3rd overall in the Coppa Intereuropa. Sadly, this was the year and the place that the great Jochen Rindt died during practice at the wheel of the Lotus 72. The author was at this race also, and so witnessed not only the Grand Prix, which was won by local F1 hero Clay Regazzoni, but also the impressive drive by Ernst Seiler in that support event.

In Spain, at the beginning of September, José-María Fernández, having raced in Seats in the earlier part of the year, along with his brother Juan, who raced with the Tergal-sponsored team Escudería Montjuich, had made contact with Porsche with a view to acquiring one of the new 914/6s. Chassis 043 1569, which the brothers acquired, was one of five injection-fed 914/6 GTs, as confirmed by Walter Näher to the author. We will hear more of the injection cars in a moment; Roland Kussmaul remembers they were mechanical injection.

José-María Fernández told the author: "The car was initially bought by my brother Juan, who drove it in the 2nd Rally Osona, 18 August 1970, in which he had to abandon because of a breakdown. He practised a lot, but couldn't get used to the car – he had no patience! And so I bought it from him. You have to bear in mind that the cars were our own property in those days: the drivers bought them themselves. Escudería Montjuich, our team, sponsored us and paid our costs for the season – entries and travel, mechanic support, etc. The costs of maintenance, repairs, improvements and accidents had to be paid for by us drivers. We were amateurs who charged for some assistance and also got some money from minor publicity. If you won a race you got a financial prize, which helped a lot to finish the season without putting our own money in, apart from the car, of course. If you didn't win or you had an accident, it was a big problem which sometimes meant that you had to miss a whole season's racing until you could get your money back.

"At that time, in Spain, there were very few who made a living from cars as professionals – rather, they lived badly! The drivers of Escudería Repsol and the Seat and Renault factories were

95

professionals, and yet we often beat them, although we were not able to put in as much practice and we had fewer resources. One of the advantages for them was that if they had accidents, they didn't have to pay from their own pockets. For us, from early Monday morning we were working in the factory (we worked in the family textile business) all week, and at the weekends we practised or raced, wherever it might be. It was hard, but we were very enthusiastic. Escudería Montjuich was financed by Tergal, which was a textile fibre brand and was the main supplier of textile fabrics to the Juncadellas, founders of the Escudería Montjuich. Anything not covered by the Escudería's funds had to be covered by the drivers' own money.

"Driving the 914 mid-engine car helped me to adapt very quickly to the 908/03. It was technically similar, but the devil to drive. My 914/6 GT was on injection, with 220hp+. However, I think that, at Porsche at the time, they didn't have much patience with this car, which, in my humble opinion, was better than the 911 on fast open corners, ie in 4th or 5th gear. Also, very important, it was much lighter than the 911S. But it seemed as if they didn't want to develop it and they put all their efforts into the 911." We will hear more from Sr Fernández a little later on.

On 13 September the racing circus in Germany returned to Hockenheim, the home to no less than 25 sports car races in 1970, this time staging another round of the German GT Championship, part of the Preis der Nationen für Rennwagen Formel 5000 Hockenheim race meeting. Gerd Quist was out in the 914/6 No 87 Autohaus Max Moritz entry, Günter Steckkönig with a new drive in the 89 Strähle car and Rolf Göring driving the Hahn Motor Sports car. Günter Steckkönig says: "I was driving, testing and doing some racing, but always as a private entry. Herbert Linge had been with Porsche for many years; he knew the Strähle people well and when he decided to stop racing he brought me into the Strähle team, and that's how I started driving with Strähle. I can say it was a fantastic time, because more and more the 914 was being improved by our team and it was getting better all the time. I remember Hockenheim; the racing car was a road-going car so we used to drive it from Schorndorf on the autobahn to Hockenheim and after the race back to Schorndorf. That was the usual procedure for us. Schorndorf to Hockenheim is not too far. Especially for Strähle it was normal, because Mr Strähle was a rally driver, and because he drove on the road he said, 'It's normal for you to drive with the race car. Be careful if you see a police car!' At the circuit all my racing colleagues used to ask me every time: 'Where is your trailer for your race car?' So I explained: 'I drove it here!'" As the reader may know, in the '50s and '60s it was quite usual to drive a race car on the road to an event, but by 1970 a tow car and trailer had become the norm, with some even going to car transporters if it was an affluent team. Today, of course, dozens of huge transporters are seen at championship sports car races.

At Hockenheim, on this occasion, the 10-lap race saw Quist finish 2nd overall and 1st in the 2L GT class, Steckkönig 4th overall and 2nd in 2L GT, and Göring 8th overall and 3rd in 2L GT in this mixed 3L and 2L event.

The Tour de France Auto was always a great marathon event, held on the roads and various race circuits around France, and for 1970 the event would run from 19-27 September, starting at Bandol on the Mediterranean and taking in the race tracks of Rouen, Dijon, Albi and Pau, with other tests at La Baule, continuing to Aix-les Bains before finishing in Nice. A total distance of 4525km (2812 miles) with 1218km (757 miles) of timed stages.

Running with No 120 was one of two Sonauto-entered 914/6 GTs, chassis 043 1020, of Claude Ballot-Léna/Jean Claude Morenas, last used in the Le Mans 24 Hours. They would climb up the leader board to finish in 6th place overall, just behind the incredible lightweight 911R Porsche of Gérard Larrousse/Maurice Gélin in 3rd, Guy Chasseuil/Christian Baron 4th, and Jacques Rey/Jean-Marie Jacquemin 5th, all in 911s. The second 914/6 GT of the Sonauto team, running at No 121, was chassis 043 0457, the entry of Henri Balas/Roland Imbert, which finished in 8th place overall.

The 1970 Tour de France Auto was one of controversy amongst the non-French teams and fans. It came about because the 1st and 2nd cars overall were the sport prototypes from Matra Simca, both super-fast Le Mans 650 prototypes minutely converted for road use, with a passenger seat for a co-driver. It was felt that running these cars was not in the spirit of the game, though they were just legal!

On 27 September, the final day of racing on the Tour de France Auto, several thousand miles away in Sweden the 914/6 of Leif Hansen was racing in a non-championship event at the Kinnekulle Ring in the same car he had used earlier in the year. In practice he ended up setting pole position in the up-to-2L class, took fastest lap in the class in the race and finished 2nd overall and 2nd in GT. Back in Germany on 4 October at the Mendig Airfield 3.59km (2.5 miles) circuit, Ingo Hopp and Jörg Vogelsang competed in the ADAC Flugplatzrennen Mendig non-championship GT race. Vogelsang would dnf, whilst Hopp finished 4th overall.

Austria, 11 October, and Ernst Seiler was to be seen at the International Österreichring 1000km, round 10 and final round of the International Manufacturers' Championship: 170 laps of the 3.673 mile (5.911km circuit). It was warm and dry, and pole was

The competition begins Racing in Europe 1970

Scrutineering before the start of the 1970 Tour de France Auto: the Claude Ballot-Léna/Jean-Claude Morenas entry. This was the Sonauto car used at Le Mans. (NM)

Service at the Mont-Dore hillclimb section: an anxious Morenas looks into the camera. (NM)

Hard cornering in the second Sonauto entry: the 121 car of Balas/Imbert en-route to 8th overall on the 1970 Tour de France Auto. (WG)

set by Pedro Rodríguez in the Gulf Porsche 917K in a time of 1min 40.8sec, an average speed of 131.594mph (211.779km/h). Ernst Seiler/Peter Ettmüller qualified Seiler's regular chassis 043 0181 car 25th on the grid in 2min 9.8sec. One look at the time difference will show the reader that the task for the very fastest cars was challenging in the extreme when arriving behind a slower car on this fast and undulating circuit.

Seiler was joined in practice by the Georg Loos/Franz Pesch No 48 car and the No 51 car of Günter Steckkönig/Prince Ferfried von Hohenzollern, starting from 23rd on the grid with a time of 2min 9.55sec, the car being the selfsame Strähle 914/6 used earlier at Hockenheim.

With 34 cars taking the start, including eleven 911s, it would be a long afternoon for the two 914/6 GT teams to survive the onslaught of the big boys and try to win the heavily 911-populated 2L class. The overall winners, Jo Siffert and Brian Redman in the John Wyer-entered Gulf Porsche 917 K, covered 170 laps. However, on 139 laps was the No 51 car of Steckkönig/von Hohenzollern, 12th place overall and taking victory in the up-to-2.5L class. The Seiler/Ettmüller car was just a couple of places back, 14th overall and 2nd in the 2.5L. Günter Steckkönig told the author: "With Prinz von Hohenzollern in the 1000km, we beat all the 911s in the same class and won the GT class overall ahead of the 2.5L cars. Our 2L Strähle 914/6 was very good; we had received good help from Porsche, but it was Strähle who had developed the car step-by-step, and for us it was an important step."

By now it was evident that, with more development, Porsche could have had a great car in its hands. However, as we know, Porsche's intentions at that time were to target overall victories, not class wins. All the development money was going into the overall race-winning 917s and 908s. From the point of view of marketing the Porsche product 'brand,' it was overall victories that put the name up in lights.

Günter Steckkönig again: "I remember after the race in Zeltweg Erwin Kremer from the famous Kremer Porsche team came to me – I had driven for Kremer in 911s and he had driven a 911 at Zeltweg (19th place overall) – and said maybe it's now the time for us to also build a 914 for racing. Mr Strähle was very pleased."

On 18 October at the Nürburgring, round 22 of the DARM German GT Championship brought the following results: car 142,

Porsche The Racing 914s

Austria: the well-developed 914/6 Strähle entry of Günter Steckkönig (at the wheel here) and Prince Ferfried von Hohenzollern shows a clean pair of heels to all the fancied 911 runners in the GT class – proof that with development the 914/6 GT could have been a formidable competitor. (©P)

Ernst Seiler in the pits during practice at the Österreichring. (MaxPP)

Alexander Nolte, chassis 043 0462, 5th overall and 1st in GT 2L; car 141, Thomas Kruger, 4th in GT 2L; car 138, Gotthard Egerland, 5th in GT 2L.

That same weekend in France, at the Paris 1000km held on the 7.821km circuit of the famous Montlhéry track, two Porsche 914s were entered, but only the Fabrizio Pravedoni/Mike Franey 914/6 would show up on the grid. The No 34 car would classify 22nd overall, though some records say it did not finish. Whatever the final result, it was a quiet day for this team, completing only 40 laps compared with the winning Matra Simca's 128!

Following the dnf in his first event, a rally, José-María Fernández in Spain entered a hillclimb, the Pont de Vilomara, organized by the Moto Club Monresa on 11 October, with the 914/6 carrying reg No VD-5248. Here, his brother, driving the Escudería Montjuich Porsche 908, in very

98

The competition begins Racing in Europe 1970

wet and indeed muddy conditions, took the victory, but with a remarkable drive on the slippery surface in the new car José-María Fernández came 2nd overall, 1st in the 2L class and 1st in Group 4. He followed that result with another class victory, finishing 9th overall at the 24th Carrera en Cuesta de la Rabassada on 18 October, a hillclimb of some 4.5km organized by the Barcelona Motor Club. His brother, Juan, finished 2nd overall in the Tergal-sponsored Escudería Montjuich Porsche 908, the winner being Jorge Bagration in a similar 908.

José-María Fernández, a textile industrialist by profession from Barcelona, had considerable talent in rallying, and decided to try his luck in the big league of racing at the Jarama 6 Hours on 1 November. The 914/6 GT Group 5 (injection) car, chassis 043 1569, of José-María Fernández would have Javier Juncadella of the Escudería Montjuich as number two driver, carrying race No 40. The pairing would finish 11th overall, and 1st in Group 5, in this round 6 of the

The private entry of Georg Loos/Franz Pesch, practised but did not race, Austria 1000km. (©P)

Return to the 'Ring: round 22 of the 1970 GT championship. (JS)

Only in its second year, but already a serious event on the sports prototype and GT calendar: the 6 Hours of Jarama. (JMF)

99

Porsche The Racing 914s

11th overall, 1st Group 5: round 6 of the Spanish Drivers' Championship for sports cars in Groups 3, 4, 5 and 6, the Jarama 6 Hours, 1970. (JMF)

Spanish Drivers' Championship for sports cars in Groups 3, 4, 5 and 6.

The Porsche 914/6 with the injection engine was found to be an interesting beast, the norm being the two banks of triple Webers. The Spanish cars racing in Group 5 had the 911S 2182cc engine with 226hp at 7200rpm, duel ignition, Bosch mechanical injection, central front oil radiator with separate 12L oil tank, brakes with monobloque aluminium clamps, close ratio gears with limited-slip differential, 8in and 10in rims for asphalt rallying and racing, with wings, doors, bonnets and rear boot lids in glass fibre, polycarbonate windows and an overall weight of 850kg. The rear sway bar crossed over the top of the gearbox. Spanish driver Julio Gargallo reported that this sway bar was the Achilles heel of the 914, along with the gearbox, which he considered too fragile for the engine's 226hp. However, mechanical injection was a modification that was not taken up for volume production of the 914/6 GTs – a case of what might have been, perhaps?

By the end of 1970, the 914/6 models were being tried by many privateers who had previously been closely involved with the Porsche 911s. They were now proving to be good road cars, but for the general public they were not generally recognized as such and Porsche was struggling for sales. For the works drivers, the jury was out regarding handling and performance of the 914/6 GTs, in spite of their victory at the Marathon de la Route and successes at world level in sports car circuit races in private hands. The top rallying professionals had found the car unpredictable in testing when pushed to its limits.

In Zuffenhausen various meetings were taking place behind the scenes to determine where the 914's future lay in competition. Management at Porsche wanted to push its new baby to the forefront. After all, racing sells cars; successful racing sells even more cars; and they had a lot of 914s in production and for planned production to sell. However, as already mentioned, most of the money for development was going to the Porsches with the chances of overall victory in the big racing events, rather than development of the 914, which was being left to the privateers like Strähle, Max Moritz, Hahn, etc. It was decided, however, that more effort would go into testing and getting other drivers to use the 914/6. To this end, a decision was made in the summer to make an updating kit available to all private buyers. It was back on 26 February that the go-ahead had been given to get several outside suppliers to make parts for the aforementioned sport kit to supply the main dealers. GT kits of special parts were initially only supplied for certain client cars and to the dealer teams. Now the kits would be available to all private customers, to bring their 914/6 production model up to the race spec of the factory cars. Various options would be available: a sport kit and a rally kit were the two principle choices. The kits could be bought as a whole or in parts, according to requirements. We do not know how many cars were eventually converted with the kit, but at least 400 are said to have been supplied. They were outsourced from various suppliers, namely Karosseriewerk in Weinsberg, Karosserie Baur in Bad Cannstatt and Waggonfabrik in Rastatt. Porsche would go on selling these kits for a number of years. A sport kit consisted of the following main components:

Part number	Item
914 503 905 00	Wing extension front left
914 503 906 00	Wing extension front right
914 503 907 00	Wing extension rear left
914 503 908 00	Wing extension rear right
901 104 094 25	Twin-ignition cylinder head
901 108 110 00	Carburettor kit
901 108 046 00	Air intake kit
914 501 905 00	Front oil-cooler kit

Plus various ancillaries to go with the above, purchased at client's request.

More items could be obtained and some chassis were finished off at Karmann, the body maker, who prepared GTs to customer order at Porsche's request.

On 19 October 1970, Dunlop representatives met with Porsche in Zuffenhausen to discuss tyres for the 1971 season. With the dark

The competition begins Racing in Europe 1970

A simple programme for the annual season finale at Hockenheim. (Vin)

The mixed classes at the Hockenheim finals, with the Max Moritz 914/6 ahead of a group of cars in the sports class. (©P)

nights drawing in, Germany's final circuit race of 1970 would be held on the 2.630km small circuit of the Hockenheim Motodrome in an event organized by the Mannheim-Heidelberg Sports Touring Club.

A non-championship field saw the 914/6 of Autohaus Max Moritz in the hands of regular driver Dietrich Krumm. He completed the season finals in 4th place overall, with the Robert Stoddard entry in 5th and Hermann Neureuther in 6th. However, out in front of two vastly superior cars in terms of power was the 914/6 GT entered by Hahn Motorsport and driven by Rolf Göring, taking overall victory ahead of the Shelby GT 350 of Martin Rath and the Autohaus Max Moritz Porsche 911S of Klaus Utz in 3rd place.

We have mentioned hillclimbing previously, and as stated before there is not space here to go into great detail. However, the statistics shows that, out of the sixteen hillclimbing events (not definitive) in our list for 1970, Porsche 914s took a class win on eight occasions. As regards the slaloms/sprints, from the records of the ONS alone we find nineteen events in Germany and two class victories.

Production of the new 914/6 had already contributed to 17% of the sales of all Porsche cars in 1970, acknowledged in the company report as follows: "The 914 echoes the Targa 911, though its detachable roof is easily stored in the rear trunk. The 914/6 carries a 2L six-cylinder engine of 110hp, but thanks to its being some 220lb (99.79kg) lighter, it has better acceleration than the 911T in the lower ranges."

Also mentioned in the annual report is this fact for the future: "One year has passed since the seven Porsche American sales importers became Porsche+Audi, a branch of VW America." The 914 was being imported in the USA and, in a little over six months of sales, 7000 914s had been sold, 600 of them being the 914/6. The USA was already being seen as the major market for this model. In fact, the report recorded that the largest share of Porsche sales in the USA went to the new 914.

Of the 914/6s produced in 1970, a total of 17 cars had received the GT kit treatment for racing, loosely termed M471 customer cars. Several of the 914/6 GTs run during 1970 would be sold on to teams and drivers in the USA at the end of the 1970 European season. Amongst them were chassis 0691, which was sold to Ralph Meaney, and 0705, along with 0315, which went to Brumos and Peter Gregg. We will learn more of these cars in chapter 8. For now, it's time to move on: 1971 beckons.

Dietrich Krumm at the Hockenheim finals in the Max Moritz 914/6. (©P)

4

Good times
Racing in Europe 1971

As we know, in 1970 the staple diet was still the 911; this fabulous car, which would undergo continuous development, just kept on going. But there were signs at that time that certain members of the management team were thinking of a new design to replace it: the 914/6 GT was on their radar. As with all car manufacturers, Porsche was no different in looking towards the next model. The 356 had been replaced; Porsche needed to look at what might follow the 911. It may seem strange now, but of course we are viewing the situation with hindsight. Even the 911 suffered a lot of problems in its early days – the kind of problems clients would not put up with today. It took a couple of years to get it right – maybe the 914 would be the same, though at this point there were few problems with the car, only problems with perception by the market. By 1970, the Porsche 911 was seen by owners as the be-all and end-all model; why would they want to buy a car with a Volkswagen badge?

Likewise, the reality was that comments on the car's handling at the limit in feedback from the top drivers during testing meant that management had a problem. With the popularity of the 911, it was going to be an uphill struggle for the 914/6 to topple it. The Porsche Sports Department, however, was determined to give it a chance and issued a statement at the beginning of 1971:

"The 914/6 is being homologated in Group 4 special GT under FIA No 626. Copies of the document can be obtained from the Porsche Sports Department.

VW-Porsche 914/6 – Racing version
a) Chassis: Lowered, competition shock absorbers, stabilizers front and rear. Brakes with ventilated brake discs. Callipers of the Carrera S. Wheel hubs with long studs and 27mm spacers to mount larger rims with racing tyres.
b) Body and interior: Simplified interior, black with bucket seats, rear window Plexiglas. Extended fenders front and rear. Underskirt, front and rear bumpers glass fibre. Additional oil cooling system installed in the front of the car.
c) Engine: The production 914/6 engine is specially prepared for higher performance within the regulations of the International Automobile Sports Code. Production crankshaft and connecting rods. Light alloy cylinders hard chromed, with racing pistons, cylinder heads with carefully polished intake and exhaust ports, special intake manifolds with 46 IDA Weber carburettors, racing camshafts, racing exhaust system, competition clutch, transistorized dual ignition system. Performance 210hp (DIN) at 8000rpm.
d) Transmission: 5-speed with main shaft which permits interchangeability of each gear set. Ring and pinion: 7.3:1 with limited-slip differential.
e) Homologation note: It is possible to order as an option the 914/6 titanium connecting rods. However, at this moment the rods are not yet homologated, the FIA requiring a minimum production number of vehicles equipped with these rods."

Porsche The Racing 914s

The 914/6 in GT format would be the flagship of the 914s; it was hoped that its image, performance, handling and racing persona would rub off onto the cars for the street. (©P)

The 6th place at Le Mans in 1970 had been no fluke (well, maybe a little – they had been 7th, remember, but the Corvette that was 6th across the line had been 'not classified' as a finisher) and the victory at the Marathon de la Route proved the car's reliability. Now, at the start of 1971, the Monte Carlo Rally beckoned, and a major attack on the US motorsport scene was planned. (As mentioned in our previous chapter, the US side of things warrants significant study in its own right and as a separate entity to the happenings in Europe. 914/6s had started racing in 1970 in the USA and we will pick them up in chapter 8.)

Before we go circuit racing in Europe, it's worth a mention that ice racing has always been a favourite winter pastime for rally drivers and racing drivers alike. In Garmisch Partenkirchen on 2 February we find the ADAC-run Eibsee-Eisrennen. Sepp Greger was there and took 1st in production and special GT. A second 914/6 was driven to 3rd in the same class by one Herr Neuseiter.

Good times Racing in Europe 1971

Ernst Seiler at the Hockenheimring, 21 March 1971. (MaxPP)

As spring warmed up in Germany, the racing season began for the 914/6 at Hockenheim, with the SAR Rundstreckenrennen German national race meeting, a non-championship event, over the weekend of 20-21 March. Race details elude us, but we do have a photograph, above – Ernst Seiler in the familiar 043 0181 914/6 GT.

A week later, 28 March, we see more new cars and drivers in 914/6s come out to play for the start of the new season of championship racing in Germany: round 1 of the DARM (Deutsche Automobil-Rundstrecken-Meisterschaft) National Championship, held at the Belgian Zolder race track.

This was the Internationales Rundstreckenrennen Bergischer Löwe Zolder, held over 24 laps of the 4.184km circuit, and in which Porsches dominated. In the over-2L class it would be 911s that took the overall race honours. However, not so far behind was one of a number of new names to the 914s: Friedhelm Theissen in the No 284 914/6 of the Porsche Kremer Racing Team, and owner/driver Werner Kastner, No 283, 3rd place in the class. Six 914/6 GTs had started, but only four finished – the entries of Horst Godel (8th) and Henry Balas being down the field.

28 March had seen early spring tarmac action in Spain at the Montserrat hillclimb. It was the 13th edition and a round of the Spanish Championship. José-María Fernández, in the 914/6 GT Tergal-sponsored injection car, would come home 6th overall, the 7km climb being won by Jorge Bagration, the famous Georgian nobleman, in a Porsche 908. 91 entries were on the start list. A week later, at the Montjuich Castle hillclimb on 3-4 April, Fernández put in a storming drive to take victory overall. For cars only, this interesting event was held at night! With 3km of flat-out twisting turns and steep gradients, the format was two runs up the hill, starting at Paseo de Colón. The Peña Motorista Barcelona (Barcelona Motor Club) organized the event, which started at midnight and ran through to late morning. 50 cars took part; Fernández completed the course in 2min 9.2sec in the 914/6, 1.29sec ahead of the 2nd-

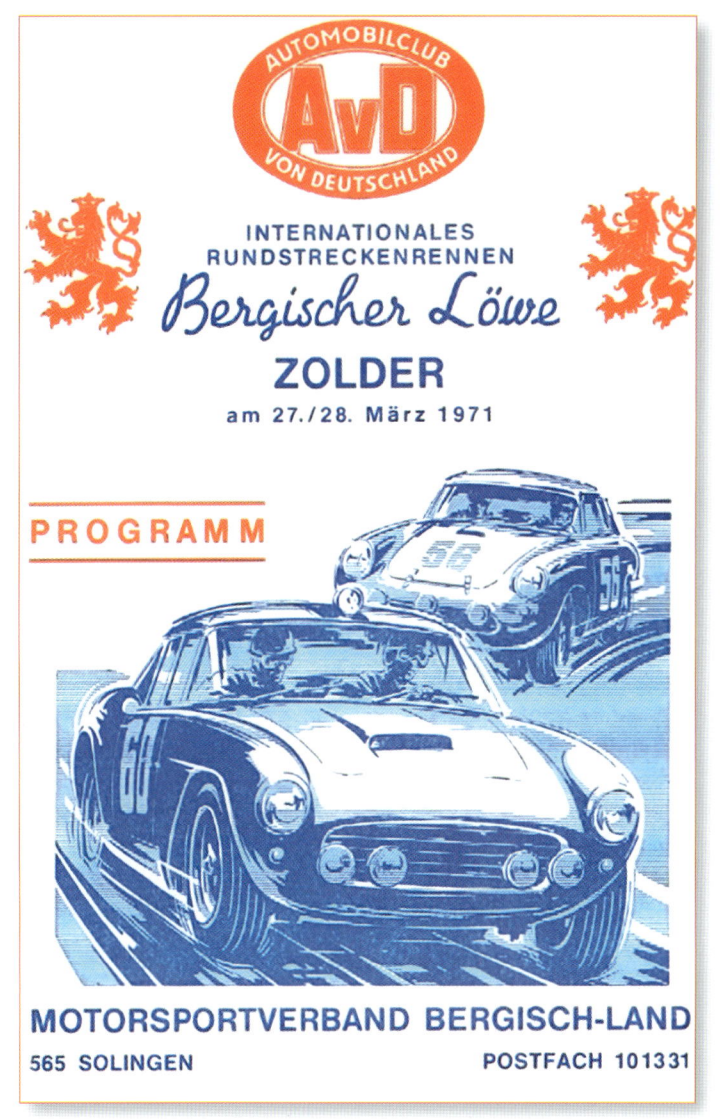

105

Porsche The Racing 914s

I SUBIDA EN CUESTA AL CASTILLO DE MONTJUICH

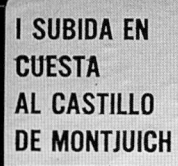

JOSE MARIA FERNANDEZ, BATALLADOR COMO NUNCA

JOSE MARIA FERNANDEZ INAUGURA EL PALMARES DE LA PRUEBA CON 2' 9" 20/100, A 94,734 KILOMETROS POR HORA

El vencedor de la prueba, a bordo del 914/6, registró en los entrenamientos un tiempo de 2' 14" 99/100, que rebajó en su primera escalada a 2' 11" 58/100. En la segunda su crono fue de 2' 9" 20/100, cubriendo los 3,4 kilómetros de recorrido con un desnivel del 5,6 por 100, a una media de 94,73436 kilómetros por hora.

Juncosa, que pilotaba su Abarth de dos litros, se clasificó como segundo mejor tiempo, seguido de Kutz, quien realizó su trepa con el Carrera 6. Juncosa, en entrenamientos, registró 2' 15" 10/100, y en primera manga de carrera, 2' 10" 10/100, y en la primera manga de carrera 2' 10" 67/100, mientras que Kutz lo haría en 2' 17" 76/100 y 2' 13" 50/100, respectivamente.

Miguel Brunells logró marcar 2'22"94/100 con su Mini.

J. M. FERNANDEZ («PORSCHE-914»), GANADOR DE LA PRIMERA CUESTA AL CASTILLO DE MONTJUIC

Fernández, con «Porsche 914», se adjudicó la I Subida al Castillo de Montjuich

CLASIFICACION GENERAL

		1.ª Subida	2.ª Subida
1.°	José María Fernández (Porsche 914-6)	2' 11" 5/10	2' 09" 2/10
2.°	Manuel Juncosa (Fiat Abarth 2000)	2' 10" 6/10	2' 10" 4/10
3.°	Juan Kutz (Porsche 906)	2' 13" 5/10	2' 10" 6/10
4.°	«Pepe Sauquet» (Alpine 1440)	2' 21" 9/10	2' 18" 8/10
5.°	Miguel Brunells (Morris Cooper)	2' 25" 3/10	2' 22" 9/10 1.° G. 2
6.°	Jorge Caton (Porsche 911-R)	2' 25" 1/10	2' 24" 5/10
7.°	Diego Cañas (Morris Cooper)	2' 28"	2' 32"
8.°	Alfonso Marcos (Alpine 110)	2' 29" 8/10	2' 28" 1/10
9.°	José Teixidó (Alpine 1300)	2' 29"	2' 28" 5/10
10.	Pedro Bassols (Morris Mini)	2' 32" 8/10	2' 29" 8/10
11.	Pedro Fábregas (Morris Cooper)	2' 33" 7/10	2' 30" 6/10
12.	«Toni Riba» (Seat 1430)	2' 34" 1/10	2' 31" 6/10 1.° F. N.
13.	José Marcos (Renault 8-TS)	2' 34" 5/10	2' 34"
14.	Luis López (BMW 2002)	2' 37" 4/10	2' 35" 3/10
15.	Daniel Ferrater (Renault 8-TS)	2' 38" 2/10	2' 36" 2/10
16.	«Goliath» (Morris Cooper S)	2' 38" 2/10	2' 37" 7/10 1.° G. 1
17.	Claudio Caba (Seat 600-D)	2' 38" 5/10	2' 36" 7/10
18.	José López (Seat 600-D)	2' 46" 4/10	2' 39" 6/10
19.	Antonio Mir (Renault 8-TS)	2' 40" 2/10	2' 39" 8/10
20.	Andrés Pérez (Renault 8-TS)	2' 42" 8/10	2' 41" 3/10

A 'nocturne' hillclimb: Fernández fastest – press cuttings from the archives of the Fernández family.

Good times Racing in Europe 1971

From this photo we may assume a front-row start for Günter Steckkönig in the Strähle-prepared 914/6 GT. The front left of the No 2 Chevrolet Camaro can just be seen in this official Porsche photo. Out-powered over the full distance, Steckkönig finished 6th overall. (©P)

(Vin)

placed Abarth of Manuel Juncosa, who was closely followed by Juan Kutz of the Escudería Corunesa in a Porsche 908.

This is interesting, because we now see that the 914/6, not exactly favoured by the very top drivers for either rallying or racing because of what is said to have been their feelings of insecurity due to instability and unpredictability at the limit, was proving to be an extremely useful vehicle in the hands of some drivers who, while perhaps not at the top of the tree, were nevertheless regarded as very good and perfectly capable of excellent results. We saw this at the 1970 Le Mans and through numerous class victories throughout the rest of that year. Now, in 1971, we see not only the car's class-winning capability continuing, but also outright victories, each type of event demanding a different mindset and driver capability.

For the circuit-racing 914s in Germany, the next outing would be the Jim Clark Memorial Meeting at the Hockenheim Motodrom on 4 April. Race 4 on the programme was the Hockenheim GT race for 3L/2L classes over 10 laps of the 6.7km circuit for this non-championship race for the AvD Europa Trophae, organized by the Automobil Club von Deutschland. Peter Kaiser, in the Motorsport Club Stuttgart-entered 914/6, would finish 4th overall and 1st in

Porsche The Racing 914s

Horst Godel with the Sixtant Racing Team sport kit-built 914/6 GT. (©P)

2L GT behind two Chevrolet Camaros and a hot 911S in the 3L class. Günter Steckkönig, having started from the front row after a storming practice lap, finished 6th overall in the Strähle KG-prepared and entered car. In 10th, 11th and 12th (5th, 6th and 7th in GT 2L) were Robert Stoddard, Horst Godel and Günther Schwarz, the latter in the Scuderia Lufthansa car. Peter Kaiser's car was the one attributed to the Sports Car Club of Stuttgart, and was often also driven by Heinz Blind. Chassis No 914 143 0306 would compete in over 35 races in the years that followed.

On 11-12 April, over in Spain at the St Bartomeu de Grau hillclimb, José-María Fernández took his faithful 914/6 GT along to claim 8th overall and 2nd in Group 4 in this highly competitive event.

Good times Racing in Europe 1971

Robert Stoddard in his privately-entered 914/6 GT sport-kitted car. (Vin)

José-María Fernández, 8th overall, 2nd Group 4, at the St Bartomeu de Grau hillclimb. He followed it up with an overall victory at Lurdes hillclimb. (JMF)

The following day, Fernández was out again, this time at the Subida a Lurdes hillclimb. Same car, different place, a new day – victory time for Fernández!

It was tradition in the 1970s that the middle of April saw staunch sports car racing enthusiasts head for Le Mans for the test weekend. This was a chance for teams to run on the full circuit to assess their car's ability, get a feel for lap times, etc. This year there was to be a new introduction: in addition to the timed testing, there would be a 3-hour race that did not count for any championship, but was intended for the ACO (Automobile Club de l'Ouest) to see those cars that had tested and were on the reserve list running in race conditions, the idea being to facilitate a final selection for the

109

Porsche The Racing 914s

Before it became the famous 'Pink Pig,' here we see the 917 short-tail as it appeared on the grid at the start of the Le Mans 3 Hours in April 1971. (©P)

24 Hours reserve list. However, the reality was that those that did race were either already accepted for the 24 Hours or were running in the race for the fun of it, and never planned to run at the 24 Hours itself. For the established teams, it would be an hors d'oeuvre before the main event in June.

The official test session held on the 17th and 18th had seen the John Wyer-entered Gulf Porsche 917 long-tail of Jackie Oliver come out on top, with a fastest lap of 3min 13.8sec. For the 3-hour race on the 18th, practice was held on the 17th in a 1½-hour session. Willi Kauhsen came out fastest for pole with a 3min 21.7sec run in the Hans Dieter Dechent-entered white short-tail 917 that would become the famous 'Pink Pig' at the 24 Hours a few weeks later. 28 cars lined up out of 51 that had entered the spring Le Mans 3 Hours; 27 were classified as finishers.

Two 914 GTs would run with ten 911s of varying degrees of tune, and, of course, other typical Le Mans entries: Ferrari 512s, Porsche 908s, 917s and even an ageing GT40. Three hours would equate to 47 laps for the winners Georg Loos/Franz Pesch in a Ferrari 512M. In the photographs and records in the Porsche Stuttgart files and those of *Christophorus* magazine, we see the 88 914/6 GT in the hands of Claude Haldi and Bernard Chenevière, listed as finishing 11th overall from 17th on the grid.

The second 914/6 entered was the Lufthansa-sponsored car of Günther Schwarz, running No 92. Having qualified 20th, it had a sorry time in the race, being the first to dnf.

In Germany on 25 April, the non-championship AvD/ISCC-Flugplatzrennen Sembach, a mixed race of sports prototypes and sports cars, saw a large entry of some 12 914/6s scheduled to race,

Good times Racing in Europe 1971

The Porsche Club Romand No 88 914/6 GT driven by Claude Haldi and Bernard Chenevière would finish 11th overall at the April running of the 3 Hours of Le Mans. (©P)

though on the day only six turned up. All six finished, and Rudolph Sauter came out on top in the Max Moritz racing team car to win the up-to-2L class. We then have to go down the class records to 5th place to find the next 914/6GT, that of Walter Bauer. Alexander Nolte's 914/6 GT was 6th with Hermann Dorner 7th.

That same weekend was the Monza 1000km in Italy – round 5 of the 1971 International Championship for Marques. Running at No 58 would be Peter Ettmüller/Ernst Seiler in the Tartaruga racing entry, Ernst Seiler's car, chassis 043 0181.

Three other 914/6 GTs were entered, but only two of those turned up: the Elvio Maria Zanini No 56 entry for himself and Luigi Calzani, along with the Porsche Club Romand 57 entry for Bernard Chenevière and Paul Keller. Neither qualified, failing under the rules of the championship to achieve a sufficiently low lap time, the 56 car only achieving 2min 3.61sec and the 57 car 2min 28.2sec. The Seiler/Ettmüller 58 car did qualify fastest in the up-to-2L class, with 1min 53.96sec. The fastest qualifier of all, though, and on pole position, was the great Vic Elford in the long-tail 917, with a time of 1min 32.93sec at an average of 138.41mph (222.748km/h). Starting from 18th overall on the grid on a warm and dry 25 April, the No 58

Porsche The Racing 914s

The Lufthansa-sponsored 914/6 of Günther Schwarz was, unfortunately, the first to dnf at the April Le Mans 3 Hours. It is seen here ahead of the No 69 911S of Dechaumel/Parot that would also dnf. (©P)

914/6GT gradually worked its way up within the highly populated GT class to take the victory in the 2L section – a fine result for the reliable private entry of Ernst Seiler.

Three weeks after the Monza 1000km, on 16 May, it was the Targa Florio: as mentioned, a successful hunting ground for Porsche. At the Targa Florio it was vital to have the drivers fully acquainted with the circuit and conditions, and that meant practising. This was set to happen the week preceding the race.

In between the Monza 1000km and the Targa Florio was the Spa 1000km on 9 May, which we will come to in a moment. First, we need to go back to February, where we see a memo in the Stuttgart archives dated 17 February 1971, stating: "For training, three 914/6 rally cars are to be prepared for the John Wyer

Ernst Seiler's armband from the Monza 1000km. (MaxPP)

Good times Racing in Europe 1971

team drivers." It is signed off by Helmuth Bott. A second in-house memo to Paul Hensler, Peter Falk and Herr Flegl, again signed off by Herr Bott, states that five Porsche 914/6 in rally specification were to be made available for the purposes of course familiarization (three cars for the John Wyer Gulf team and two cars for Hans Dieter Dechent's Martini team).

Another memo to Mr Wyer and Mr Piëch and Mr Flegl, dated 3 March 1971, states:

"H Dieter Dechent team will use the 908/3 for the race.

It will be necessary for the drivers to familiarize themselves with the course. Two Porsche 914/6s will be made available to him (Dechent) to do this. The 914/6s are to be collected from the Porsche factory before the race at Monza (suggest 20.4.71). After the race at Monza, the cars will be driven to Sicily for one week of practice. The 914s are to be delivered back to Stuttgart after the test. The insurance for the cars will be looked after by H Dechent.

The transporter of H Dechent will carry a spare engine, spare gearbox and spare parts. These items, which are for both the Martini Team and JW A E (Automotive Engineering), will afterwards be transported from Sicily to Stuttgart. H Dechent will see to petrol, oil and tyres in Sicily.

The race participation will be managed by Porsche."

A third memo to John Wyer, Mr Piëch and Mr Flegl, dated 11 March 1971, reads:

"Mr Wyer has stated that the amount of money to be spent on the Targa Florio race is to be limited.

Drivers for the Targa Florio suggested by Mr Wyer (for the Gulf team):

P Rodríguez

Monza 1971: the 58 car, chassis 043 0181, awaits the grid call. (MaxPP)

Monza 1000km 1971: Peter Ettmüller/Ernst Seiler, 13th overall and winners of the GT 2L class. (SB)

113

J Siffert
D Attwood
H Müller

Porsche will supply two cars 908/03 (Gulf colours), as it is the view of Mr Wyer that to race only one car is unwise in case of a problem. The agreement is that there will be training and circuit familiarization before the race. For this Porsche will supply three 914/6. These cars will be collected in Stuttgart before the Monza race. After the race in Monza the cars will go to Sicily for a week of test driving. Mr Wyer will be in contact with Gulf to obtain a secure garage, so that the 914s may be stored until required in Sicily, if they do not need to be brought to Stuttgart for repairs. The 914s will all be available for pre-race testing the week before the (Targa Florio) race. Porsche will manage the race. The paint of the cars will be from the proposal of the Studio."

From this information we can see that five of the 914/6 GTs were made available for training at the Targa Florio. From the archive records dated 25 April, we see they were (in house) numbers:

49	Chassis 043 2451	Engine No 640006
50	Chassis 043 2542	Engine No 640005
51	Chassis 043 2543	Engine No 6301863
56	Chassis 914 143 0139	Engine No 6301828. This car had an injected engine.
58	Chassis 914 143 0141	Engine No 610002

In interviews with team members from the time, the consensus is that three cars were driven from Stuttgart to Monza, two by team technicians and one by Derek Bell, who was new to the team that year. The other two cars went by transporter. There is an interesting anecdote from Porsche racing driver Derek Bell about the 914 Porsches getting to Monza: "During my season with JW Porsche (John Wyer Porsche), they decided that, as it was to be their last attack on the Targa Florio with a sports prototype, where of course they would run the 908/3 cars, it was unwise and unnecessary to have me, the new boy, spending considerable time learning the Targa Florio course. But Porsche did ask me to contribute to the exercise by driving one of several 914/6 down from Stuttgart to Monza, where we were racing with the 917 previous to the Targa. At the Monza 1000km I was driving the John Wyer-entered 917K with Jo Siffert; we finished 2nd. I think on the drive to Monza there were three of us, each in a 914/6. These cars would then be driven on down to Sicily for the drivers doing that event to use for familiarization training to save wearing the race cars out. We had a great high-speed drive in the 914/6s from Stuttgart down over the Alps in great weather. A trip I shall never forget! So I had my share of hairpins over the Simplon Pass, etc!"

Author's note: some articles on the web and in magazines state that the two other drivers were Vic Elford and Gérard Larrousse. However, I put this question to each of them, and both told me that neither of them drove 914-6 GTs from Stuttgart to Monza. It is also to be noted that the Spa 1000km was held on 9 May and the Targa Florio followed on the 16th. Both suggested that the other two drivers in the 914s were other team members – technicians. Derek Bell confirms that, too.

Now we come to the aforementioned Spa 1000km on 9 May. Two 914/6 GTs were entered in this race, which was round 6 of the International Championship for Makes – 71 laps of the then 8.761 mile (14.1km) mighty circuit of the Ardennes. Rated as one of the great fast circuits of the world, and being close meteorologically to the equally notorious Nürburgring, it shares the experience of similar weather conditions. The full circuit, being used here for the 1000km, had been judged unsafe by the Grand Prix Drivers' Association for the 1971 Formula 1 Grand Prix. The sports car fraternity was under different pressures, and whilst maybe prudence should have been the better part of valour, it was valour that won out at this cauldron of high speed that always provided a daunting spectacle, and this year it did not disappoint. In fact, it is worth mentioning that at last, after the many tragedies that motorsport had experienced since the war, the circuit owners and race organizers were now being forced to improve safety for the men and women who provided the drama of racing and attracted the spectators who spent considerable sums of money at and around the circuits.

It would be new John Wyer team boy Derek Bell, who had driven at Daytona, Sebring and Brands Hatch and finished 2nd with senior teammate Jo Siffert at Monza a couple of weeks previously, who proved the bravest at Spa, driving on a surface that was proving rougher with every race. The pole time set by the Siffert/Bell team was set by Bell at 160.923mph (258.98km/h) – so fast that it threatened to eliminate the entire field in the GT class if the 130% rule were applied. (According to the rules at the time, all qualifiers had to be within that percentage to get on the grid and start.) Had that happened, the field would have been reduced to just 13 cars. Not good! The organizers and officials decided, on this occasion, that a waiver would be applied. The GT cars were allowed in, but the speed and time per lap gap, from Siffert/Bell in the fastest car, the 917K, to the last car on the grid, Jacky Dechaumel/Jean-Claude

Good times Racing in Europe 1971

Clockwise from top left: After 71 laps, 1000km, in just 4h 1min 9.7sec, the 917K of Rodríguez/Oliver got the better of Siffert/Bell with a storming finish from both teams, with the No 21 917K taking victory over the No 20 917K by just 0.004 of a second! The average speed had been 154.765mph (249.069km/h). Amazing! (©P)

The Gerd Quist/Dietrich Krumm 914/6 GT rounds La Source at Spa in the 1971 1000km race, on its way to winning the GT 2L class. (©P)

The Porsche Club Romand entry of Sage/Keller at Spa: disqualified after receiving outside help to regain the track following a spin. (©P)

Parot in their 911S, was 1min and 34sec. Slower cars are obliged by the rules of racing to keep out of the way of the faster cars. Of course, a racing 911 – or even the 914s – were pretty quick in their own right, and needed a lot of concentration to drive fast, so having to keep one eye on the rear-view mirror all the time was a taxing experience.

The race started with a little rain falling, but quickly dried out to give a warm and dry event. As ever, it was the John Wyer-entered 917Ks at the front, qualifying 1st and 3rd on the grid, the two cars separated only by the Hans Dieter Dechent-entered 917K of Vic Elford and Gérard Larrousse. After 71 laps, covering the 1000km in just 4h 1min 9.7sec, the JW Gulf Porsche 917K of Rodríguez/Oliver (3rd on the grid), got the better of the Siffert/Bell car with a storming drive from both teams, the No 21 917K taking victory over the No 20 917K by just 0.004 of a second!

The average speed had been 154.765mph (249.069km/h) for the race, and the race lap record went to Siffert with a sizzling 3min 14.6sec, an average of 162.080mph (260.843km/h). Breathtakingly fast, in what was arguably the greatest period of racing of all time, where the cars were mighty and the drivers not only brave but possessing huge amounts of talent and skill.

In the GT class, amongst the many Porsche 911s were the two 914/6 GTs: Gerd Quist/Dietrich Krumm in the Max Moritz-entered 043 0178 chassis car, No 49, and Jean Sage/Paul Keller in the Porsche Club Romand entry, No 51. With the challenging task of trying to beat their fellow competitors and at the same time keep out of the way of the Porsche 917s, 908s and Ferrari 312s, it was the 914/6 GT of the Max Moritz team that took the up-to-2L class victory. The Sage/Keller 51 car was unfortunately disqualified due to receiving outside assistance to regain the track after a spin with 38 laps completed.

The class victory by Quist/Krumm brought the total of class race victories in senior races for the 2L 914/6 GTs to 22 in the last 12 months, proving that, in the 2L GT Class, the 914 was indeed a formidable competitor. However, we reach a point in the life of the 914/6 GT when the decision is made within Porsche to cease any further development; as a factory team, they were not interested in entering these cars officially anymore. We need to qualify why, of course. The facts were, as we know, that most support was going behind the loosely-termed customer teams of John Wyer and Hans Dieter Dechent with the 917s. The desire of the Porsche Management at the time was to put the Porsche name ahead of all others by taking overall victories; there would be little money left over for a Porsche factory effort with the 914s. That said, the factory Competition Department did continue to support the teams like Strähle, Max Moritz and Hahn Motorsport very well, ensuring that development parts that might be useful were made available to them.

In Germany on 8-9 May at the Nürburgring, the International Eifelrennen took place. Run under the auspices of the ADAC, this was the fourth running of the 18-hour race known as the Eifelland Rallye, an event sponsored by the Eifelland Caravan Company. Titled a rally, it was in fact a circuit race. We see in the records the 914/6 GT of Horst Hoier/Walter Simonis carrying No 3. The May date

Not so much a rally as a circuit race on the Nürburgring. (JS)

Preparation before the start for the Rubenach Automobile Club entry: the Simonis/Hoier 914/6 at the well-supported 18 Hours Eifelland Rallye on the Nürburgring circuit, 8-9 May 1971. (©P)

could have been risky in terms of the famous weather in the Eifel mountains. Luckily it was warm and, most of all, dry. 107 starters set off on 8 May at 17.00hrs in a rolling start. The race had many twists and turns, including a mishap when the previous year's winners Rang/Lieb went out early – 18 hours is a long time in the saddle!

Ninety-nine laps of the Nordschleife – that's the total that winners Clemens Schickentanz/Hartmut Jacques completed. However, in 2nd place was the No 3 914 Rubenach Automobile Club entry, Horst Hoier/Walter Simonis. In fact, they thought they had won when, on passing the pits, they saw that the eventual winners were stopped at their team counter, but there had been a miscalculation in the No 3 team, as Schickentanz/Jacques had a two-lap lead, not one lap, and even after the stop they still had a lead of 16sec over Hoier/Simonis after the 18 hours.

Friedhelm Theissen was also racing on 8 May, driving the Kremer team-entered 914/6 to 1st in production and special GT up-to-2L class at the non-championship AvD-Rundstreckenrennen Fassberg race.

Whilst the club and national races were taking place in the homeland of Porsche, the factory team with the prototypes had headed south earlier in the week for the 55th running of the incredible race that was the Targa Florio. If Le Mans is the longest (barring events like the Marathon de la Route), Spa the scariest and Nürburgring the most technical, then the Targa Florio is the most spectacular. The Hotel Santa Lucia in Cefalù, where Porsche garaged their cars, would be their home for a few days.

The Targa Florio went back many years – in fact to 1906, when it was first held on a much longer circuit on roads that would be unthinkable today. By 1955, when the event became part of the World Sports Car Championships, a 44 mile (72km) circuit had been established as the set course. A Porsche first went to the Sicilian circuit in 1953: a private entry of Frenchman Jean-Paul Keck, who was taking in both the Mille Miglia, in which he failed to finish, and the Targa Florio, where he finished in 20th place. Porsche would next make an appearance in 1956, when Umberto Maglioli took the victory in a 550A Spyder. Porsche returned again in 1958, finishing 2nd with Jean Behra/Giorgio Scarlatti in the 718RSK. Porsche would win outright in 1959, '60, '63, '64, '66, '67, '68, '69 and '70. So it could be said that Porsche had form on this circuit!

They came back in 1971, ready to do it again, but times were changing. The mighty but difficult to drive sports prototypes would soon give way to more manoeuvrable, and almost as quick, GT cars in the years to come. The signs were there that year, when Bernard Chenevière/Paul Keller finished 4th overall in a 911S. Ahead of this pairing were three of the super-quick sports prototypes, their days not yet quite over. The Autodelta Alfa Romeos had foregone the race at Spa to concentrate on the Targa Florio in the hands of the masters of the event, Nino Vaccarella/Toine Hezemans and Andrea de Adamich/Gijs van Lennep, as well as Rolf Stommelen/Carlo Facetti. However, this year the starting procedure had been changed, and it was announced after practice that the cars would be released by class, then by practice time, with the bigger cars going first. This gave Nino Vaccarella the advantage of being first on the road on the first lap (well, it is Sicily!). But this procedure didn't help Rolf Stommelen, who crashed his T33-3 and failed to start. The Alfa of Vaccarella/Hezemans went on to dominate the race, completing 11 laps, the same distance as the 2nd place car of de Adamich/van Lennep. The Targa Florio is essentially a time trial over 492 miles (792km). As ever, it was hot and dry, and those 492 sweltering miles took some 6h 35min to complete. The Chenevière/Keller 911 finished ahead of 24 of the 27 prototypes entered. As mentioned, the era of the Grand Touring car was arriving.

Porsche as a factory team was there to support its customer-entered cars: John Wyer Automotive and the Martini team of Hans Dieter Dechent. Running 908 Porsches that came direct from the factory, these fancied runners from Porsche had a torrid time, the John Wyer 908/3 of Brian Redman/Jo Siffert crashing out in an accident on the first lap when Redman understeered off the course and the car caught fire, causing him burns to his face and hands. He was followed shortly by the Pedro Rodríguez/Herbert Müller 908/3, also under John Wyer management, when Rodríguez hit a curb and broke his suspension, meaning he too was out on that first lap! Then on lap 7, with Larrousse at the wheel and with a minute lead over Vaccarella, the final 908/3 of Larrousse/Elford collected a puncture. He was carrying a spare –a space saver – and so set to work to change it, limping on to an intermediate service point, 30km away! It seems that the Larrousse Martini Porsche was contracted to Goodyear Tyres, but when he had to make his emergency tyre repair stop, he did it at the John Wyer team emergency base, and they were contracted to Firestone! As he came to the pits eyebrows were raised, but a diplomatic incident was averted. An interesting little aside with the tyres to excite the Porsche management. Getting away quickly, Larrousse was back up to speed, but a radius arm broke on the next lap and that was it.

Four 911s took places between 3rd and 12th. Then in 13th overall we see the 914/6 No 56 car of Willi Kauhsen/Günter Steckkönig/Ferfried von Hohenzollern, chassis 043 2542, registration WN-V1 entered by Paul Ernst Strähle Porsche. Günter Steckkönig says: "Oh, I remember this race very well. That was my first Targa Florio as a race driver, and it's like it was only yesterday.

117

Porsche The Racing 914s

Our book cover picture: the 914/6 No 56 car of Willi Kauhsen/Günter Steckkönig/Ferfried von Hohenzollern, chassis 043 2542, registration WN-V1, entered by Paul Ernst Strähle Porsche, at the Targa Florio 1971. (©P)

The Targa Florio is, in my opinion, the most fascinating race. Of course, the Nürburgring Nordschleife is a favourite, but the Targa Florio is special. I remember with Strähle we drove on the road to Sicily with the trailer. I had a BMW from Strähle as a tow car, with the 914 on my trailer and, with another tow car, Mr Strähle brought the 911 – we had two cars. I was to drive with Willi Kauhsen in this race. Before practice and the time allowed to get the car prepared, we had technical verification and here came the first problem, because we had our roll bar only behind the driver – you know the type, a single roll bar. It did not cover the passenger seat. In

Good times Racing in Europe 1971

Pressing on in the sun amidst a huge crowd spread all around the circuit. (©P)

Germany this was okay, and we had a certificate from the ONS, the German governing body for motorsport, and we showed it to the scrutineers, because the car as standard had its integral roll bar. But the scrutineers said: 'What is ONS? We go only by the rules from the FIA – the full-width roll bar, triangulated back to the chassis. You have to change the roll bar and you have to fit one tube through the window to go to the suspension turret.' The shock absorber is, of course, fitted to this point. 'There's no chance,' they said, 'that you can start without this.'

"Fortunately, Mr Strähle had a lot of friends in Sicily. They told us there was a blacksmith in Cefalù, the little village where we worked and where the main Porsche mechanics were also based. We took our car there and spoke to the blacksmith about the problem. He said okay, he would do it, and we asked if he wanted a mechanic from our group to help, and he said no. I think he said it would be ready maybe in the evening or the next day, a very short time, '... you can fetch the car.' I was very worried – fingers crossed! But he called us later on in the day; it was late evening: 'Okay, you can come, the car is ready.' You know, it was really perfect – amazing, even painted matt black, just like as-new. I think this roll bar is still in the car now. The car was last heard of in a museum in north Germany. Well, at the next scrutineering, the blacksmith turned up, dressed very smart, and watched what happened. The scrutineers found no problem: the car was okay and our blacksmith was standing just behind the car, very proud and smiling.

"So now the race: we had a good race, but in the final laps when I was in the car, we were fighting against two Opel GTs prepared by the engine tuner Conrero. These two Opel cars were very fast, and so I had a lot of work to catch them, but I did catch them and I was in front on the final lap. As you know, at the Targa Florio there is a long straight 5.5km, along by the sea. On this straight, suddenly I felt and heard my engine cough and I thought it was a fuel problem. It was, and it got worse. All the time I could just see the Opel, a dot in the distance at first, but it was getting bigger and bigger in the mirror! He passed me, and although the last part to the finish line was normally nice to drive, my car had this problem. It stopped. I tried driving it by using the starter motor, but it was only good for a few metres. Then I started to push the car uphill round the curve until my own engine, my heart, was getting tired! Then I tried it again and it started, but stopped soon after. Just then, Herbert Müller, who had abandoned (he had crashed on the first lap), suddenly appeared from the spectators. I said, 'I've no fuel.' He ran off and came back within seconds; as he arrived, he craftily threw a small can under the front of my car – a little can of fuel. It all happened very quickly. He came round the car and said to me very quietly that there was fuel under my car! But I thought by now I would be disqualified. There was no solution but to put the fuel in – at least to get home. I started the car, threw the can into some bushes further on where

Piero Monticone/Luigi Moreschi in the Brescia Corse Italian team 914/6. Unfortunately, they went out on the first lap. (EM)

there were no spectators and got to the finishing line. We managed to get 3rd place in GT (up-to-2L) and no disqualification. Nothing was said – I think the organizer was also a Sicilian friend! The reason why this problem occurred with my fuel was that, during the last stop for refuelling (you refilled from a big tank above the pit box on the roof), they must have had an airlock. Because the fuel flushed back and the mechanic operating the filler decided it was full, it was okay, and pushed the fuel tube away. I started, but the tank was not full."

Without this problem, the 914/6 of Steckkönig/Kauhsen would have finished in 9th place overall. The Strähle team had a good Targa Florio, and at the finish their No 40 Porsche 911S came home 6th overall and 2nd in the over-2L GT class with Dieter Schmid/Giulio Pucci. Incidentally, although Steckkönig's 914/6 had finished behind one 911 2L (the 4th-placed car), they were in front of ten other 911s of varying capacities.

Also competing at the 1971 Targa Florio with a 914/6 GT was the Brescia Corse Italian team with Piero Monticone/Luigi Moreschi driving. Unfortunately, after qualifying to leave the start in position 34, they did not come round at the end of the first lap.

Good times Racing in Europe 1971

The Strähle 914/6 GT of Günter Steckkönig/Dieter Schmid – 15th overall and 2nd in the 2L GT category at the Nürburgring 1000km. (©P)

Further north in Europe, in Germany on 16 May, the 1971 Flugplatz Kaufbeuren mixed motorcycle and car race meeting, which included a non-championship GT race, was held. Gerhard Fetzer would take his 914/6 to victory in GT 2L with Horst Godel 3rd. The following weekend at the Bremgarten International, in another non-championship race programme, Peter Zbinden in his privately-entered 914/6 GT took victory in the over-1600cc class, beating several 911s, two other 914s and a Corvette! While Zbinden was winning in Bremgarten, at the Nürburgring on 23 May in the non-championship Nürburgring 750 miles, a race organized by the ADAC, Simonis/Hoier, 914/6, were pipped at the post by the 911T of Rieder/Degen for victory in the 2L GT class. Both private entries, they were followed home by two more 914s, the 914/6 of Schimpf/Matthiess and the 914 four-cylinder of Römer/Dimmendaal, these three 914s finishing ahead of 41 other starters, a dominant performance at the hands of privateer owner/drivers. This being at the Nürburgring, too, where handling is at a premium, tells its own story. At the Neuhausen DARM race in Germany on 30 May, Friedhelm Theissen, in the Porsche Kremer Racing Team car, came 2nd in the DARM Meisterschaft (round 6) race, while at the Salzburgring in Austria, finishing in the top spot in yet another non-championship race on the 4.238km circuit was Hermann Neureuther, driving 914/6 GT 043 0734.

The reader will by now see that this work covers as many of the 914 Porsche racing activities as we have been able to trace, in homage to the smaller teams as well as the major championship races. Sadly, the quality of some cameras in the 1970s and that of some of the private 'snaps' from the period are not up to standard for the publisher to be able to reproduce effectively here. There are also not so many images still available from the period to show the cars from the smaller races. However, we still feel it is very important to mention these events, even without images.

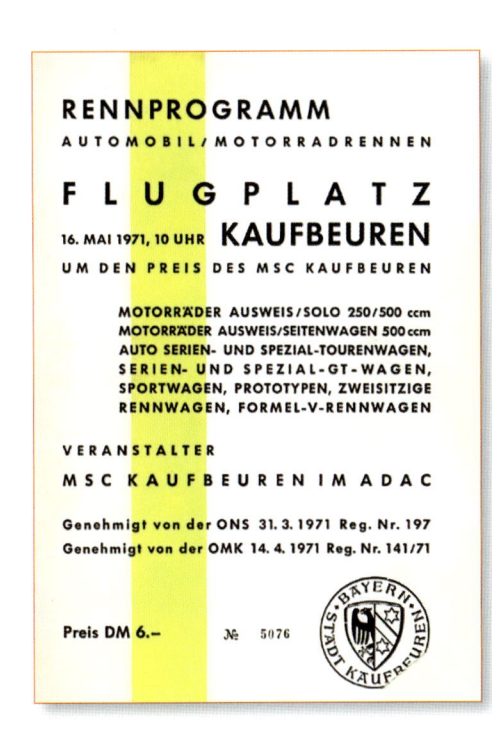

(Vin)

121

Porsche The Racing 914s

With the 914, mostly in six-cylinder form, performing successfully, we return to one of the Blue Riband races, those involving a World or European Championship. Next up in 1971 would be the Nürburgring 1000km, also on 30 May. An entry of 92 was whittled down to 56 qualifiers, of which 53 started on a warm, dry day, and 51 finished. Pole had been set by Jacky Ickx in the 312P Ferrari with a time of 7min 36.1sec, an average speed of 111.994mph (180.237km/h) for the journey round the 14.189 mile (22.835km) circuit. However, come the race, the Ickx/Regazzoni combination went out with only 21 laps of the scheduled 44 completed. It would be Porsche who again took the top spot, this time with the Hans Dieter Dechent team Porsche 908/3 in the hands of Vic Elford and Gérard Larrousse. (They, of course, were in the sports prototype class.) Prototype sports-class cars filled the first 11 places, followed by two 911Ss, a Kremer entry and a Porsche Club Romand entry, in 12th and 13th, finishing 1st and 2nd in the over-2L GT class.

In the up-to-2L GT class were nine cars, of which six were 914/6 GTs:

Max Moritz Porsche	94	Gerd Quist/Dietrich Krumm	Chassis 043 0178
Paul Ernst Strähle	95	Günter Steckkönig/Dieter Schmid	Chassis 043 2542
Rubenach Automobile Club	93	Walter Simonis/Horst Hoier	Chassis 043 0185
Kremer Brothers	96	Frans-Josef Rieder/William Scheeren	Chassis 043 0653
Alexander Nolte	108	Werner Christmann/Willi Nolte	Chassis 043 0462
Tartaruga Racing	104	Ernst Seiler/Peter Ettmüller	Chassis 043 0181

This time, the No 108 car of Werner Christmann/Willi Nolte qualified fastest of the 914/6 GTs, 24th on the grid, with the eventual class-winning No 94 Max Moritz-entered car of Gerd Quist/Dietrich Krumm, 914/6 GT chassis 043 0178, in 31st.

The results would show the No 94 Max Moritz-entered car of Quist/Krumm in 14th place overall and winning the 2L GT category. 15th overall and 2nd in the category was the No 95 car of Günter Steckkönig/Dieter Schmid. For the record, the No 93 914/6 GT of Walter Simonis/Horst Hoier came home 18th overall, with the No 96 car of Frans-Josef Rieder/William Scheeren 19th. Nolte Christmann, along with the usually very reliable Seiler/Ettmüller team, failed to finish.

Class winners at the Nürburgring 1000km 1971: Gerd Quist/Dietrich Krumm, 14th overall and 1st in the 2L GT category. (©P)

Walter Simonis/Horst Hoier: 18th overall at the 1971 Nürburgring 1000km. (©P)

Good times Racing in Europe 1971

The Nolte/Christmann team failed to finish this time, coming to a stop on lap 32. (©P)

All the major teams would now look to the next International Championship round, the big one: the Le Mans 24 Hours 1971. Before we get there, though, it's worth noting that Hans Christian Jürgensen, racing the same weekend as the 'Ring 1000km, was at the Zolder track to record a 3rd place in GT2.

Le Mans, the 24 Hours of 1971; hopes were high in the 914/6 GT camps of the Porsche Club Romand and the Max Moritz Racing Team.

Paul Keller/Jean Sage were in the No 46 car and set a qualifying time of 4min 27.4sec, putting them 44th on the grid of 49 starters,

Porsche The Racing 914s

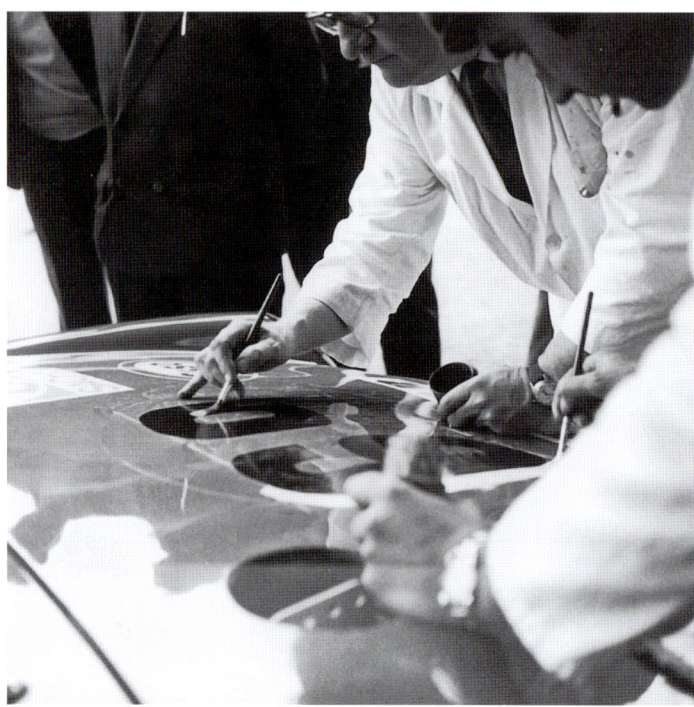

Officials paint the numbers onto the 69 Max Moritz Racing Team car. (©P)

(JS)

and Gerd Quist/Dietrich Krumm in the No 69 car, chassis 043 0178 were on position 37, having set a time of 4min 24.3sec. However, this year's race would be fraught with attrition for those down the field. Up front, two 917K Porsches dominated affairs, completing 397 and 395 laps for the 1st- and 2nd-finishing cars; 1st being the 917K of Helmut Marko and Gijs van Lennep, a Hans Dieter Dechent entry, and 2nd being the John Wyer entry for Richard Attwood, last year's winner, and Herbert Müller. They were followed by the David Piper and Luigi Chinetti Ferrari 512s. Then came the André Wicky-entered Porsche 907 of Walter Brun, followed by a plethora of 911s, stamping their authority on the GT class again. Things had started well for the two 914 teams, and as they went to the grid the prospect of a long run was high in their minds.

And as the race got under way, both the 914/6 GTs looked to be performing well. However, the Keller/Sage car hit a problem just before midnight, when the oil pressure started to fluctuate. The drivers soldiered on, but the efforts of the Porsche Club Romand team were to no avail when, nine hours into the race, the pressure dropped further and engine failure followed shortly after.

As the night-time period passed and daylight arrived on the Sunday morning, the Max Moritz team, having performed so well at the Nürburgring 1000km, was hoping that another class podium would be on the cards. But as they entered the morning period, the gearbox suddenly shouted "enough!", forcing the abandonment of the 914/6GT when it hit the guard rail as a result of the gearbox failure, leaving the car stranded out on the circuit.

The 1971 Le Mans would be the last time that the 914 would compete on the hallowed tarmac of La Sarthe in that period. In the Porsche Racing Department, it was already decided that there would be no further development. The 911 was the flagship model; it was the car that the racing teams preferred to moved forward with. The shadow of Volkswagen and what Volkswagen stood for in the 1970s did not suit the image of the Porsche name in the eyes

Onto the grid: preparations begin. No 69 is the Quist/Krumm entry; No 5 is the Teddy Pilete/Gustave Gosselin Lola T70 Chevrolet; No 40 is the Jean Egreteaud/Jean-Marie Jacquemin 911S. (FRA/AJ)

"Excuse me!" The No 69 car of Quist/Krumm moves over to allow the flying 917LH of Jo Siffert/Derek Bell to make a clean pass. (©P)

Porsche The Racing 914s

The Paul Keller/Jean Sage (46) Porsche Club Romand 914/6 tucks in ahead of the Quist/Krumm 914 and the 12th place finisher (44) of Richard Bond/Paul Vestey and the (63) 6th place finisher, the French pairing of Raymond Touroul/'Anselme' of the Porsche Club Romand. (©P)

Quist/Krumm storm up the start/finish straight as the No 9 Ferrari 512M of Hughes de Fierlandt/Alain de Cadenet leaves the pit lane. (LAT)

For 12 hours the Max Moritz 914/6 GT performed impeccably, but as the sun came up the team's hope faded when the gearbox started to show a problem. (FRA/AJ)

Good times Racing in Europe 1971

Stranded out on the circuit, its race over: the No 69 car of Quist/Krumm is passed by the eventual race-winning 917K of Helmut Marko/Gijs van Lennep. (©P)

of certain influential customers. It's certain that fans of the 914 model today will be dismayed to hear that statement, especially as many eminent drivers and team members have since said that it could have been very successful with a bit more development. The fact is that the 1970s was a different time from today, when in our much more open, less aloof society, the 914/6 is now fast becoming acknowledged as an excellent machine, and the 914/6 GTs are desirable, high-value items on a par with (and in many cases above) several of the 911 models. Even the humbler 914-four-cylinder, especially the 2L model from 1973 onwards, provides a performance and roadholding experience that is a revelation to today's generation of classic motoring and motor sports enthusiasts.

America would become the market where the 914/6 and four-cylinder would have the greatest impact and developments for racing that would stretch way into the '80s and '90s, and today they are regularly seen there racing in historics. However, we are getting away from our European story – we will return to the USA scene in a little while.

27 June 1971, and the Zeltweg Circuit Austria would provide the setting for the Österreichring 1000km, round 10 of the International Championship of Makes. Six 914/6 GTs were entered. Sadly, the Kremer brothers' 914/6 didn't turn up, and there was trouble in store for four of the remaining cars. The Gerd Quist/

Dietrich Krumm Max Moritz car failed to qualify, having turned in a 2min 10.71sec time in qualifying. Likewise, the Brescia Corse 914 of Mario Ilotte did not qualify; neither did the Willi Nolte/Werner Christmann Alexander Nolte-entered car, due to the rules of the required achievable time, 130% of the fastest in practice. Ernst Seiler/Peter Ettmüller fared no better, although they had recorded a 2min 08.4sec in practice and qualified to start. For some reason unrecorded, the car did not appear on the grid.

This left the sole survivor, car 37 of Günter Steckkönig, last year's runaway class winner, this year with Dieter Schmid/Roland Bauer, taking 23rd place on the grid of the 25 cars that did start. In an undramatic race in terms of incidents, though cold and foggy, only 11 cars were classified at the end of the 5h 4min 26sec that it took to cover the 1000km on this year's 3.673 mile (5.911km) circuit.

This event would be the last time that the incredible 917 Porsche appeared at the top of the podium in a World Championship qualifying round. The winning team were pole-sitters Pedro Rodríguez/Richard Attwood/Jackie Oliver, with a time of

Porsche The Racing 914s

Amongst the 914s failing to qualify at the Österreichring 1000km was the usually quick Gerd Quist/Dietrich Krumm Max Moritz car. A far cry from earlier in the year, the pace of the competition had begun to heat up. (©P)

Ninth overall, and 1st in the GT 2L class: the sole surviving 914/6 GT 043 0163 of the Strähle team with Günter Steckkönig/Dieter Schmid/Roland Bauer. (©P)

1min 39.4 sec in the John Wyer Porsche 917K. They won by a clear two laps. The Jo Siffert/Derek Bell Porsche 917 sister car failed after only four laps, due to a rare mistake by Siffert after he burnt the clutch at the start. However, the good news continued, because Porsche would also be on the podium in the GT 2L class, where in 9th overall and 1st in the GT 2L class once again we find the 914/6 GT 043 0163 of the Strähle team, with Günter Steckkönig/Dieter Schmid/Roland Bauer on-board. As Günter Steckkönig says: "The Strähle team always provided a well-sorted and reliable car."

On 4 July 1971, at the Avus Ring for the Internationales Avusrennen 50 Years of Avus races, a non-championship DMV-organized GT race, two privateers took to the track in 914/6s. Running in the up-to-2L class, they would take the honours, the class winner being Hans Christian Jürgensen, with Eckhard Schimpf, also in a 914/6 entered by Keipel RRT, in 3rd place. The 911T of Peter Rumpfkeil was 2nd in GT 2L. There was little coverage for this round, though it is said in some reports to have been one "with plenty of excitement."

Nothing to do with racing the 914s, but definitely racing support, the French F1 Grand Prix, also on 4 July, would see Jackie Stewart set pole position, take fastest lap and win the race held on the Paul Ricard Circuit in the south of France. In a promotional coup, the French Porsche importer Sonauto had arranged for the drivers to parade in a string of standard 914 Porsches before the race, as can be seen opposite.

In grid position order: a collection of Porsche 914s is used to present the drivers of the 1971 French Grand Prix at Paul Ricard, Le Castellet. Jackie Stewart, seen here in car 11, set pole and eventually won the Grand Prix. (P)

Good times Racing in Europe 1971

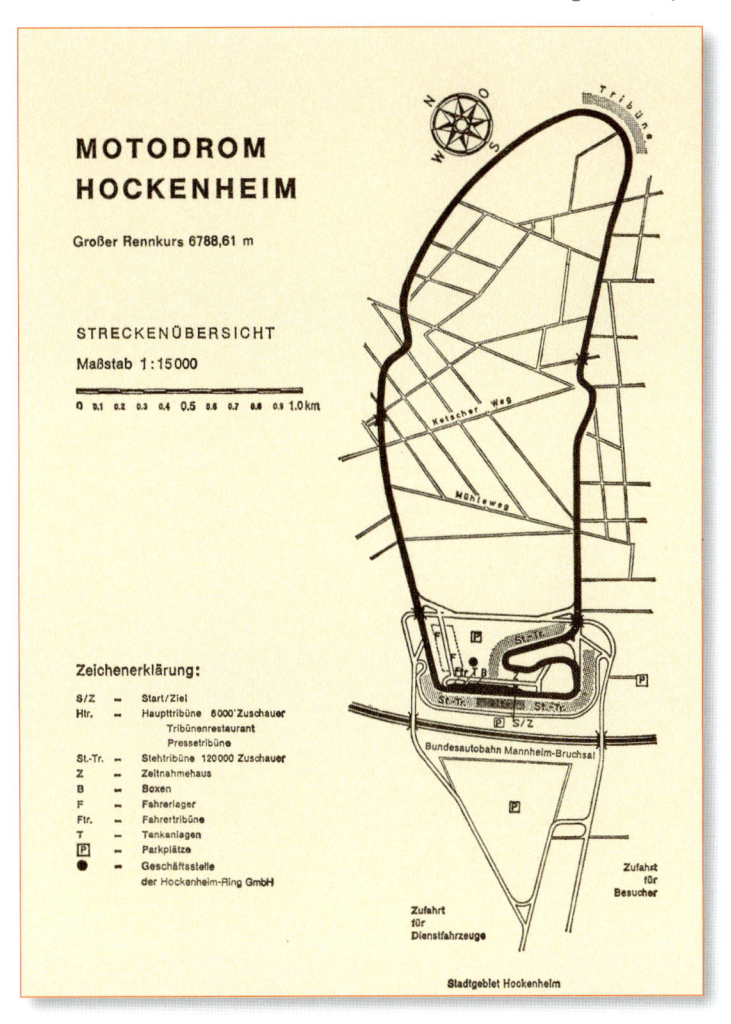

The Hockenheim circuit circa 1971.

The same weekend, over at Hockenheim, a round of the German national series of GT races was part of the programme for the European 2L Sports Car Championship. Eight of the ten 914/6 GTs entered would start:

16 Écurie Biennoise	914/6 GT	Gustav Schulp
19 Apag Racing	914/6 GT	Martin Maraggia
23 Sixtant Racing Team	914/6 GT	Horst Godel
20 Strähle KG	914/6 GT	Günter Steckkönig
17 Squadra Tartaruga	914/6 GT	Ernst Seiler
15 Heinz Blind	914/6	Peter Kaiser
22 Autohaus Max Moritz	914/6 GT	Gerd Quist

Twenty-six cars got away in the Südwest-Pokal Hockenheim Internationales Solitude-Rennen for touring and GT cars over 1.6L. An impressive line-up of other GT racers saw the Motorsport Club Stuttgart Ford Capri of Dieter Glemser take victory. A plethora of Porsche 911s and BMWs in other classes filled the next seven places. Then in 8th we see the up-to-2L GT winner Gerd Quist in the No 22 car of Autohaus Max Moritz. Second in the class came Peter Kaiser; 3rd Ernst Seiler; 4th Günter Steckkönig; 6th Horst Godel.

On 11 July at the Norisring there was a supporting event to the 200 Miles meeting (another race in the Deutsche Automobil Rundstrecken Meisterschaft series, round 10) was a supporting event. In a large turnout of 914 GTs, Ernst Seiler was in car 22, joined by Friedhelm Theissen in 21, Peter Kaiser 23, Hermann Dorner 24, Horst Godel 25, Gerd Quist 26, Roland Bauer 27, Hermann Neureuther 28 and Hans Heinrich Timm 29. The race had 27 entries, all either 911s or 914s, so a Porsche would win whatever the circumstances!

129

Porsche The Racing 914s

GT 2L class winner at Hockenheim on July 4: the now well-known Max Moritz team car of Gerd Quist, chassis 043 0178. The other two 914s in the background are just a little too far back to identify clearly, though we can guess at the Strähle and Tartaruga Racing entries. (©P)

Horst Godel prepares in the pit lane at Hockenheim, 4 July 1971. (©P)

This interesting shot shows how relaxed and informal a race paddock was in the early 1970s, even at a major meeting such as a round of the European Championships. (©P)

130

Good times Racing in Europe 1971

Five entries failed to turn up – all 911s – whilst one, the 914/6 of the Écurie Biennoise, car 30 of Gustav Schulp, arrived but did not start. That left 21 cars to take the first corner, split into two classes: over-2L and up-to-2L. Curt Wetzel in a mighty Chevrolet Corvette led home a multitude of 911s in the over-2L class. In the up-to-2L class it was Ernst Seiler who would take the honours, with Dorner 2nd in the class and Bauer 3rd.

It is important to mention the main event of the day, the aforementioned Norisring 200-mile race, round 4 of the Interserie challenge. Amongst the many sports prototype Porsches and Ferraris present that weekend was a Ferrari 512M, entered by Herbert Müller and driven by the great Pedro Rodríguez, who had just become World Sports Car Champion for the second time. Rodríguez had been at Silverstone testing a BRM the previous day, and arrived at Nuremberg late on the evening before the race. A special practice session was allowed for him the next day before the race. On that race day, with the weather extremely hot, Rodríguez shot into the lead as the Norisring 200 got underway – he was lapping back markers by the 10th lap.

Just two laps later, approaching the sharp right-hander that led on to the back straight of the circuit, he suffered tyre failure and the car ploughed into the Armco, shot across the road straight into a wall and bounced back on to the left-hand side of the track, catching fire. The race was stopped. Rodríguez was trapped in the wreckage. The fire took several minutes to extinguish, following which he was rushed to hospital in Nuremberg, where he later died from horrific multiple injuries. The motor racing world had lost one of its finest, if not the greatest driver of the time. This was not the only tragedy in 1971, for just a few months later at Brands Hatch in October, in a memorial race to Rodríguez, his team-mate at the Gulf John Wyer team, Jo Siffert, was killed in a BRM Formula 1 car. A sharp reminder of the fragility of the man behind the wheel, and the price often paid for being there.

Pedro Rodríguez, allowed to practise on the morning of the race due to prior commitments. He had just been acknowledged as World Sports Car Champion for a second consecutive year. He was leading the race comfortably when tyre failure caused a tragic end to the day. (FL)

131

Porsche The Racing 914s

The DARM Championship moved on to Diepholz for its next round. Here, for the Grand Touring over-1300-cc race, another huge entry across the classes in several races saw Hans Christian Jürgensen finish 4th overall behind the Swiss-O-Pass Racing Team Chevrolet Corvette of Curt Wetzel in 3rd, Åke Andersson in a 911S in 2nd, and the race winner, Frank Gerlach, in the Hülpert Racing Team Dortmund Porsche 911S/T, those first three being in the 2L+ class. In the up-to-2L class, Jürgensen, as mentioned, 4th overall, took victory in his privately-entered 914/6 GT. Friedhelm Theissen was 3rd in up-to-2L, with Willi Nolte 4th (043 0462), Heinz Blind and Hans Joachim Bartsch following, also in 914/6s. Hans Christian Jürgensen's car, chassis 914 043 0306, was an early 1970 machine supplied initially to Hahn Motorsport along with a GT kit from the factory. Jürgensen had acquired it in 1971 and would race it successfully, as we will see, right through to 1973 when it was sold on. The car still exists today and competes in historic racing.

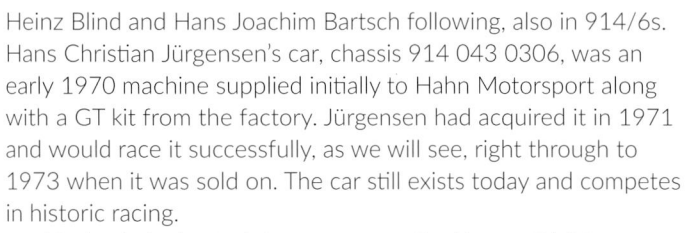

Hockenheim hosted the next event, the Hessen DMV non-championship races on 24-25 July. Six 914/6s took part. However, on this occasion, all the 914/6s were outshone and got nowhere near the

Clockwise from top left: Roland Bauer in the Strähle car normally used in 1971 by Günter Steckkönig: he would finish 3rd in the GT 2L class. (©P)
Friedhelm Theissen, 4th in GT 2L, leads the No 4 911 of Eckhard in the Norisring German Championship at the DARM support race. (©P)
Hermann Neureuther, the Team Matter-entered 914/6, 9th in GT 2L class. (©P)
Ernst Seiler (22), 1st in the GT 2L class ahead of Hermann Dorner (24), who finished 2nd in GT 2L at the Norisring, 11 July. (©P)

Good times Racing in Europe 1971

Seiler takes the class victory at the Norisring. (MaxPP)

As in our earlier image, racing in the 1970s, even at a National Championship round, took place in an almost party atmosphere – no big motor homes to be seen. Ernst Seiler (r) is taken by surprise by the camera, whilst a mechanic works on the front wheel of the Tartaruga Racing Team 914/6 GT in the Norisring paddock. Little did they know that a tragedy was about to unfold in the Norisring 200 Interserie race. (MaxPP)

podium.

The same weekend over in Spain, the La Bien Aparecida Hillclimb, near Santander, promised a smooth and fast surface where speeds of up to 185km/h could be achieved with ease. A mix of cars came to the start line, headed by the three Porsche 908s of Juan Fernández, Jorge Bagration and J Kutz, the Abarth 2000 OT of Luciano Otero, a single seater Selex and Hispakarts. Julio Gargallo was in the fuel-injected 914/6 GT of the GES team. In practice, Gargallo climbed very fast, being 8th fastest overall, behind the three Porsche 908s, the Abarth, a couple of single seaters and the Alpine A110 of Sunsundegui. Gargallo, having fitted new Firestone semi-slicks of soft rubber, was very strong again on the second ascent, stopping the clock at 2min 22sec and ending the day 5th fastest overall.

In Denmark on the weekend of 7-8 August, German driver Hans Christian Jürgensen took his 914/6 GT to the Djursland Jysk Grand Prix at the Djursland Ring, Kolind. It was a combined Groups 1-4 event and in the Group 2 and 4 race over 1000cc Jürgensen finished in 5th place. Also on 8 August in France at the Mont Dore European Championship Hillclimb, Piero Monticone in a 914/6 would finish 4th in the Group 4 category.

On 15 August, at a non-championship race organized by the ADC at Niederstetten, four 914/6s would race; three of them

José-María Fernández in Spain on 28 August 1971, tackling the Cresta Terrassa-Rellinars hillclimb: 1st overall and 1st in Group 4. (JMF)

133

failed to finish: regulars Sauter, Bauer and Godel. However, it was a victory for Jim Docherty, this time in his 914/6 entered by the Mannheim-Heidelberg Sports Touring Club Team.

That same weekend saw another 914/6 victory over at the airfield circuit of Wunstorf, at the Internationales Flugplatzrennen Wunstorf race (another ADAC-organized non-championship race) – our old friend Hans Christian Jürgensen again – beating two 911s in the process before the second 914/6 of Hans Heinrich Timm in 4th place, and taking fastest lap as a consolation! Regular 914/6 competitor Willi Nolte came 5th.

22 August at the Kassel-Calden airfield 2.646km (1.2 mile) circuit saw round 15 of the DARM Championship series. Nine 914/6s were entered, with only Opel and the 911s turning up to do battle in the up-to-2L class, the over-2L class being dominated by the 911Ss.

Werner Christmann took the win in the up-to-2L class with his privately-entered chassis 043 00462 car, beating the Steinmetz-Automobiltechnik GmbH Opel of Gerhard Schüler. In 3rd, though, was the 914/6 of Friedhelm Theissen, chassis 043 0653, with Hans Christian Jürgensen 4th and Hans Heinrich Timm 5th. Two more 914/6s also finished, but Gerd Quist in the Autohaus Max Moritz VW-Porsche-Sportwagenzentrum car was a non-finisher, as was Hermann Dorner in the Mannheim Heidelberg Sports Touring Club entry.

On 29 August in Switzerland, the famous Ollon-Villars hillclimb took place on the International Bergrennen climb. François Cévert was fastest in a Tecno F2 car, but down in 25th overall, and in 3rd place in the Group 4 class, was the familiar name of Gerd Quist. Bernard Chenevière was also competing with a 914/6, coming 6th in Group 4, with Peter Zbinden 8th.

Also on the 29th at the International Flugplatzrennen at Mendig, a non-championship event attracted a large field to race on the 3.95km circuit. Five 914s were entered again for the usual suspects – Bauer, Jürgensen, Timm, Christmann – plus a new entrant, Bert Lips, driving a Kremer Racing 914/6 GT, chassis 043 1034. The records indicate that this was the car originally supplied to Werner Kastner (it would later become a Jägermeister team car). Thirty cars had entered; 22 started. Two 911s dominated the 14-lap race, but on the podium in 3rd overall was the Opel of Gerhard Schüler taking the 2L class, with Werner Christmann 4th overall and 2nd in GT 2L in the Willi Nolte-entered 914/6 GT (043 0462). Timm was 4th in GT 2L, Jürgensen 5th and Lips 6th.

The Nürburgring 500km was next up on 5 September, round 6 of the European Championship. Only the serious need apply! Three serious entrants did turn up: Autohaus Max Moritz entered Gerd Quist in their chassis 143 0178 car, Porsche-Kremer Racing had Erwin Kremer and Jürgen Neuhaus in chassis 043 0653, and AFG Dortmund put in an entry for Werner Christmann and Willi Nolte in 043 0462. Erwin Kremer was double driving, as he was also the co-driver of the Kremer Racing 911T with Günter Huber.

83 cars lined up to take the start. The full 22.835km circuit was being used for the 22 laps that would take just under three hours for the winning car, the Lola of Vic Elford. Fifteen of the 83 starters to finish after the Lola were sport prototypes, but in 17th place came Erwin Kremer in his No 1 drive with Günther Huber, winning the GT 2L class with the Kremer-entered 911T. Second in GT 2L came Gerd Quist in the 914/6, and 3rd in GT 2L was, again, the dexterous Erwin Kremer in the 914/6, this time with Jürgen Neuhaus. A commendable result in any circumstances, but at the Nürburgring it was a veritable feat of endurance! Out of luck,

The Kremer brothers' 914/6 GT for double-driving Erwin Kremer, co-driven by Jürgen Neuhaus. (©K)

though, on this occasion, was the 914/6 of Christmann/Nolte, though they did have the honour of the fastest lap in the class with 9min 21sec.

At the Hockenheim Motodrom on 11-12 September, the featured race in the DARM GT Championship meeting would be round 18 for GT cars. The GT 2L touring class would be won by the very rapid Ford Escort RS 1600 of Christian Schmarje. The GT 2L sports class was won by Ernst Seiler, running his regular car under No 52 this time and finishing 2nd overall to the Escort in a class field of 20 cars that started the race. Second in GT 2L was Wilhelm Siegle in the privately-entered Porsche 911T. The Autohaus Max Moritz 914/6 GT entries of Dietrich Krumm (55) and Gerhard Fetzer (54) came 3rd and 4th. Friedhelm Theissen (53) came 5th in GT 2L.

The following weekend, 19 September, at the Mainz-Finthen

Impressive performance from Kremer at the Nürburgring 500km European Championship race. (K)

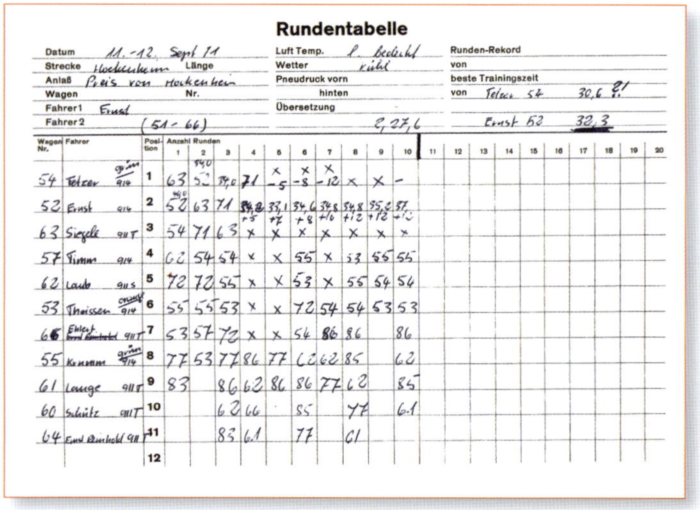

Porsche The Racing 914s

Part of the Hockenheim lap chart records of Ernst Seiler. (MaxPP)

Qualified as reserves but no race place this time as the 914 GTs were outpaced – an early sign that the writing was on the wall for the short-lived 914/6 in Europe. Ernst Seiler thought so, and would shortly after sell his car and move on to a Ferrari. (MaxPP)

Airfield Circuit, another 914/6 victory in the GT 2L class fell to Stephen Behr, with Hans Christian Jürgensen 3rd in GT, the 914s being split by the 2nd-placed 911T of Horst Lange.

Into October, and to France this time. On 16 October at the multi-circuit layout of Montlhéry, south of Paris, 32 cars started the Paris 1000km held on the 7.856km circuit. The overall winners after 128 laps would be Derek Bell and Gijs van Lennep in the JW Automotive Porsche 917K. This time, though, the already multi-winning 914/6 of Ernst Seiler and that of Dieter Spoerry only qualified as reserves. Was the competition starting to reveal flaws in the 914's performance?

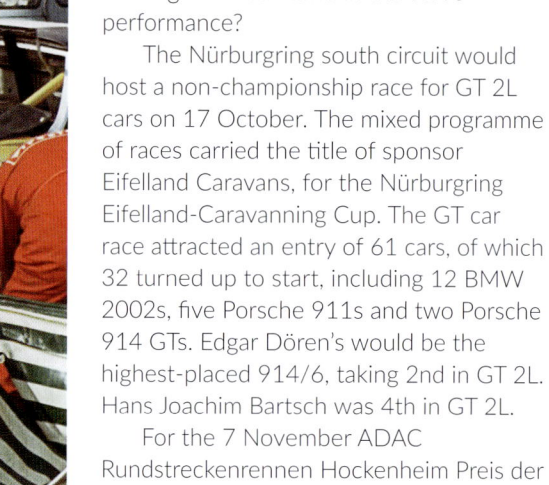

The Nürburgring south circuit would host a non-championship race for GT 2L cars on 17 October. The mixed programme of races carried the title of sponsor Eifelland Caravans, for the Nürburgring Eifelland-Caravanning Cup. The GT car race attracted an entry of 61 cars, of which 32 turned up to start, including 12 BMW 2002s, five Porsche 911s and two Porsche 914 GTs. Edgar Dören's would be the highest-placed 914/6, taking 2nd in GT 2L. Hans Joachim Bartsch was 4th in GT 2L.

For the 7 November ADAC Rundstreckenrennen Hockenheim Preis der Stadt Karlsruhe non-championship race, Autohaus Max Moritz had entered Gerhard Fetzer in a 914GT. He won the race ahead of two 911s, followed by Gotthard Egerland in the Kamei Racing Team 914/6, in 4th overall. Three more 914/6s would also finish this 20-lap race. The same weekend, Bernard Chenevière was taking the Porsche Club Romand 914/6 GT to the Jarama 2 Hours in Spain. Carrying No 57 and starting from No 11 on the grid, he came home 9th overall and 3rd in the GT 2L class, a fine result in this round of the European Sports Car Championship.

The Hockenheim Finals on 28 November were a series of races that traditionally closed the season. This time, Walter Bauer would be the only 914/6 competing; he finished in 5th in GT.

Summing up 1971, one can say that, for the 914/6 GTs, it had been a fairly successful year with 22 GT 2L class victories, though these were mainly national category events. Internationally, the 914/6 GT was suffering from a lack of ongoing development from the manufacturer. Only the Strähle and Max Moritz teams were making headway, with several podiums for class wins at international level. Porsche, via the John Wyer Gulf team, once more took the Manufacturers' Championship, the Challenge Mondiale, the GT Trophy and the Marques Points Championship. So it was a good year in the end for Porsche, apart, that is, from the tragic accidents involving two of its top drivers, Pedro Rodríguez and Jo Siffert.

The 914/6 would go into 1972 with question marks over its true performance against the rapidly developing cars in the GT series in Europe. It was not a favourite of the Porsche factory, and 914/6 production itself was slowing rapidly and would survive only one more year. As we will see in chapter 8, it would be in the USA that its life was extended way beyond a time not even considered in Europe.

Before we leave 1971, we will briefly look at the statistics for this year as regards the discipline of hillclimbing. A look at the charts shows 34 events and 13 class victories. There were undoubtedly many more in other European countries. Looking at the slaloms results (usually the domain of the club driver), in Germany there were an astonishing 71 events where 914s took part, with 28 class wins. Clearly at this point these cars, even in road-going classifications, were proving to be useful in the hands of amateur drivers, who had found that the mid-engine principle gave them a chance advantage. In Spain, too, Fernández and his fuel-injected 220bhp 914 would race almost every weekend, winning at the Montjuich Castle hillclimb in April, then in July at the Gironella-

At the Hockenheim 3 Hours on 29 October, Ernst Seiler and Dieter Spoerry were having a final run in the faithful car – not so faithful this time, however, as it suffered from mechanical maladies leading to a dnf. (MaxPP)

Casserras hillclimb, again beating the Abarth of Juncosa and, this time, the Alpine A110-1600 of Jorge Pla in 3rd – no mean feat when both the Alpine Renaults and the Abarths were at the peak of their careers. Ernst Seiler, having had a fine couple of years in his car up to the latter part of the year, was feeling the pinch with development and decided to move on. Development was, and is, an expensive business beyond the pockets of the private entrants, who, though usually with sufficient funds to race, had to rely on advancements from the supplier – Opel, Porsche, Ford, or whoever. We will leave racing the 914 for a chapter now and examine how it became the car at the forefront of the (then) new thoughts on motor racing safety.

5
Rescue: 914/6 GT
The first racing fire/safety quick response vehicle

When Ray Harroun won the first Indianapolis 500 in the USA in 1911, the race began with a rolling start, and leading the pack was a pace car, now commonly call a safety car. Over the years, the rolling start format has been adopted by other races, but it wasn't until recently that the pace car began to resemble the safety cars that we know today. Prior to this, setting the pace of the cars behind it was its sole purpose – it carried no safety equipment, doctors or fire marshals.

Pace cars are for the front of the race; for our purposes we need to look at the back of the grid – or more precisely, behind it.

Motor racing has always carried risks; the drivers take them and sometimes the spectators feel the effects, as was the case in the horrific disaster at the 1955 Le Mans 24 Hours. Safety equipment and facilities were, at that time, the responsibility of the circuit owners, but they were in business to earn money, and circuit improvements and the safety of spectators were low in priority up to as late as the 1970s. Safety consisted merely of keeping the cars racing on the black stuff, and the spectators had to learn to stand back! Many postwar tracks were resurrected out of old airfields, and those race tracks that had existed before the war were put back into use, with little consideration given to driver facilities or spectator protection. Safety was something that no one wanted to talk about, though it was a fact that too many lives were lost due to the time it took to respond to incidents, and because

Weissach: there is still some snow around as the first sponsored racing fire/safety quick response vehicle is wheeled out in 1973 for the press to examine. (©P)

Rescue: 914/6 GT The first racing fire/safety quick response vehicle

The 15-year-old Herbert Linge's pass/identity card from the period under the Nazi regime of World War II. (©P)

the facilities available to those who arrived at an accident scene were very basic.

Apart from the horrors of the 1950s, in 1967 Lorenzo Bandini died in a fiery accident, as would two of the greatest drivers of the 1970s, Pedro Rodríguez and Jo Siffert. None of the cars had onboard extinguishers, and the suits the drivers wore were inadequate. Readers knowledgeable about motorsport will be familiar with the ambassadorial work done by Jackie Stewart in the mid 1970s regarding safety, continuing to this day. His efforts, and those of the late Professor Sid Watkins, who began in 1978 to get track medical facilities developed, are to be applauded – not to mention the huge involvement of the man that made things happen, Bernie Ecclestone.

However, one man and his efforts pre-date the work of these highly respected men. He is Herbert Linge, a man who was to become a key player in the rise and success of Porsche from the 1950s onwards. We have already seen his name in the earlier chapters. Let us, then, hear from the great man himself – who Herbert Linge is, and how he became the first to think of driver rescue and the use of a true safety car, fully equipped to save lives. (Author's note: from an interview in Stuttgart, March 2015.)

Herbert Linge: "How did it all begin? Okay, I'll tell you. In 1943, I was 15 years old and was learning to be a mechanic at Porsche, where old Dr Ferdinand was the big boss, of course; it was during the war. I was supposed to have finished the course in late 1945, but the war ended before that and I had to take my exams half a year early." (Author's note: see chapter 1 for Herbert Linge's progress within Porsche.) "Then, after the war ended and all the turbulence, along with my few years in Baden-Baden, I went back to Stuttgart, to Porsche." As we have already seen, Herbert Linge's racing career was meteoric; not only that, but he was involved in all the testing and development of cars and saw first-hand the good and the bad side of motor racing, including the lack of safety and the assistance response in the event of an incident.

Herbert Linge continues: "I was so involved with the development and testing of the cars, for me racing was the masterpiece at the end of our work. We had done a lot of work; we had tried to make it the best marque. That's why I always drove the test cars, to make sure that all was well, using my experience in each car."

As a driver, Herbert Linge drove in 95 races between 1954 and 1970, including the Carrera Panamericana, Mille Miglia, Sebring 12 Hours, Daytona 24 Hours, Le Mans 24 Hours, the Targa Florio seven times, and many, many more. Podium positions are too numerous to list. He became one of Porsche's legendary drivers. But it was at the 1963 Le Mans 24 Hours, where he finished 8th overall with Edgar Barth, winning the 1601cc-2000cc class, that he really started to think about driver safety. Christian 'Bino' Heinz, sales manager for Willys in Brazil, agents for Alpine Renault in South America, was driving one of the new Alpine sport prototypes when he lost control on the Mulsanne straight and crashed the car, which immediately burst into flames. There were no marshals at this point; no one came to the rescue and Heinz perished in the fireball.

From that moment, Herbert Linge began to think about how things could be made safer for the drivers. He started making notes and writing down ideas while continuing to work at Porsche in his day job, becoming responsible for the Competition and Development Departments. Herbert Linge: "Yes, from 1949 I was actually driving the 356, right up to the 917 – everything we made. As you have seen, when the 914 came along I was very much in at the start of that project. Here in Stuttgart, I was in charge of the complete shop: experimental mechanics, racing, transmission – everything. I had a big group here. The first cars were not very good, but I was very happy when they came out with the six-cylinder in 1969 and I said: 'Now it's going to be a car.'

"Away from the racing, Monte Carlo, the Marathon, etc, I was having the ideas about safety." In fact, Herbert Linge had, for a number of years, been trying to get circuits to improve protection for drivers and spectators, but his words were falling on deaf ears. He spoke with many of the drivers in sports car racing and, increasingly, Formula 1. Herbert Linge: "I had a good contact with Jacky Ickx and all the top drivers, and these drivers were pushing and saying if nothing happened with the circuits and the cars, they would make their own decisions about racing. It was about this time that Mr Ecclestone became involved – 1973, I think. I was the speaker for the German drivers [drivers' representative] and I had to go to the meetings in Paris. Eventually they set up a Safety Commission, where I met Professor Sid Watkins later in 1978, and we worked together afterwards for almost ten years."

It was in 1971 that discussions started within Porsche with Ferdinand Piëch and Professor Helmuth Bott, recently returned to Porsche. In 1971 they gave Herbert Linge the okay to go ahead with a project to create a safety car alongside his own day job. Herbert Linge's technical workshop had been moved from Zuffenhausen in 1970 to the new site at Weissach. By now, the team had grown to almost 300 people.

Herbert Linge: "I had already started to think about what was required, but when I was putting my ideas down on paper and talking to the circuits, a lot of people didn't like the idea. The owners of most of the circuits immediately said: 'Oh, it's going to cost a lot of money, what Linge wants to do.' A lot of pressure came from the organisations who were putting on the races, especially if they had had their own system in place for many years. Most of their equipment comprised of old cars or breakdown trucks that couldn't be used on the road anymore, along with old ambulances, etc. Then somebody comes up – me – and tells them to change everything around. I didn't have too many friends at this time!

"The governing body for motorsport in Germany had also decided that it would not allow any car other than a race car on the track during a race. They had their ways of working and they did not want to change. They said they wanted to improve safety, but the reality was they did not want to spend any money on it! I was starting to think my idea was dead. But I was determined I was not going to give up; we were going to have this, because on the other side I was also under pressure from the drivers to push the safety angle at the circuits. No one would listen to the drivers; they were seen as paid performers: provide the spectacle or else. The circuits did not want me or the drivers criticising their organisations. So I decided I would build a car and show them that this was the best way with what we had at the time [1971]. I had also recently seen a big accident in 1968 at Le Mans, where a car flew over a guard rail and another one had a big fire [Author's note: it was Mauro Bianchi's

A classic hazard at the Nürburgring in 1970: the top picture shows the situation before the marshals arrived. The bottom picture shows that the photographer had time to move to another position to photograph the No 88 car of Huhn/Schwarz passing the still-burning wreckage, and the marshal, who has just arrived. (©P)

Alpine Renault]. They rescued the guy, but back in 1963 with the Bino Heinz incident, I think the race cars passed this place three or four times; his car was on the other side of the track to the marshals and it was so bad, by the time anyone got there it was far too late. It should not happen and we had the same thing in Zandvoort, when the fire truck just came too late. Always too late.

Rescue: 914/6 GT The first racing fire/safety quick response vehicle

"Because Professor Bott was actually a friend of mine – he had started working at Porsche early in the 1950s and I was already here then, so we knew each other well – I asked him if I could have a car to convert into a 'safety car' so we could show the public and the industry, and he said the only car he had available was this test car for the 914. I said okay, that's not so bad. It had a six-cylinder engine and space in the back for the equipment."

The car chosen for Herbert Linge to use to convert to a 'fire car/safety car' was 914-57, the 914/6 GT chassis 914 143 0140. Its engine was 6408007, the car that carried the registration S-Y7715 for Åke Andersson on the 1971 Monte Carlo Rally. It had also seen training duties on the 1971 Targa Florio. That is how the first safety car came to be a 914.

As we have heard from Herbert Linge, many of the circuits had their own way of dealing with incidents on track. By 1971, this procedure basically consisted of marshals spaced out around the circuit, usually positioned at the points where the flag marshals' posts were located. At the better-organised circuits, such as Silverstone in the UK, each of these posts was connected by a telephone system, and each flag marshal's post was in sight of the next one, placed on either side of the track. The same idea in principle applied at the Nürburgring, but here the circuit is huge – 22km+ – in mountainous and wooded surroundings. To attend and put out a fire on such a circuit, where the furthest point away from the start can be at least 11km, was an extremely difficult task with the regular fire/rescue vehicles. As those vehicles were standard road-going versions, they lacked the necessary pace, and the one thing that is desperately needed in an emergency is speed of reaction to attend to an incident. They were also usually placed at the start/finish area.

Not yet a safety car, but a marshal's circuit car at the Nürburgring, 1968. (©P)

141

Herbert Linge: "Having got the car [the 914/6 GT] I had to decide which tools we needed when we got to an accident. At this time fire was the first danger, always, and that's why I told them we had to have a fast mobile fire extinguisher, and not the regular circuit arrangements, where the regular fire tender would attend. [Author's note: as mentioned, usually it was a fire tender that was no longer in service with the regular local fire brigade – better than nothing, but far too slow, and there were not usually three or four parked around a circuit.] It took too long for the fire tender to get to an incident. You have to be there in 1-1½ minutes."

Herbert Linge's vehicle would be equipped with fire extinguishers, and with at least one of the team of two, both already being mobile track-marshalling experts, also being a medical specialist. Numerous organisations started to take notice, including the Grand Prix Drivers' Association. Linge's requirements were:
A competition car from Group 2 or 4.
Fitted with a rollover bar.
Full four-point seat harness.
Tow hooks front and rear.
The car should have the letter 'R' in place of a number where the race roundels were sited, representing the fire rescue car, or 'S' for safety marshal at the track.
A white flag with a holder/support fitted to the car.
A rotating emergency light on the roof.
Radio set with helmet earphones and a throat microphone.
Fire extinguisher set: one of 4.5lb and one of 9lb.
Fire extinguisher unit with 220-230lb extinguishing agent and nozzle feed.
Asbestos gloves, face mask, asbestos blanket (two of each of these items).
Spade.
Crowbar with a hook.
Bolt cutters and large tin snips.
Two tow ropes.
Hand-operated block and tackle.
Dispersion material (in a container of around 20lb).
Scissor jack.
Axe and a large machete.
Reserve fuel for stranded vehicles.
Complete mechanic's tool kit.
Flashlight and hand-held flasher.
Warning triangle.
First aid kit.
Note pads, writing materials, regulations and plans of the marshals' posts.

A memo notice of the rescue car whilst undergoing aero test. Note: it is not yet fully converted, as the extinguisher cannon hump is not present on the rear cover. (©P)

The vehicle must be maintained in first-class condition and under contract.
Drivers must be licensed, race competent, of high calibre and with fire and first aid training.
Drivers must be equipped with fireproof suits and helmet.
Vehicles should be located in such a position as to have instant access to the track.

Herbert Linge: "The car was converted and tested, with the two drivers in it and fully equipped. They must never take longer

Rescue: 914/6 GT The first racing fire/safety quick response vehicle

than 1½min to get to the accident. That was the big idea. I went to the German ONS (Oberste Nationale Sportkommission) and said I was trying to show all the owners of the race tracks that this was needed and wanted by the drivers: would the ONS support it? They said: 'No! The way we work is fine; we don't need this.' So I went to Austria when they had a big conference to talk about the same thing. I gave a three-hour speech about the safety ideas I had, and they, the Austrian race authorities, agreed to implement a plan. One day later, back in Germany, I was called by the German head of the ONS who asked why the hell I had gone to Austria to give information on my ideas. I said, because you said no!"

It was then that the governing body of German motor racing decided to pay greater attention to safety on German race tracks. Herbert Linge was given the authorisation to create what was basically the first emergency rescue race car. In fact, there were plans afoot to have a safety 'R' rescue car at the German Grand Prix of 1971. These ideas appear in an in-house memo from Rainer Bratenstein and Herbert Linge to Peter Falk and Paul Hensler. The memo is dated 7 July 1971.

Herbert Linge: "At that time, the fire extinguishers we had were either simple water ones, or the powder type, which was not good for the driver – very bad when you sit in the car and powder is flying

Hockenheim 1971: Herbert Linge with the first attempt at a safety car equipped as an emergency rescue car: chassis 914 143 0140, used by Åke Andersson/Bo Thorszelius at the 1971 Monte Carlo Rally. (©P)

143

Porsche The Racing 914s

The perfect fire engine: a racing car with special extinguishing equipment, seen here at Hockenheim. (©P)

The fire extinguisher supplier Deugra had come up with a product that did not leave powder deposits on anything or affect breathing. In those days, powder was a favourite extinguishant. The new product to replace powder was Halon 1211; it put out the fire and, for a short space of time, allowed the driver to breathe without affecting his vision or health, giving him time to react. (©P)

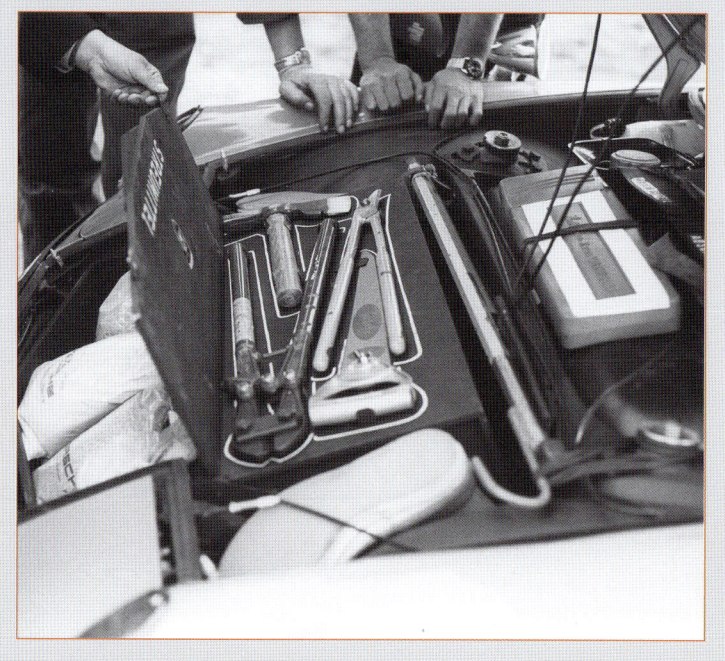

The Linge-designed emergency rescue tool kit, located in the front boot of the 914. (©P)

Rescue: 914/6 GT The first racing fire/safety quick response vehicle

around; also, when you had an engine fire and you used powder, afterwards the team would have to take the engine out to clean it.

"At that time, in 1971-72, we were experimenting with a new fire protection system inside the military tank – the Leopard tank. The Leopard tank was constructed by Porsche and the test driving was being done in Weissach. We had to install the fire extinguisher system for the tank, inside, and the supplier Deugra had come up with a product that did not leave deposits on anything, but you could still breathe. It was Halon 1211; it put the fire out, and for a short time it was not bad for the driver. I said, that's going to be the way for our cars, so I went to the manufacturer and told them this is the size of the 914, and they made up these three containers to fit exactly." (Halon is forbidden today for motorsport, but at that time it was perfectly acceptable.)

Herbert Linge: "I tested the process at least five or six times, sitting in a burning car, with my friends with the fire extinguishers putting out the fire, and I never had a problem!

"The next thing we had to make sure of was to have a doctor in the car. ONS agreed, and once we had the okay for the fire/safety car, I went to take the idea to all the German car companies: Mercedes, Opel, plus Ford, and in Italy Alfa Romeo. I knew many of these people, because over the years in my work I had regular contact with them. Within a couple of weeks, ONS had at least ten cars promised for the race tracks."

The idea was that if the manufacturers saw one or more of their cars being used in front of the public in a safety role it would do several things. First, it would increase the number of safety/rescue cars at a circuit; second, it would allow more safety teams to be created; and third, response time to an incident would be reduced dramatically. Of course, for the manufacturers the publicity was priceless.

Little did the ONS or Herbert Linge know, but they would be able to prove his

The famous image of the Herbert Linge fire/rescue car: the three Halon tanks can be clearly seen. (©P)

Nürburgring at the 1972 Rheinland-Pfalz-Preis, Interserie race: Willi Kauhsen in the 917/10 leads the pack onto the south curve, while the column of smoke of a major drama is visible in the background. (©P)

145

Porsche The Racing 914s

ideas and the worth of the new fire/rescue car very soon, at the Nürburgring in the 1972 Rheinland-Pfalz-Preis, the 7th round of the Interserie race series, on September 24.

Herbert Müller was starting on the last row due to a problem in practice. In the rolling start, which ran on the old Nordschleife circuit into a little loop behind the pits before returning out of a corner onto the start/finish straight, the last rows were just coming out of the corner as the race started. At the back, the inexperienced Franz Pesch in the No 5 McLaren M8, not being used to the torque produced in the McLaren, spun coming on to the starting straight, and in the process crashed into Herbert Müller's 512 Ferrari. The Ferrari became airborne, flew across the track, turned upside down and hit the pit lane guardrail; the guardrail sliced into the car right behind the driver's seat, causing an explosion. The car landed in the pit lane, upside down and fully engulfed in burning fuel.

Herbert Linge in action just as the circuit's firemen and their equipment arrive. The 914 rescue car is clearly visible. (©P)

A sight no one ever wants to see. (©P)

Linge's work is completed; as he climbs over the barrier, it's over to the firemen, now. (©P)

Rescue: 914/6 GT The first racing fire/safety quick response vehicle

Huschke von Hanstein, Porsche Press and Publicity Manager at the time of the event, surveys the work done by Linge and his safety car as the track firemen, using powder, finally ensure the fire is completely out. (©P)

Müller recalled afterwards in a news report: "There was a tremendous crash. I knew that I was flying through the air, because I saw the blue sky behind the pits, and I knew that the car was on fire, and I thought: 'This is not going to be good.' I braced myself, waiting for some kind of impact, which is what happened, twice! All I was worried about was not to hit my head anywhere. Then the car came to a stop and I immediately released my seatbelt, and since I didn't know that I landed upside down, I fell into the burning fuel. I turned

147

Porsche The Racing 914s

myself around and tried to kick open the door ... no go ... considered knocking out the windshield ... didn't work ... so I tried the other door ... and it opened enough for me to get through ... and I knew then that I was on fire."

Müller later told the press that it had actually been a good place to crash, because it was very near to some fire extinguishing equipment. Herbert Linge: "There was a big crash at the start; one car went into another and Müller in the Ferrari looped over. There was a huge fire, and I was behind the race cars in our 914 ONS car with the doctor. [Author's note: The ONS 914/6 GT followed the race cars on the starting loop as the safety and doctors' cars do today.] I was out of our car and on the scene immediately. I already had the fire under one of the cars extinguished before the Nürburgring circuit firemen with the fire engine, which was parked 100m further down the road, got to the accident. I was right there. And this was at the start, in front of all the prominent people – they saw it all." From that moment on, there was to be no doubt in the minds of the German race organisers and the ONS.

There would be more fire drama, too, in a support race the same weekend, as we see here.

Jim Doherty follows the No 25 Jean Canonica car past the Porsche Club Romand 911T of Horst Klauke, about to be engulfed. (©P)

148

Rescue: 914/6 GT The first racing fire/safety quick response vehicle

The big hump on the back of the car covers the cannon nozzle for quick access to the pipe attached to the extinguisher tank. (©P)

Ten-minute laps were perfectly possible with the fully-loaded 914/6 GT rescue car, speeding emergency response to a new level. (©P)

It had taken a quick response and avoidance of a tragedy to wake up the German motorsport fraternity, but by 1973 more safety and rescue cars had been added to the team. Herbert Linge: "You know, we could do 10min laps of the Nordschleife with a fully-equipped car and two people inside. The big hump on the back of the car was to cover the cannon nozzle, so that I could get the pipe attached to the extinguisher tank quickly. It was a cannon with 25m of hose to take to the fire.

"In 1971, when we first started, I was on the track in the 1000km at the Nürburgring during the race: not too fast, but always in position if something happened. And then along came Bernie Ecclestone. He came up to me at a race meeting at Hockenheim, maybe. He had two people with him – I don't know who they were – but he said he wanted me to be in F1."

Already the matter of driver safety when racing was being brought to the

First outing: A trial run of the new idea, 1971 Nürburgring. (©P)

149

The ONS Linge rescue car at the 1973 Essen Motor Show. (©P)

forefront. Jackie Stewart had been raising the subject and had managed over the years to get seat belts made obligatory, fuel tanks on the cars improved, and, along with the other drivers, had been pushing the organisers to listen. A lot of drivers had lost their lives in the late 1960s and early 1970s. Stewart was three-times world champion by the end of 1973 when he retired. He had had a serious crash in 1966 at Spa, and on his recovery he set out to become a leading spokesman on the subject of safety in motorsport, campaigning for improved emergency services and better safety barriers around race tracks. Along with the mandatory use of seat belts, he pushed forward the design of full-face helmets for drivers. He was even instrumental in organising driver boycotts – at Spa in 1969, the Nürburgring in 1970 and Zandvoort in 1972 – unless safety barriers, run-off areas, fire crews and medical facilities were improved. Stewart and Linge were moving in a similar direction.

Their ideas and actions would lead to the next phase: improved off-track and infield medical services, finally instigated by Professor Watkins in 1978.

Herbert Linge: "After the result in Germany at the Nürburgring, where both drivers had emerged virtually unscathed, we had cars put in place in Austria, and then we went to Canada, Japan and all over the world with the 914 to demonstrate what we were doing. I was once even in the German sports studio, where all the big sporting people were for a show. I was there with this car, and we had a fire in the studio. It was quickly put out!"

It was in 1973 that Recaro (famous for seats), previously known as the Reutter Carrosserie Company and very closely associated to Porsche, took over the running costs of the 914 rescue car. By now, with the other manufacturers on board – Ford, Mercedes and Opel – word was spreading.

Rescue: 914/6 GT The first racing fire/safety quick response vehicle

Nürburgring 1973, now in Recaro colours (not visible here!). The red paint had the same colour code as the fire engines of the period. (©P)

In 1973, a pace car was tried for the first time at a Grand Prix in Canada. It was a limited success at that time in F1; as we have read, there was resistance from some of the circuits. In years to come it would become the norm. (©P)

Hockenheim sports car race 1972: the Linge rescue car in attendance, following the grid of cars round to the start of the race. (©P)

151

Porsche The Racing 914s

More cars were made available, including a 911 for the ONS. On the back row we see a Ford Capri, a Ford Escort, a BMW 2002 and two Volkswagen estates. On the middle row are two Opels, another Capri and a Mercedes. Safety on the circuits was now (1973) being taken seriously. (©P)

Porsche added a 911 to the rescue group. Herbert Linge: "The 911 and all the cars from the other companies were converted into safety and rescue cars at Weissach, where we had a space especially set aside in the workshop. That was, of course, my work. The supplying company, such as Mercedes, would call us and tell us they had a car ready for us – most of the time they wanted to use a new type because it was good publicity – and we would collect them. With Mercedes, we had to change every second year; they called up and said: 'We'll get you a new one now!'

"My wife was always picking the cars up at the companies and taking the old ones back. Bernie Ecclestone started to get more involved with F1, and he took the decision to bring the other countries into line with what we were doing in Germany. We went to Italy, to Monza, with our rescue cars with the backing of the teams, but they [the Monza authorities] wouldn't give us the okay to have the fire safety car on the race track. They said: 'We don't need the

The full ONS rescue team at Hockenheim in 1973: Herbert Linge sits on the bonnet. (©P)

Rescue: 914/6 GT The first racing fire/safety quick response vehicle

Germans here!' I told them it had nothing to do with Germans! Ecclestone intervened in practice – we had three cars positioned out around the circuit and at the correct points, ready to go on track instantly if there was a crash. But the guys in the cars called me up and said: 'We are not able to go out on the track because we are blocked in [Author's note: an action by the circuit's management], so I went to Bernie and told him that our cars were not in a position to help if something happened, because they were blocked by two cars. Ecclestone went up to the Race Control steward and said: 'No F1 car can go for practice until these cars are positioned the correct way.' And he succeeded. He made them change their ideas. This helped us a lot. I think it was as late as 1979 that this happened, because in 1978, when the big crash occurred and Ronnie Peterson died, we weren't there then with the safety car. I was there personally, but not with our cars."

The reader might like to read the late Professor Sid Watkins' book, *Life at the Limit*. Professor Watkins came on the scene when Bernie Ecclestone was President of the Formula One Constructors' Association (FOCA); he was still running Brabham then. Bernie, of course, knew what Herbert Linge was doing, but wanted to go further. Professor Watkins went to Hockenheim in July 1978 and met up with Herbert Linge and saw the set-up for the ONS system in three Porsches with paramedic-trained teams.

He was disgusted to find however, that although the first part of any accident was taken care of on track, behind the scenes the medical centre consisted of an old converted bus! This at a circuit with all the latest facilities in every other respect, including a new hotel! The circuit owners just would not pay for better medical facilities. It was at this point that the whole scene was to come into sharp focus. The circuit's chief medical officer explained his frustration, all down to the circuit not investing in the need for driver safety, a shortage of doctors on practice days before the race, too few ambulances – the list went on. To cap it all, Professor Watkins was refused access to Race Control on race day, with no liaison between race direction and the medical teams in the event of an incident. It seems a request for a talk was met with abuse.

Bernie Ecclestone was called upon; he spoke to the race direction and said that if the rescue and medical teams were not given access to Race Control to monitor emergencies, he (Bernie) would go onto the track and get the drivers out of the cars. A pre-arranged signal was agreed; Bernie went down on the track and stood at the front of the grid. Professor Watkins went to Race Control; he was let in and gave the thumbs up to Ecclestone, and the race went ahead. From that moment on, the ONS system began to be introduced worldwide. Professor Watkins, along with Bernie Ecclestone and Herbert Linge, were responsible for having Appendix H of the 1980 FISA Handbook rewritten, declaring a much higher standard for medical facilities and support – developments which have been ongoing to this day.

Herbert Linge: "You know, when I got to know most of the race managers at the circuits, and when I came down to Hockenheim

Here we see the legacy – a news cutting of the safety/fire rescue car used in Sweden. Note the date on the paper: August 1973. (FF)

This is that safety car today. (FF)

153

Porsche The Racing 914s

Waldegård in the former Monte Carlo and Recaro rescue car in the UK in 2012. The vehicle, which, at that time, was owned by a pop star, was looked after by Maxted Page and Prill. It was then re-acquired by Recaro to be returned to its place as probably the world's first fast-response emergency rescue vehicle. (PA)

The restored 914/6 GT as it was in 2015, following many months of work. (©P)

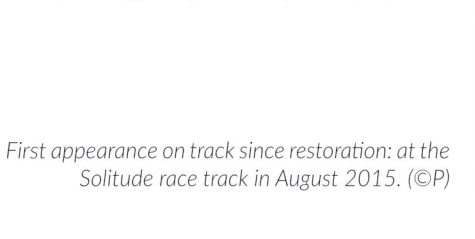

First appearance on track since restoration: at the Solitude race track in August 2015. (©P)

or Nürburgring, it was: 'Oh my God, he's here again and it's going to cost us a lot of money!'

"We started to get involved in lots of other things relating to safety at circuits. After every race, I was asked to send a letter to the FIA in Paris where I described the accidents and what could be done to improve things. Without Bernie Ecclestone, I don't know if I would have made it. As far as safety was concerned, he told the circuits: 'That's the way I want it and I'll pay for it.' Sometimes I had big arguments with the ONS and others when we told them they needed five or six rescue and safety cars for a race. The circuit owners always asked who was going to pay for it. I had to explain that Bernie would see to it. At first they did not believe it; it took some persuading, but once they saw that he paid, they were much more cooperative. I told them that was the cost for the cars – we were not paid, just our food and hotel and daily expenses. Bernie always saw to it – he never let us down. I was very proud of our teams; they were fantastic, all of them."

The work done by Herbert Linge, which is little known outside of Germany, had an effect worldwide as race circuits started to realise that, if they wanted to put on events, they had to think of the drivers' and spectators' safety.

For a while, the original rescue car, chassis 0140, moved from one private owner to another, returning to its former colours as the historic motorsports movement gained in popularity, as can be seen here, when the late Björn Waldegård drove the car, which at the time was owned by a British pop star. Since then, it has been re-acquired by the Recaro Company, and its life has come full circle as it has been transformed back to its position as the first race-track fire/rescue quick-response vehicle.

6
Privateer time
Racing in Europe 1972-1976

The 914/6 had a short life in terms of a production run. As we have seen, the reality was that it needed development, for which there was little or no desire. The top European drivers liked the known factors and predictability of the 911 design, even if it was tail happy; it was more powerful than the 914 and would get even more power in the years to come. By 1972, the new crop of 911s had an engine with a lot of torque, and rally drivers especially prefer torque over pure bhp every time. For racing, outright performance is required, and even with 220+bhp in the quickest examples of the 914/6 GT, it would only ever be good enough for class podium positions on the international scene. The competition was moving forward rapidly – Ford, in particular, with the new Capri. There was also another problem for the Porsche Company in the general market place: price. The six-cylinder, and in fact the four-cylinder version were not proving to be the much less expensive alternative entry-level Porsche that the company's Sales and Marketing Departments had anticipated in the beginning. Performance-wise, the 914 four-cylinder cars were okay, but not as fast as regular Porsche buyers would have liked. Porsche had to correct the situation. In Europe, the 914 was selling moderately in four-cylinder form and very well in the USA, while the six-cylinder version had, by 1972, been picked up by the privateer racing guys in the national classes, with a few competing at international level on home ground. Several factory-created examples were moved on.

One arena where the 914/6 was still to shine was in the hill and mountain championships which, as already mentioned, were a big deal in Europe. The names of the venues – Mont Ventoux, Ollon-Villars, Freiburg-Schauinsland, Rossfeld – ring bells throughout the racing fraternity. There would be plenty of class wins for the 914/6 on the tracks and on the hills, but it is in the latter where, even by 1977, the 2L and 3L classes would still see the 914 performing effectively.

It was April before any of the racing 914/6 GTs hit the tracks in 1972. On the European international racing calendar, the Nürburgring 300km, a round of the German National Championship and also a round of the Interserie challenge, would kick things off on 3 April. The race, its full title being the International ADAC-300km-Rennen Nürburgring um den Goodyear-Pokal, held on the familiar Nordschleife, had attracted a huge entry of impressive machinery and drivers, including Howden Ganley in the BRM Chevrolet, Willy Kauhsen and Leo Kinnunen in Porsche 917s, Mario Casoni and Guy Edwards in Lolas, and many more. Fifty-one cars took to the start. In the GT class, 17 of them were Porsche 911Ss, eight were 911Ts and just three were 914/6s: No 155 Willi Nolte, 156 Edgar Dören and 158 Horst Sasse. Fourteen laps later, on the damp to wet circuit, the winner overall would be John Fitzpatrick in the Porsche-Kremer Racing 911S, ahead of former 914 drivers Claude Haldi and Günter Steckkönig, also in 911s. Willi Nolte was the highest-placed 914/6,

155

Porsche The Racing 914s

300km of the Nürburgring opened the 1972 season.

Willi Nolte in what is thought to be chassis 914 043 0462, splashing his way to 14th overall and 5th in the GT 2L class at the Nürburgring 300km. (©P)

John Fitzpatrick, a force to be reckoned with in 1972 – soon to be European GT Champion. (K)

The Jim Clark Memorial, paying tribute to the late World Champion and one of the greatest-ever racing drivers. Jim Clark died at Hockenheim in a Formula 2 race on 7 April 1968. Another car suffered clutch disintegration, dropping debris on the track; it is thought this caused a puncture that led to the high-speed fatality when Clark's car left the track. (RS)

finishing 14th overall and 5th in the GT 2L class – the GTs ahead of him being an Opel (6th overall), which won the class, and three 911Ts. Edgar Dören came home 16th overall and 6th in the up-to-2L GT class, with Sasse 26th overall and 7th in the class. The event was a two-race affair with results based on aggregates.

It was already clear that the competition had moved on, and the 914/6 was struggling in international racing. Opel was showing the way, but even the privateer 911s frequently topped the 914s. As we enter the national series challenges for 1972, there was a class win at the Zolder round of the DARM German Championship on 9 April, when Hans Christian Jürgensen came home 2nd overall and took the GT 2L victory. Twenty-two cars started. Finishing in 5th overall was Horst Klauke, and in 7th Willi Nolte.

Privateer time Racing in Europe 1972-1976

On 15-16 April the annual Jim Clark Memorial meeting was held in Hockenheim, where on the Saturday the 914/6s of Günther Schwarz, Walter Bauer and Roland Bauer finished in 5th, 8th and 11th overall, with Schwarz collecting a podium place with a 2nd in the GT 2L class. At Sembach, for the ISCC Flugplatzrennen race on 30 April, three 914/6s finished, with Hans Christian Jürgensen coming 3rd overall and 3rd in GT2 behind two 911s. A return to Hockenheim on 13 May saw four of the regulars taking part in a GT-only race, a non-championship round. Fetzer, Schwarz and Bauer were competing; some records state that Jürgensen also started and finished, collecting a 2nd place; however neither his name nor his number appears in the race programme. On 21 May, at Zolder, there was no doubt Jürgensen was in the game this time, beating the 911s and taking a victory in the DARM championship round 12, with Edgar Dören's 914/6 coming home in 2nd place.

Several hundreds of kilometres south, also on 21 May and with the sun shining, teams were getting ready for the 56th running of the Targa Florio. A problem was brewing at this fabulous race – a victim of its own success. More spectators than ever before turned up during the week before race day, and if 1971 had been busy, 1972 would see the island of Sicily absolutely packed; crowd discipline was a real problem. In addition, the circuit had undergone a lot of refurbishment – much needed, of course, but in fact, in the view of some reporters, these updates might actually make the race more dangerous, as higher speeds could be attained following the road improvements. Negative publicity for a race that was of great historical significance intensified with an increased rate of accidents amongst the locals, who frequently came to grief as they tried to emulate their heroes. Several F1 drivers of the time refused to race on the Sicilian circuit; there were calls, too, for the race to be removed from the World Championship. However, the CSI (Commission Sportive Internationale) in Paris was not to be moved – not yet, anyway.

It was against this backdrop that the days of practice and the race itself took place. Porsche, under the instruction of Dr Fuhrmann, would not be there with the sports prototypes for a challenge on the overall victory, the normal target for Porsche. The mood of the marketing people was changing, and the new plan was to race cars more like those on sale to the public. The cost of running sports prototypes was becoming prohibitive at a time when sales of sports cars were under pressure. For Porsche, it was the 911 that needed to be sold in greater numbers. The marketing people would be pretty well satisfied with their profile at this year's Targa Florio, as nineteen 911s and one 914/6 would turn up to run in the GT class.

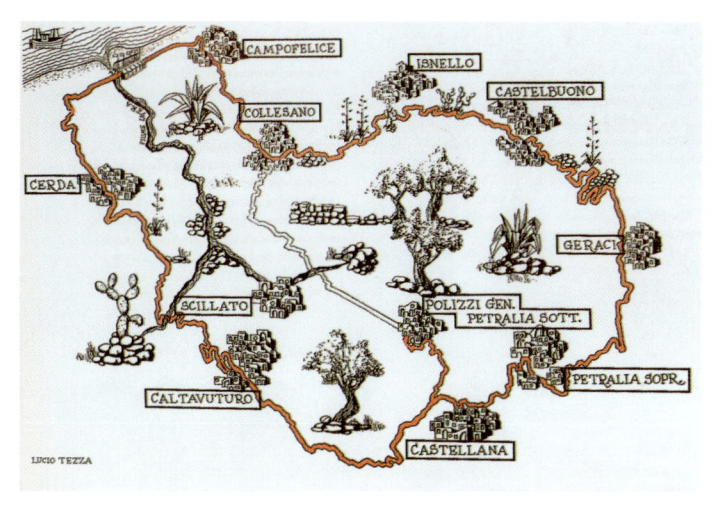

A fairly accurate (if ornate) drawing of the Targa Florio circuit from the 1930s, showing the incredible twisting route with some 710 corners. (JS)

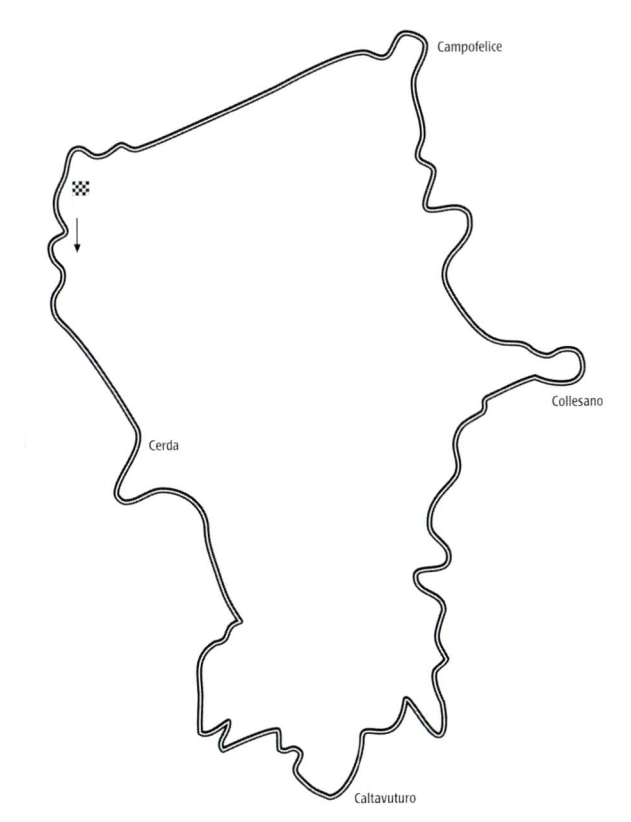

The 72km of the Piccolo Circuito delle Madonie: a more clinical plan, with the start/finish point clearly visible. (JS)

157

As practice got under way, the public services departments, including the police, decided to go on strike, causing chaos. One entrant was to have trouble even reaching the start! The story goes that Ennio Bonomelli, owner of one of the cars, had an argument over a bill in a local restaurant and left in a state of agitation without paying. Next day – race day – he went to the garage to find his car gone! This is Sicily, after all ... It seems that while he was fuming at the garage, the phone on the wall rang and a voice told him he would get his car back after the race!

Because of the practice fiasco the organizers decided that any times achieved would be null and void, and the starting order was instead decided by drawing lots, which meant that the local hero, Nino Vaccarella, did not start at position one on this occasion: Vic Elford did. Elford's race was over in minutes, though, when, as he was nearing the Campofelice section, his engine let go, with a conrod going through the block.

Eighty-one cars got away at the start, with the race run as usual on a time-trial basis, like the Isle of Man TT, the winner decided by total time over a given number of laps. It was Arturo Merzario and Sandro Munari who stood out as the class of the field in their Ferrari 312B, with a sizzling time of 33min 59sec over one 44.739 mile (72km) lap. If you think that was quick on this tortuous course, Helmut Marko eventually set a time of 33min 41sec in his Alfa Romeo 33 TT3, an average speed of 128.253km/h (79.693 mph).

It was hot and very dry on race day, when Merzario/Munari completed the 11 laps of the race, taking victory in a time of 6h 27min 48sec, with 2nd being taken by Marko/'Nanni' (Giovanni Galli) in their Alfa Romeo 33 TT3/3.0 on 6h 28min 4sec, then de Adamich/Hezemans, also Alfa-mounted, in 3rd on 6h 46min 12.3sec. Amongst the many 911S Porsches in the GT classes was the Paul Ernst Strähle-entered Porsche 914/6 GT, believed to be the former works car chassis 2542 used the previous year by Günter Steckkönig. This year it was No 35 and was driven by Dieter Schmid and Italian Armando Floridia. Their 914 was obviously still no slouch, and in the practice period that was later declared void (due to the reasons mentioned above), they returned a time of 41min 34.5sec. Come the race, though, it was the 911 2L car 38 of Gabriele Gottifredi/Pino Pica that finished best out of the GT Porsches, coming 5th overall and winning the GT 2L category ahead of the 2.5L 911S of Günter Steckkönig/Giulio Pucci), also entered by Paul Ernst Strähle. Finishing 9th overall and 2nd in the GT 2L class came the 35 car, the 914/6 GT, after a battle royal with No 23, Jürgen Barth/Michael Keyser in their 911S, in 10th. Seven 911s came behind the 914/6. The Strähle team, then, had a mixed result, but in general were delighted at seeing the 914 so far up the leader

Paul Ernst Strähle-entered No 35 for Dieter Schmid/Armando Floridia: a good practice time, later annulled, of 41min 34.5sec for the 72km. (EM)

911S 2.5L of Günter Steckkönig/Giulio Pucci, entered by Paul Ernst Strähle. An accident on lap 9 meant they were not running at the finish. (EM)

board, a car that Porsche was already planning to drop from the range.

28 May was the date set for the annual Nürburgring 1000km. Four 914/6s were entered. Two cars, those of Gotthard Egerland/

Privateer time Racing in Europe 1972-1976

In a battle royal for 9th overall with the No 23 car of Jürgen Barth/Michael Keyser in the 911S at the Targa Florio: it was the 914/6 GT that got the better of the 911 at the finish, ahead of seven more 911s. (EM)

The famous Jägermeister 914 of Eckhard Schimpf at the Nürburgring. (ES)

Friedrich Tonne and the Paul Ernst Strähle entry for Roland Bauer, did not qualify. A third 914/6 GT was privately-entered by Walter Simonis, and raced carrying No 81. Driven by Simonis and Horst Hoier, the car started 49th on the grid of 51 starters. It was a non-start for Eckhardt Schimpf in the fourth, Jägermeister car; we will see the reason why in a moment!

It was raining as the race unfolded. After just over six hours and 44 laps, the winning car, which had started from pole position, was that of Ronnie Peterson/Tim Schenken, a Ferrari 312 PB. Down in 29th place, some ten laps behind, but classified as finishers, was the 81 Simonis/Hoier 914/6.

At this point it is interesting to point out the influence and effect of the Jägermeister involvement in the sport, due in great part to Eckhard Schimpf. Though the first outing wasn't so successful. Schimpf told the author: "You know, there are always cars which play an important role in a person's life. For me, this was the Porsche 914/6. The Roadster and its concept fascinated me on its debut. I had my reasons, of course. Two men who I admired were the protagonists of this mid-engined car. Ferdinand Piëch, the 'father' of the magnificent Porsche 917, and Huschke von Hanstein, the legendary race director. Both aroused an enthusiasm for the 914/6 within me. I didn't have money at the time, but I had borrowed a standard Porsche 914/6 from the Porsche dealer Voets in Braunschweig, and competed at the Monte Carlo Rally. My cousin, Günter, came to see me – he had been the CEO of Jägermeister. I wanted 500 marks for racing, and offered to place Jägermeister stickers on the Porsche. He gave me 1000 marks!

"Sadly, the 'Monte' ended for me in a pile of snow, but our conversations afterwards would lead to the founding of the Jägermeister racing team, which I would manage until the year 2000. I signed a legend for Jägermeister: Graham Hill. In 1972, he drove a Formula 2.

"I myself was also able to buy a race car – a Porsche 914/6. I bought the car I thought to be the fastest in Germany; it was the 914/6 that had been the Max-Moritz-team car of Gerd Quist – it was very successful ... winner of its class on the 1000km Nürburgring and Spa.

"In 1972, I unfortunately only drove 12 times because I also had to work as a sports journalist, which of course often involved working at the weekends. That Max-Moritz-914/6 was so good that, at the Grand Prix of Germany weekend at the Nürburgring, I managed a fastest practice time of 9mins 32.7sec, though in the end I came 'only' fourth in the 2L GT class, but I was satisfied. At another race on the South loop of the Nürburgring, I was the overall winner by a 100th of a second ahead of Edgar Dören. And he was brilliant in the Porsche 914/6, a champion! That balanced my disappointment at the misfortune at the 1000km race on the Nürburgring where I didn't even start. [As mentioned earlier!]

Porsche The Racing 914s

Hockenheim, home of the Jochen Rindt Trophy for 1972. (V)

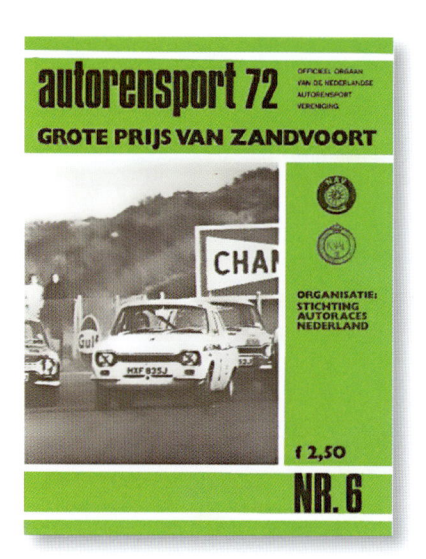

Wonderful period cover of the Dutch Grand Prix programme. (V)

"As I rolled out there on Friday to the training, I realised that the mechanics had incorrectly rebuilt the transmission. I only had a forward gear! When I wanted to qualify on Saturday, it was raining. DNQ! Off!

"Later on in 1973 I did a full season with the 914/6. But times were moving on, and I traded it in with Max-Moritz as part payment for a Porsche Carrera RSR. However, the 914/6 was always my first love. It formed the backbone of the Jägermeister team sponsorship programme. The car is now in the hall of '72 Stagpower,' our collection, which continues the tradition of the Jägermeister racing team."

As we enter June 1972, the familiar pattern of DARM and AvD races continues each weekend as the semi-professional and private racers took to the tracks. On 11 June at the Jochen Rindt Trophy meeting at Hockenheim, the highest-placed 914/6 was the No 62 car of Jochen Engel, the STC Mannheim-Heidelberg Racing Team-entered car finishing 13th overall and 3rd in the up-to-2L class. The Max Moritz entry No 75, driven by Gerhard Fetzer, was a non-finisher. Roland Bauer, in the final 914/6 entered, finished 9th in the up-to-2L class. Forty-one cars had entered, 30 took the start.

The European GT Championship race, supporting the Dutch Grand Prix at Zandvoort on 18 June, saw 12 of the powerful 911s in Division 3 and Division 2 of the Championship dominate the over-2L class. We have to look down to 4th place in the up-to-2L class before we find a 914/6, this time that of Theo Kinsbergen, 13th overall of the 16 finishers.

Theo Kinsbergen at Zandvoort in 1972; Dutch team Stichting Team Radio Veronica, 13th overall and three laps down. (K)

18 June was the date set for the Martini International Race Meeting at the HMSC Flugplatz-Rennen on the airfield circuit of Mainz-Finthen. Organized by the Hesse Motor Sports Club and run to the rules of the AvD, it was round 15 of the AvDs championship. Twenty-four cars took the start flag and set off on 30 laps of the 2.15km circuit. 911s dominated, but down in 9th overall and 4th in

Privateer time Racing in Europe 1972-1976

the GT 2L class was the No 77 914/6 GT, the former Max Moritz car, now running under the colours of Jägermeister and driven by Eckhard Schimpf.

Also on 18 June we find the Sarnano-Sassotetto hillclimb, run on a testing 12.4km course near Macerata, Italy, for the Trofeo Lodovico Scarfiotti. Groups 1 to 4 touring cars were eligible. In 8th overall and 4th in the Special GT Group 4 section was the 914/6 of Francesco Migliorini.

Into July, and on the 9th, at round 6 of the European Hillclimb Championships held at the Sestriere hillclimb near Turin, Italy, in the Special Touring Car class was the Italian 914/6 of Carlo Fabri and the German 914/6 entry of Dieter Bonhorst. Fabri would get a 5th in the up-to-2L class, and Bonhorst 9th. A week later, at a non-championship DRM race in Germany, this time at Diepholz, Jim Doherty finished 4th overall. The same weekend, over in Austria, we see for the first time in 1972 a 914/6 return to the podium when

2 July 1972: the Coupes Benelux at the Nivelles Circuit in Belgium. Jean Canonica in the No 11 car is chased by the Jean-Pierre Gaban, entry 12. The result has eluded us, but a close look might suggest the following car is either a standard 914/6 or a four-cylinder 2L. (Ferret)

161

This image is included to give a flavour of the 1970s: note the big hair and flared trousers! The identity of the image has escaped us, but is believed to be Nivelles at the Euro GT 1972, though the author has not been able to confirm this. (Ferret)

Roland Bauer, in an entry believed to be a Max Moritz car, took 1st place in the up-to-2L class. This non-championship race was won by former 914/6 driver Ernst Seiler in a 365 Ferrari GTB/4. Then in Italy on 23 July, at the XI Coppa Paolino Teodori Hillclimb, the Italian 914/6 driver Francesco Migliorini was out and about again, finishing 5th overall – this time in the Group 4 class – and 2nd in the up-to-2L section.

The 1972 German F1 Grand Prix was scheduled for 30 July at the Nürburgring, the main event on that weekend's programme.

Jacky Ickx in the 312 B2 Ferrari was on pole, and went on to take his tenth, and as it turned out last, Grand Prix victory. One of the support races was the fifth round of the European GT Championship. Held on the full 22+km circuit of the Nordschleife, the European Trophy for GT cars would see an entry of 30, amongst which would be the 914/6s of Mannheim-Heidelberg Sports Touring Club for Jim Doherty, Jägermeister Racing Team for Eckhard Schimpf, and the Porsche Club Romand entry for Jean Canonica. 911Ss would dominate the entry again and the results, with the first

Privateer time Racing in Europe 1972-1976

seven places going to the 911s. A lone Camaro sneaked into 8th place ahead of another five 911s, filling 9th to 13th; then in 14th we find Docherty, 3rd in GT 2L; 15th Schimpf, 4th in GT 2L; and 15th Canonica, 5th in GT 2L.

One of the support events for the Interserie race meeting on 6 August at the Norisring was round 17 of the DARM Championship. Christian Neureuther was running in the race but it is suspected that he dnf'd, as there is no reference to him in the ONS Germany records.

13 August was the date of the non-championship race on the Wunstorf airfield circuit, the competition being mainly between privateers in a race organized by the ADAC. Jägermeister, Strähle and Mannheim-Heidelberg Sports Touring Club 914/6 teams would have drivers Bonhorst, Bauer and Engle, respectively, at the wheel. Into the mix would come Hans Christian Jürgensen and Eckhart Gutowski; these two private entries would scoop the victory and come 1st and 2nd. Third would be Engle, and 4th Bauer. The

Christian Neureuther at the DARM Championship races at the Norisring. (JL)

163

Dieter Kilb at the non-championship meeting run by DMV at Mainz-Finthen on 10 September. (K)

Jägermeister car did not finish. At Zandvoort, also on 13 August, Edgar Dören finished 2nd in a DARM national race. Another 2nd place went to Horst Sasse the same day at the Nürburgring in a national GT race. At Karlsruhe on 20 August, Walter Bauer took 3rd in GT 2L, and on 27 August at the European GT Championship race

Gerhard Fetzer finished 11th overall and 3rd in GT 2L.

Over in north Portugal, at the Villa do Conde circuit near to Porto, we see one Miguel Correia finish 4th in a non-championship race for GT and prototypes on 27 August.

Into September in Germany, and Dieter Kilb, Hans Christian

Privateer time Racing in Europe 1972-1976

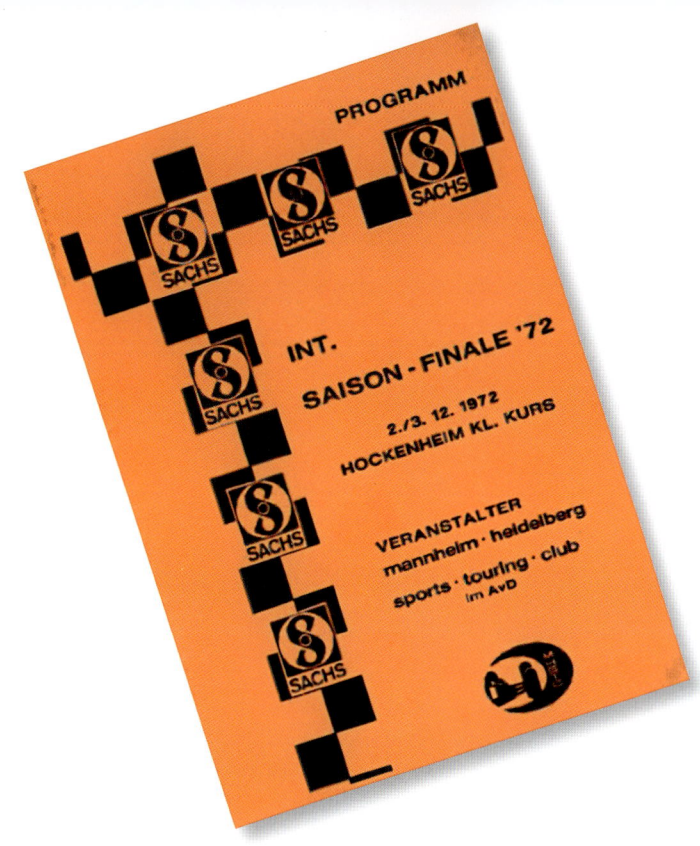

Jürgensen and Walter Bauer took part in the non-championship meeting run by DMV at Mainz-Finthen on the 10th. The 25-lap race had 19 starters, and once more the 911s filled the first seven places. That 7th place was held by the Autohaus Max Moritz 911T, taking the top spot in GT up-to-2L; 8th would be Walter Bauer in the Autohaus Max Moritz 914/6, taking 2nd in the up-to-2L GT class; then came three more 911s before we get to the Kilb and Jürgensen 914s.

Hans Christian Jürgensen took his car up to the Jyllandsringen in Denmark on 16 September for a national race meeting and came home 2nd overall. He followed that trip with a journey to Zolder on 1 October for a 60-mile race, where he took the victory overall in a 20-car field of mixed GT capacities. On 17 September at Zolder, Edgar Dören had finished 2nd in GT 2L. He would return to Zolder on 1 October, finishing 3rd in GT2L, behind Hans Christian Jürgensen. Miguel Correia, running in a GT race – this time at Estoril in Portugal – was on the podium in 3rd place.

Swiss driver Jean Claude Canonica became a regular with the Porsche Club Romand team. He ran in seven races in the team's 914/6 GT during 1972, including two races in Spain in November, driving for the Bricolens Interracing team. The first was the Jarama 2 Hours, the ninth round of the European Sports and GT Championships. In race one, won by Nanni Galli in an Abarth Osella, Canonica finished in 13th place, eight laps down on the sports prototype. In the second race, won by Derek Bell, also in an Osella, Canonica was again eight laps down, but this time finishing 10th overall, with Claude Haldi in the Porsche Club Romand 911S in 9th, six laps down. Canonica would be credited with a 10th place overall in the final rankings.

A week later, on 12 November, and only a few months since its inauguration, the new Estoril Autodrome was host to an event for the European GT Trophy. With six 911s taking the first six places, we have to look down to 7th overall before we see the Bricolens Interracing 914/6 of Canonica (car 81), reputed to be chassis 914 023 0032. Miguel Correia in his 914/6 (car 82), thought to be chassis 914 043 0418, also finished but did not classify. According to the records, he promptly put his car up for sale!

At the Sachs-sponsored Hockenheim Finale meeting in Germany on 2-3 December 1972, organized by the Mannheim-Heidelberg Sports Touring Club, only Jochen Engel in his privately-entered 914/6 put up anything of a fight, finishing a credible 6th overall. Hans Christian Jürgensen would be a distant 23rd overall this time.

It had been an up-and-down time for the 914/6s racing in Europe. With no factory interest apart from the supply of the GT kits, it was left to the private teams of the dealers or sizeable motor clubs to continue to support the 914.

As we reach the end of 1972, we find a depleted production run of the six-cylinder model. Just over 3300, it is said, were built from 1969 to the end of 1972 – way below the 6000 initially foreseen. The buying public was not keen, and only a little over 240 914s were sold in the UK – including both four- and six-cylinder versions! The famous M471 kits were still being supplied to those who wanted to uprate their cars or tune them for racing, but the six-cylinder would not be made in 1973.

A few teams would be seen racing with the new 'Porschified' four-cylinder 2L unit in Europe, about to be supplied in the road cars, and it is known that this engine would show huge potential – as we have heard, Vic Elford thought the four-cylinder 2L a better option for the 914 than the heavier six-cylinder.

Whilst the chassis and suspension remained pretty much the same from 1970 onwards, the power units of the four-cylinder cars did vary. The road cars had started off with the Volkswagen W80 engine, a 1679cc unit with some 80bhp available on fuel-injection; then in 1972 the EA80 engine was installed for just the 1972 and 1973 model years. The new 2L engine was a four-cylinder electronic injection engine of 1971cc, a development of the earlier, well-proven

165

1679cc unit, this time with design input developed by Porsche. The European versions had 100bhp available, and because they were lighter in weight they were almost as quick as the original 110bhp six-cylinder unit. For the road, this was a cracking engine, although in the USA emissions requirements ensured that it lost a good 10bhp! With no more six-cylinder 914s being produced, the rush to obtain them for racing continued in the USA, where quite a few of the cars raced in Europe during 1970, '71 and '72 had found their way to new owners. But, as we will see, many of those who had tried the 914/6 even in 220bhp GT format would return to their first love, the 911.

Over the next and final three years of production, the four-cylinder versions would receive many minor upgrades, mostly to suit the American market, where sales were buoyant. These details, however, are not for this work, and we refer the reader to eminent works by Brian Long, Thomas Lang and Michael von Klodt for a detailed study of the road cars. We will carry on with racing in Europe from 1973 to the end of the time period of our study.

The first major event of the 1973 season, the Monte Carlo Rally, would not see any 914s taking part – not even private entries. However, many 914s were once more appearing in sprints (slaloms) and hillclimbs. We turn first to Spain on 11 February, where Juan Bautista Martínez Gemar appears under his pseudonym of 'Crady' on the Col de Rates hillclimb in southern Spain. He was racing under the colours of Escudería GES, the team he established in 1969. For 1973, Gemar had acquired the 914/6 from Julio Gargallo, who had gone back to the 911. It was one of the five factory-produced Porsche 914/6s made in 1971 with a mechanical fuel-injected engine. It was not homologated in Germany, and raced in Group 5 in Spain. Run by the Automóvil Club de Alicante, the Col de Rates hillclimb saw Gemar make the fastest time in practice with 4min 46sec. Sunny February weather had brought out large crowds, who were there to see Gargallo ascend very fast in his newly acquired 2.5L 911, clocking 4min 28sec – a new record for the event. In 2nd, though, was Juan 'Crady' Gemar 914/6 in 4min 42sec.

As we move on to the end of March (the 25th), we're off to Belgium and the Zolder circuit for the Bergischer Motor Club race meeting, and for the 914/6s it would be the Deutsche Automobil-Rundstrecken-Pokal: round 1 of the championship and advertised as an international event. Of the 24 cars entered in the GT race, 18 lined up at the start, including Edgar Dören in the 914/6 chassis 0165. Racing with No 228, he finished 2nd in the 2L GT class ahead of the 914/6s of Lothar Ohren, Peter Nowak and Werner Christmann.

The weekend of 31 March-1 April saw both the European GT Championships, the Interserie Can-Am Nürburgring 300km and round 2 of the DARM-ONS Championship take place all in the same race, labelled as the Interserie Can-Am 300km Rennen um den Goodyear Pokal, Europa-Meisterschaft GT-Wagen Nürburgring – basically the Can-Am and GT Trophy meeting. It would be a busy race weekend. 37 cars lined up on the grid of the two-heat (each of 150km) GT race from the list of 55 that had entered. Three 914/6s failed to show. The field was brimming with 911 RSRs, 911Ss and Alfa Romeos. Three RSR 911s and two 911Ss took the first five places, but there in 6th overall appeared Werner Christmann in his privately-entered 914/6 GT No 155, taking 1st in 2L and winning class 3 – a fine performance up against formidable opposition. Edgar Dören in the No 143 Bergischer Motor Club entry was 11th overall in the first heat and 8th in the final, finishing 4th overall in GT 2L.

A week later and miles away in terms of status from the Nürburgring, though not so much in distance, a small field started the non-championship regional GT race at Zolder on 8 April, worthy of a mention in that it was the 914/6 of Karl Heinz Schrey that won the 24-lap race. Meanwhile at Hockenheim, the same weekend, it was 'Ronald Knudel' who won the GT 2L class at the annual Jim

Privateer time Racing in Europe 1972-1976

A timely reminder of what the Nürburgring Nordschleife was like in 1973. (JS)

Werner Christmann, beaten only by 911 RSRs and 911Ss to finish 6th overall in both heats of the gruelling Nürburgring 300km and winning the GT 2L class, proving there was still life in the 914/6. (©P)

Jochen Engel at the Nürburgring 300km Euro GT Championships, chassis 043 1415; 13th in heat 1, he dnf'd in heat 2, running in the GT 2L class. (P)

167

Porsche The Racing 914s

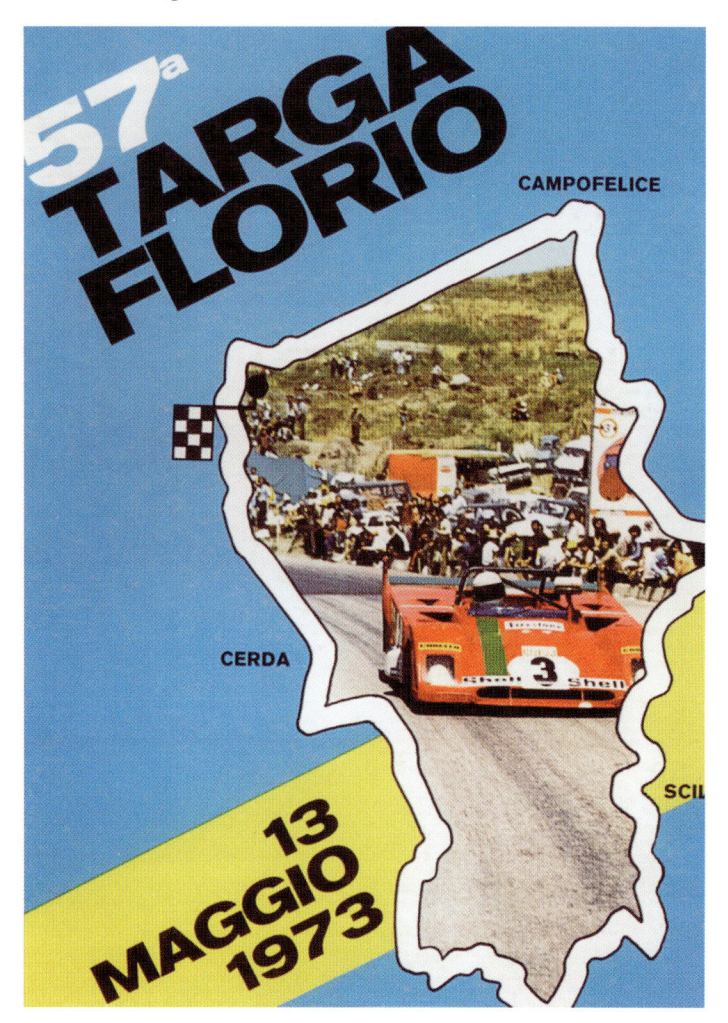

The promotion shows a sports prototype, but it would be the turning point for the Targa when a 911 took victory. The sports GT era had arrived. (EM)

that next year the Targa Florio would not be included as part of the World Manufacturers' Championship. It was, perhaps, the beginning of the end of one of the great races of the past. The surface of the road, unpredictable at the best of times, the narrow streets, the increased crowd attendances – all contributed to the rule-makers' decision as they sought to run the World Championship series on smooth tarmac tracks with no street furniture – the non-racing-enthusiast public's perception of motorsports on public roads, and the demands of the relevant authorities were starting to have an effect. A good decision, or a necessary one – the reader must choose. Either way, one of the world's longest running and greatest races was drawing inevitably to its close, as a new world order in the sport arrived. For 1973, though, let's make the most of it.

As usual, the entry list alone was staggering. 125 cars were on the sheet, including three training (T) cars. Of those 125, only 80 qualified to start, and amongst them were two Porsche 914s. Giuseppe de Gregorio privately entered his 914/6, running with No 127, but would find the task ahead a daunting one in the GT 2L class, facing a gaggle of 911s and other GT cars, including a second 914/6, that of the experienced Carlo Fabri/Antonio Nieri running with No 123. Up front, the pole-sitter – if that is what it can be called in this annual race against the clock – with the fastest time was the No 3

Giuseppe de Gregorio privately entered his 914/6, running with No 127; he found the task ahead a daunting one, but would make the finish and take 2nd in the GT 2L class. (EM)

Clark Memorial meeting. On 15 April, Hans Christian Jürgensen took 1st place in the GT 2L class at the Zolder 60 Miles race, while a week later in round 3 of the DARM Championship, on the same Zolder track, Werner Christmann would finish 2nd in the GT race with Edgar Dören 3rd, both 914/6 GT-mounted. Round 4 was held at Sembach on 6 May, and here again Edgar Dören was the one on the GT 2L podium in 3rd place.

As we arrive in May 1973, we return once more to Sicily and the Targa Florio. This year the weather was warm and dry again, but was not matched by the mood of the organizers, who had to announce

Privateer time Racing in Europe 1972-1976

Ferrari 312B of Arturo Merzario, with a time of 33min 38.5sec, an average speed of 79.97mph (126.412km/h) for the run round the iconic 44.739 mile circuit (72km). Ferrari would be pushed hard by the Autodelta Alfa Romeo team as the two giants slugged it out to be the quickest on the days before the big event. However, they weren't looking over their shoulders carefully enough, for in fifth fastest came the first of the new superlight Porsche 911 Carrera RSRs, that of Herbert Müller/Gijs van Lennep, a formidable pairing with the backing and organization of the factory works team personnel. Porsche Club Romand and the Brescia Corse team were also there with 911 RSRs, all with hopes that reliability would win through; they might not need ultimate speed.

Practice sadly brought tragedy when the Lancia of British entry Charles Blyth had an altercation with another car, which led to the Lancia tumbling into a ditch, claiming the life of the driver. Top driver Jacky Ickx had a close shave when his Ferrari left the road and went careering down a slope. Incidents were unfortunately too common this year, perhaps justification for the aforementioned decision of the authorities. Come race day, the realization was dawning that this may well be the last Targa Florio. As it happened, it was not quite the last – not yet, at least.

As the race unfolded, the mighty Ferraris and Alfas began to fall by the wayside. But even so, after some five hours it looked as if one of the remaining Alfas, that of Rolf Stommelen/Andrea de Adamich,

Herbert Müller/Gijs van Lennep's car charges into the lead as the factory Alfa Romeos and Ferraris fall by the wayside. The GT era at the Targa Florio is about to begin. (EM)

169

Carlo Fabri/Antonio Nieri: 4th in GT 2L on the 1973 Targa Florio. (©P)

would claim the victory, running some six minutes ahead of the nearest challenger, which was now the Porsche 911 Carrera RSR of Müller/van Lennep. At the final pit stop, de Adamich appeared to have it in the bag. A steady lap would do it – the Porsches were not so fast that they could catch him – but fate took a hand. Driving quickly but cautiously, de Adamich got stuck behind a Lancia Fulvia and, as the seconds started to tick away, the tension inside the Alfa mounted. He got alongside, but the Lancia driver must have thought de Adamich was going to pass on the other side, for he moved over and collected the Alfa, which crashed into a distance marker stone. The damage was too much as the Porsche No 8 shot past with only a few miles to go.

The history books recorded that it was the tenth Porsche victory in the Targa Florio during its World Championship status period. Clearly the 914/6s were no match now for the speed of the front runners, but nevertheless reliability and roadholding put the No 127 car of Gregorio/Mannino into 21st overall and 2nd in the GT 2L class, with the 123 car of Carlo Fabri/Antonio Nieri 4th in GT 2L and 36th overall of the 42 cars classified out of the 80 starters.

Everyone left the Targa Florio fearing they had witnessed the last one; however, by a quirk of fate due to an oversight in the offices of power, the event was to be included in the Challenge Mondial series the next year. Fabri would return in 1974.

Whilst excitement was at fever pitch in Sicily, up in Germany at the famous Avus circuit, in a non-championship event organized by the AVD on 13 May, Dieter Bonhorst was to be seen finishing 3rd overall in a race for GT cars over 1.6L, the 1st and 2nd places being taken by 911s; 14 cars finished. A week later, the Hockenheim 100 miles, also a non-championship race, had 29 cars lined up with five 914/6s amongst them in the up-to-2L class. Sixtant Racing's entry, with Horst Godel aboard, would finish 2nd in the class. Eckhard Schimpf (in the Jägermeister entry), Lothar Ohren and Hans Stähli were down the field. Up the Autobahn at the Zolder race track on 1 June 1973, Edgar Dören in the Bergischer Motor Club entry took a 2nd in the 2L GT class and a week later, at the same track, prolific performer Werner Christmann won the Division 2 class in a non-championship event.

As the reader will see by now, the type and status of the races involving 914/6s were not, one might say, 'top-drawer' internationals. The 914/6, though, was still being regularly campaigned by the stalwarts, especially in Germany, as the statistics show. The 914/6 GTs could still, in certain cases, dominate the regional level 2L GT class in Europe. However, on the national and international scene we see a different set of performances. Take the Imola European GT race on 2 June as an example: an international field of cars that would be dominated by the Porsche 911 RSR and the French Alpine Renaults, now with 1800cc engines. In this race Carlo Fabri, no slouch behind the wheel and veteran of races like the Targa Florio, was down in 20th place overall and only 6th in the GT 2L class. One or two competitors do stand out though:

Privateer time Racing in Europe 1972-1976

Werner Christmann, for one. From June to December 1973, he took a class win at Zolder on 17 June, Diepholz on 17 July at the 6th International ADAC-organized Flugplatzrennen, and at Zolder again on 30 September at the Düren-Nordheim meeting. Autohaus Max Moritz and Walter Bauer also continued to perform well. On 12 August at the Hockenheim-Hessen meeting, Bauer won the GT 2L class, took another class victory at Hockenheim in the Swiss Trophy meeting, and then at Mainz-Finthen on 9 September won the GT 2L class and Group 4; added to those victories were several other podium positions. Albrecht Schütz had arrived on the scene, also driving for Max Moritz, and would claim three victories from three starts during the latter part of 1973. So although the 914/6 was now filtering down to more privateers, several of the 'dealer' teams, like Autohaus Max Moritz, were still able to turn in good results – mainly, one suspects, because they had made the effort to develop the suspension and engines where possible. A look at the race charts here in this work will show the full story without boring the reader by having to wade through pages of information on the DRM, DARM, and ADAC minor championship rounds.

For the remainder of this part of our story we will cover primarily those premier events that command a closer look.

First, the Nürburgring 500km: a full international event held on the mighty Nordschleife, a qualifying round (round 6) of the 1973 European 2L Sports Car Championship for Makes, and also, strangely perhaps, round 5 of the Spanish Drivers' Championship for GT and Sports Cars. A serious, high-profile event, Abarth-Osella, Chevron, Lola, March and Alpine Renault headed the list of entries for the Coupe de l'Eifel – a race, one might think, that was by now

Nürburgring 500km International: European Sports Car Championship round 6. In 13th overall, behind 12 sports prototypes in a 43-car field, came the class-winning Porsche 914/6 GT of Werner Christmann, once more proving his, and the ageing car's, capabilities. (©P)

Porsche The Racing 914s

The traditional fuelling arrangements at the Nürburgring: Christmann fills up. (©P)

way out of the class of the 914/6 GT. Forty-three cars lined up at the start with drivers of the quality of Vic Elford, Derek Bell, Arturo Merzario, Giorgio Pianta, Guy Edwards, Jean-Claude Andruet, Jean-Pierre Jabouille in the Alpine Renault, and the future USA Porsche star driver, Jim Busby. Amongst this line-up was the 914/6 GT 140306, entered for Werner Christmann. With two races, each of 11 laps, the aggregate score would determine the final positions. It will come as no surprise to learn that the first 12 places in each of the races were taken by the 2L sports prototype cars, but there

in 13th overall and 13th in both races was the regularly capable Werner Christmann, completing 21 laps compared to the 22 laps of the first six cars, and taking victory in the GT 2L class ahead of formidable opposition. Like the 6th place at Le Mans in 1970, victory in the Marathon de la Route in 1970, equal 3rd on the Monte Carlo Rally in 1971, class podium positions in 1972 at the Nürburgring and the Targa Florio, this was a standout result for the 914/6 in 1973.

Records show that most of the racing action with the 914 in

Privateer time Racing in Europe 1972-1976

competition in Europe took place in Germany during 1973. 914/6s were a rare sight in competition in France, Italy, Scandinavia and the UK, with just a few taking part in club events. Turning to Spain, 10 June 1973 was the date of the Morcuera hillclimb to the north west of Madrid. The aforementioned GES team entered the 911S for Julio Gargallo and the 914/6 for Juan Guemar. The Morcuera hillclimb followed the traditional plan of a practice session and two official ascents, the fastest of which was counted. The day began badly for Guemar when he went wide on a corner and damaged the wing of the 914/6 in practice. In the first official ascent, Gargallo led the field, followed by the two Abarths of Otero and Costas, and in 4th place Guemar in the 914/6. As far as we know, that's how it stood! (Author's note: we failed to find the official result, but Gargallo is quoted as saying that he won it.)

The 1973 season had seen the Escudería GES take part in 26 hillclimbs and rallies, with 12 1st places and nine classifications between 2nd and 5th. However, the writing was definitely on the wall for the 914/6 in Europe, with no upgrades coming from the factory to keep it at, or near, the front in national competition. Internationally, the ongoing developments with the 911 ensured that that model, the Porsche Company's flagship, now in RSR format, would continue to dominate.

As we come to 1974, there were, however, still some signs that the 914/6 GT was not quite ready to lie down. There would be 23 2L GT class wins during the year, and 33 other GT 2L class podium places. Taking in the German national events, we see some 160+ entries, so it is evident that total dominance by others, or even other Porsches, was not a foregone conclusion. But we should not kid ourselves. The reality is that, in the big league of rallying and racing, the days of the 914/6 GT were over.

1974 kicked off with a trip to Zolder – 24 March, to be precise, and round 1 of the DARM-ONS Championship. Overall from the 30-car field, at the head of the 2L GT class we find Edgar Dören taking the victory, with the 914/6 GT of Albrecht Schütz in 2nd. At Hockenheim in the Formula 2 support race for 2L GT cars it was Albrecht Schütz this time who took an overall race victory in a 21-car GT field, chalking up another podium for the very successful Autohaus Max Moritz team. Edgar Dören, in the Bergischer Motor Club entry, was 2nd.

At the Nürburgring on 28 April 1974, in a support race for that year's German Motorcycle Grand Prix, the DARM Championship round 1 saw 30 cars qualified to start, and whilst after seven laps of the full Nordschleife circuit it was the then very popular Cologne Ford Capris that dominated the big class, Edgar Dören would come home 10th overall.

173

Porsche The Racing 914s

Salvatore Geraci/'Sven Hassel': unfortunately, their race lasted only two laps before they had to retire – reason unknown. (EM)

Carlo Fabri/Marco Micangeli recovered from this mishap, thought to be in practice, to take victory in the GT 2L class. (EM)

Gérard Larrousse/Amilcare Ballestrieri, in the 2.4L Lancia Stratos, won the 1974 Targa Florio, round 3 of the Challenge Mondial. Eight laps, taking 4h 35min. (EM)

On 4-5 May it was back to Hockenheim, where the 100-mile event, a non-championship GT race organized by the Motor Club of Switzerland, saw Wilhelm Siegle in his privately-entered 914/6 take the top spot in the 2L GT class. The same day at the little-used Neubiberg-Munich race track, an airfield circuit, a 31-car GT field was dominated by the big Carrera 911s in the over-2L class. However, once more in the up-to-2L class we find a Porsche 914/6 GT, this time with Manfred Laub driving the Autohaus Max Moritz entry, finish just 37sec down on the front-running Carreras after ten laps of the 5.75km flat circuit – a class win in strong company. A week later on the 12th, at the Sembach track, it was Edgar Dören who led home six 914/6s, finishing 5th overall behind the 911s, but winning the 2L GT class.

As May flowed into June, it was time for the Targa Florio again in Sicily. Thought to be off the championship programme, by some quirk of fate it was still included in the Challenge Mondial: a reprieve of sorts. Although the Porsche, Ferrari and Alfa Romeo factory teams all stayed away, 59 cars lined up, among them the two 914/6 racers of Carlo Fabri/Marco Micangeli and Salvatore Geraci/'Sven Hassel.' Following his 4th place in the GT 2L class in 1973, Fabri overcame a practice incident to start the race from 35th place, completing seven laps of the full circuit on a hot 9 June. It was a race lacking the elements of the big teams, and one report says that a club racing atmosphere prevailed throughout the weekend. For the record, Gérard Larrousse/Amilcare Ballestrieri won in a racing version of the Lancia Stratos.

The same day as the Targa Florio, up in Germany at the DARM race, round 4 of the championship on the Wunstorf circuit, Edgar Dören took another GT 2L class victory, repeating that performance on 17 June at the Nürburgring in the ADAC International 300km race, round 5 of the ONS Championship. The first 25 places were taken by the Porsche 911s, RSRs, RSs and Carreras, but in 26th place and 1st in the 2L class was Mr Dören, with 24 more cars

Privateer time Racing in Europe 1972-1976

Prolific finisher and victor on several occasions, Edgar Dören, 1st in GT 2L, seen here at the 300km Nürburgring ahead of the 8th overall Dieter Franke's 911 Carrera. (JS)

behind him. At the Avus Ring, round 6 of the ONS Championship, a support race to the main race for Formula 3 cars, it was Albrecht Schütz's turn to take the victory ahead of three more 914/6s. Edgar Dören only managed 4th this time; ahead of him in 3rd was the Jägermeister Racing Team car of Dieter Bonhorst, and in 2nd Herbert Mohr in the Autohaus Max Moritz second entry, the first being that of Schütz.

Hockenheim, 21 July, brought another Autohaus Max Moritz victory in the 2L class, with Manfred Laub taking overall victory in a non-championship race on the Motodrome. 914/6s also took the next four places. On 18 August at the Kassel-Calden track, the overall victory swung in Edgar Dören's favour as he won ahead of five more 914/6s in the GT2 class in this the ONS Championship round 7, although on this occasion it was a mixed 1.6L and 2L race. RSRs dominated at Mainz-Finthen airfield circuit on 1 September, where round 9 of the ONS Championship brought victory to Werner Christmann in the GT 2L class after 31 laps and 66.5km of flat-out racing, which again saw the first eight places falling to the 911s, with a lone De Tomaso Pantera entering the fray.

15 September saw class win number 20 of 1974 at the Zolder circuit. This time it was Hans Christian Jürgensen who won the ADAC GT 2L national category race. However, 6 October at Zolder would see Edgar Dören on top in a non-championship race in which Hans Christian Jürgensen failed to finish. Dieter Ankele would be the last driver to take a class victory for the 914/6 in 1974, this time at Hockenheim in the Max Moritz team car in a non-championship ADAC regional race on 10 November.

Salzburgring 1975: believed to be the Edgar Dören GT 2L class winner at the annual DARM-ONS Championship round 4. (SP)

Hans Christian Jürgensen in the 914/6 (car 239) won the ADAC GT 2L national category race at Zolder on 15 September. This car still exists and is raced regularly, according to the owner. (NN)

1975 would bring another crop of class wins, but on a lesser scale than in previous years, the total of podium class positions being around 33. There were no class wins at the higher international championship level. That the 914/6s were still popular amongst the club racers is beyond dispute. The German championship and non-championship races continued as before at the various airfield circuits and the tracks of Hockenheim, Nürburgring, Zolder and Norisring, though as time passed the airfield circuits would become less used. From the records it appears that there were no new-build 914/6 kit GTs in 1975, and likewise through into 1976, the final year of the production of the 914 four-cylinder. Numerous owners would turn to tuning the 914/4, and quite a number of specials would appear, but their impact on the racing scene would be limited, and there are no recorded international successes.

1976 saw even fewer successful performances, with only four class victories in the annual circuit racing series. The 914/6, of course, had ceased production in 1972, with just the final 229 cars being completed. Porsche stated that 400 kits were supplied to convert the production 914/6 models into GT models. However, it is possible that more than this number were converted to GT spec, as other aftermarket manufacturers began to produce the wider wings and different suspension components. Many 914/6 race cars would find their way to the USA, and this is where the 914 model in its entirety was most popular, though it took a while to gain acceptance, again due to perceptions in what was then a very conservative era in the US. For racing in Europe, the 911 continued to be the dominant model. The 914/6s and 914/4s ceased to be mainstream. Many were parked up in garages, until in recent times interest in the historic road and race movement has seen them come into their own

Privateer time Racing in Europe 1972-1976

Dieter Ankele on the grid; he would finish 2nd in GT 2L at the Nürburgring 300km DARM support race on 3 April 1976. Ahead of him overall were seven 911 Carreras. 1st in GT 2L was the BMW 2002 of Peter Kuhlmann. (JS)

again, with good examples being hard to come by, leading to a demand that is seeing values rise.

But enough of the current situation: our work here is to cover the story in the period, and having seen how the 914/6 GT faired in racing, we will turn our attention to the rallying scene in the next chapter, before turning to the big country that is the USA.

For hillclimbing (Bergrennen) between 1972 and 1976 there were around 130 events, and among those we find 51 class wins for a 914! As usual, the number of occasions for those inclined to go sprinting or competing in slaloms in Germany alone was huge – in fact, over 300 'races,' netting 72 class victories over the four years. If we take the records from 1970, then we see in the world of racing up mountains more than 72 occasions when a 914 claimed the trophy for fastest in class. On the usually level track of a sprint or slalom, there were 102 fastest in class achievements. Perhaps, therefore, it comes as little surprise to see that it was two of the circuit racing car/driver combinations that performed best on the majority of occasions. The most successful appears to be Herrmann Neureuther, with under-2L class victories in 17 hillclimbs. On the sprinting/slalom side, Gotthard Egerland comes out on top with 13 victories. With this collection of facts, we will move on!

Undergoing restoration in 2015 in Sweden: on top is chassis 914 143 0306, formerly driven by Werner Christmann in 1973; below it is 914 043 0462, formerly driven by Willi Nolte. (FF)

177

7

Tarmac and dust
The 914 rally story

Following the conclusion of our European racing story, we now go back to the early days of the 914 to look at rallying. In order to promote the new 914 to the general public beyond the recent exposure garnered from the 1969 Frankfurt show, it was believed within Porsche that motorsport – the company's lifeblood – could prove the 914's competence. The form of motorsport chosen at this point was rallying, which, in the late 1960s, was high profile and had a huge following. As already mentioned, the first evidence we find in the archives is an internal memo dated 25 September 1969 from Herr Piëch to Herr Bott, where Piëch sets out the desire to prepare three 914/6s and three 911Ss for the 1970 Monte Carlo Rally, the 914s to be powered by the 911S 2.2L engine, using many Carrera 906 parts, including the twin-plug system. Shortly after this, in a 'to be actioned' memo dated 9 October 1969 bearing the signature of Ferdinand Piëch, we see these statements:

Type 914 rally specification
KW (Karosseriebau Weinsberg) will build the 914 series cars to the rally specifications (homologation requirements).
Herr (Rainer) Bratenstein from Porsche will be responsible for the build at all times.
On 10 October KW will be supplied with one 914 (a 914/6) and the work must be completed by 20 October 1969.
KW is to make sketches of the specified work for conversion, to be used as a guide for the build of four more 914s.
These four 914s are to be built by November/December 1969.
This is the list of changes for the proposed rally cars:
1. Oil cooler with oil hoses (if it is allowed/necessary to find a way to move the oil hoses and cooler from the back of the car to the front).
2. Fit a tank filler through the front bonnet.
3. Mounting for the front bonnet (updated mounting for motorsport purposes).
4. Rebuild of the engine cover to ensure a wider, mesh-covered opening.
5. Making the rear suspension arms stronger.
6. Fitting of sway bars front and rear.
7. Removable targa roof – make the roof stronger and rigid by bolting a secure fixing to the chassis.
8. Fit wider front and rear arches.
9. Mounting points for racing six-point harness.
10. Removal of all carpets in the interior of the car.

The memo was copied to Herren Tengler, Knoll, Bratenstein, Steckkönig, Engels and Bott. From it, we can see that the actual chassis/body 'monocoque' of the first four 'factory' 914/6 GTs was to be built by another company, Karosseriebau Weinsberg, not at Karmann, which was building the production models, or at

Tarmac and dust The 914 rally story

Zuffenhausen, where the cars would be fitted out with components in Werk 1. In fact, the author was informed that at least two other companies were involved in the manufacture of special parts.

Next we see internal memo 1162/69, dated 17 October 1969 from Rainer Bratenstein, giving the fully detailed perceived requirements; this would be the first full specification:

Front bumper and air dam in glass fibre, with new shape for fitting of oil cooler.
Rear bumper in glass fibre.
Wider arches front and rear, 50mm, with glass fibre fittings to attach (the bodywork/bumpers).
Front and rear bonnet in glass fibre, opening for filling of petrol tank in the front bonnet, mechanical operation of the front headlights, to the regulations.
100 and 110L tank, to be filled through the front lid. Hood pin, straps to hold the bonnet and no lock.
Doors with aluminium skin.
Felt for interior, dashboard with no trim, plain door trims, felt for rear bulkhead.
Scheel race seats with new subframe [Scheel was the manufacturer].
Different handbrake (discussions had taken place to relocate it away from the standard position).
No silencing mat for the engine bay.
Windscreen and side screens in Plexiglas [author's note – This was the first specification, of course].
Heated front windscreen.
Heating of petrol tank: electrical type, not heating from the engine/exhaust system.
Oil cooler at the front, opening for cooling air through the front bonnet.
Piping for the oil cooler in the left door sill.
Standard oil tank with oil filter console from the model B with fitting.
Mounting of overpressure valve for the oil filling pipe.
Front and rear sport springs and dampers of choice, as with torsion bars; sway bars front and rear.
Wheel hubs with spacers and longer wheel bolts.
Tyres at the rear 4.75/10.00-15 on 7in wheels; at the front 5.00 M-15 on 6in wheels.
At the rear, vented brakes, callipers from 911 S.
Thinner sheet metal around all the parts for cooling of the engine.
Stronger mountings for seatbelts.
Paint to be minimal thickness.
No under-body rust protection.
No silencing mats or 'wax oil treatment'.
No polishing or finishing on the body.
Engine lid only with cover as light as possible.
No rear valance.

Two types of under-body protection were prepared for the rigours of rallying – one a steel slatted sumpguard and the other a steel sheet, more suited to the less rugged events.

Homologated sumpguard for the rallying 914/6. (©P)

Secondary under-plate for the sumpguard or used alone for less arduous events. (©P)

In addition to underneath protection, FIA rules called for driver protection by a separate roll bar in addition to the integral one included in the cars' design.

Sheet metal parts on the cars would all be lightened to a thinner gauge steel for rally-purposes:
1) Rollover hoop thickness to go from 1.25 to 1.0mm.
2) Side members between front bulkhead and rear bulkhead from 0.88 to 0.75mm.
3) End of rear bulkhead from 0.75 to 0.63mm.
4) Cover of top for front headlights from 0.80 to 0.75mm.
5) Cover of front headlights from 0.88 to 0.75mm.
6) Front of front wall from 0.88 to 0.75mm.
7) Front wall from 0.75 to 0.63mm.
8) Front inner arches from 1.0 to 0.88mm.
9) Front wing from 0.88 to 0.75mm.
10) Side parts of front headlights from 0.75 to 0.63mm.
11) Mounting for light switches from 0.75 to 0.63mm.
12) Seat mounts from 0.88 to 0.75mm.
13) Rear wings with side parts for rollover hoop from 0.88 to 0.75mm.
14) Front and rear dams from 0.75 to 0.63mm.
15) Outer skin for front bonnet from 0.75 to 0.63mm.
16) Outer skin for rear bonnet from 0.75 to 0.63mm.

FIA requirements allowed Porsche to install a cage design, which also stiffened up what was deemed to be a rather flexible chassis floor. (©P)

Of course, the above information was the first 'wish list,' it would undergo several changes to meet standards of safety and other eventualities found during testing, but this is how it all started in 1969. One can imagine how much weight can be shaved off by applying the above ideas. Rainer Bratenstein told the author that not all were applied, and records do not exist as to exactly which were adopted. From the detail in the archive, we can see everything was to be done quickly, to be ready by January to race in the most prestigious rally of them all, the Monte Carlo. However, whilst the Racing Department was under pressure to produce, it was eventually – and sensibly – decided to hold back, and not play its hand with a new untried car too quickly. Questions were asked, of course, and the answers from the development team, led by Rainer Bratenstein, deemed it too early. He told the author in an interview in 2015: "We were actually more or less against the 914 concerning the rally business, because we thought the 911 was the better basis."

As the reader will have seen earlier, Walter Näher says: "It was Huschke von Hanstein who was pushing us; then, instead of the 2.2L S we had planned to use, we found that we would have to use the 2L engine for homologation reasons – the engine of the 911T."

Herbert Linge, already mentioned, was in charge of making the parts and putting it all together. Here are some of his words to set the scene: "As you know, when we started to make a car for the planned attempt on the Monte Carlo, I was the man doing the first tests on the original road car. The first connection with the 914 was at the test in 1968, and I was saying immediately: 'You're going to have another engine at least in this car, because this is too slow.' It was only 1.7L – the four-cylinder one. We talked to Piëch, because he was the man behind Mr 'Ferry' Porsche, saying what we should do. And at this time I think nobody, not even Piëch, knew what was about to change within Porsche because of the ideas of the new VW man [Kurt Lotz], so everything was a little mixed up. Too many people were involving themselves with this car."

But the problems did not end there. Some of the drivers were wary of trying the new 914/6 GT on the 1970 Monte Carlo, preferring to stick with the known product, the successful 911S. In fact, as the now sadly late Björn Waldegård told the author: "When we actually got to test the car we found it was not the easiest car to get used to. We drivers were used to the rear-engine 911. It could be positioned by our own skill on a loose surface stage; the swinging tail of the car was, when used correctly, an advantage to making quick progress.

"We had got used to this style, and of course it was similar to that of a front-engine rear-wheel drive car too. With the 914, I found it very difficult to come to terms with its strangely stable condition. I did not like it as a rally car. It was better as a race car

Tarmac and dust The 914 rally story

The late, great rally driver Björn Waldegård in the UK in 2012. (PA)

on a smooth track, where many things are more predictable. The technical guys, though, thought it was the ultimate, because it had a near 50/50 balance – on paper perfect for a racing car – but they didn't understand that as a rally car on mixed surfaces I found it very unpredictable."

The decision was therefore taken to cancel the idea of doing the 1970 Monte Carlo Rally. More development was needed and a confirmed final specification decided upon, dependent on what was found in further testing. The first time we see a 914 in competition, though, is on a rally: a four-cylinder model, on 6-8 February 1970 on the Bayerische Winter-Rally Marktredwitz, where the pairing of Hans Weinberger/Volkhard Trübsbach is recorded as driving a 914/4 to 5th overall in the GT Unlimited class. Their next outing would be in the ADAC-Rally Ulm International on 4 April. At this time all the models were placed in entry lists as VW-Porsche, so it is a little tricky to determine which are six-cylinder and which are four-cylinder from the records. The statistics in chapter 10 for rallying, apart from the internationals and known use in rallying outside of Germany, come from the then-named ONS (Oberste Nationale Sportbehörde – the German governing body for motorsports) records. On the Rally Ulm, Weinberger/Trübsbach are recorded as coming 1st in the GT class with a VW-Porsche. Then came a 3rd overall and 3rd in Special GT up-to-2L in the Rally Trifels International on 11 April.

The first victory for a 914/6 had come on 22 March in the ADAC-Automobil-Slalom Fürth, where one Herr Röthke took his car to 1st overall in the GT Unlimited class. It is worth mentioning here that slaloms/sprints in Germany were much the same as those throughout the rest of Europe, including the UK. They were often the starting point for many a budding rallying or racing driver; a place where they could learn to hone their car-control skills. (Author's note: the volume of events can be viewed in the statistics section in Chapter 10. However, as already mentioned, the lack of good-quality images precludes a full study of that side of the sport here. Nevertheless, the presence of these events and their importance to the sporting scene should not go unrecorded.) Rallying in Germany, as in many other countries, took place all year round. Hundreds of these events preclude total coverage, and because of this we will concentrate only on those of a regional and national status, or of special interest, and in the case of Germany, run under auspices of the ONS. Of course, 914s did find their way into rallying in other countries, but the majority of entries in the early 1970s were certainly in Germany.

As mentioned at the beginning of this chapter, Porsche originally foresaw the 914 as ideal for rallying. Within the team, however, several drivers, having done a considerable amount of testing, were of the opinion that it might be better for racing, due to its handling characteristics. Günter Steckkönig, in that period one of the fast-rising Porsche drivers, said in an interview with the author: "I think one of the reasons we felt the way we did was the disadvantage on the engine side. By then the 911 had a well-developed Bosch mechanically fuel-injected 230hp engine, and the 914/6 rally car had the old-style Weber-carburetted 220bhp engine. We found the reaction time for the driver with a carburettor engine car made it more difficult to handle for rallies compared with the injected 911. It was a question of response and driveability." If we combine this comment with the feel of the car, as mentioned earlier by Björn Waldegård, the reader can see that the 914 had certain limitations. The new 'strange' handling meant driving 10/10ths was a gamble. Drivers take calculated risks, but they do not gamble.

However, in spite of the reservations, and driven by the demands of the sales and marketing departments, Porsche pressed on with preparations for rallying. As described earlier, a lot of tyre testing was conducted by the Competition Department, and in conjunction with Dunlop, the tyre supplier. Tests were conducted in Sweden, where Björn Waldegård and Åke Andersson spent many cold hours working out how the 914 would perform in such circumstances. One of the first professional teams to try the 914/6 was the Bosch Racing Team, who acquired a pair of 914/6s in GT trim from Porsche, with which Bosch entered the International Austrian Alpine Rally held on 6-10 May 1970.

Bosch Racing Team entered two cars in the Austrian Alpine Rally in 1970. This was thought to be the first time a 914/6 GT was to be seen in top international rallying, but the two pairings of Günther Janger/Walter Wessiak and Carl Christian Schindler/Gustav Hruschka both had bad luck and dropped out of the rally. (WG)

Günther Janger/Walter Wessiak, car No 2 on the Austrian Alpine Rally. (WG)

The two cars were car No 2, the Sunkist-sponsored 914/6 GT of Günther Janger/Walter Wessiak, and that of Carl Christian Schindler/Gustav Hruschka, car No 1 (in spite of detailed investigations by Porsche Werk Archives and Bosch, precise details, eg chassis numbers, have escaped us). Neither was destined to finish on what was, by the look of things, a very tough event. Björn Waldegård won the event, driving his favourite, the 911. As the Alpine Rally was finishing, the previously mentioned Weinberger/Trübsbach were bringing their now 914/6 home with a 1st in Special GT up-to-2L class on the Rudolf-Diesel-Rally on 9-10 May 1970.

Four 914 Porsches would compete on the International Rally Wiesbaden in Germany on 22-24 May. The highest placed was the Jürgen Müller/Werner Säckel entry, taking 3rd in the up-to-2.5L Production class. A few days later, on 28-30 May, two 914s competed on the Bodensee-Neusiedlersee Semperit Tyres Rally, a 30-stage round of the European Rally Championship. Carl Schindler/Gustav Hruschka took their Bosch Rally Team Porsche 914/6 GT to 3rd place overall. It is thought that this was the same car used previously on the Austrian Alpenfahrt Rally. A second 914, the standard model driven by Müller/Säckel, finished in 31st overall, but won the Production class.

In France that same weekend, 30-31 May 1970, the 17th edition of the famous International Rally Lorraine was won by Jean-Claude Andruet/Guy-Michel Vial in an Alpine Renault A110 1600. On this rally a Porsche 914/6 was seen, possibly for the first time in an international rally in France: a customer car without the Sportpaket. The French pairing came home 26th overall. As can be seen, this was a production 914-6.

4-5 June was the date of the ADAC Nordgau-Rally Amberg. Three 914 VW-

The 914/6 of Messieurs Robert Barret/JP Thomas: 26th overall on the 1970 International Rally Lorraine. (NM)

Stage start: 17th International Rally Lorraine, thought to be the first time a 914/6 appeared rallying in France. (NM)

Porsche The Racing 914s

Porsches, six-cylinder cars, were entered, one of the three being the Weinberger/Trübsbach car, which finished 3rd in Special GT over 1600cc.

Weinberger/Trübsbach would be out again on 6-7 June on the ADAC-Sud-Rally 24 Fränkische Zuverlässigkeitsfahrt (ie reliability trial), coming home 2nd in the Special GT class, while Hermann/Schiller won the Production class in their 914/6. On 11-12 July, at the Nordbayerische ADAC-Grenzlandfahrt Rally, the pairing of Hartsch/Wesol finished 1st in Special GT up-to-2L.

Round 11 of the European Rally Championship, the Rally Danube, would have two 914/6 GT entries this year. Run from 29-31 July, this long-established and tough rally saw Carl Christian Schindler/Gustav Hruschka in the Bosch Racing Team car finish in a well-deserved 2nd place, with Pöltinger/Hartinger in 7th overall in the second Bosch Team 914/6 GT.

Pöltinger/Hartinger, 7th overall on the Elan-Elf Danube Rally in the Bosch Racing Team 914/6 GT. (FG)

Over the weekend of 8-9 August, the aforementioned Horst Hartsch/Reinhard Wesol repeated their July success by taking 1st in Production GT/Special GT over 1300 on the ADAC-Rally Wolfsburg. At the International ADAC-Rally Avus Berlin on 28-30 August, they were again on the podium, 3rd in Production GT up-to-2L. At the end of September, on 27-28th, they were back on top in the ADAC-Zuverlässigkeitsfahrt 'Mittelholstein' rally, taking 1st in Production GT Unlimited. A fortnight later, they repeated the result on the AvD-Rally Hamburg: 1st in Special GT over 1600. Clearly, with consistently strong competition in the Production classes, the 914/6 was, in spite of the reservations of the professionals, proving to be a useful weapon, at least for this pairing.

The 914/6 had demonstrated that, in spite of certain negative vibes from some of the more aloof amongst the Porsche-loving public, and in fact some of the press, it was no lemon. A class win at Le Mans added to the fact that here was a car that could get results in competitive conditions. It had now been proven on national and regional rallies by private entry teams – the class wins and that 2nd place overall on the Danube were no fluke. Porsche as a factory

Tarmac and dust The 914 rally story

team, however, was not going to put the factory cars into the firing line of rallying just yet. As we saw in chapter 3, the Marathon de la Route-86 Hours of the Nürburgring was their immediate key target.

The news of the 914 and its developments were the subject of inquisitive interest in other parts of Europe by mid-1970, and in Spain at the beginning of September José-María Fernández, a private competitor but who was racing with the Escudería Montjuich, was one of those taking an interest. Having raced in SEATs in the earlier part of the year, he had turned to the Renault R8 Gordini, a favourite in Spain at the time. He had also been joined by Alfredo Cortel, who was to become his regular co-driver. In their first event together, the Rally Anoia on 28 March, they finished 2nd overall and 1st in Group 1. They followed this with an 8th overall and another Group 1 victory on the Criterium Luis de Baviera a week later. It was after this that Fernández and his brother Juan made contact with Porsche with a view to obtaining one of the new 914/6s. Chassis 043 1569 was suggested, which they acquired. As we saw in the racing section, this was one of five injection-fed 914/6 2.2L cars built.

José-María Fernández told the author: "My brother Juan drove it in the second Rally Osona on 18 August in 1970. However, he had to abandon because of a breakdown; in reality, he was finding

The new 914/6, ready to rally. This factory-built car, one of five built with injection-fed engines, is seen here at a local event – the Rally Osona in Spain – in the hands of Juan Fernández, brother of José-María. (JMF)

RALLYE INTERNACIONAL DEL SHERRY

8·9·10 SEPTIEMBRE 1970

Superado en las pruebas iniciales por los primeros clasificados del rallye, el Porsche 914-6 de J. M. Fernández se vio forzado prontamente al abandono.

Tipo 914.
Homologado en Grupo 4.

Posee las mismas características que el 911-S Rally, salvo:

Suspensión: posee, detrás, brazos de amortiguación y resortes helicoidales.

Carrocería: extensión de aletas y acoplamiento de un radiador de aceite en el frente.

Medidas: distancia entre ejes, 2.450 milímetros; vía delantera, 1.377 milímetros; vía trasera, 1.427 milímetros; largo, 3.985 milímetros; ancho, 1.700 milímetros; alto, 1.205 milímetros; altura libre al suelo, 140 milímetros, círculo mínimo de giro, 11 metros; peso en estado de marcha, sin gasolina ni conductor, 880 kilogramos; capacidad depósito de gasolina, 100 litros; depósito de aceite, 11 litros; caja de cambios, 2,5 litros; líquido de frenos, 0,3 litros.

Motor: tipo 901/25; número de cilindros, seis en plano horizontal; diámetro por carretera, 80 x 66 milímetros (1.991 c. c.); 10,3 : 1 de relación de compresión; 220 CV (DIN) a 7.800 r. p. m.; 13 kilogramos por centímetro cuadrado de presión máxima media; 20,5 mkg. de par máximo a 6.500 r. p. m.; 110 CV/litro; 167 kilogramos de peso; alimentación por dos carburadores Weber-Vergaser de triple cuerpo.

Relación peso/potencia: 4 kilogramos/CV. Velocidad máxima, 240 kilómetros hora.

CLASIFICACION GENERAL

Clasif.	N.	Concursante	EQUIPO	VEHICULO	PENALIZACION
1.°	1	E. Repsol	A. Ruiz-Giménez-R. Castañeda	Porsche 911 S	4.053,5 puntos
2.°	3	J. Gargallo	J. Gargallo-R. Guerrero	Porsche 911 S	4.123,2 "
3.°	2	J. Learsson	J. Learsson-S. Bostrom	Porsche 911 S	4.187,8 "
4.°	7	E. Mille M.	"PEDRO"-"SYMENS"	B.M.W. 2002 S	4.443,9 "
5.°	10	E. Montjuich	C. Perejoan-J. Juncadella	B.M.W. 2002 TI	4.474,2 "
6.°	4	E. Hipocampo	J. A. Castillo-J. Marsa	Porsche 911 S	4.657,1 "
7.°	23	Dunton	Peacock-D. Skittrall	Ford Capri	4.750,4 "
8.°	17	Keating	J. Keating-R. Keating	Ford Scort GT	4.788,5 "
9.°	18	O'Connell	M. O'Connell-A. O'Connell	Ford Scort	4.860,4 "
10.°	26	S. Roig	S. Roig-M. C. Marin	Morris Mini	4.929,5 "
11.°	30	Milner	Milner-T. Brunskaill	Austin Healey	4.975,0 "
12.°	28	Salido	S. Salido-A. González	R-8 Gordini	4.978,3 "
13.°	16	Pond	T. Pond-P. Shilds	Lancia Fulvia	5.131,8 "
14.°	42	Romero	A. Romero-M. Barahona	Simca GT	5.228,9 "
15.°	36	González	S. González-Agu	Morris Mini	5.302,2 "
16.°	20	R. Pricce	R. Pricce-Hedg	Morris 1800 MKI	5.345,6 "
17.°	38	C. Madueño	F. Yusta-J. Rubio	Seat 1430	5.377,0 "
18.°	27	Garnarez	E. Garnarez-J. L. Mompin	Morris Mini	5.381,4 "
19.°	31	Ozanne	P. Ozanne-P. Wrist	A. Maxi	5.459,8 "
20.°	40	Leo	"LEO"-M. A. Giménez	Seat 124	5.598,9 "

After running well at the beginning, a malfunction on the Sherry Rally caused the No 5 car to drop back and eventually to dnf – contemporary newspaper cuttings. (JMF)

Tarmac and dust The 914 rally story

he couldn't get used to the car (he had no patience!) and so I bought it from him. Once I had learned its secrets it was excellent, and by the end of 1971 on the rallies it often beat the Repsol-sponsored 911Ss with their professional drivers! I think at that time the 914/6 was the fastest car in Spain on the rallies. On fast open corners, ie in 4th or 5th gear, it was better than the 911. Also – very important – it was much lighter than the 911S. But Porsche didn't want to develop it, and they put all their efforts into the 911."

On 8 September, Fernández (JM)/Cortel started the Sherry Rally in Spain in the 914/6, then carrying registration VD-5248 and running with No 5, but it did not prove a successful outing, as an engine malfunction first slowed, then stopped the car.

In Germany on 10-11 October, at the AvD Rally Hamburg, Horst Hartsch/Reinhard Wesol took the top spot prize in the Special GT class over 1600cc. Turning to the archives in Porsche Zuffenhausen, one finds a letter dated 9 November from the Automobile Club Monte Carlo to the then Rally Team Manager, Rico Steinemann: "We are in receipt of your application to run three teams in the 40th Rally Automobile Monte Carlo." The decision had been made. 1971 would see the 914-6 GT make its appearance in a full factory-entered effort.

There is also an interesting letter from the Automobil Club of Almería (Spain), inviting the Porsche Company to utilize the facilities available, all free of charge, and to use Almería as the start point for the concentration run for the rally. Porsche, though, had already decided to start in Warsaw.

Whilst the plans were being made for 1971, there was still one important International Championship event to be completed for Porsche. On 13-18 November, the RAC Rally of Great Britain would decide the 1970 International Rally Championship. Porsche could win that championship, but so could Alpine Renault. As

The Åke Andersson entry for the Monte Carlo Rally; there were two more similar documents for the other factory cars. (P)

the teams arrived at London's Heathrow Airport, that year's starting point, it would be the Porsche team that had the most to lose, leading the championship by just three points; it was close with just

187

this one event to go. The French Alpine Renault team, led by Team Manager Jacques Cheinisse, was snapping at their heels and would throw everything at this event, including enlisting the help of several UK-based contacts who knew the ways of the British event (the full story of this can be read in this author's work *Alpine Renault – The Fabulous Berlinettes*, published by Veloce). Porsche, however, only needed to finish in the top six to win the championship. According to contemporary reports, this year's event saw the greatest array of factory teams ever assembled: Ford, Saab, Lancia, Alpine, Porsche, Vauxhall, Fiat, Toyota, Opel, Chrysler, Triumph and Renault. Seventy-seven special stages awaited the protagonists over private roads, military land and forest tracks, with no reconnaissance allowed. At 11am on 13 November, it was raining as the rally got under way from Heathrow Airport. Porsche had decided to give this event maximum effort – mechanics, servicing and general backup. In the previous events for 1970, Porsche had loaned factory cars to the drivers who had to supply their own mechanics, because, as mentioned, the major effort and investment had gone into the sports prototype racing team. In addition, all was not really well financially within the company. We have seen that sales of the 911, though still strong, were dwindling; it was hoped at the time the new 914/6 and 914/4 would help the company out of its difficulties.

At the RAC Rally, the Zuffenhausen team was out in strength. Three factory 911Ss were entered for Björn Waldegård/Lars Helmer, Åke Andersson/Bö Thorszelius, and the third for Gérard Larrousse and former BMC works co-driver Mike Wood. In addition to the three factory 911s, Porsche had also decided to enter one of the 914/6 GTs for Claude Haldi/John Gretener, the latter being an Anglo-Swiss who was once a member of the British Triumph team.

It was to be only the third test of the 914/6 in serious international rally conditions, the other attempts being with the Bosch Rally Team on the Austrian Alpenfahrt and on the Danube. What would happen on the RAC Rally would determine tactics for 1971: whether to stick with the 911s or run with the 914s. The weather was atrocious, with constant snow and rain, and the surface was ultra-slippery. Larrousse, in a 911, had a problem and dropped down the field. Alpine Renaults were looking good, with the berlinette A110s of Nicolas/Stone in 7th, Cowan/Cardno in 10th and star driver Jean-Luc Thérier in 3rd. After the halfway re-start in Blackpool, Thérier moved into 2nd place. Källström found himself in the lead at Machynlleth, just 37sec ahead of Thérier. All the while, the two remaining Porsche entries – Larrousse in the 911 and Haldi in the 914/6 – had been gradually progressing up the field.

RAC Rally: A factory-built 914/6 GT, chassis 043 1732, a former Marathon training car. (MH)

Tarmac and dust The 914 rally story

Prestatyn (Wales): service for the Alpines. Thérier/Callewaert. (CD)

Battered and bruised, but Haldi/Gretener press on. (JS)

Porsche The Racing 914s

The second half of the rally would see the Alpine team lose the J-P Nicolas/David Stone 1600S, leaving only two Alpines still running: Jean-Luc Thérier and Andrew Cowan. Gérard Larrousse, in the 911, had moved up the leaderboard, as had the 914/6. Through the next night and day of rain, the battle continued. Porsche needed to improve on its score of 27 points.

On the last stage before the run to the line, disaster struck Alpine. Thérier/Callewaert got stuck in the mud as the track worsened, then a universal joint gave way. Larrousse, running a few places further back, arrived to find that the organizers had decided to cancel that final stage and nullify the times of those that had got through! The later-running cars were told to skip the final stage and to get to the finish by the most direct route. Andrew Cowan, in his A110, moved into 5th place and gained two points, thus making a total of 26 for the Alpine team. It was not enough. Gérard Larrousse, in a magnificent fight-back, finished 6th, winning one point; Porsche took the title by 28 points to 26. Claude Haldi/John Gretener reached the finish in 12th place. The 914/6 GT had survived its most serious test yet.

Whilst the RAC Rally was taking place in a cold Great Britain, in warmer Spain the season's programme had reached the sixth running of the Rally Barcelona-Andorra, taking place on 14-15 November: 505km with seven stages, all timed, totalling 68.8km. Eighty cars were entered for the rally, with 52 being finally classified as finishers. And who do we see in the overall placings? Just behind two 911Ss, a Fiat Abarth 2000 and an Alpine A110 1600 came the 914/6 of JM Fernández/Alfredo Cortel in 5th overall.

A week later in France, on the Critérium des Cévennes, Claude

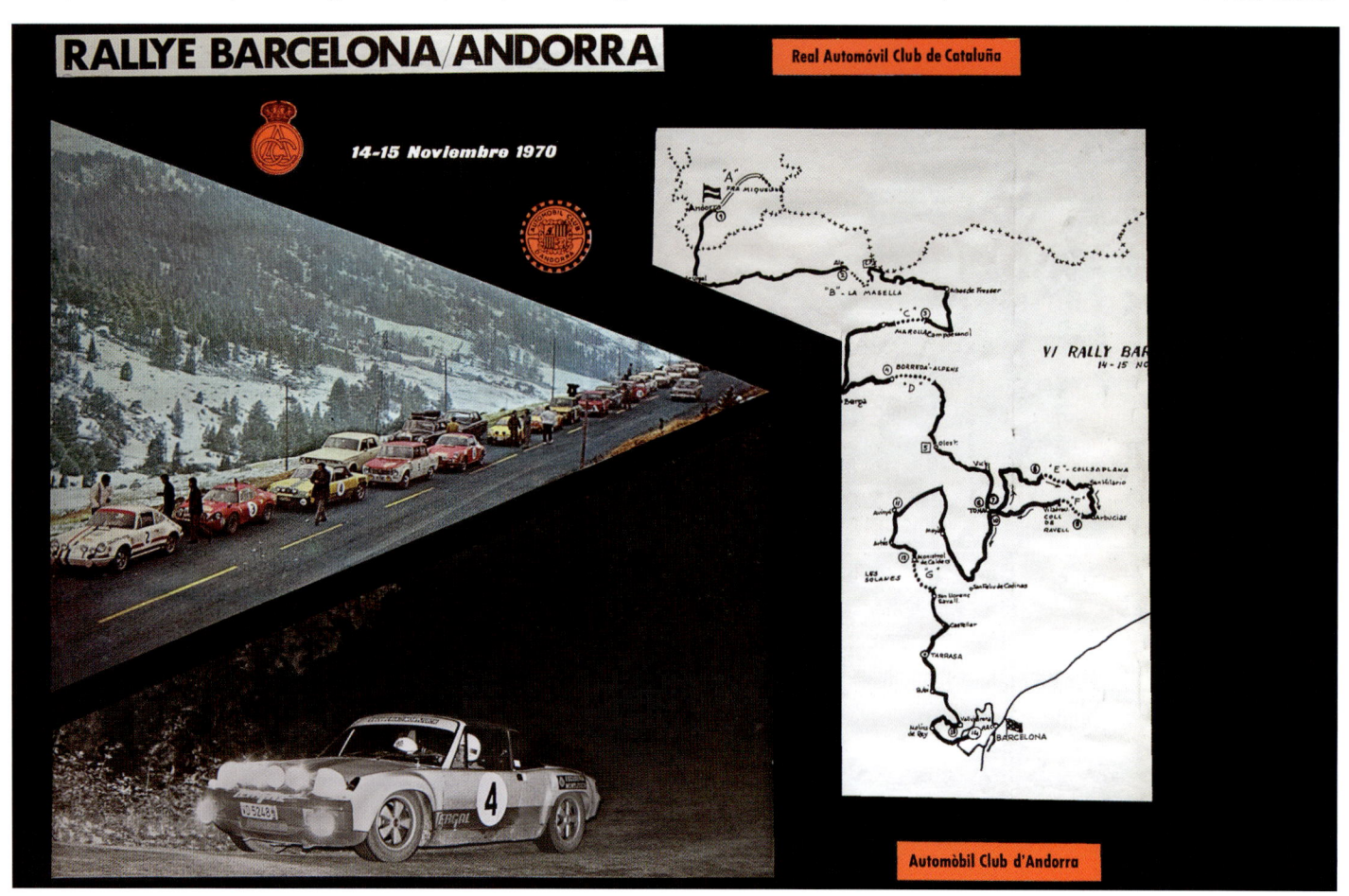

The all-purpose 914/6 of JM Fernández/Alfredo Cortel in 5th overall at the Rally Barcelona-Andorra. (JMF)

Tarmac and dust The 914 rally story

Ballot-Léna/Claude Morenas took the Sonauto 914/6 GT (the former Le Mans and Tour de France Auto car), chassis 043 1020, to 9th overall and 3rd in GT, running with No 87 on this annual road race.

In Weissach and Zuffenhausen, much development work, preparation and training for the Monte Carlo 1971 Rally was going on. It was going to be a flat-out effort: practice, practice, practice were the orders, and components were tested to destruction. The three cars used on the Marathon de la Route were pressed into service to do much of the donkey work. Porsche knew that Alpine Renault would be throwing everything at this rally on its home territory. There would also be plenty of snow, and testing of the 914 in these conditions was vital. Based in Grenoble, the team started work on 8 December through to the 16th. Björn Waldegård told the author: "Our tyre testing was very important. As I told you, I was not so happy with this car after my experiences with the 911. It seemed quite light, which was good, but it was difficult to control when you have been brought up on rear-wheel drive cars. The skill required becomes natural; the handling of the 914, whilst incredible in the dry on a race track, did not lend itself to the nature of rallying. At the beginning of 1970 I had a new technique to learn."

Roland Kussmaul was involved in the test driving, using car 043 2543, SW-1949. It was listed in-house as car 51. Roland Kussmaul: "My first connection with the 914 had been in the Test Department in 1970. We made a lot of tests at this time because of a number of little problems. My task was to sort out a driveshaft problem – initially we used this car only for driveshaft tests. The problem was that the gearbox was a special one for the 914; the driveshaft was not really good. The grease was not good and the diameter was too small for the

Hard-charging Åke Andersson in training, December 1970, with the No 3 car from the Marathon de la Route. This car now had mechanical injection installed, as confirmed by Roland Kussmaul in handwritten notes from the period. (©P)

The engine installation is prepared to go into one of the former Marathon de la Route cars to be used in tyre testing and practice for the Monte Carlo Rally. As can be seen, this car was on carburettors. (©P)

191

Porsche The Racing 914s

Mind the walls! Threading a sliding test car through a tunnel ... or is it the eye of a needle? (©P)

Björn Waldegård (left) discusses stud and tyre types with Gérard Larrousse at the workshops before a test. (©P)

bigger engine; we had too much torque, so the driveshaft broke all the time. We made a bigger flange and a new upright, because the flange on the shaft didn't fit in the hole in the original trailing arm upright. It solved the problem, but in fact the gearbox was not good. It was a 901 gearbox as used on the Marathon, but the power had been reduced for that race. To use it for the Monte Carlo, the 901 was really no good when you have 200+hp. So my job was to develop a new unit together with the gearbox guys. Called the 915/20, it was the gearbox made for the 914, and tested in my test car (51). Externally, it was the same gearbox that we did for the 916, but inside it was all 911/915. The 51 car had been put on mechanical injection at that time (it was used by Åke Andersson during the winter tests), and so was the 50 (Waldegård's car). The other two on the tests were carburettor cars. Larrousse tested the injection car, but his had Webers for the rally."

Björn Waldegård: "Porsche knew we had a problem driving the 914/6 on the limit in difficult conditions. The 86 hours at the Marathon de la Route had proved they could be reliable, but that was on a race track, not snow and ice. We did a lot of testing, including tyres, to help me and Gérard [Larrousse]; he had his opinions about these cars." We will hear from Gérard Larrousse in a moment, but we can see the efforts going into preparing the cars and the tyres. We will also return to a meeting held in the September, where tyres and studs dominated discussions, according to the minutes. Wheel sizes were to be 6in x 15in, and both crossply, which they called 'konventionell,' and radial tyres were to be tried. Remember, although radial tyres had been developed, this was still early days for the new technology. This is where Krupp-Widia came in; it was to be the adviser, and supplier of the studs, the tyres to be tested being the 'konventionell' Dunlop 35 and the Dunlop 185/70

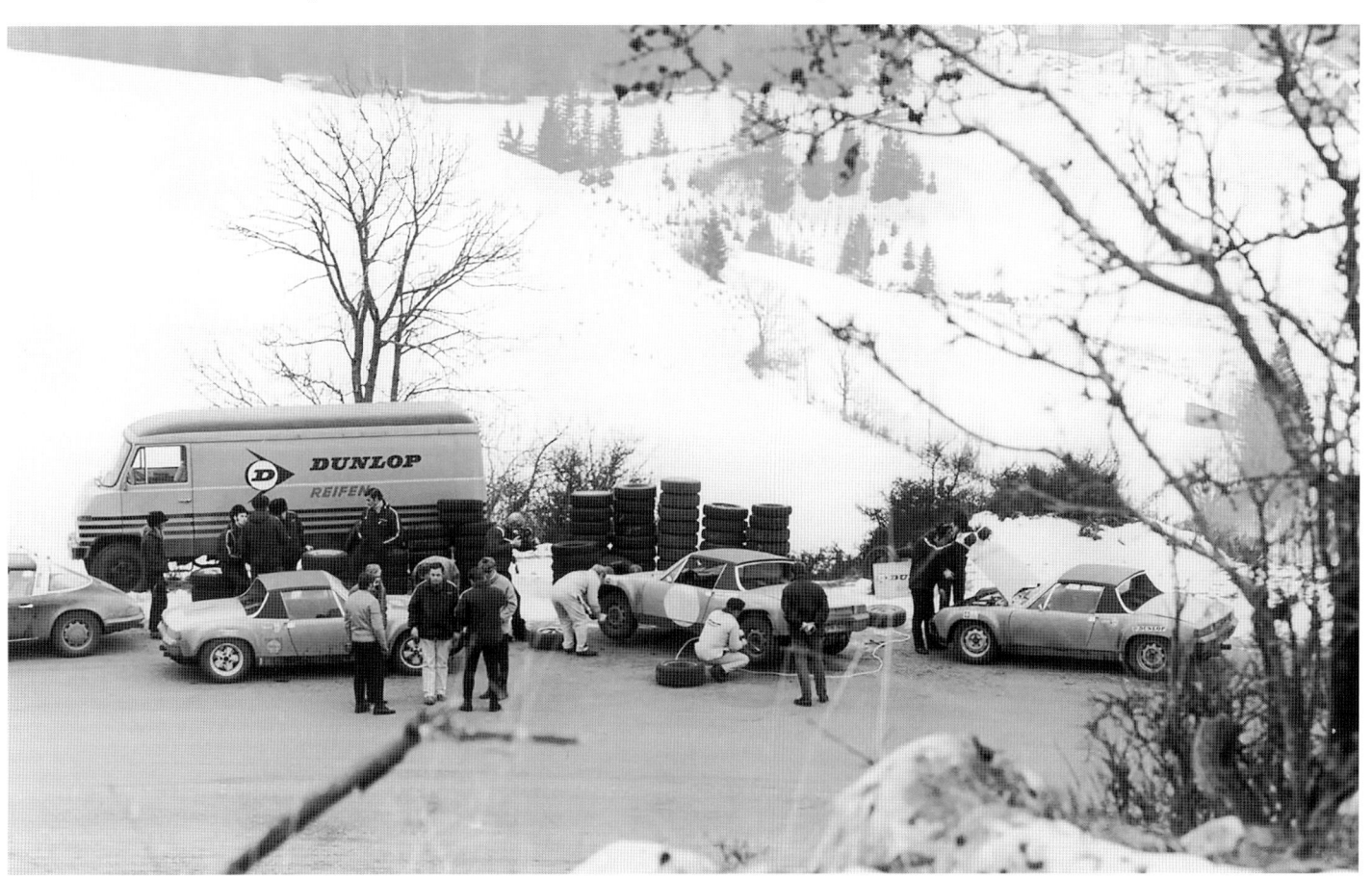

January 1971: a tyre test in the high Alps; snow obligatory. The three Marathon cars pressed into service. (©P)

Porsche The Racing 914s

Waldegård, with sledge, observes the fitting of a tyre. "Oh yes," Waldegård told the author, regarding the sledge, "I think it was used to move tyres around, but we had some fun, too!" (©P)

Here we see four of the 914/6 GTs undergoing detailed preparations. (©P)

Larrousse returns. Waldegård (left) stands by his car looking down the road thoughtfully. The car is the very well-used chassis 043 0709. Dunlop technicians used Dunlop Racing 350 tyres on the Monte, as well as Dunlop M+S Normal and both Dunlop Snow 50% with 260 spikes and Dunlop Snow 100% with 520 spikes. (©P)

Tarmac and dust The 914 rally story

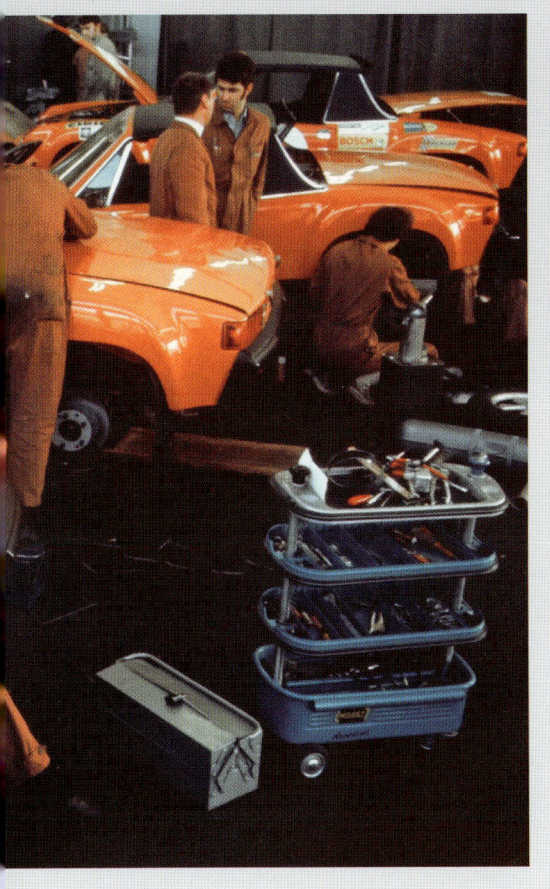

Service! A lot of equipment and spares are required to run a team in any rally. Here we see a selection of components, ready to be loaded into the service truck. (©P)

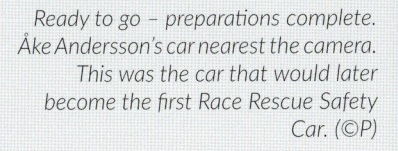

Ready to go – preparations complete. Åke Andersson's car nearest the camera. This was the car that would later become the first Race Rescue Safety Car. (©P)

195

Porsche The Racing 914s

SR 15 SP tyres. The snow studs would be of varying lengths from 1-1.5mm up to 3.5-4mm.

The factory-entered team consisted of three Group 4 cars:

S-Y 7714 – Chassis 914 143 0139 – Engine 6408002 Björn Waldegård/Lars Helmer, No 7

S-Y 7715 – Chassis 914 143 0140 – Engine 6408007 Åke Andersson/Bö Thorszelius, No 17

S-Y 7716 – Chassis 914 143 0141 – Engine 6408008 Gérard Larrousse/Jean-Claude Perramond, No 1

At least, that's what the press release and the rally organizers thought. However, Lars Helmer had to drop out just before the rally began, and Hans Thorszelius was drafted in to replace him as co-driver for Björn Waldegård. Hans was the twin brother of Bö, and over the years this has led to much confusion in the reports of rallies, organizers' line-ups and, indeed, as someone in the know said, "women, too!" Hans was a regular co-driver for Björn, and so was a natural choice.

Everything, then, was at last ready, including all the service crews. Jürgen Barth

The office: Waldegård's home for the next week. (©P)

A little more comfortable than the 908 racer seen in the background in Zuffenhausen. (©P)

The tools of the trade, neatly stowed in the rally car, ready for action. (©P)

Tarmac and dust The 914 rally story

The presentation: Hans Thorszelius/Björn Waldegård, Claude Perramond/ Gérard Larrousse, Bö Thorszelius/Åke Andersson. (©P)

told the author: "I was there to organize the service crews, and did some ice notes ahead of the cars coming through the stages to recce and inform the team by telephone." For those who are not familiar with the format of the Monte Carlo Rally back in the 1970s, it is necessary to know that, unlike today, the event was a challenge of endurance even before the timed stages began. The rally involved starting at different points in Europe chosen by the entrants.
The start points for the teams were Almería, Athens, Bucharest, Frankfurt, Glasgow, Marrakech, Monte Carlo, Oslo, Reims and Warsaw. This year there would also be an early high-speed test after the concentration run, starting near to the small town of St-Pierre-d'Albigny, between Montmélian and Albertville in south-eastern France.

Other 914/6 entries were No 181, an Italian entry for 'Toakai'/ Angelino Lepri, No 118 of Juan Fernández/José-María Fernández, fast becoming well-known Spanish Porsche campaigners, and No 69

The sign of a rally car: the necessary sumpguard! (©P)

197

for Manfred Gudladt/Florian Altmann, one of the GT-kitted cars. Ahead of the rally, José-María Fernández gave an interview to the press, in which he said: "The way I see Monte Carlo is as a truly impressive and very difficult rally for both machines and drivers. Just imagine: the first stage covers 3200km, and this is considered to be the easiest, because then comes a stage completely in the mountains, which is where the rally proper really begins. The 60 best survivors will then cover a stage of 600km around Monaco. The Dunlop service guys have an impressive stock of tyres, and during the event we will see how many we need. We are starting in Marrakech; the reason is that it saves you one of the passes through the Alps. We will have a time check in Barcelona and this itinerary is the one which allows you to reach Monte Carlo the least tired. The official Alpine Renault team will also start in Marrakech, as will most of the Spanish drivers."

Porsche chose to start from Warsaw on 22 January to cover the 2790-mile run to Rouaine, where there would be a 24-mile special selective stage to Pont des Miolans. This would be used to set the initial classification. Thirty-five private Porsches were entered, mostly 911s, but, as we see, other teams were also trying the new 914/6. Vic Elford told the author: "I discovered Warsaw as a start point in 1966 with Ford. Then, when I was with Porsche as a driver, I was the first of the Porsche drivers to start from there in 1967: that was the year we (David Stone and I) finished 3rd. Warsaw was

Monte Carlo or bust – complex ways to reach Monaco. (JMF)

The Tergal/Escudería Montjuich-supported entry, car No 118, of Fernández/Fernández; unfortunately they would fall by the wayside, but this car would be very busy in 1971. (JMF)

José-María and brother Juan Fernández (l) at the start in Marrakech. (JMF)

Tarmac and dust The 914 rally story

Larrousse looks a little frustrated. No wonder – it was necessary to carry out suspension adjustments en-route. (©P)

New tyres, please! Waldegård's car undergoes examination, refuel, tyre change – all at speed. (©P)

a dream start point: big, wide roads with virtually no traffic and virtually no speed limit, since even if there was one, the cops were so enthusiastic about us they didn't care. I have great memories of sitting at a bar with Paddy Hopkirk, eating caviar with spoons out of a huge crystal bowl while drinking ice-cold Vodka. The secret was out, and in 1969 Björn and Gérard joined me at Warsaw."

Returning to 1971, we find after the start that all was not well in the No 1 914/6 GT. As they entered France, Gérard Larrousse, who had not been happy with his car's handling, decided to take things into his own hands. Gérard told the author: "My opinion of my car was not very good. We had done a lot of testing to establish the set-up, but somehow mine was not good. Porsche had decided to go very conservative on the adjustment of the car, and they did not want to do some of the things I wanted – the Dunlop people, too, because we were racing on Dunlops – they too were being so cautious. I liked a car with a good, grippy rear. And as we travelled across to France from Warsaw on the concentration run I became angry, because it was so difficult to drive in the snow and ice.

"As soon as we entered France, I stopped at a Porsche garage somewhere – I don't remember exactly where – without saying anything to our team. I decided to check a few things and found that the adjustment on the rear camber was at 0°. I had asked for at least 1° of negative. So with the help of the mechanics at the garage, I changed all the adjustments to suit my more finger-tip, balanced style of driving. Björn, too, complained, but he was a big guy – very strong – and could drive around the set-up they had given us. When we left the garage we had more toe-in and increased camber, and now the car felt good as we drove to Rouaine."

There was another problem, too, when rallying the 914/6, which had become very apparent during the 1970 events: space. Whilst there is room front and rear in the road cars, the paraphernalia involved in rallying left no room for the stowage of helmets between stages in the rally cars, and it's not possible to recline the seats to rest – and where does one put all the paperwork?

The 1971 Monte Carlo Rally, and indeed all of northern Europe, would see snow in abundance that year. Alpine Renault chose to start in Marrakech in Morocco, hoping that the weather would be better than at a more northerly starting point. They were right: Andruet, Darniche, Nicolas, Thérier, Vinatier and a new recruit from the previous year, Swedish driver Ove Andersson, would drive 1600cc and 1800cc cars, running in Group 4, and all starting in Morocco. Of course, all the top teams would have done reconnaissance and prepared pace notes. Here we see from the Porsche archives an example of the pace notes of Larrousse and Waldegård, each driver/co-driver preparing in his own way.

The convergence point for all the routes this year was at Gap. Reaching this point had been stressful: nearly a third of competitors were eliminated on the way there. The British starters from Glasgow were nearly all excluded, due to gale force winds hindering the Channel crossing. Further delays and a horrendously rough crossing saw the competitors arriving at the control in Boulogne with just 30 minutes to spare.

Driving from Gap, the teams came to the special 38km (24 mile) selective that followed after the concentration run. It was to be a difficult one, run on minor roads and winding and twisting downhill. It was very cold, icy and peppered with snow. It was the frequently used Rouaine to Pont-des-Miolans stage, well known to the locals, though this time with frozen railway crossings, humps and pot-holes adding to the hard-packed snow on the sides of the road. It was also an unseeded stage, meaning drivers started as they arrived, which would add to the hazards. Passing was difficult, and there would many incidents as the route and the conditions caught out the unwary. Alpine, running early, got the best of it, but those starting from Athens, who arrived later, ran into a snowstorm to add to their problems. There would be many eliminations and time penalties on

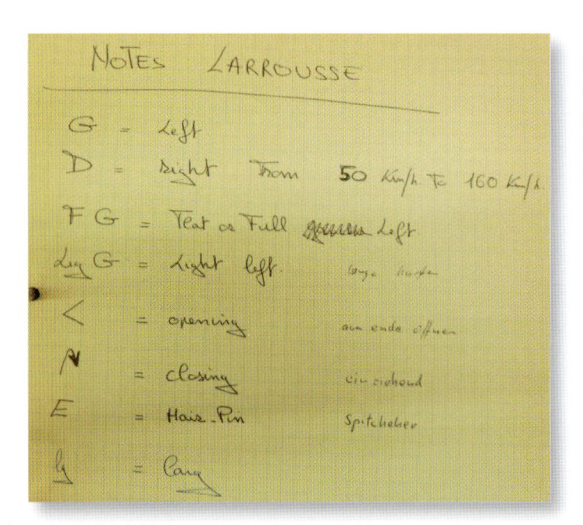

Perramond's handwritten pace notes for Larrousse. (©P)

In German, the notes of Thorszelius. (©P)

Tarmac and dust The 914 rally story

Larrousse: an icy stop for refuelling during the 1971 Monte Carlo Rally. (©P)

this stage, the end of which would see Ove Andersson/David Stone (Alpine Renault) in the lead from Jean-Luc Thérier (Alpine Renault), then Sandro Munari in the Lancia, followed by Björn Waldegård in the 914/6 GT Porsche, who was experiencing a misfire at one point. Many teams, though, were not in such a fortunate position, as this 'special' stage had left many cars hors de combat, and having to abandon in the stage or soon afterwards. 241 cars had started from the various cities of Europe; only 171 were still classified as the cars reached Monte Carlo ahead of the 'common run' section to continue into part two of the rally.

Twenty stages would make up the common run, 1514km from Monte Carlo to Vals-les-Bains to Chambéry, and back to Monte Carlo. It would prove a decisive section. With nine tests totalling 252km against the clock, tyre choice was crucial. With the exception of the Moulinon to Antraigues and Levens stages, where one could fit racing tyres, the other seven special stages presented a procession of changing conditions – dry, wet and snowy roads – where choice of studs was critical. Race 'sweepers' would set off an hour before the competitors prior to closing the roads; their job was to report back details of road conditions by telephone to

Åke Andersson/Bö Thorszelius: clutch problems would start to affect the works 914s. (©P)

their respective team at the start point. On the early stages, Ove Andersson, who held the overall lead, made a perfect choice of studs. It is reported that Alpine had 13 trucks, carrying 1132 tyres – Dunlops and Michelins – for just six cars! Porsche had 740 tyres, all Dunlops. Andersson took the first stage (Saint-Auban), followed by Andruet, then Waldegård.

As the stages were ticked off, first it was Munari in the Lancia who led affairs, then Waldegård. On the famous 45km Burzet stage, Ove Andersson (Alpine) had a throttle problem in a snowstorm; it was chaos everywhere and many lost time. Lindberg in the Fiat 124 Spider took it; Waldegård in the 914/6 GT was 3rd. At Saint-Jean-en-Royans, Munari stepped up again. On stage seven, Saint-Barthélemy-de-Séchillienne, Simo Lampinen in a Lancia took the stage. Waldegård was 1min behind, back in 3rd.

Then it started to rain on the hard-packed snow. It was Aaltonen who got the stud choice spot-on, this time taking the Saint-Apollinaire test from Andersson and Andruet. Waldegård was 5th. The sun came out to shine on the final Larochette 7km climb, won by Waldegård by 6sec from the Alpine of Darniche this time.

Åke Andersson/Bö Thorszelius in the No 17 914/6 had been the first of the factory Porsches to go out, due to an accident caused by clutch failure. Roland Kussmaul: "All three cars had clutch failure."

Tarmac and dust The 914 rally story

Then the fancied Larrousse-Perramond team fell by the wayside, also with clutch failure. As the scene began to be set for the final efforts, Waldegård began to have the same problem. Thérier and Andruet in the Alpines, who were both battling for 2nd, had Waldegård hard on their heels.

On this World Championship Rally, arriving at a checkpoint more than 30min late meant elimination. Many suffered this fate, and as the teams arrived back in Monte Carlo on 27 January, there were only 30 cars still in the race out of the 171 that started the common section. Ove Andersson/David Stone were in the lead, followed by Andruet/Vial, Thérier/Callewaert, and Waldegård/Thorszelius, still in the hunt in 4th place.

There was no time to rest before the mountain circuit stages began – 12 hours at high speed on ice and snow, going up and down the mountains north of Monte Carlo, including three passages on the Col de Turini. The race restarted with the rough and pot-holed Col de la Madone, due to be tackled twice. Waldegård set the pace, closing on Andruet, who at that point was in 3rd overall; the Alpine

It wasn't all work! Someone takes advantage of a brief moment of rest during a rare moment of sunshine. (©P)

Porsche The Racing 914s

Privateers No 69, Gudladt/Altmann: a dnf after a brave showing. (FL)

team began to worry. More worries came as their fancied driver, Jean-Pierre Nicolas, retired with his gearbox broken. Next it was into the lion's den of French fans on the hard-packed snow of the notorious Col de Turini, where Andruet collected a puncture, while the Alpines of Andersson and Thérier were out front. Waldegård, though, looked menacing in 3rd. Porsche engineer Walter Näher says: "Little did the other teams know that Waldegård had the same problem as the other 914s: his clutch was failing!"

Alpine was working its socks off, changing wheels and getting the balance of the correct studs to suit each of its drivers as the teams tackled the Couillole test. Thérier was revelling in the snow, and his choice of studs saw him return the fastest time. Back to the Turini, and it was now Lampinen who showed he was far from out of it with a blistering time. Alpine wanted the Frenchman to win; as things stood, it was an Alpine in the lead, but driven by a Swedish guy and co-driven by an Anglo-Saxon!

Waldegård had capitalized on a few problems in the Alpine camp, and by the last pass on La Madone, was equal 3rd with Andruet, having been consistently quick: 4th on the Col de la Couillole test 3, 4th again on test 4, the Col de Turini second time

Tarmac and dust The 914 rally story

Waldegård, so close but so far from victory. He had lost his clutch long before the final stages, but his brilliance put him in joint 3rd overall by the end of the 1971 Monte Carlo Rally. (©P)

A rare result: joint 3rd overall along with Andruet's Alpine. (©P)

round, and 5th on test 5, la Couillole again. "Think about it," says Walter Näher, "all that, and without a clutch!" By then Waldegård was ahead of Andruet, but on the third pass of the Turini he slipped out of the top six. However, on the 7th and final test, the last pass of the Madone, he was third fastest. Thérier had tried everything, but Andersson was better in the end by 40sec. Waldegård, always close, drew level with Andruet and that was it – both of them just 1min 51sec behind victors Andersson/Stone, and a dead heat for 3rd between Porsche and Alpine. José-María Fernández: "Unfortunately for us things did not go so well; we had to drop out before the finish when we got stuck in a culvert in the ice trying to avoid a BMW that was on its side in the middle of the road."

A great result for Alpine and a good result for Porsche, but not what they were looking for. Many internal discussions took place; maybe politics were also in play. We will see the result as we continue with our story.

The big rally story over the years is always the Monte Carlo, just as the big race for sports cars is Le Mans and for Formula 1 the Monaco Grand Prix, while in the USA the big name is the Indianapolis 500. Behind these flagship events are many small races and rallies, and the next one up on the rallying calendar in France

was the annual Rally des Routes du Nord. However, this would be the last one in the period for an event which had been held every year since 1951. Run as both an international event and a French National Championship round, the 1971 edition took place on 5-7 February. It brought some success to two privateer teams when Jacques Bedet/Philip Ronet took their 914/6 to a podium position in the national event with a 3rd-place finish, with a second 914/6 coming home in 9th in the hands of Christian Letesse/Dominique Danger. In Germany, on the International Bayerische ADAC-Winter-Rally Marktredwitz, on 5-7 February, we find in the ONS records Feiler/Niedermeyer finishing 18th overall and 1st in Special GT.

A plethora of local and national rallies in 1971 saw 914s frequently on the podium in the GT classes – at this stage of the story they become too numerous to mention them all. We will continue with the international and important nationals from this point on, though a look at the statistics in chapter 10 will allow the reader to get the picture.

Spain, always a hotbed of rallying, would field in excess of 60 rallies during 1971, ranging from small regional events through to the internationals. One of the early events that year would be the Rally Costa Brava on 13 February. José-María Fernández/Alfredo

205

A good start for the No 8 914/6 of Fernández/Cortel, but a spin on the sixth stage put an end to any chance of victory. (JMF)

A first victory for the 914/6 in Spain on the Rally de la Lana: Fernández/Cortel. It had been a very cold night, and the lead had changed several times, but various accidents and breakdowns finally gave the victory to the 914/6 of the Escudería Montjuich's Sabadell pairing. (JMF)

Cortel were entered in the selfsame 914/6 used on the Monte Carlo Rally. Escudería Montjuich had entered three teams of drivers, though in the end only two would start.

Fifty-two cars got away, and a good start saw Fernández/Cortel in 2nd position midway through the rally, but the victory would not be theirs, as a spin on the sixth stage saw the 914/6 needing five minutes to regain the road, putting them out of contention.

A few days later, on 27 February, came the Rally de la Lana. ('Lana' is Spanish for wool, this rally being associated with a textile company. It is to be remembered that Tergal, sponsor of Escudería Montjuich, was connected to the textile industry.) The rally, organized by the Escudería Sabadell, ran overnight. José-María Fernández was entered again, with Alfredo Cortel in the hot seat. According to contemporary reports, this fourth edition of the Rally de la Lana tarmac rally "… was to be one of the most competitive in the history of the event. A large entry saw 90 cars registered, excepting No 13, which was by superstition left blank. 77 cars set off, the favourites including Juncosa/Salsas (Abarth 2000), JM Fernández/Cortel (Porsche 914/6), 'Jean-Claude'/'Michel' (Alpine 1600) and Catón/Figueras (Porsche 911 R), who had won this event in 1969. Starting and finishing on the outskirts of Sabadell, the event included five high-speed stages totalling 47.75km, to be driven twice – a total of 95.5km, about a third of the total course. Juncosa, in his usual Abarth 2000, went into the lead early on. At the halfway point, the time gap was in Juncosa's favour – more than 4sec. Fernández set off determined, patiently grabbing back fractions of seconds until a notable drop in the car's performance forced him to slow. It looked as if Juncosa could seize the moment, but he had to retire his Abarth when an irreparable problem occurred in his gearbox. Fernández overcame his difficulties, managing to improve on his times on the first pass of the course to take victory, winning three of the five final sectors, though he was chased hard at the end by Fidel Riba in his BMW 2002."

Staying in Spain, on 20-21 March the Rally Anoia brought another win for Fernández, again in the 914/6 used on the Rally de la Lana. A contemporary report about the Anoia from Spanish newspaper *Mundo Deportivo* states: "The first surprise on arriving at the parc fermé for the event was the quantity and quality of the entry … The route comprised 354km, including 107.1km of timed sections. It was cold. The Fernández/Cortel pairing in the 914/6 would be among the favourites, though it was the A110 Alpine Renaults that dominated the first part of the rally. As the early starters found, the afternoon's rain had left the tarmac in poor condition. Jorge Babler went off the road when in 3rd, not helped by the poor conditions in the Montserrat sector, with a lot of standing water on the road and many small rock-slides that required caution by the leading drivers, all of whom had opted to use 'dry' racing tyres in the hope of it drying out. Serious challenges started to come when conditions improved. Fernández, coming to life in his 914/6, set his mind to narrowing the small gap between him and his rivals. Times were improving considerably and the Sabadell driver was fighting for every tenth of a second. On the second pass through the Montserrat stage, Fernández improved on his previous time, while Jorge Pla in the Alpine A110-1600 recorded a time of 1min 1sec behind José-María Fernández. There was talk that a control had made a timing error, but it is impossible to prove. Error or not, Pla lost the rally in Montserrat. In the remaining sectors, the struggle had been fierce, with more tyre changes; in places, surface water with the potential of turning to ice as it got colder slowed things down. Pla had returned the Alpine A110 to the parc fermé and it was here that he took some penalty points (30) when his starter motor was found to be out of action. This left the way clear for Fernández, who would go on to win the event."

There would be many more small rallies like this one that featured the 914; unfortunately, after so many years a lot of records from that pre-computer age have been lost.

On 6 June in France at the Rally d'Antibes, otherwise known in 1971 as the Rally des Roses, we see a 914 driven by the pairing of Calais/Jullian recorded as finishing in 9th overall. The weekend of 3-4 July was a busy one, including the 8th Rally del Cid Internacional in Spain, which took place over 374.8km. The records tell us there were 13 timed stages, totalling some 92km on the event, organized by the Escudería Los Cangrejos. Overall winners were Doncel and Gutiérrez in a Group 6 911S Porsche; 2nd, also in Group 6, was another 911S, that of Giménez and Muñoz (all well-known in Spain); then in 3rd, the Group 5 914/6 mechanical injection-fuelled car of the now equally well-known rally pairing of Julio Gargallo and Jaime Ramón. More used to the 911, Gargallo was getting to grips with a 914, having acquired an identical car to that of Fernández. He said in a report: "In slow corners, hairpins and where short gears were required, the 914 was lazy and slow. It was impossible to slide the rear end, and the Alpines and Porsche 911s could dominate it. But in fast corners, between 100 and 140km/h, both uphill and down, it was difficult to beat. Pushing braking until you were in the corner, the 914 gave confidence and security, and you could repeat this bend after bend. It was unbeatable on any relatively smooth surface with rain or mud. But it had to be remembered that on very bendy, slow sectors, the 914 lost its front end without warning, and would proceed for a metre or more in the middle of the road."

Gargallo remembers that selecting the right stabilizing bars was always a problem, and in his view was never completely solved. He is reported as saying: "The greatest difficulty of the 914 was that, in rallies, you had to adapt to its qualities and not vice versa. It was never a polyvalent Porsche, hence its low acceptance by several drivers in Europe. Then, too, by the end of the 1972 season, the best 911 Carreras had 250hp, and so it was the end for the 914/6."

It is worthy of note, however, that Gargallo would go on to do 18 more events with the 914 before moving it on to Juan 'Crady' Gemar, who drove it for another 14 events as the second car of the GES Team. For Gemar, it was a car to learn on, as up to then he had only driven Minis and a SEAT 1800 Proto. It was his first Porsche, and he soon learned that it was not as easy to drive fast with 220hp under your foot, especially in the rain.

For the class classifications, Groups 4, 5 and 6 were often put together. On 25 July, José-María Fernández/Alfredo Cortel took part in the Rally de Benicàssim. Organized by AC Castellan, this event ran over a course of 249km, with timed sectors totalling 39km, taking in roads around Cabanes, Oropesa and Borriol, then into the rough mountain countryside around San Mateo, Tírig, Alcalá de Chivert, etc. The rally itself didn't present great difficulties, but the long, monotonous neutral sectors between stages had to be limited to an average of 50km/h. News was getting around about the 2.2L injected six-cylinder Group 5 914/6 and a contemporary report states: "No doubt this was partly the reason for the huge crowds at the stages. Fernández was on fire: he won the first five special stages without having to go flat out in any of them. Behind him, the local drivers did their best not to lose sight completely of him."

It was at this event that we first see a change in the car's registration to VD-35227. Such was his lead that, in this regional rally, entered to test the car rather than to win a round of a championship, Fernández won easily.

25 July, Rally de Benicàssim: Fernández/Cortel, 1st overall. The observant will note that the registration has changed from the usual VD-5248. Sr Fernández advised the author that it is, in fact, the same car. It was changed for administrative reasons. (JMF)

Staying in Spain, on 12-13 August 1971 we find the 9th Rally Rías Baixas, held on a Thursday and Friday to avoid the weekend traffic. Run over two long sections, the first was a 403km run with eight timed sectors. A short break to grab a coffee and a quick service and it was on to the second section: 150km with seven timed sectors, one of them a sprint. Ninety-nine crews were in the entry list, and among them were the two 914s: the first the Escudería Montjuich 914/6 GT for José-María Fernández/Correia, and the second the 914/6 GT of the GES Team for Gargallo and his trusty co-driver Jaime Ramón, plus three service vans to assist. Firestone supplied rally tyres: dry, semi-slicks and wet. Also running in this event was Estanislao Reverter in the Alpinche (Porsche-powered Alpine). The first sector included the notorious descent from the Alba mountain, with lots of loose gravel. Bernard Tramont (Alpine) got the best time, followed by Pavón (Alpine). After a few timed sections, Gargallo was up to 4th behind Reverter, but then leader Tramont in the Alpine went off and Gargallo moved into 3rd place. On the Negros timed sector, Gargallo was fastest with 1min 56sec, Alberto 1min 57.3sec, Doncel 1min 58.4sec, Reverter 1min 59.8sec. All was going well, until on the Fornelos stage Gargallo spun off, taking four minutes to recover the 914 back to the road with the help of spectators. As he drove off he found he had broken his clutch, though he was able to continue and pressed on through the final sector at Camos to finish 7th overall. The rally was won by Eladio Doncel from Alberto Ruiz Giménez, both in Repsol Porsche 911s. Third came Reverter in the Alpinche.

21 August saw the third running of the Rally Osona, Barcelona. Outright winner would be JM Fernández again, this time with José Adell in the hot seat. Second in this event were Marcos/Vial in an Alpine A110. On 7-8 September, the second Vuelta Andalucía tarmac rally was held over 650km and 12 high-speed timed sectors in the Huelva mountains, Ronda, Antequera, Marbella, Sierra de Ubrique and Algeciras. Originally, the Escudería GES had not planned to enter the Vuelta, as it was preparing for the Rally del Sherry two weeks later, but financial rewards would be good. Having had an excellent season in his own region, dominating many of the events entered, José-María Fernández decided to take some holiday in another region, where he would face stiff competition from the likes of Julio Gargallo, Bernard Tramont and Manuel Juncosa. Arriving in Cádiz, the Fernández team planned to stay in the area near Jerez for the upcoming Sherry Rally.

The concentration stages on this Vuelta Andalucía would prove to be more difficult than expected. Beginning in three different cities: Córdoba, Almería and Málaga, it would be a concentration run rather like the Monte Carlo Rally, on the way to the concentration

Victory on the Rally Osona; this time with José Adell as co-driver. (JMF)

point in Granada. Arrival was followed by a neutralization time of one hour in Granada before the rally proper began. The first two special stages, in the early morning, saw Fernández (José-María – note that his brother Juan was also competing on this rally) bedding himself in. The Alpine A110 berlinettes of Marsa and Hoffman were suited to the twisty road, but the two Porsche 914s of Gargallo and JM Fernández were close, and the third stage was won by Fernández. At the end of the first sector, one of the worst of the rally, Fernández had a three second lead over Tramont's Alpine, with Gargallo 12sec behind as they arrived at the checkpoint in Jerez. Starting the night stages, Gargallo closed in as the pair of 914/6s took 24 and 25sec respectively from Tramont. The short 'special' around Medina Sidonia was won by Gargallo. Fernández took the longest sector of the rally, near to Barrios, where Gargallo was 11sec behind and Tramont 40sec behind the leader. In the fast Atajate 'special,' Fernández took 5sec from Gargallo and 24 from Tramont. So it went on, the two 914s swapping times. On the very fast last special stage, Gargallo took 2sec from Fernández. However, it was not enough, and at the end, with all the results in and checked, it was victory for JM Fernández ahead of Gargallo.

Directly after the prize-giving it was back to their temporary workshop in Jerez for the mechanics to prepare for the Rally del Sherry. Held on 21 September, this was the main target for Julio Gargallo. In contrast to the fast tarmac rallies, the Sherry Rally was known to be rough. The team raised the 914/6 by 3cm, aluminium plates were added to protect the underside, the close-ratio gears

Tarmac and dust The 914 rally story

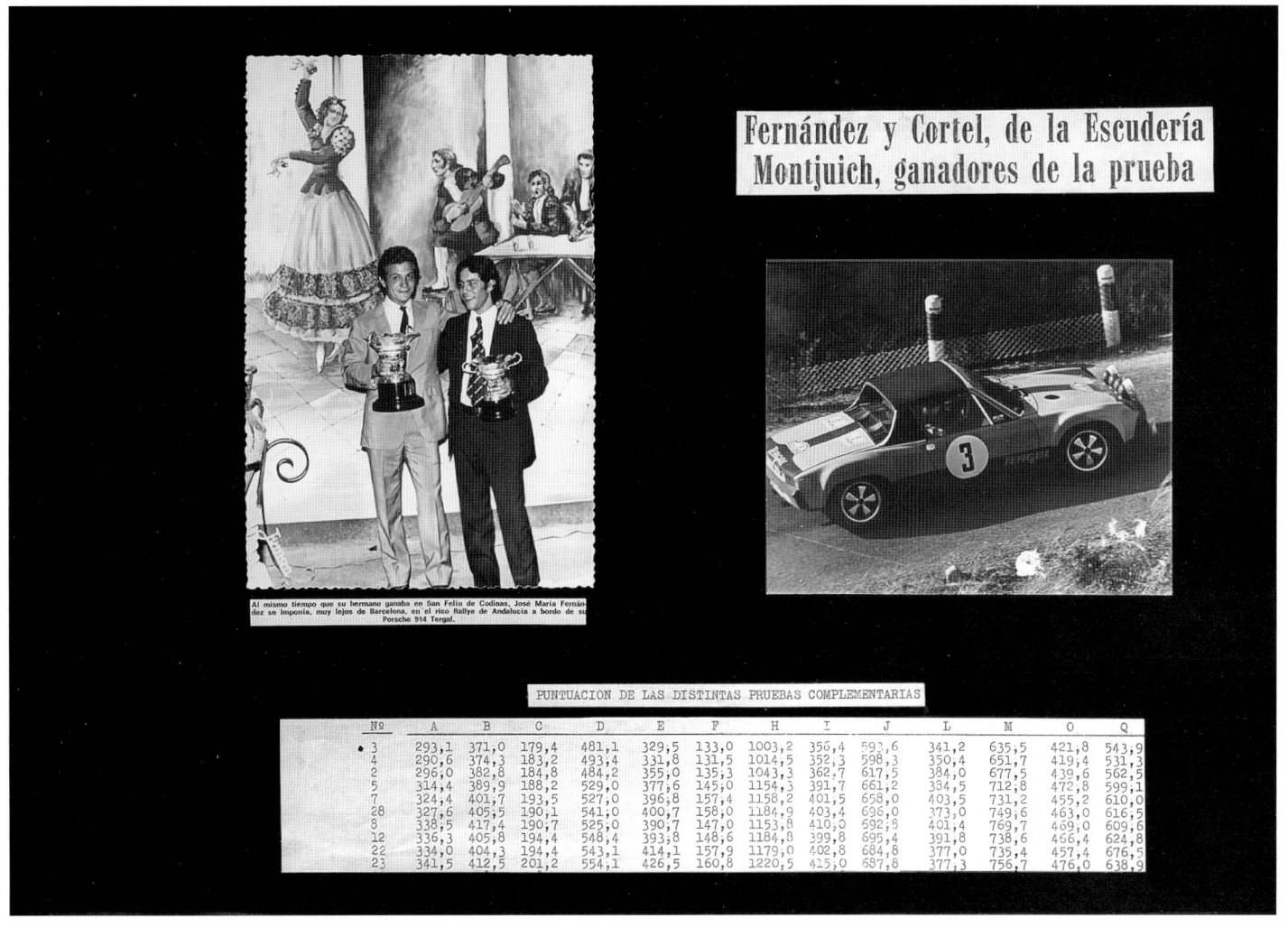

Victory on the Rally Andalucía for the JM Fernández/Cortel duo: 1st JM Fernández (914/6), 2nd Gargallo (914/6) at 38sec, 3rd Tramont (Alpine). A souvenir. (JMF)

were set to give a max 168km/h in top, and the suspension was adjusted ready for the rough stuff. For this event, run over 970km in three sectors, going as far south as Almería with neutral sectors in Granada and Málaga, and 20 timed stages on asphalt and the rough off-road terrain, attention to service was very difficult. Impressive prize money for the top ten places, though, had attracted top teams from all over Europe. Fifty-two teams lined up, the usual suspects being joined by the hot shots of rallying from England, Germany, Belgium and Portugal.

Julio Gargallo and José Ramón setting out to target victory on the 1971 Rally del Sherry. (JMF)

Porsche The Racing 914s

Flying down the rough, loose-surface roads on the descent of Mount Veleta: Gargallo's Group 5 914 takes four stage wins. (JMF)

Tarmac and dust The 914 rally story

From the start in Jerez, Gargallo went on the charge, taking the fastest time on the first stage ahead of the Repsol 911 Porsche. On the off-road, tough 20km stage of Puerto Galix, Gargallo again took fastest, 11sec ahead of Ruiz Giménez (911). Of the following stages, Gargallo won four and Ruiz Giménez two, with Reverter in the Alpine Porsche closing in. Planning ahead, Gargallo fitted the 914 with tyres that were not so good on tarmac but ideal for the descent on the Mount Veleta stages. Reverter's Alpinche took an advantage of 2min ahead of Gargallo on the ascent, while that stage was won by Giménez. The descent, though, was a different matter: 20km of narrow, loose surface, big drops, and no protection for the wayward and much damage to the cars that were unprepared. Exhausts and steering were broken, accidents ... many cars didn't make it to the control point at Capileira. But running fast, Gargallo caught and passed Reverter's Alpine. Gargallo's tyre choice had been right: he did not have to stop during the next several stages to the neutralization zone of Málaga. He had won four stages.

Alberto in the Repsol 911 had suffered damage. A five-hour rest break came to his rescue and it is recorded that Gargallo's mechanic, Satur Martín, together with Porsche workshop chief Antonio Santés, worked furiously together to help keep the 911 in the race. At this point, Gargallo was 1st, Alberto 2nd, Reverter 3rd, and Lucas Sáinz, in the works Alpine, 4th. The final phase of the rally played into Gargallo's hands when Alberto's 911 and Reverter's Alpinche sustained more damage. Rain added to the fun, but there was no holding the 914/6 of Gargallo/Ramón, and they charged away to take the victory ahead of Ruiz Giménez/Muñoz in the second Repsol 911S; 3rd was Reverter in the Alpinche; 4th Lucas Sáinz in the works Alpine 1600. Only 15 cars made it to the finish at 6pm at the Casa del Vino after 55 hours of driving, having covered over 1000km. With the added bonus from Firestone for winning with its tyres, the GES team walked away with some 400,000 pesetas.

Gargallo would take another 914/6 victory on 17-18 October 1971 on the non-championship Torre del Oro, taking home another 50,000 peseta first prize.

The famous International Rally Firestone was held in Spain on 13-14 November. As usual, it attracted large, high-class entries: this time, 89 cars were entered. There were 13 special timed stages, totalling 100.4km. Overall victory was taken by the Group 6 Porsche 911 of Egreteaud and De Sauto; Giménez/Muñoz were 2nd in a 911S; 3rd were Etchebers/Rives; then in 4th overall was the pairing of Gargallo/Ramón in the 914/6 (this time running in the Group 6 class).

The rallying challenges continued in Spain on 22 November with the 7th Rally Barcelona-Andorra, a night rally that saw 70 starters

A fill-up, but a dnf on the Barcelona-Andorra Rally on 28 November 1971 for Fernández/Cortel. (JMF)

come to the line. This time the 22 dnfs included the 914/6 of Fernández/Cortel; they went off in a spectacular way, crashing down to the bottom of a ravine. Fortunately the surrounding terrain in this particular area, the Mina sector, was largely unobstructed by trees and boulders on the way down, and the lucky pair escaped unhurt, which is more than could be said for their well-campaigned 914/6.

The Rally Costa del Sol, 7-8 December, organized by the Automobile Club of Almería, saw 83 equipes entered in a tough rally; only 34 teams classified at the finish. On scratch overall were the pairing of Giménez/De Sauto in their Group 6 Abarth 2000; 2nd came the Lencina/Caballero Group 6 911S; then, on the podium again, the Gargallo/Ramón Escudería Montjuich pairing in their 914/6. Gargallo would have won more events with the 914 had it not been for frequent electrical faults and breakages, which several times cost him victory when he seemed to have it within his grasp.

News was coming that the new 911s had 250+bhp available, so when, during a visit to the Porsche factory in January 1972, Gargallo and Juan Gemar saw the new rally version of the 911S, a widened machine which looked very impressive, and the 911 2.5RS, with two engine versions, Gargallo decided to return to the 911. Juan 'Crady' Gemar would take over the team 914/6 for 1972.

As we saw in the racing chapter, by 1972 in Europe the 914/6s were frequently outclassed in the international arena. In the national echelons of the sport, they would still hold their own for a while. Now, too, we find the 911 re-establishing itself as the

211

preferred option in rallying. This was the case at the Monte Carlo Rally, the first major event of the season. Larrousse/Perramond would return to their familiar car, a 911S, but now with 2.5L and this one putting out 270bhp. They promptly finished 2nd overall, pipped to the top spot by the light and fast Lancia Fulvia HF 1600 of Munari/Mannucci. For the Porsche factory team, rallying the 914, as with racing, would now become history. It was the privateers and dealership entries who kept the 914/6 in their line-up, at least for the time being. At the Monte Carlo Rally, the well-known Jägermeister team entered a 914/6 GT (race No 279, registration BS-HM663) for Eckhard Schimpf/Zauner, but a dnf would be the result.

Following the Monte Carlo Rally, we see several winter rallies where the 914s performed well in the Production classes to kick off the season, whilst over in the warmer climes of Spain, the first round of the Spanish Rally Championship, the Rally Fallas on 29-30 January, had 61 entries, including the 914/6, still initially in the hands of Julio Gargallo. After the start in Valencia on the Saturday night, torrential rain and treacherous road conditions caused some 34 crews to fall by the wayside, including the Eladio Doncel 911S that had started the rally as favourite but went out with broken suspension early in the second timed section. Gargallo failed to make it to the halfway mark.

If the Rally Fallas had been a disappointment, Gargallo/Guerrero turned that result around on the Rally Torre del Oro. Having won the Torre del Oro in 1971, Gargallo's hopes were high for the 1972 edition on 11 April. His hopes were justified as he and his co-driver took a resounding victory ahead of the Simca 1000 Rally of Muñoz.

The Spanish *Mundo Deportivo* sports newspaper for 8 May shows that Julio Gargallo again took his 914/6 out in the IX Criterium Luis Baviera, but his victory at the Torre del Oro would not be repeated, as this time his engine failed. Interestingly, though, the race was won by a Porsche-engined car, not a 911, but the aforementioned, so-called Alpinche of the man from Orense, Estanislao Reverter. The Porsche engine in the Alpine had come from a 911. Let's take a short look at this remarkable pairing of arguably two of the best cars of the period: the 911R and the Alpine Renault A110 berlinette. Originally called a 'Realpor,' it became better known as the Alpinche, created by Estanislao Reverter, a well-respected rally driver from Orense in Spain, where he had set up the Escudería Orense, which became an organizer of rallies. His obsession was weight. Even the orange paint characteristic of the team's Porsche was lighter than the paint used by others. When this Porsche was irreparably damaged by José Pavón in the Orense Rally

Gargallo/Guerrero, in the fuel-injected 914/6 GT, took a resounding victory on the Rally Torre del Oro ahead of the Simca 1000 Rally of Muñoz. (JS)

Reverter/Rodríguez: the 'Alpinche.' The Porsche-powered Alpine of Estanislao Reverter became famous during 1972 – a fascinating car that finished on the podium on many rallies in the mid-1970s before succumbing to an accident. (LR)

Tarmac and dust The 914 rally story

in 1970, Reverter had the option of going the new Porsche 914 route, or following an idea he had already thought of: to create the lightest possible rally car paired with the most reliable and powerful engine – Alpine berlinette A110 + Porsche. He acquired an Alpine A110 1300, registration OR-31516, and fitted the components that would affect the transformation. The car had its debut at the Rally Rías Baixas in 1971, painted in the orange colours of the Escudería Orense. In 1971 it had been 3rd in the Rally of Spain, 2nd in the Rally Bosch de Bilbao and 3rd in the Asturias Rally. In 1972 Reverter won the Luis de Baviera, Rías Baixas and Asturias, and came 3rd in the Bosch Rally and in the Sherry Rally. In 1973, he won again at Rías Baixas, was 2nd in the Rally de España and 3rd in the Alicante 500km. With rule changes for the 1974 season prohibiting the Group 5 special cars, Reverter could not use it on rallies that counted towards the European Championship. The Alpinche reappeared with a new Porsche 2.7 270bhp engine in the Costa del Sol, where it finished 6th. There followed many adventures, until a big accident brought its career to a halt. The car is being restored (2015); like the 914, it's a design idea that required more development, and once more, an 'if only' situation!

A new kind of sport saw the light of day in the late 1960s/early 1970s, although not yet as a mainstream interest: rallycross was to become a major off-road event in the 1980s-'90s and through to the present day. Back in the 1960s, a popular form of racing was

Estanislao Reverter (L) with the Realpor/Alpinche. (LR)

autocross, held on marked-out courses in friendly farmers' fields, all on grass which inevitably turned to mud as the day's events wore on. All kinds of cars took part, from standard production to autocross specials. The rallycross form of the sport, which involves tarmac sections as well as off-road, continues to this day. It began in Britain in response to a British government suggestion that they were going to ban rallying. Rallycross spread rapidly and really took off in continental Europe, where in 1973 the first European Championship came into being. On 21 May 1972, we see the beginnings of the use of 914s in rallycross, when at the International ADAC Rallycross Niederelbe Dieter Bonhorst is listed as taking victory in the Production Special GT class. As we will see in the statistics chapter, 914s became very popular machines in this form of motorsport.

Returning to rallying, we come to the 1972 Olympia Rally on 13-19 August, a one-off event run in conjunction with the Olympic Games of that year. Those Games will be remembered for the terrorism that marred the great occasion, but the rally itself was not affected, and whist Alpine took a victory, we see in 4th in Special GT the 914/6 of regular rally competitors Karlheinz Franke/Jürgen Eirich. A second 914/6 entered but failed to finish.

After a few months away doing other things, Spanish rally men Gargallo and co-driver Ramón were seen again on the 1972 edition of the Rally de España on 27-29 October, a 21-stage event with 218.1km of timed sections within the 1422.2km route. One hundred cars started the event, but only 37 would be classified – amongst them in 4th place the 914/6 of Gargallo. The aforementioned Porsche-engined Alpine A110 'Alpinche' was 2nd.

Gargallo had begun using the 2.5L 911 more than the 914/6 in 1972, and indeed JM Fernández had also gone back to the 911 model. In Germany, the 914/6 had continued to be rallied, but now predominantly only in the Production classes, regularly netting class victories. It would be a similar situation in 1973, and the years that followed. No 914s were entered in the first major event of the 1973 season, the Monte Carlo Rally – not even private entries.

Whilst some appeared in smaller regional events, it was not until 31 May that year that a 914/6 featured in an international event – the Semperit Rally in Austria. Leistner/Scholz finished 2nd in the Production GT over-1600 class. From the records it appears there were only seven rallies where the 914/6 managed to achieve a result. Rallying was moving on, and in Spain Julio Gargallo moved his 914/6 on to Juan 'Crady' Gemar. However, there are few records of success with the 914/6 in Germany, France and Spain until we reach the International Rally Spain on 26-28 October 1973. Organized by the Real Automobile Club of Spain, this tough event was run over

Juan 'Crady' Gemar with the 1973 version of the team GES Group 5 914/6. Note the even wider wheelarches at the rear. (JS)

1640km with 26 timed sections totalling 247.5km. 'Crady' Gemar/ Juan Fernández were amongst 47 teams that started the event; they would finish 7th overall in the 914/6, running in Group 5. Jorge Babler/Ricardo Antolín just beat the Alpinche of the Reverter brothers for the victory. The Escudería GES team took victory on the Rally Paz de Santander, dominating it from the beginning. The Rally Costa del Sol on 8-9 December, the last rally of the year, had 52 entries for what was a relatively short event of 675.6km, one of the shortest of the 1973 season. 'Crady' Gemar was accompanied again by Juan Fernández. Here the 914 was on good form, finishing on the podium in 3rd overall, ahead of formidable opposition.

By 1974, in the period of operation when the 914 was a current model, we find no recorded victories in rallying, and it is only on 25-26 April 1975 that we see a 914, a four-cylinder version, take a class victory on the ADAC Rally Berlin, coming 1st in the Group 3 up-to-2L class. It was pretty much the final throw of the dice in this period for the rallying 914s, and it would not be until the rise in popularity of historic motorsport that they would be seen again.

There is, however, one final twist to the rallying story of the 914/6: the possibility for a Group B vehicle, noted in an internal memo dated 13 September 1982. It is a record of a discussion at a meeting that took place on 10 September. The memo was addressed to Helmuth Bott, and the document was brought to the attention of the author by Jürgen Barth, who was at the meeting along with Peter Falk and Roland Kussmaul. The 914/6 GT was the subject. Let's see what the minutes of this meeting said:

"In order to have a competitive vehicle available once more across the motorsport sector, the following points were considered. Around 80% of our customers attend track events, but only 20% attend rallies. Although many firms are developing four-wheel drive versions of their road cars with the specific aim of success in rallying,

Tarmac and dust The 914 rally story

The idea was to create a four-wheel drive mid-engine concept rally car. This drawing, done by Jürgen Barth in conjunction with Roland Kussmaul and then-team manager Peter Falk, demonstrates a reworking of the 914 GT design. But it was a 'what might have been': the project was not taken forward. (©P)

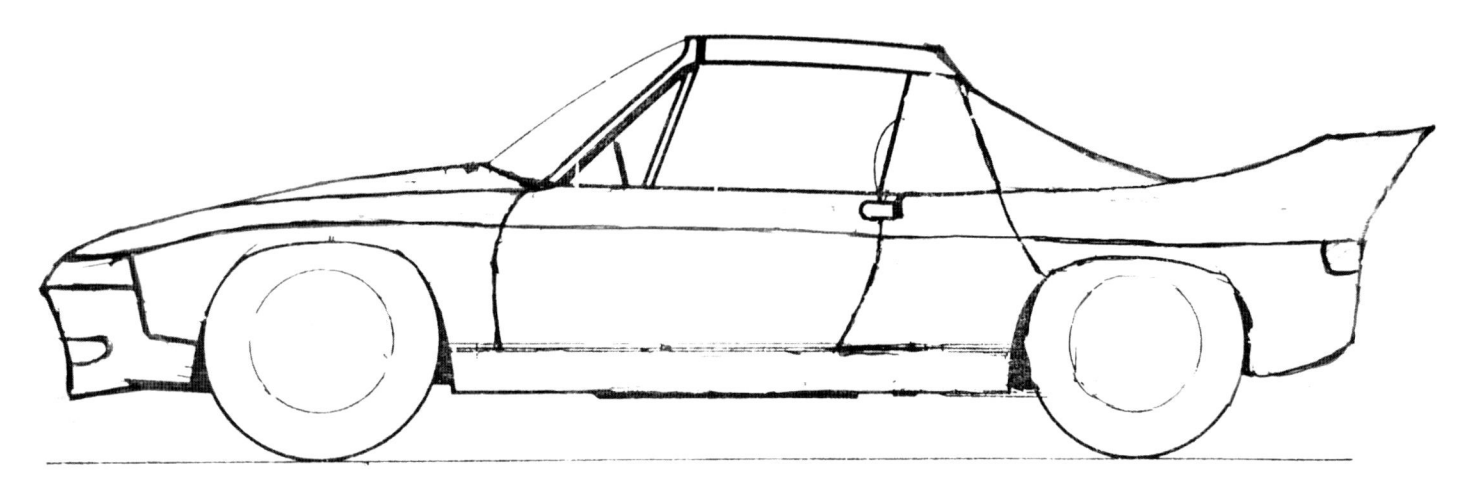

we are of the opinion that a mid-engine car will be most suited to our likely clients. In order to be able to guarantee eventual success in the rally sector, we need to investigate the possibility with FISA of any handicapping of four-wheel drive vehicles in relation to allowing a mid-engined (4WD) car to compete.

We foresee that such a vehicle would comprise the following:

Engine: 2.1L 2-valve engine, air-cooled, intercooled, bi-turbo, twin-spark, Motronic pressure-controlled (the former Le Mans 936 engine can apparently be made roadworthy according to engine division).

Transmission: Group C transmission, suitable for suspension pickups. The new 911 transmission unit could be a possibility here, given the power.

Running gear: Front axle from either 911 or 924 GTS possible, but with new coil springs. The best solution, however, would be a new double-wishbone arrangement.

Rear axle: No existing modularity with current programme is applicable, so a new double-wishbone layout would need to be designed.

Chassis: Since the manufacture of a new monocoque is too expensive, the most cost-effective solution would be to rework the 914 – similar to Group C – with a central cockpit and front and rear subframe.

Bodywork: Fibre-glass front and rear bodywork, also doors.

Summary: In order to make such a vehicle available for test as soon as possible, we request a budget of DM500,000. Herr Kussmaul could then create a prototype under collaboration with the Customer Repairs division."

With this stillborn idea, we see that the key men of Porsche, all talented engineers and already experienced in the world of rallying in 1982 (the car of the moment at that time being the new 924 Carrera GT Club Sport), could see the limitations of the idea. Walter Röhrl had used the 924 Carrera GT in the German Rally Championship during 1981 and Barth himself, along with Kussmaul, had developed the 924 Carrera for rallying. The Almeras brothers in France had also experimented with one. But in the end, with Audi and Lancia already experimenting with 4WD, later to be joined by Subaru, Porsche were thinking they needed four-wheel drive for sure. This concept was the first investigation into this idea. We can only surmise that it may well have been a success; we will never know!

8
Big country
Racing in the USA 1970-1975

Racing with the 914 in the USA can be traced right back to the very beginning of the 914 racing programme. It is not by accident that the 914/6 was to be introduced to the market in the USA from the early days of 1970. The USA, always a major market for Porsche, had been immensely successful with sales of the 356 model and the 911 cars that did much to raise the profile of Porsche in the 1950s and 1960s and establish its authority as a maker of fine, reliable cars. They were also quick enough and strong enough to be race winners in the right hands, in a country where motorsport was a major pastime for many. Motor racing had grown rapidly after World War II; America was in love with the automobile and the '50s and '60s were boom time – new roads and many new race tracks all helped the sport appeal to the competitive psyche of those financially able to indulge, while those of lesser means turned out in their thousands to support drivers who would become heroes to their followers. NASCAR was, and is, the big-money motorsport, but the heritage of the Indy 500 also provided a solid base. Then there were the postwar races for sports cars, as soldiers returned to their homeland after World War II with examples of European sport and racing models that started to beat the home-grown marques on the North American tracks, often airfield circuits. By 1970, the Daytona 24 Hours and Sebring 12 Hours were flagship events that were becoming well established, attracting international competition.

It was inevitable, then, that when the 914 was created, America beckoned.

Gestation started when the newly created Porsche+Audi USA's Competition Manager, Josef Hoppen, set up facilities for three different two-car 914/6 Porsche teams to compete in the SCCA (Sports Car Club of America)-governed races in three geographical regions of the USA. Each Porsche+Audi-assisted team would get $50,000 and cars to run for the season in the 'C' Production class. In the east, it was to be the team run by Peter Gregg of Brumos, while the Midwest effort would be headed by Art Bunker, Bob Hindson and Kendall Noah. In the west, Hoppen initially spoke to Volkswagen-Pacific, suggesting Richie Ginther could manage their team, as he was already Competition Manager for the VW-Pacific concern. Alan Johnson, the test driver of the first car, told the author: "Jo Hoppen sent the car to the VW-Pacific Porsche dealership of John Von Neumann. I drove that first car at Willow Springs for a test – that was when Richie Ginther got involved. At that time, the car did not have the second mandatory roll bar. The test was good, though, and we looked forward to racing it." However, a report shows that VW-Pacific demanded triple the original cash figure, because, as they said, they had to do all the development. The negotiations were taking too long, and in the end Ginther went his own way rather than wait for VW-Pacific to decide. On the instructions of Hoppen, Richie Ginther, already renowned for his

Big country Racing in the USA 1970-1975

racing exploits, prepared four other cars in addition to his own two: the two 914/6s for the Art Bunker-run team, and two for the Peter Gregg-run team.

Well known for the 911s coming from his workshop, Ginther and his chief mechanic Harold Broughton had plenty to do. They would have stiff competition, too, because two other major car importers were entering the field of play at the same time. Triumph from the UK appointed Bob Tullius in the eastern side of the USA and Kas Kastner over in the west to look after its interests in racing the TR6s. Datsun would appoint Peter Brock to look after its 'C' Production interests in the west. Sports cars were big business and victory in the Production classes sold cars.

Ginther had been running Alan Johnson and Milt Minter in various cars in the preceding years, and this would be his line-up at the start of 1970. In the Midwest, based in Kansa City, the Bunker-Hindson Racing team would have Bob Hindson and Kendal Noah driving. In the east, Peter Gregg drove one car himself and Pete Harrison drove his second car. Production cars running in the 'C' class had inevitably developed over the years, to a point where, if you wanted to win, it was necessary to be as close to pure racing car specification as the rules would allow. It will, then, come as no surprise to hear that on receiving the 914s in the USA in 1970, the first job deemed necessary was to completely strip them down and rebuild, incorporating, removing or changing everything permissible to get an end-product as light and as fast as the team could make it. Engines, too, were stripped and rebuilt using new parts from other Porsches, such as the 911T, with crankshafts in the standard engine being immediately changed for 911S items. Each of the cylinder heads received valve modifications, plus polishing and porting treatment; Carrera 6 camshafts and specially tuned exhaust systems were also fitted, as were other items permissible within the regulations. Shocks were changed, spring rates altered and extra oil coolers fitted. Bodywise, although the 914 had an integral roll bar forming the rear part of the cabin, the SCCA rule makers at first insisted on it being removed, and a regular tubular one fitted. Heated discussions took place and eventually Porsche won out: the original could stay, as long as a secondary one was installed!

(l-r) Richie Ginther, Jo Hoppen, Elliott Forbes-Robinson – key players at the introduction, and for the next two years of the 914's fortunes in the USA. (©P)

The windscreens on these cars were removed, as was the window behind the driver, to leave what would be a low, sleek-looking racing car.

Interestingly, although things were pressing ahead now for racing, only a few months earlier there had been big discussions within the Porsche Club of America as to whether the 914, being part Volkswagen, would actually qualify its owner to join the Porsche Club of America! Such was the class distinction and conservative thinking in those days, reflecting in fact exactly the initial opinions in Europe. As John Baker records in the June 1988 *VW and Porsche Magazine*: "The 914 was viewed as a compromise car, rather than an exciting and totally new model." Incredible when one can see today the 914/6 and also now the 914/4 becoming admired, collectable items among the new generations of enthusiasts; as the author was told by a very respectable and experienced present-day journalist: "Those are really cool cars!"

Back to the racing. As mentioned, Ginther and Johnson carried out a first test session at Willow Springs only a few days after the introduction of the car at the 1970 New York Motor Show. Cooling was immediately a problem with the mid-engine set-up, and it is said that, due to the rules, Ginther had to be creative in this area,

217

Peter Gregg, owner of Brumos, said in an interview in 1972: "The handling and visibility were both good; I found the 914 much underrated." Seen here is one of the two cars prepared by Richie Ginther under the instructions of Jo Hoppen for the east division competitions of the SCCA 'C' Production class, 1970. (Brumos)

especially where the oil cooler was placed (remember, this was pre-GT, with cooler in the front). Throughout the first season, any change of position from standard within the car was protested by the Triumph and Datsun teams, as the 914/6s were starting to show speed and were therefore a threat to the established front runners. It is said that engine tuner Art Early was getting 212bhp out of the early standard 914/6, once tuned, in 1970.

The SCCA regional championships are split up into further, different regions, due to the sheer size of the USA, with a decider to choose the Champion of Champions usually held at Atlanta in the autumn. In 1970, racing started early in the USA; on 1 February in a national race at Holtville, California, south of San Diego, film star Steve McQueen won in his personal 908. A 914/6 was competing in this combined event (classes A-B-C-D) in the hands of Alan Johnson, who set the 'C' class pole and led the 'C' class for three laps before succumbing to engine failure. It was only a month before the selfsame 914/6 claimed its first victory on 1 March at the Phoenix International Raceway. A précis of the contemporary report of the race that appeared in *Porsche Panorama* states: "Alan Johnson captured a first-category victory for the new 914/6 Porsche. It was a damp track at the start and Johnson chose to start the race with rain tyres, whilst his main competitor Jim Dittemore chose dry tyres on what they thought was a drying track. As it turned out, this was a mistake by Johnson: no more rain fell during the 17-lap feature race. Johnson lost nearly 2sec a lap, as the track had dried by lap 4. He had put his car on pole position in qualifying, breaking the 'C' Production official lap record. But fortune smiled on the Richie Ginther-managed Porsche team when their principal adversary Jim Dittemore in his TR-6 was forced to pit with a loose wheel. He lost a minute and half, enough to allow Johnson to take the 'C' class lead. However, Don Roberts in his 'B' class Production GT350 got by to put Johnson 3rd overall at the finish. The winner overall in an 'A' class sports racing car, his own Porsche 908, was again none other than actor Steve McQueen, who in fact lapped the field, never being contested. Fellow Hollywood actor and also car enthusiast James Garner led a band of well wishers at the finish line."

Alan Johnson told the author: "In the first race before that class victory, we had a problem with too much advance and ended up burning a piston. At the end of February we fixed that – we put in a Bosch distributor and that was just fine. For our second national championship race we qualified on pole and won the class. As you know, it was Richie Ginther's car. VW of America (Porsche cars North America) set Richie Ginther up for four more cars to prepare for two other regions."

We see in the archives from around this time a copy of an invoice for parts. Volkswagen Pacific is in this case the supplier of special parts to Rico Steinemann – racing parts for the German cars, likely to be the same as the items being fitted to the Ginther racers. The invoice includes: Teflon bushes, 21 and 22mm torsion bars, Teflon front stabilizers and rod-end bearing modifications – all items that were definitely non-standard on 28 April 1970, the date on the invoice.

Alan Johnson continues: "The cars of Art Bunker and Peter Gregg were all a sort of tangerine colour except for the original car – the original show car that came over – which was signal orange. Richie said that because we'd had some problems with that original car, he sent that with another to Peter Gregg, which I always thought was kind o' funny. Two cars went to Bunker in Kansas City and then we had two cars out here. Richie hired Elliott Forbes-Robinson to drive the second car. I don't remember a whole lot about the various races during the year, but we did quite well and we won our division and qualified for the national championships at Atlanta."

The Porsche Club of America has always had a strong racing contingent since the early days in the 1950s, with a lot of good-quality motorsport competitions running at grass-roots level.

Big country Racing in the USA 1970-1975

Alan Johnson in the Richie Ginther-prepared 914/6 – one of the early appearances of the 914 on the west coast. (AJ)

May 1970: Alan Johnson wins the 'C' Production category, again in a race at the Riverside National Meeting. (AJ)

Porsche The Racing 914s

Practice at Watkins Glen, 1970: the Ralph Meaney 914/6. Note that the body has the standard 914/6 shape, without the bigger wheelarches of the GT pack. (MK BO)

The No 94 Porsche 914/6 of Meaney/Behr tussling with the 41 Lotus Europa of 13th finishers overall Jim Bandy/Bruce Cargill. (MK BO)

For those who wanted something more, however, the SCCA races were the starting point for some of the great US drivers: Bob and Al Holbert, Alan Johnson, John Hotchkis, Hurley Haywood, Peter Gregg, Dick Barbour, to name but a few.

For the Watkins Glen International 6-Hour Race on 11 July, Porsche specialist Ralph Meaney had acquired one of the early 914/6s, chassis 043 0663. At this stage it did not have the GT kit wheelarches installed and was built to the standard spec body-wise, unlike the 'C' class Production cars. Kendall GT-1 Racing Oil would put up the sponsorship to support the Meaney 914/6, No 94. It was one of two Porsches entered by Meaney that day, the other being a faithful 911S. Ralph Meaney and Stephen Behr shared the 914/6. All 26 cars that started the race would continue to the end, though only 20 were classified as finishers. With 181 laps under their belt from their 19th position on the grid, Meaney/Behr got over the line at the end, but were not classified due to insufficient distance covered. They had been delayed by clutch and ignition problems. The race winner, on 308 laps, was Pedro Rodríguez/Leo Kinnunen in a Porsche (of course!) – the 917K of the John Wyer Gulf Team.

Ralph Meaney, interviewed in 2015, said: "I've done so much stuff with Porsche. In the 1960s in New Jersey I started watching, then my mother bought a factory car and my father raced it – it became a family thing – oh, so much stuff! When Porsche brought out the 914/6, I got two cars – one was a gift; the other I bought. It was then that I started to develop the cars; in fact I invented a lot of the parts on the car. Then they brought out the GT that ran in Europe and I ended up grabbing one." We will hear more from Ralph, one the pioneers of 914 development and racing in the USA, in a moment.

Big country Racing in the USA 1970-1975

Uneven contest? Well, it's certainly not the 914 passing the 917K of van Lennep and Larrousse. Watkins Glen 6 Hours. (©P)

mentioned future star Elliot Forbes-Robinson. They were 1st and 2nd on the grid in the 'C' Production race. A contemporary report tells this story:

"As the race progressed, the 914/6s showed their metal, and with a lap to go EFR was in the lead overall with Johnson hard on his tail, when they came upon a Cobra that was a lap down. EFR got past, but somehow Johnson got tangled up with the Cobra, incurring a blown tyre. He rapidly pitted and tore out of the pits like a man possessed, storming round the final lap to finish 4th." The report also states "... in his seven-wheeled car!" Seven wheels? Yes, the three on his car, and the four on the jack wedged under the left rear! He had left the pits thinking the wheel was on! The SCCA races were once more providing as much excitement as anyone could have wanted.

For the remainder of 1970 the SCCA Production 'C' class was the arena that would mostly see the 914/6s being campaigned. Racing being high on the Porsche+Audi agenda, it was certain that publicity for the 914s would be guaranteed, and its profile as a new car on the market was raised further with a celebrity race that took part at the Ontario Raceway, just east of Los Angeles, California. The driver line-up included Bobby Unser with US TV star of the time,

Unlike the 12- and 24-hour races, the 6-hour events were flat-out sprints – no place for taking it easy and saving the car. Vic Elford, driving the 4th placed 917K of the official Porsche+Audi team, said: "The cars were all so reliable by then that you could not sit back and hope that one of your competitors broke. It was flat out all the time – a sprint from start to finish."

12 July would see SCCA regional racing over at the Sears Point International Raceway, where the Richie Ginther-managed team had their two cars in the hands of Alan Johnson and the already

A Le Mans-style run across the track would add to the excitement – but for the celebrities only, who had to touch the hand of the pro driver already seated in the car to set off at the start. The reader will notice that attendance was somewhat limited! (©P)

221

Bobby Unser does a lap of honour with the chequered flag. (©P)

Dick Smothers; Al Unser with golfer Ken Venturi; Indy car driver Roger Ward with US entertainer Dino Martin; Dan Gurney with tennis player Pancho Gonzales; Mark Donohue with US TV man Hugh Downs; Parnelli Jones and Paul Newman, and Mario Andretti with astronaut Pete Conrad, who would go on to race 914s again. The race would be over 12 laps of the Ontario Motor Speedway (note: USA, not Ontario, Canada), with each driver taking two turns at the wheel, changing over after three laps. With just seven cars, it would not be crowded. Film star Kirk Douglas waved the starter's flag. At first Andretti would lead, and he and Pete Conrad would hold it for ten laps, until Al Unser/Ken Venturi moved into the lead with two laps remaining. However, it was Bobby Unser/Dick Smothers who held on and took the chequered flag first.

If the celebrity race was a bit of fun, it had been set up with serious intentions to attract the public, because there were a lot of rumblings from the 'stuffy' brigade: Porsche owners who saw the 914/6, with its VW and Porsche badges, as 'not a proper Porsche,' even though it had a Porsche engine, was designed in the Porsche Design Studios and was being raced by the factory in Europe. VW was regarded as the poorer brother.

None of this mattered to the racing men: they were only interested in the serious stuff, and at the SCCA Bonneville US National Race Meeting on 7 September, Elliot Forbes-Robinson took an overall race victory ahead of Alan Johnson, both again in the Ginther Team factory Porsche 914/6s. EFR repeated the performance at the SCCA Portland National Meeting on 13 September. He also took 3rd place at the SCCA Ontario Race Meeting on 19 September, 2nd overall at Phoenix on the 27th, and 4th overall at the SCCA Atlanta Finals Meeting on 29 November. At the latter race, Peter Gregg of Brumos would be 8th, with Alan Johnson 5th overall.

Alan Johnson told the author: "During the season we ended up having some new, fresh engines done. Art Early was an engine maker with a lot of respect on the west coast. He had run Indianapolis engines, and so Richie got him in and he worked over our engines, and they were really running well on the dyno. We went to Atlanta and found they wouldn't pull in top gear and we tried to get the mixture right and everything like that. It turned out that the fuel pumps in the car were not sufficient to supply enough fuel, because the engines were using more than before. We went off down the straights and couldn't get a really top speed; we were off by a few miles an hour, because we were getting a misfire, like you were running out of gas. We qualified okay, but in the race the car ran the same. The whole time it was missing on the straights and Richie was really mad. That's the reason we really didn't run very well in the champ finals at Atlanta in 1970. At the end of that year the 914/6 'C' Production racing programme came to an end and they took the car that I had – they felt it was the best one – and the team converted it to a 914/6 GT."

Although already somewhat maligned by some, the 914 was also meeting pressure from those running the 911s of the time, the point being that, with development by the teams in the USA, it was proving to be quicker than some liked. In addition to this, it's fact that, as the 1970 season progressed ,both Datsun and the Triumph teams were lobbying to keep the 914/6 away from their classes. Something had to be done for 1971.

This was all about road car sales strategies, of course, and Jo Hoppen, the Porsche+Audi motorsports boss, decided on a new

Big country Racing in the USA 1970-1975

1970: a starter year for Porsche in 'C' Production. At Atlanta, though, Datsun cleaned up with a 1-2-3. Porsche struggled: here we see No 42 Hindson (9th), No 16 Stroh (10th), and No 55 Peter Gregg on the inside, fourth in line in this image, near the back of the grid on the starter lap. (News cutting from the period.)

Famous father, soon-to-be-famous son: Bob Holbert (standing) with a young Al Holbert and the Holbert dealership's 914/6, acquired from Peter Gregg. (U)

strategy for 1971: to run the 914/6 in a modified format, reflecting the GT available in Europe. The entries would be supported by Porsche+Audi and their dealers. They would also encourage privateers to campaign the less-exotic 914-4. Hoppen still had to keep the 911 owners sweet, too, because in various ways he was also supporting plenty of top drivers racing with the 911s, and they regularly took the honours in the SCCA races right up to the Trans Am category. On the other hand, he was under pressure to promote, launch and sell the 914s to a much wider audience, spending his budget promoting the new cars.

In another building, the SCCA was listening to the protests from the Datsun and Leyland teams regarding the 914/6: they had also heard about the 914/6 GT, which looked as if it would be more powerful than the regular 914s run in 1970, and that the GTs were being specially built in Stuttgart. They were not happy. The SCCA had also come into conflict with the Porsche teams of the last few years, concerned about the domination of the 911s. If things went on the way they were, it looked as if no one but Porsche would get a look-in. They did not want Hoppen to run the 914/6 GT in Production 'C,' so decided, for 1971, to allow the growing number of Hoppen's 'racing in Production class' customers to run in class 'E' with the 914 four-cylinder cars, but to ban the six-cylinder cars from this class.

Hoppen mulled it over, because, in fact, the results in 1970 had been a mixture of good and disappointing. In the Midwest, Art Bunker took six SCCA national victories, while Kendall Noah got three more wins. On the eastern side, Peter Gregg's team did not have it all their own way, Gregg and sidekick Pete Harrison finishing with 2nd places several times, and only scoring two wins for

223

Porsche The Racing 914s

An 'E' Production 914 four-cylinder example. Note the slightly flared rear arches: allowed by the regulations, but not the full GT kit. (CF)

the 914/6. In the west, Alan Johnson, driving for Richie Ginther, won four times early in the season.

Going into 1971, Hoppen, being sensitive to the SCCA comments, decided on a different plan. Certainly, getting hold of the 914/6 GTs was one thing, but when the SCCA found out that only a few of the true factory cars had been built officially at Porsche, they banned them Protests from Datsun and the Triumph teams under the British Leyland banner were upheld. Things did not look good; the GT kits being offered convinced the SCCA to think that all the 914/6s would be to the same specification as the few factory cars.

If the SCCA would not play ball, Hoppen decided, he would outflank them. In addition to running in the national series, he would also enter a new series: the new International Motor Sports Association organization, formed only a few years previously.

The IMSA had been in the mind of Bill France, the founding father of NASCAR, for some time. In 1969 Bill France met with John Bishop, then executive director of SCCA, who, having set up the Trans Am programme, had become frustrated with the internal politics of the SCCA. IMSA was born, and Bishop was given sole control of the organization. France liked sole control – boards of directors were not for him. Bishop agreed, and was made the principal manager of the new organization.

The first race to be organized by IMSA in October 1969 at Pocono saw the SCCA threatening the circuit's management. The event went ahead, but with a lot of fighting between the parties, and it is said that it cost an extra $10,000 in rental fees for IMSA. The struggles went on through 1969. Then Bishop decided to establish a link with the FIA (Fédération Internationale de l'Automobile) 'Appendix J' World Championship for Makes sports cars, and in the closing months of 1970 a new championship emerged for Group 2 and Group 4 cars, with regulations set to allow equal competition between the groups. In 1971 a new class of Grand Touring (GT) was added, bringing international endurance racing to North America.

The series was to grow from strength to strength, and was the area that Jo Hoppen had in mind. Hoppen asked if the GT version of the 914/6 could be raced under IMSA rules, and the organisation said yes. That decision would be the start of a long association between Porsche and IMSA racing.

Richie Ginther Racing announced a programme to race a 911 at Le Mans, and to run a team of Porsche 914/6 GTs in the USA SCCA Production 'B' class, the same cars he raced in Production 'C' in 1970. Back then they were just 914/6s; now they would have the big-valve engines with twin-plug cylinder heads, fed by 46mm Webers from the GT programme, and race with considerably more bhp. He said at the time that they would also reduce the weight by 200lb by the extensive use of glass fibre panels. However, there was a snag – we will hear from Alan Johnson what happened in a moment.

Turning to Brumos Porsche, owned since August 1965 by Peter Gregg: they had a new driver, Hurley Haywood, and in 1971 they would win their class in six out of seven IMSA GTU events in a 914/6 GT, and by so doing win the series championship. Hurley Haywood told the author: "It was a good time. The 914/6 GT was great to drive. It was the first car I drove when I got back from National Service in Vietnam, having been there for most of 1969-1970. I had started racing with Peter Gregg in 1969. We won our class at the 6 Hour at Watkins Glen in the Brumos 911. When I came back from 'Nam in the later part of 1970, I rejoined Brumos and restarted with Peter for 1971. We still have that 914/6 GT car today. The livery was Brumos Porsche+Audi on the car; we were pretty excited. The colour was orange – the white, red and blue paint scheme didn't come until 1973."

The first race for Haywood on his return would be at the Daytona 24 Hours, but it didn't last long: the car, chosen by Peter Gregg and specially prepared in Stuttgart (chassis 914 043 0705), would go out after 260 laps. It's interesting, though, how fate takes a hand. Peter Gregg had flown to Stuttgart to see two cars that were being prepared in Zuffenhausen and to choose which one he wanted. The story goes that he spotted a cigarette burn on the seat of one of the cars, chassis 1017. Peter was a perfectionist, so he chose the 0705 car, which had been a training car for the 1970 Targa Florio. Had he chosen the other, it might have been him and Hurley Haywood who won their class at Daytona.

The Daytona 24 Hours, 30-31 January, round 2 of the International Championship for Manufacturers, was run for prototypes Group 6, sports cars Group 5, Grand Touring Group 4 and Touring Cars. Fifty cars started of the 63 that qualified; remarkably, 48 finished. The winners, Pedro Rodríguez and Jackie Oliver, covered 688 laps in that time in their John Wyer 917K, having qualified 2nd on the grid to pole-sitters Mark Donohue and David Hobbs in the Ferrari 512M. Most importantly to our study, the class winners of the up-to-2.5L GT class were Jacques Duval/George Nicholas/Bob Bailey in a 914/6 GT (No 5), said to be chassis 043 1017. Finishing 7th overall, this was a fine achievement for this car. Listed as being originally delivered on loan to the French Porsche importers Sonauto in 1970, it was returned to the Porsche factory and rebuilt as a GT race car in Zuffenhausen and prepared to go to the Daytona 24 Hours for Jacques Duval, who had placed the order for a 914/6 GT through his Montreal Porsche dealer. Had Peter Gregg not been put off by the cigarette burn, he could have

Porsche The Racing 914s

Two 914/6s and a 911 were used as pace cars to start the Daytona 24 Hours in 1971. (©P)

been in Duval's position instead! It is said that Duval was not happy when the car arrived, having paid a tidy sum: $12,000 – a lot in 1971 for what was a relatively unproven racing car. He had expected it to be 100% immaculate, though he was unaware at the time of why Gregg had chosen the other car. He found out after the race and had a good laugh!

In 8th overall and just a few laps back was the team of Stephen Behr/John Buffum and, from Germany, Erwin Kremer (No 19) in chassis 043 0691, previously raced in 1970 by Autohaus Max Moritz utilizing the factory GT kit upgrade, and now having been supplied to Ralph Meaney Inc. In the No 18 car, chassis 043 663, was Ralph himself. Ralph, who had won the GTU 2L class at the 1970 Daytona 24 Hours in a 911, told the author: "I had three GT cars and with the development work we had done on 1970 when we got the new ones, I stripped them out and made all the modifications

The No 59 914/6 GT, chassis 043 0705, of Peter Gregg/Hurley Haywood, prepared especially in Zuffenhausen for the Daytona 24 and Peter Gregg's team. The Porsche orange-liveried car suffered engine failure after 260 laps, putting an end to their challenge. Had Peter Gregg chosen another car over this one, the result may have been different. (©MK BO)

226

Big country Racing in the USA 1970-1975

A great image of Daytona: the No 18 car of Ralph Meaney low down on the inner line, with the No 19 of Behr/Buffum/Kremer at the front of the image. (©P)

The Ralph Meaney-tuned 914/6 GT, duly modified after a year's experience in 1970. This is the Stephen Behr/John Buffum/Erwin Kremer car, tussling with 4th place finishers DeLorenzo/Yenko/Mahler's Chevrolet Corvette at the 1971 Daytona 24 Hours. (©LG)

Class winners Jacques Duval/George Nicholas/Bob Bailey: 7th overall first time out for the remarkable 914/6 GT, beating 43 more powerful cars. (©P)

that I knew we could do. At Daytona I was clocked at 170mph and no one else could get that then. I mean, it was quick!

"It was orange originally, and then I changed it over to green. It was at Daytona that some of the guys got dirty: we found fine shotgun pellets in the fuel tank. The car was seen to be too quick, I guess; anyway, I was all the time trying to guard everything."

Ralph continues: "Bill Bean drove with me at Daytona. In 1970 we had finished 14th overall and won the up-to-2L class in the 911. The 914 was a blessing to drive. That car – I couldn't believe it, even though I was making them really fly." Ralph Meaney's trio of cars had been acquired with help from Jo Hoppen pressing the right buttons with Porsche in Europe. Hoppen had all the right contacts, including communications with the Max Moritz organization, prominent Porsche customer/partner company at the time. Along with the Sun Oil team car and the Brumos-entered 914, this year Meaney was part of the push by Porsche+Audi to promote the 914/6 GT big time.

The Sun Oil (Sunoco) No 5 car had qualified 28th on the grid with a time of 2min 15sec, actually tying the time of the No 19 car of Behr/Buffum/Kremer, putting them on 27th spot by dint of doing the time before the Sunoco car. However, the Brumos-entered car was the fastest in qualifying in the up-to-2.5L GTU class, on 23rd spot with a time of 2min 12.01sec. It had been a steady climb up the ladder for all of the 914/6 teams and it was looking good for all three, until the No 59 Brumos car started to have the engine maladies that sidelined them at the 260-lap mark. The No 18 entry of the Ralph Meaney team, with Ralph on board with Bill Bean and Gary Wright, had qualified in 33rd with a time of 2min 16.59sec. All was looking good, until several niggles slowed the car, including a clutch change that took just 34min! On into the night they went, but it is reported that, at 3am, Ralph arrived in the pits with his exhaust manifold gone. More time was lost, and he returned a little more than an hour later with more problems. They pressed on manfully, but were not running at the finish and had covered only 470 laps – effectively a dnf, but would have been 18th overall.

It had been a successful Daytona for Porsche, with the Rodríguez victory overall in the 917, the class victory for the Sunoco car, a 2nd in that class for the second Ralph Meaney-entered No 19 car and 3rd in that class for the 911T of Everett/Locke/Netterstrom, No 3. Generally a good day at the office.

Before we leave Daytona, there is a little anecdote attributed to Jacques Duval: "When we arrived at Daytona we found that we were in the stall alongside the other Sunoco-backed team of Roger Penske with the 512S. Penske was not at all happy to see this little unimportant team pitted right next to his!" As we have seen, in fact, it was the little guys from Canada who took a class victory, while Penske's team was only 3rd in their class!

The chassis number of the Peter Gregg/Hurley Haywood car, as listed in Janos Wimpffen's fine work, *Time and Two Seats*, is 914 043 0705. As we have already seen, chassis 0705 was one of the training cars at the 1970 Targa Florio. It has been suggested that Peter Gregg only had two 914/6 cars; however, the records show three: 0705, 0315, 2563 – all 1970 chassis. Not forgetting that he had one SCCA car left from the 1970 SCCA season (the second SCCA car is believed to have been sold to the Holberts). The new (to Brumos) 0705 car was to be used at Daytona for the 24 Hours, and at Sebring for the 12 Hours. It was the 0315 chassis that was used for the rest of the IMSA championship races.

Hurley Haywood confirmed: "The championship winning 914/6 GT that we have in our showroom today is 914 043 0315."

914 043 0315 is listed in one famous (or infamous) telex of the time as being supplied to the Luxembourg Porsche dealer André Losch, but it is more than likely that the 0315 car was diverted to Brumos. This was at a time when Porsche in Stuttgart was helping Jo Hoppen in the USA to get the 914/6 show on the road. Sadly, Peter Gregg is no longer with us to answer this point, but the 0315 car was certainly at Brumos in 1971. Hector Rebaque bought this car from Peter Gregg at the end of 1971, and would race it at the 1972 Daytona 6 Hours. Rebaque was no stranger to the 914/6, because Peter Gregg already had that 914/6 left over from the 1970 season, and this is the car he rented out to Hector Rebaque/Guillermo Rojas for the 1971 season (the fourth car). The important point here is that Brumos ran several 914/6s in 1971. On 14 February, a 914 in road trim, probably a 914/6, was seen again on the famous banking of Daytona, when it was utilized as pace car.

Moving on to the next race, we find four 914/6 GTs entered. This was the Sebring 12 Hours, run on 20 March 1971 on a warm, dry day. Fifty-seven cars lined up to start, and all 57 finished. It was round 3 of the International Championship for Manufacturers,

Tom Adams, Lieutenant Governor of the State of Florida, drives the 914/6 pace car on the 14 February at the Daytona 500 NASCAR race. The aforementioned Bill France is in the passenger seat. (©P)

Big country Racing in the USA 1970-1975

Stephen Behr/John Buffum/Pete Conrad's 914/6 GT, the second Ralph Meaney entry at Sebring 1971. (LG)

and round 2 of the Triple Crown, which consisted of the Daytona 24 Hours, the Sebring 12 Hours and the Le Mans 24 Hours. The Brumos (No 59) car 043 0705 was again present for Gregg/Haywood, who were joined by the Ralph Meaney-entered (No 28, chassis 043 0663) car with Ralph himself, Gary Wright and Forry Laucks, along with class winners from Daytona, Jacques Duval/George Nicholas/Bob Bailey in the yellow Sunoco 0431017 car (No 5), and finally Stephen Behr, John Buffum and former astronaut Pete Conrad in the No 29 car – a second Ralph Meaney entry, chassis 043 0691.

Feathers would fly in the big classes during the race, as it seems an incident occurred involving the Roger Penske-entered Ferrari of Mark Donohue, which was hit from behind by John Wyer's entry, driven by Pedro Rodríguez. Both cars needed work, but Rodríguez left the pits with a fair portion of his bodywork missing. Penske complained about the actions of the John Wyer car, but the officials saw it differently, and it looked like Donohue would be penalized. Penske then made official protests, and it started to get out of hand. Eventually it was sorted out, and didn't affect the overall positions in the race.

The Gregg/Haywood 914 is passed by the No 34 Alfa Romeo of Vaccarella/Hezemans. The Alfa went out after 27 laps, whilst the 914/6 GT went on to 14th overall and 2nd in the 2.5L class at the Sebring 12 Hours 1971. (LG)

Another good performance from Jacques Duval/George Nicholas/Bob Bailey in the Sunoco 914/6 GT: 17th overall; 4th in the 2.5L class. (©P)

The race was won by Vic Elford/Gérard Larrousse in the Hans Dieter Dechent-entered Porsche 917K, with 2nd the Autodelta works Alfa 33/3 of Giovanni Galli/Rolf Stommelen, and the second Autodelta entry of Andrea de Adamich/Henri Pescarolo/Nino Vaccarella in 3rd. This race showed the pace that the 914/6 would have to muster at this level of racing, the highest-placed 914 being the Brumos car of Gregg/Haywood in 14th; 2nd in the GT up-to-2.5L class. Next to finish was the No 28 car of Meaney/Wright/Laucks, but they were classified as not running at the finish after their gearbox failed on lap 187. Also on 187 laps and classified 17th were Duval/Nicholas/Bailey. The No 29 car finished but was not classified, having covered only 112 laps.

The next race on the calendar for the 914 was the start of the aforementioned IMSA GT Championship series, a new series created to meet the demands of the manufacturers of Grand Touring cars. Entered for the championship in this first race was the Brumos team 914/6 GT new chassis 043 0315. There were to be six races in the championship: the Danville 300 Miles at Virginia International Raceway, 200 Miles at Talladega, Charlotte 3 Hours, Bridgehampton 3 Hours, Summit Point 250 Miles, and the 200 Miles of Daytona. At the first race on 17-18 April 1971, 27 cars entered, including two 914/6s. One, of course, No 59, was the Brumos car, the second being the No 29 car of Ralph Meaney. Ninety-four laps would decide the outcome, with the 914/6s running in the GTU class. The Danville

Big country Racing in the USA 1970-1975

300 would see first blood go to the pairing of Peter Gregg/Hurley Haywood. Haywood told the author: "Peter and I were battling like crazy with the Corvettes and Camaros, and we beat them all. It was our first win in the successful hunt for the championship at that race in Danville, Virginia. We found we now had a great car; that mid-engine concept was something really important for Porsche. We started to sell a lot of them because of the racing at this higher level."

For what happened in the race, we can do no better than turn to a report from the period magazine *Competition Press and Autoweek*, 8 May 1971, by Phil Allen: "Danville, Va, 18 April – Peter Gregg and Hurley Haywood, driving a Porsche 914/6, took advantage of an off-course excursion by the leading Corvette of Dave Heinz to post a two-lap margin of victory in today's Danville 300, first event in the new International Motor Sports Association

A first outright victory for the No 59 Gregg/Haywood 914/6 (chassis 0315) at the Danville 300 on the open-track, limit-free Virginia International Raceway. (MK BO)

Porsche The Racing 914s

By now, the advertising boys were taking advantage of the early success. (JS)

(IMSA) Grand Touring series. A field of 24 starters took the green flag before a crowd estimated at 10,000. The race, billed as a showdown between American horsepower and European handling, proved to be just that. Although the event was to be the debut of American subcompacts, Chevrolet's Vega and Ford's Pinto, neither of the two marques made an appearance here this weekend. But, even without the debut of the new subcompacts, the race was marked with close competition. Never more than 10 seconds separated the Gregg/Haywood Porsche 914/6 and the Heinz Corvette. Pole-sitter Heinz slipped off-course near the end of the 94-lap contest and had to pit for repair work to his left-front fender. 1st – (59) Peter Gregg/Hurley Haywood, Porsche 914/6 (1st under-2.5L GT); 2nd – (57) Dave Heinz, Corvette (1st over-2.5L GT); 3rd – (29) Ralph Meaney, Porsche 914/6."

A 1st and 3rd in this IMSA championship race was a fine performance that included beating two 911Ss into 4th and 5th places, namely Pete Harrison and Jack Rabold.

Just a few weeks later came the Talladega 200 Miles IMSA (US national) race, held at the Talladega Superspeedway on 15 May 1971. It would be over 50 laps on the 4-mile road course, a total distance of 200 miles. This time, Dave Heinz in the mighty (No 57) V8 7L Chevrolet Corvette got the better of the 914/6 GT of the Brumos boys in the No 59 car, taking a lap out of them and finishing in 1st place. Second on 49 laps were Peter Gregg/Hurley Haywood, with Michael Keyser in his (No 48) 911S in 3rd. However, by finishing 2nd overall, the 914/6 of Gregg/Haywood took the top spot in the GTU IMSA class. Canadian Harry Bytzek would make an appearance at this race in his 914/6 GT (No 19), said to be chassis 043 0033 – a privateer team that was to

Big country Racing in the USA 1970-1975

become quite well known, having started with his 911 in 1970, and taking three podium positions. At Talladega, though, he came home 5th overall in a 914/6 built into a GT, utilizing the factory GT kit. The car, originally built in November 1969, was one of the early 914/6s.

A week after Talladega, on 23 May 1971, came the IMSA GT Piedmont 3 Hours of Charlotte, held on the 1.75-mile road course at the Charlotte Motor Speedway, over 146 laps, a distance of 255.5 miles. Chevrolet driver Dave Heinz had Or Costanzo as second driver, since 1967 a man well familiar with handling the big Corvettes. The 7L power should have proved too much over the longer distance, and in terms of final positions it did, as Heinz/ Costanzo took the top spot overall. But here again, the relatively small 914/6 GT of Gregg/Haywood only lost one lap of the 146 to the 'Vette. A fine performance, and another race GTU class victory ahead of several hot 911Ss. The Ralph Meaney-entered 914/6 (0691), driven by Stephen Behr (No 29) was 5th on 137 laps.

Over in Europe, the Americans were racing in force at the Le Mans 24 Hours in June, mainly Ferraris and Porsche 911s – but not in 914s. Whilst our work now concentrates primarily on IMSA, we cannot overlook that racing in the SCCA championships was ongoing, and on 23 June it's worth a mention that, at Laguna Seca, a race report from the period states: "Most of the excitement for the crowd came in the 'E' Production race won by Elliott Forbes-

Harry Bytzek's 914/6 (No 19) sits on the grid (l). The No 59 car receives attention, whilst it looks like a drivers' briefing is taking place by the trackside. (DP)

233

Robinson in the works Ginther Porsche 914 (one of the cars changed from the previous year's 'C' Production to 'E' Production). Twenty cars started but only 11 finished." The report continues: "Dwight Mitchell, who was leading in his 914 (40mm Solex carburetted and going as if Rudi Caracciola himself were in pursuit), sailed up the banking on the outside of the downhill turn 7 and let Forbes-Robinson through into the lead." Another 914, it seems, had dumped all its oil while a marshal was looking the wrong way, and all hell let loose, with cars going off in all directions, "... except for the cool Forbes-Robinson, who kept his head and took victory."

Interestingly, Walt Maas, who we will hear of later, was also in this race in a Datsun 240Z. Elliott Forbes-Robinson would take over the Dwight Mitchell car that was being run by Garretson's, future sponsor of Walt Maas, who would win the GTU championship in a 914/6 in 1977.

Those in the IMSA championship would look now to 27 June and the 93 laps of the 2.85-mile road course that formed the inner part of the Bridgehampton Raceway for the IMSA 3 Hours of Bridgehampton, some 265.05 miles of high-speed driving. Six of the Chevy Corvettes were there, and starting on pole was the Rodney Harris/John Paul 427 Corvette of the ESPA Racing Team (No 18). David Heinz, the regular challenger to the Brumos team for overall championship honours, but running in the GTO class, was giving this race a miss. Thirty-two cars lined up. Peter Gregg, doing a double stint driving, would be in the championship-contending car with Haywood, the regular No 59 914/6 (043 0315), but would be joined at Bridgehampton by a second Brumos 914/6 (thought to be the 043 0705 chassis used at Daytona and Sebring) driven by Harry Theodoracopulos (No 58), a long-time friend and business acquaintance. 'Superman' Peter Gregg would switch from car to car to co-drive not only with Hurley Haywood, but also with Harry Theodoracopulos. Theodoracopulos was a very experienced driver, having started racing in the bigger classes back in 1961. Harry Bytzek was along, too, with brother Klaus this time, running in the No 19 914/6. The race result saw a storming overall victory for the Gregg/Haywood combination, with the Corvette snapping at their heels, both on 93 laps. Peter Gregg also achieved a 3rd place on 92 laps with Harry Theodoracopulos. Harry Bytzek finished off a great weekend for the 914/6 GTs by coming home in 4th on 91 laps. Once again a magnificent victory, and more points in the championship.

Garretson sponsored: the modified 'E' Production 914/6 in the Garretson Electronics factory, one of the previous year's SCCA Production 'C' cars no longer allowed in that class. (JS)

Big country Racing in the USA 1970-1975

Gregg: 1st and 3rd in the same race: doing a double stint driving in the championship-contending car, the regular (No 59) 914/6 (043 0315), with Haywood at the IMSA 3 Hours, Bridgehampton. (MK BO)

The second Brumos car, driven by Theodoracopulos at Bridgehampton and used also as a second car for the Guillermo Rojas/Hector Rebaque racing team later in 1971/early 72, according to an article in the Porsche magazine *Excellence* of October 1992 was "... totalled at Mid-Ohio in July 1972." In the same article, former Brumos crew chief Jim Bailie is quoted as saying: "It was rolled up into a ball and burned." It apparently went to the yard belonging to Denis Aase, well-known in Porsche circles, and subsequently to the crusher. That No 58, if we take a view from the fact that the 2563 still exists today, is implied to be chassis 0705.

Porsche The Racing 914s

At the Watkins Glen 6 Hours on 24 July 1971, although not an IMSA-counting round, Brumos Porsche+Audi would put in an entry for the showpiece event. This year, this major calendar event would be held in warm, humid conditions, and had attracted all the front runners, being the 11th and penultimate round of the International Championship for Manufacturers.

The motor racing world was reeling from the death of one its greatest ever sports car drivers: Pedro Rodríguez (as mentioned in the earlier chapter about racing in Europe) who had died as a result of horrific injuries incurred in an accident with his Ferrari 512 at the Norisring in Germany. Although mourning his passing, everyone at Watkins Glen would have to cope with this familiar risk, remember a great personality, and move on.

Thirty-five cars practised; 26 would start and all 26 would finish. Five 914/6s were entered; two did not arrive. Of those that did, only the Gregg/Haywood car qualified to start under the 130% rule in place in this international race. Left watching would be the Sunoco car of Jacques Duval/George Nicholas, No 5, and the No 12 car of US astronaut Pete Conrad, driving with Raymond Caldwell. The track layout was to have been improved, but due to delays it was an interim circuit that faced the drivers on the first day of practice.

Alfa Romeo was about to challenge Porsche's lead in the top class of the International Championship – it had even prised Vic Elford away from Porsche for a one-off drive. Pole position, though, would be set by Mark Donohue/David Hobbs in the Roger Penske-entered Ferrari 512M, nearly a second faster than the Porsche 917K of Jo Siffert/Gijs van Lennep. For four of the Porsche 911s in the 2.5L class it was a bad day at the office, as they were to be humiliated by the pesky 914/6 GT of the regular IMSA podium attendees Peter Gregg/Hurley Haywood, the quick 914/6 even out-qualifying the 911Ss. Gregg/Haywood sat on pole in the GT up-to-2.5L class and converted that into a fine class-winning performance, finishing 6th overall in the race, which finished after 279 laps had been completed by the winner on the 2.428-mile (3.907km) circuit. The race was won by Andrea de Adamich/Ronnie Peterson in the Autodelta Alfa Romeo 33/3. Second came the Siffert/van Lennep Porsche 917K, and 3rd the second John Wyer Gulf 917K of Derek Bell/Richard Attwood. Those finishes gave Porsche the title in the Manufacturers' International Championship, ahead of Alfa Romeo. The 6th place of Peter Gregg and Hurley Haywood helped Porsche to win the Grand Touring Trophy section of that championship, trouncing Corvette by 70 points to 32. Porsche also won that year's Challenge Mondiale and the Marques' Standard Points Championship, again ahead of Alfa Romeo.

Back on the IMSA GTU Championship trail, the Summit

Watkins Glen 1971: the No 49 Greenwood-entered Corvette of Robert Johnson/John Greenwood. No 68 is the Baker Racing entry of Patrick Keating/Levon Pentecost/Anthony Torgersen. No 59, of course, is the Peter Gregg/Hurley Haywood 914/6. (JG)

The No 59 914/6 GT car run at the Watkins Glen 6 Hours, according to the results in Time and Two Seats by Janos Wimpffen, is chassis 043 2563, another 1970 chassis Brumos car. Peter Gregg/Hurley Haywood would finish a very credible 6th overall and take the class win in the up-to-2.5L category. (MK BO)

Point 250 Miles, the penultimate race in the first IMSA GTU Championship series, was held on 19 September 1971 over 125 laps of the 2-mile road course at the Summit Point Raceway. It turned into 250 miles of flat-out racing. Dave Heinz in the big Corvette was there; he took pole, the No 57 car being co-driven by Don Yenko, a very experienced driver who had started his racing career in 1957. Second on the grid would be the No 1 911S of Michael Keyser/Bob Bailey. Third on the grid would be Robert Hennig/Charlie Cook in an AMC Javelin, and alongside the No 21 car and fourth on the grid was the No 59 of the Brumos-entered 914/6, the regular car (chassis 0315) of Peter Gregg/Hurley Haywood. Fifth on the grid was the second 914/6 GT, No 19, of Harry Bytzek. A third was the No 12 car of Ralph Meaney/Sam Perry (043 0691).

As the race got under way, fireworks began when Dave Heinz in the Corvette went out on lap 37, followed soon after on lap 63 by the AMC Javelin. Excitement was building as the special 911 of Bruce Jennings, starting from P15 on the grid, carved his way through the field and the Brumos 914/6 had got past the 2.5L 911S of Keyser/Bailey. As the chequered flag came out, it was another class victory for the Peter Gregg/Hurley Haywood team. That win was sufficient to clinch the IMSA GTU title, and would launch Haywood onto an illustrious career in the years that followed.

The 125-lap race had lasted 3h 27min 21sec; the 914/6 average speed had been 72.336mph, including pit stops, of course. For the record, Bruce Jennings also got past the 911 of Keyser to take 2nd on 124 laps, along with Bob Beasley in his 911, also on 124 laps. Fifth overall was Harry Bytzek on 122 laps, a lap ahead of the 6th-placed Chevrolet Camaro. Ralph Meaney/Sam Perry had a quiet drive from 13th on the grid to 28th. This would be the last professional race for chassis 0691, as the car was sold and repainted, and would eventually appear in historic racing in later years.

The final race of the IMSA Championship season would be at Daytona on 21 November, the outcome being a two-lap victory for the Chevrolet Corvette of Dave Heinz/Don Yenko. The Brumos boys did not take part. Having cleaned up the championship already, they were planning the 1972 season's efforts. Big smiles all round. Also, in the prestigious Porsche Cup Championship, a worldwide challenge sponsored by Porsche in Germany, Peter Gregg/Hurley Haywood were each credited with 9th place overall, with 56 points that netted them each a prize of $2700. Hurley Haywood told the author: "We had some great fun in that little car, always trying for outright victory." He also said: "We had no problems, because of course we could mount the oil coolers in the front bumper and do other modifications under the IMSA rules that we could not do in the SCCA series."

Back in August, before the Summit Point IMSA race, over the border in Canada, Klaus Bytzek/Harry Bytzek ran at Mosport Park in a round of the Canadian Endurance Championships. They took 2nd in class, and from the records it seems they also finished 2nd overall in the Canadian Championship at the end of the year. In the SCCA Production series, the 914 had continued to race on, unsupported by the Porsche+Audi competition management.

1971 saw Bob Hindson repeated as Midwestern Division SCCA Champion. With the four-cylinder cars now also racing in regional SCCA events, Hoppen saw an opportunity to win 'E' Production at Atlanta in 1971, so he got Ginther and Elliott Forbes-Robinson to campaign the four-cylinder cars. At the SCCA Central Division run-offs, Hindson lost to fellow 914 driver George Parish, while another young man, then known only as Bob Holbert's son, Al, finished 3rd.

Alan Johnson entered in the SCCA in 'B' Production class in 1971, where the bigger arches and engine modifications were allowed. However, as mentioned earlier, questions were being asked as to whether this was truly a Production car, and Jo Hoppen had serious discussions with the SCCA. In the SCCA boardroom, oozing with tradition, they were watching when, in early summer 1971, shortly after acquisition of the new car, Johnson entered an SCCA national at Laguna Seca with classes 'A', 'B' and 'C' all running together. In practice he came in 3rd fastest overall, ahead of several much more powerful 'A' Production cars. In the race, Johnson in his 'B' class car charged off after the leading 'A' class Production Corvette, driven by the then reigning Production champion, staying with him and closing until brake fade forced Johnson to drop back.

Alan Johnson told the author: "Porsche at that time had provided the kit to make a 914/6 into a 914/6 GT, and it involved twin-plug cylinder heads and ignition systems, fender flairs, wider wheels, and I think bigger brakes – I'm not sure about all of the various things that made up that car, but in April or May we had done some testing with the car and it was somewhat quicker than the regular 914/6. We took it for an SCCA National Championship race at Laguna Seca in June. I was driving, and I was doing very well. It was a top Production car race with 'A' Production, 'B' Production – all the classes in together. I was running 2nd to a Corvette, and I was staying with the Corvette very close.

"Well, what happened was the SCCA saw this, and of course the 914/6 GT was already getting the SCCA agitated. This was too fast a car, and it was deemed not to have been a Production-made car by Porsche, so they disqualified it!

237

Porsche The Racing 914s

A young Al Holbert ran in the SCCA 'C' Production class with the 914, not fitted with the GT kit, in 1971, finishing 3rd in the Central Division run-offs. (SS)

"From that point on it was not allowed to run in 'B' Prod. That car sat for about a year or so in Richie's workshop (Richie Ginther), so I bought it myself to use personally, painted it up; I had an Eagle put on the hood and a fancy paint job! I used it just for promotional purposes; I took it out at Porsche Club events and gave people laps in it and that kind of thing. It was eventually bought by Jim Cook and he used it in Trans Am for a little while.

"I did not race for a few years. I established my own business, a Porsche and Audi dealership in San Diego, and put a lot of work into it. Then the 924 came along." (Note: The full story of the Racing 924s can be studied in the author's work *The Porsche 924 Carrera – Evolution to excellence*, published by Veloce.)

As we have now seen, the 914/6 GT was too quick for the SCCA. Fine for IMSA GTU, but to the SCCA it was a no-no. Investigations had, of course, proven that the GT version, either with the kit from the Porsche factory or an actual 'works' type car, was certainly not a true Production car. After the IMSA Summit Point race, the Brumos cars were parked up, but the championship winner was to have a new life in 1972. Guillermo Rojas told the author: "Mr Hector Rebaque Sr was always committed to supporting his son, Hector Jr. When young Hector Rebaque started to race, Rebaque Sr asked me if I would like to bring young Hector, who was 15 years old, onboard and create together the Rebaque-Rojas Racing Team, later named RVR (Rojas-Van Beuren-Rebaque) with the addition of Freddy Van Beuren. To start this adventure, we bought a Porsche 914/6 – the 1971 IMSA Championship car (0315) – from Peter Gregg of Brumos Porsche at the beginning of 1972. It was agreed that we would have technical support from Brumos Porsche, and Brumos would enter us to run in a number of races, the first one being the 6 Hours of Daytona."

The author contacted Hector Rebaque, who said: "This was a crucial moment in my racing career, as I started to race

Fifteen-year-old Hector Rebaque, a star driver right from the very beginning, was brought on by his father, Hector Alonso Rebaque Sr. Guillermo Rojas took the youngster under his wing to develop his talents. Daytona was the first major race for the team. (Rojas)

Big country Racing in the USA 1970-1975

The 0315 car, now driven by Hector Rebaque/Guillermo Rojas and entered by Brumos, was the former Peter Gregg/Hurley Haywood championship car. They qualified 41st on the grid, but would come to a stop on lap 70 to record a dnf. (MK BO)

239

internationally and in a team, not by myself, and also in a faster car, the 914/6 GT. The concept of the 914 was great: lower centre of gravity, central engine and very, very trustable, which resulted in a very good concept which, I think, Porsche should have developed more. It allowed our team to win many times."

The 6 Hours of Daytona was held on 6 February 1972 and designated as round 2 of the World Manufacturers' Championship. The race had been shortened to six hours due to a fear that the new engines in the series, based on the 3L F1 format of the period, would not last the distance of 24 hours, which threatened to impact on the size of the crowd. Because of this, in addition to the fact that the FIA said they only wanted one 24-hour race, race organizer Bill France decided not to take any chances. Of the 72 cars entered, only 60 turned up and qualified. Four 914/6s were entered, though this dropped to three. The No 58, the Brumos-entered former Peter Gregg/Hurley Haywood car, was to be driven by Hector Rebaque/Guillermo Rojas. They qualified 41st on the grid. Joining them were the Lee McDonald-entered No 72 car for Lee and Bert Everett, which qualified 33rd on the grid, along with No 81 (chassis 043 0332), the former SCCA car previously run under the Art Bunker team in 1970, now somewhat modified and running like the other 914s as a GT in the up-to-2.5L class. It was entered by Daniel Muñiz, and driven by Daniel with Rubén Novoa. They qualified 51st on the grid.

All eyes would be on the front runners: three Ferrari 312PBs from the Ferrari factory team, and the works Alfa Romeo 33s. In the end, it was the Ferrari 312PB of Mario Andretti/Jackie Ickx that won by two laps. Peter Gregg/Hurley Haywood had returned to the Porsche 911S, and took the class victory in the up-to-2.5L GT class. Incredibly, Daniel Muñiz/Rubén Novoa came home 13th overall and 3rd in the up-to-2.5L GT class. The other two 914 race teams didn't fare so well, with No 72 finishing but unclassified and the Brumos No 58 going out of the race on lap 70.

The Sebring 12 Hours brought no better luck. Round 3 of the World Manufacturers' Championship on 25 March 1972 showed that the 914/6 GT was approaching its sell-by date in the kind of company it kept at World Championship level. Just a year before, at Daytona, Jacques Duval had finished 7th overall, winning the GT class, and at Sebring Peter Gregg/Hurley Haywood had finished 14th overall and 2nd in the GT class. In 1972, however, the competition had moved on. The 911S 2.5L of Gregg/Haywood was considerably more powerful and took the GT class, finishing 5th overall. This year the No 78 car of Daniel Muñiz/José Luis/Rubén Novoa did the business, finishing in the top ten, 9th overall, after qualifying 50th on the grid, 25 places down on the No 59 Brumos 911S. It was reliability, rather than performance, that had got the Muñiz No 78 car through 207 laps in the 12 hours. The winners – Andretti/Ickx in the Ferrari 312PB again – qualified on pole, and in the race completed 259 laps of the 5.2-mile (8.369 km) circuit. 15th overall and 6th in GT came the No 27 car of Robert Kirby/John Hotchkis; Bill Cuddy is also listed as driving this Bozzani Porsche-entered car on 189 laps, having qualified 29th on the grid. It is not

Daniel Muñiz, ahead of the Bruce Jennings/Bob Beasley 911S that finished 11th overall. Sebring 1972. (MK BO)

Big country Racing in the USA 1970-1975

Robert Kirby/John Hotchkis in the Bozzani Porsche-entered car completed 189 laps to finish 15th overall of the 62 starters. (MK BO)

Lee McDonald/Bert Everett – out with an oil leak on lap 22 after a credible 38th place out of the 62 starters in qualifying. (MK BO)

Porsche The Racing 914s

clear if this is the Bozzani (Johnson) 043 1571 car, though it's a fair bet that it was this car. The No 70 914/6 of Lee McDonald/Brett Everett had to park up in the pits after an oil leak stopped their progress from 38th on the grid on lap 22. David McClain/Dave White in the No 19 car qualified 49th, but got only as far as lap 51 in the race, when the engine said: "No more, thank you."

Robert Stoddard/Joe Hines Jr/Frank Harmstad in the No 68 car completed 168 laps from their 35th place on the grid, the fastest 914/6 in qualifying, before their day ended in the pits. Hector Rebaque/Guillermo Rojas only got as far as lap 152 in their Brumos-entered car from their starting position of 46th.

Next up, a week later on 1 April, came the Starlight Daytona 3

David McClain/Dave White's 914 tussles with the Ferrari 365B of Harry Ingle/Charles Reynolds. Lee McDonald is tucked in behind the Ferrari, with the Camaro of Houghton Smith/Bert Gafford about to bear down on the trio. Unfortunately, all were non-finishers. (MK BO)

Big country Racing in the USA 1970-1975

Hector Rebaque/Guillermo Rojas with the Brumos-entered No 58 (0315); mechanical problems thwarted their progress on lap 152. (MK BO)

Robert Stoddard/Joe Hines Jr about to be eaten by the 10th overall finishers Vince Gimondo/Billy Dingman in the growling 5L class-winning Camaro. The No 68 car got to the end but was not classified, having covered insufficient laps: 146 to the winners' 259. (MK BO)

243

Porsche The Racing 914s

Rebaque mixing it in Mexico 1972 prior to the Viceroy Sponsorship deal. (Rojas)

Hours and round 2 of the IMSA Camel GT Championship: 84 laps on the Daytona 3.81-mile road course. Dave McClain/Dave White in the regular No 19 car would claim 9th place overall. Charles Vincent/J Knott were in the 0-numbered Porsche 914/6, believed to be a GT-kitted car, finishing 11th. Roberto Quintanilla, in a similar car running No 48, would come home 36th. However, finishing 8th on 78 laps was the Bozzani Porsche+Audi-entered 58 car, with Hector Rebaque/Guillermo Rojas behind the wheel. Guillermo Rojas says: "We had a good try: Brumos and Bozzani had given us the support; young Hector had driven well, but we decided to return to Mexico to race in the Mexican National Championship." The Rebaque Rojas Racing Team, supported by Hector Rebaque Sr and later Freddy Van Beuren, would take the GT Championship in Mexico in 1972, then again in 1973, the 914 running with the colours and backing of Viceroy Cigarettes. They would also go back to the US to run at the Watkins Glen GT race on 10 September with Peter Gregg, which we will come to in a moment.

For now, we stay in the US and come to the Danville 250 IMSA GT race held at the Virginia International Raceway on 16 April 1972: 80 laps on the 3.25-mile road course – 260 miles total. This was the scene where, in 1971, Peter Gregg/Hurley Haywood scored their first victory for the 914 in the IMSA Championship. This year, though, both had moved on to the new 911S. Running with No 78 was the Daniel Muñiz-entered 914/6 0332 chassis for himself and Fred Van Beuren IV. Fifty-two cars were entered in this GT race, which was won by the aforementioned Peter Gregg/Hurley Haywood in the Brumos 911S No 59 car, which, due to its preparation and performance, would dominate this class in 72/73. The Muñiz 914/6 was the only 914 in the race, and gives a clue to the preparation and performance of this car, too, when one sees on the results sheet that the No 78 car came home 3rd overall, beaten only by the Gregg/Haywood 911S (2.5L), while 2nd place went to the Toad Hall Racing Team entry from Towson, Maryland, with well-known Michael Keyser/Bob Beasley driving, also a 2.5L 911S. Behind the 914 were nine more 911Ss, and many Corvettes, Camaros and Fords.

Whilst we are concentrating mainly on the major national races, we must not overlook the SCCA rules races. One such race was at the Laguna Seca circuit on 6-7 May 1972. A series of Production races saw the 914 of Bill Cuddy out racing in the 'E' and 'C' Production event. A regular competitor in this arena, he would finish 2nd in his 'C' Production 914 to future champion Walt Maas in a Datsun 240Z. Richie Ginther continued to prepare the 914s with both four- and six-cylinder engines for the Production classes, as he had done in 1970 and 1971. The 914 was still popular, and would be seen regularly in the national and regional SCCA races. In fact, back during the winter in 1971, several versions were even seen ice racing! In one case, a certain Prince Leopold of Bavaria visited the Alaska Sports Car Club ice races, taking away the class 2 victory with a 914/6.

A press cutting from 1972 shows a 914/6 at the Annual Alaska Motorsports Club ice races. (P)

Big country Racing in the USA 1970-1975

Returning to the IMSA Championship races, at the Lime Rock 200 Miles on 29 May, Lee McDonald took his 914/6, running with race No 70, to 11th overall and 8th in the GTU class. On 9 July at the Mid-Ohio 6 Hours, a national IMSA GT race run over 187 laps of the 2.4-mile road course, McDonald was out again, but this time with Harry Bytzek sharing the No 70 car; they would finish 18th overall, 15 laps down on race winners Bob Beasley/Michael Keyser on 187 laps. Dave McClain/Dave White were even further back in their 914, having covered only 164 laps.

On 10 September at Watkins Glen, in the IMSA GT race over 93 laps of the 3.37-mile road course (313.41 miles), Peter Gregg had another Brumos double entry. Along with Hurley Haywood, he would win in their famous 911S, but he also entered the Hector Rebaque/Guillermo Rojas car.

A good run to 10th overall would provide interest to a prospective sponsor for what is thought to be the remainder of 1972 in Mexico and into 1973. In the colours of Viceroy Cigarettes, the 0315 was raced extensively in Mexico, including in the 1000km of Mexico, where the then 16-year-old Hector Rebaque, along with Guillermo Rojas, took a convincing victory, ten laps ahead of the 2nd placed 911S of Bolaños/Aguilar.

Guillermo Rojas told the author: "We raced the car for just one

Run both in Mexico and at Watkins Glen, the 1971 championship car would have a good run at the Glen to 10th place out of 54 runners. (Rojas)

Running in the Mexican Championship in 1973, the successful former Brumos car would show a clean pair of heels to the other racers in the hands of Hector Rebaque and Guillermo Rojas. (Rojas)

Peter Gregg and Brumos gave a lot of assistance to the Rebaque Rojas Racing Team, supported by Hector Rebaque Sr and, later, Freddy Van Beuren. They took the GT Championship in Mexico in 1972. Hector Rebaque says: "We didn't race the 914/6 for a long period of time [less than a year], but it gave us a lot of satisfaction." (Rojas)

245

Porsche The Racing 914s

A victory at the Monterrey race track (Mexico) 1972. The Rojas racing crew: (l-r) Filiberto Rodríguez, Othon Aspe, Salvador Izquierdo. At back-centre is Mario Balderas. (Rojas)

Guadalajara in the 1970s, an open windswept airfield. The Rojas/Rebaque car towards the end of its period in the hands of Rojas Racing. The team would use 911S with Viceroy sponsorship for the remainder of 1973 and into 1974. (Rojas)

Big country Racing in the USA 1970-1975

Reported to be the very car, 0315, alongside a sister car, seen at Amelia Island Concourse in 2015. One of these two is the 043 0315 championship-winning car, as confirmed by Hurley Haywood. The other one is stated on its display panel to be the car run at Watkins Glen 6 Hours, which would be chassis 043 2563, according to the records of that race. (Sp)

year and later sold it to Fidel Martínez. He also raced in the Mexican Championship with it for around two years and then sold it in Mexico to another racer – forgotten now."

0315 then fell off the radar until it was found in 1988, and the aforementioned Jim Bailie, Brumos crew chief in the 1970s, was tipped off. He got the car back to Brumos, where the car was restored for Hurley Haywood to run in historic racing events. This is the car frequently seen today at historic gatherings; when not in action, it resides in the Brumos showroom in Jacksonville.

Returning to the remainder of 1972, we find at the SCCA Road Atlanta finals a plethora of 914/6s in this annual finale to the SCCA Production classes season. Al Holbert took a 4th place, the highest-positioned 914/6. The cars still featured the low screen/no roof design as first applied in 1970.

Throughout 1972, Richie Ginther Racing saw its 914 four-cylinder versions continuing to provide winners in Production 'E' classes, especially when driven by Elliott Forbes-Robinson. The four-cylinder unit proved to be an interesting item to develop, as 2.3 and

247

Porsche The Racing 914s

Stefan Edlis, founder of injection moulding Apollo Plastics Corporation, running at Road Atlanta – unfortunately a dnf. The car was originally built by Al Holbert and later revised by Raetech. (Ferret)

Ginther got his 914 four-cylinder cars to the Atlanta finals in 1972 and won, but was disqualified because the rain tyres were mounted on wheels that were slightly too wide. Elliott Forbes-Robinson, the man at the wheel, defeated by the rules. (AJ)

Richie Ginther crouches to talk with Elliott Forbes-Robinson. Ginther's 914 four-cylinder cars ran successfully in Production 'E' during 1972. (CF)

2.5L capacity could be obtained; when dry sumped and highly tuned, this unit could put out 250+ bhp.

Richie Ginther (Team Manager), Harold Broughton (Team Mechanic) and Elliott Forbes-Robinson were to become a formidable partnership with the 914 four-cylinder model some years before Wayne Baker became one of the top men to tune a four-cylinder car. At the 1973 Daytona race, it was back to the 24-hour format, the fuss of 1972 committed to history. 3-4 February saw only one 914/6 GT, the No 38 car for Daniel Muñiz/Roberto Quintanilla turn up at the start of the World Manufacturers' Championship and round 1 of the Endurance Triple Crown (Daytona, Sebring, Le Mans). Some 670 laps of the 3.81-mile (6.13km) circuit would be covered by victors Peter Gregg/Hurley Haywood in a new, super-quick Porsche 911RSR. It was a sign, as we saw in the European chapters, that the days of the super-fast sports prototypes like the 908s and 917s had gone. They were present, but fell by the wayside, and it was ultra-reliability that won the day. In 1972, Daniel Muñiz/Roberto Quintanilla had qualified 56th on the grid for the Daytona 6 Hours, but in 1973 they were 53rd of the 53 that started! They were hoping for a repeat of the reliability that had got them up from 56th to 13th overall in 1972, but it wasn't to be: they did get to the finish, but various maladies meant that they only covered 215 laps, insufficient to be classified.

The Sebring 12 Hours was scheduled for 23 March. With so many entries, a preliminary qualifying race had to be arranged. At one point, though, it looked as if Sebring would not happen, with the FIA having taken the race out of the World Manufacturers' Championship calendar. The previous organizers, the ARCF (Automobile Racing Club Florida), decided it was now not worth backing! However, John Bishop's IMSA, a growing force in racing in the USA, stepped in and picked up the reins to put on a grand show. It was another step on the ladder for IMSA. With the sports cars from Matra, Porsche, Alfa Romeo, Lola and Mirage missing, the field this year lacked the big guns; however, their loss still brought a huge field of 89 entries for the local teams, and 72 cars would eventually start.

On a warm, dry day – guess what? – It would again be the Brumos Porsche RSR of Gregg/Haywood that took victory. Gregg,

Big country Racing in the USA 1970-1975

The now-black Daniel Muñiz/Roberto Quintanilla 914/6. This year Daytona would be run over 24 hours. Various maladies denied the pairing a good result, and they only covered 215 laps – insufficient to be classified. (MK BO)

having brought on board and teamed up with Hurley Haywood in 1971, had brought him to a point where his capabilities and stock of experience were now in big demand. On the 914/6 front, our interest homes in on the No 67 and 85 cars, 85 being the Don Parish/Ron Jones/John Hulen car entered by Don Parish. They would reach the end but were not classified, too few laps being the problem. However, the No 67 car of David McClain/Dave White finished, credited with 23rd place of the 24 classified finishers.

By 1973, after a period of development, it was clear that the 914/6, initially thought to be a no-hoper, could be very good when developed properly, and many were surprised it had done so well, especially the cars developed by the Brumos Company, Peter Gregg's organization. But racing was getting tougher. The Daytona 250 Miles, Mid-Ohio 6 Hours and Road America would not see 914 finishes under 25th overall. At the Westwood 7 Hours, otherwise known as the Province 500 for the Molson Cup, run by the Sports

Porsche The Racing 914s

David McClain/Dave White finished in 23rd place of the 24 classified finishers from the 72 starters, seen here dicing with the Corvette of non-finishers Bill Schumacher/Rick Hay at the new IMSA-run Sebring 12 Hours of 1973. (MK BO)

Gordon Barron in the Performance Unlimited 914-4 usually run in 'C' Production in the period, here running in the Province 500 for the Molson Cup. This image demonstrates the wide range of events that the 914 was racing in – not just IMSA and SCCA. (BM)

Car Club of British Columbia, we see a reasonable result, though the competition was not the highest grade. That is not to diminish the achievement of Gordon Barron/Todd Webb, who took 6th place in a 914/4, 30 laps behind the winning Porsche 911S; it was, after all, a four-cylinder.

The much higher profile Watkins Glen 6 Hours, which had seen 914/6 GT entries in the previous years, had none this year. Trouble was now looming internationally – a war in the Middle East led to a fuel crisis, due to an embargo by the Arab oil-producing countries. The world of motorsport waited. It was not good publicity, or morally acceptable, to be seen motor racing when the world was being starved of fuel. As winter arrived in the northern hemisphere, the 1974 Monte Carlo Rally was cancelled, as was the Daytona 24 Hours, followed by the

1973 Sebring 12 Hours: Don Parish/Ron Jones/John Hulen's 914/6 got to the finish okay, but with too few laps on the board due to mechanical mishaps and long pit stops. (LG)

Big country Racing in the USA 1970-1975

Sebring 12 Hours. With its own fuel supplies in the USA, NASCAR kept going, and so did the early races of the F1 season. Needless to say, with the big sports car races off, so were all the smaller events. Things only started to ease by late spring of 1974. Road racing restarted, though not all of the regular annual races took place, and some of those that did had a reduced format, with less distance to cover. The effects would be long-lasting, and thought would be given to how fuel consumption could be improved.

In Europe, the first race in the World Sports Car Championship would be the Monza 1000km on 25 April. In the USA, 21 April was the date of the first GT race, the Road Atlanta 6 Hours. Dave McClain was ready to run, carrying No 67 on the 914/6, however, 27 laps in, his race was over.

Pretty much all the runners and riders in the 914/6s were private entries now. As dealer teams moved their cars on, so new names began to appear in them; drivers such as John Hulen, Robert Kirby, John Hotchkis, Doc Bundy and Ron Coupland – men who would make their mark in the years to come, having started in a 914. Kirby went on to drive 17 more times in a 914 in the period covered by our study. At the Ontario 4 Hours, we see the 914/6 of new 914 entrant Rich Mandella, sharing the driving with Miles Gupton; they would be rewarded with 17th overall and 6th in GT. There was a no-score at the Mid-Ohio 5 Hours. At the Daytona 250 Miles, won by Hurley Haywood in the Carrera RSR, the 914/6 of Lee Cutler/M Campbell carried No 55 on the side, and finished down in 21st place. On 10 August at the IMSA GT race over 50 laps on the 4-mile road course at Talladega, McClain/White came home 15th overall. A week later, at Charlotte, John Hulen/Ron Coupland/Dave Causey finished 12th overall behind the winner, Peter Gregg, in the Brumos RSR. The Lime Rock IMSA GT races – plural because there were two races on 2 September 1974 – saw poor results from both the John Hulen and the McClain entries. The Atlanta Championship SCCA finals saw Frank Harmstad come home 8th in the No 69 car. It had been a scrappy year for the racing 914s, and there were rule changes on the horizon for the years to come.

Into 1975, and the annual international racing season kicked off with the Daytona 24 Hours, now run by the rapidly progressing IMSA organization. Due to large numbers of entries in the Group 5 class, the organizers, wanting to put on a big show, brought in the GT (2.5L) and the GTU (under-2.5L) classes. There was a fuss, too, over what the organizers of races saw as the ongoing European domination led by Porsche, who were still winning everything! So a new set of rules was introduced that would, in later years, be reflected in the AAGT rules (All-American GT). As the dust settled and the entries came in, amongst the 23 Porsche 911s of various

Robert Kirby/John Hotchkis/Len Jones at the Daytona 24 Hours 1975 with the Johnson Bozzani 914. (MK BO)

Eighteenth overall on 528 laps: the battered but not bowed 914/6 No 85 car of Hulen/Coupland/Engels, missing its front end. A fine performance against such superior machinery. (MK BO)

251

Porsche The Racing 914s

models, Corvettes, Camaros and Ferraris, we find three 914/6 GTs. One did not start (the No 55 of Lee Cutler), but the No 51 of Leonard Jones/Robert Kirby/John Hotchkis, and the No 85 car of John Hulen/Ron Coupland/Nick Engels did compete, the 51 car starting 30th and the 85 car 37th on the grid. But this was Daytona, and in that period there was only one car that could be counted on to win! The famous No 59 Brumos Carrera RSR would take four victories in 1975, having won five times in 1974. The preparation was legendary, and indeed after 684 laps the Gregg/Haywood combination crossed the line victors. Ten Porsche Carreras, a Ferrari and a Mazda filled the first 17 places (Porsche dominant? Surely not!). However, in 18th on 528 laps was the 85 Hulen/Coupland/Engels 914/6. A fine performance against such superior machinery. The No 51 car covered 229 laps before its engine cried enough, an early bath for Robert Kirby/John Hotchkis/Len Jones.

As tradition dictated, Sebring followed Daytona. A huge entry was received for the 12-hour race held on 21 March. Sebring was beginning to show its age, with poor spectator facilities and a track that was beginning to break up. Neglect and lack of investment were the cause. However, the cars were here to race around such maladies, and indeed that is exactly what they did, with a result that saw the Porsches beaten on American soil at last. The winner, with 238 laps completed, was the BMW CSL of BMW North America, with the impressive driver line-up of Brian Redman/Allan Moffat/Sam Posey/Hans Stuck (Jr).

It was cloudy but dry for the main event, which saw 72 starters. Of course Porsche 911 entries dominated, but in fact this time we see three 914/6s. One of these, the No 85 car with John Hulen aboard, had to run in a preliminary race to determine grid places 51 to 69; this was the same car that ran at Daytona. At Sebring, the

Al Holbert had created and entered this 914 with flared rear arches but standard front. It's thought this was a four-cylinder powered car. Doc Bundy/Bill Schmid finished the course, but with only 151 laps covered they were not classified. (MK BO)

Big country Racing in the USA 1970-1975

Hulen/Coupland/Causey car was given 57th place on the grid, but in the end it was to no avail, as they went out on lap 46. The No 51 Hotchkis/Kirby/Jones 914/6 fared not much better: starting from 30th and fastest qualifier in GTU on the grid, they were to go out on lap 51. The third car would be an interesting entry, this being one of the 1975-bodied 914s that had been fitted at the Holbert Racing workshops with the GT-like bodykit at the rear for running in SCCA events. Underneath that body was a four-cylinder engine, but what type is lost in the mist of time. Amusingly, they were carrying No 914.

Aboard the Al Holbert Racing entry was a new protégé of Holbert's, a young Doc Bundy paired with one Bill Schmid. They finished the course, but with only 151 laps covered they were not classified. A month later at Road Atlanta on 20 April, John Hulen in the assumed-to-be 85 car would finish 6th in GTU, but down in 22nd overall. Ron Coupland, also driving a Hulen entry, would be 5th in GTU and 21st overall. In general, after the good result at Daytona, 1975 would follow a similar pattern to 1974, with racing entries coming mainly from the private driver/entrant. Most of the drivers who were progressing in their careers had moved on to more powerful machinery.

1975 would also be the final year for the regulations first set up in 1971 in IMSA GT/GTO/GTU. For many, this period (from 1971 through to 1976) was the GT Camel era, Camel being the sponsor. In the era of the 914s, the SCCA and IMSA had been vying with each other for the best championships. By 1975, the dust between the two governing bodies was settling, and Trans Am cars would be seen running with GTU, and vice versa. A rule change was decided, and in the years to come, as we see in part of the final chapter, some wild-looking 914s would appear in SCCA GT2 and in the IMSA classes.

Returning to the racing of 1975, still under the old rules, we see Ron Coupland finish 5th in race 1, and John Hulen 6th in race 2 of GTU in the two-race Road Atlanta 100 Miles on 20 April. In the Camel GT Road Race, the Monterey Triple Crown at Laguna Seca, on 3 May, Bill Polich would be 4th in GTU race 1 and 6th in GTU race 2, with John Hotchkis 5th in GTU race 1; Kirby, taking over the No 51 car, came home 5th in race 2.

At the Riverside 6 Hours of 1975 on 9-10 May, three 914/6s would enter the fray. A 40-car entry would see the regular 914/6 of Kirby/Mandella/Polich struggling at the back of the field, the 914/6 in GTU format being outclassed by the Datsun 240Zs and the GTU Porsche 911s. At Lime Rock for the Camel GT Challenge (round 8), two races of 66 laps each, on 26 May, only John Hotchkis in his

The BMW of Brian Redman just ahead of Robert Kirby's 914 (No 51) of Kirby-Hitchcock Racing, which would finish 2nd in GTU. Just behind the 914 are the BMW 2002 of Werner Gudzus, the Camaro of Carl Shafer, the No 59 911RSR of Peter Gregg, Al Holbert in the 911 and the eventual race winner, the No 6 911RSR of Hurley Haywood. (PR)

914/6 would take up the challenge, finishing down the field 5th in GTU.

The Camel GT Challenge continued at Mosport on 14 June. A 28-car field tackled the undulating course, where Robert Kirby finished 16th overall, 2nd in GTU.

In August at the Talladega IMSA GT Race, John Hulen claimed a 4th in GTU. The season's penultimate round at the Mid-Ohio 6 Hours on 24 August saw Hulen/Coupland managing only 10th in GTU, and in the final round of the IMSA Championship 1975 at Daytona no 914/6s were entered. It was becoming evident that the 914/6 in its original form was no longer competitive.

As this book is primarily concerned with the 914s as they were in the early original design format, we begin to draw the story to a close here. 1976 would see the final year of production in Germany for the last of the four-cylinder 914s. In the USA, 1976 brought a new set of rules for racing. The future would see space-frame and Silhouette cars in Trans Am and GTU IMSA. It was to be a whole new ball game.

We will look at that in our final chapter, as well as what came after: an era that saw some interesting cars and amazingly quick 914s, dry-sumped examples and super-light chassis. As ever, the times they were a'changin'!

9
What came next
USA and Europe 1976-present

Our study is about the racing cars in period, and as we near the end of that period and enter 1976, we see the start of a new era in Europe and internationally for the World Championship sports car races – that of the production Silhouette, the FIA now running Groups 1 to 5. The regular 914/6 GTs were, of course, in Group 4, and would continue to race in this category, but as the years went by, wilder modified cars would be seen in the USA, especially in IMSA GTU under-2.5L.

Although we now enter a period extending beyond the time of the cars in their original format, we could not leave the 914 story without discussing some 'modifieds,' and their results post-1975 in the USA and internationally. By now, any 914s still racing in Europe were few and far between, though there were certainly some competing at club level around the world. 1976 in Europe is covered in chapter 6, so here we start with 1976 in the USA.

The first major race of 1976 would be the Daytona 24 Hours, and this year a wide range of cars would compete. The Carrera RSR Turbo had been banned in IMSA; turbo cars in general were not encouraged, and only two private 935 Porsche Turbos from Europe were allowed to race in Group 5. On the other hand, the SCCA was embracing 911 Turbos in Trans Am – Al Holbert would be using one in the SCCA series. IMSA said RSR non-turbo cars were okay, but when the results came out, maybe the organizers wished they had banned those, too.

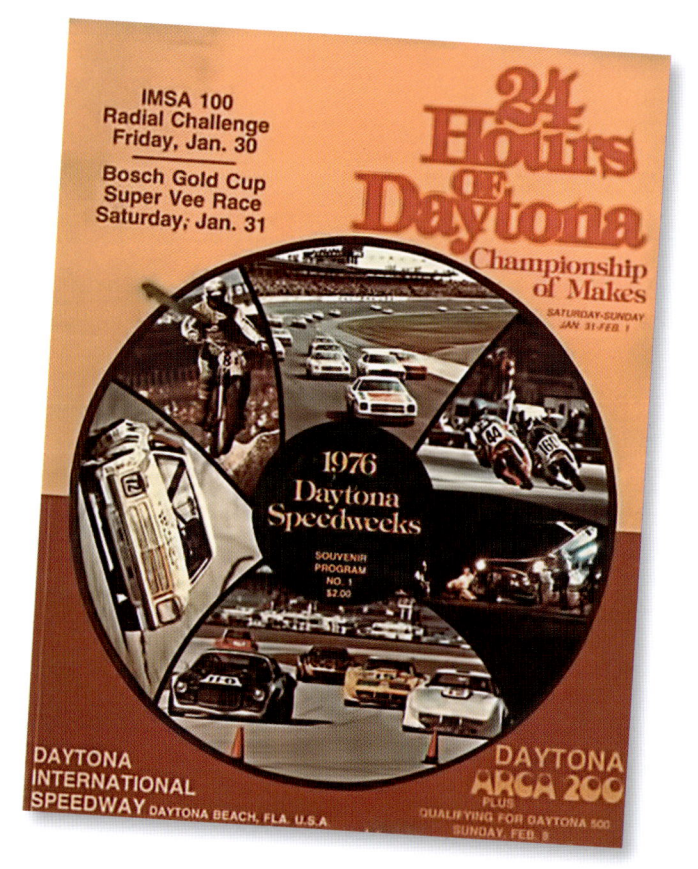

What came next USA and Europe 1976-present

NASCARS were allowed in to the IMSA classes for the first time. The BMW CSLs looked handy, and so it proved. Corvettes, Camaros, Datsun 240Zs, Mazdas, etc, made up the bulk of the GTO and GTU entry. Of the 914/6s, we see the No 51 car of John Hotchkis/Len Jones/Robert Kirby qualifying 42nd on the grid at Daytona. They improved considerably on this position over the 24 hours, in a race which was, in fact, stopped for nearly four hours at one point due to contaminated fuel being found in the race supply: they finished 13th overall and 3rd in GTU, reliability being the key over speed. Eight 911s were in front, split up by a Ferrari 365GTB, a Corvette, and two works BMW CSLs, one of which, that of Peter Gregg/Brian Redman/John Fitzpatrick, was the overall winner. The winning BMW covered 545 laps, the 13th place 914/6 covered 467. The difference in performance is evident.

Two 911s were ahead of the No 51 car in the 2.5 GTU class. A second 914, classifying as a finisher, was the 23rd and final car, the No 54 of Alex Job/Steve Southard/Hal Sahlman, on 392 laps and 9th in GTU. The regular entries of John Hulen and David McClain failed to finish.

The Sebring 12 Hours on 20 March is said to have been only a shadow of its former self – unsanctioned by the FIA, a track in poor condition, dodgy entries and, according to reports, some less than savoury spectators! That said, the front of the race saw only serious and definitely respectable professionals, and it was they who came through to fill the list of 26 finishers, the first 13 being Porsche 911s and one lone BMW, that of Peter Gregg/Hurley Haywood. Al Holbert/Michael Keyser were the victors. Three 914/6s were in attendance; the highest placed would once more be the No 51 car of Robert Kirby/John Hotchkis/Len Jones, 14th overall and 4th in IMSA GTU, 32 laps down on the winners.

John Thomas/Jim Cook: 22nd at Sebring, 56 laps down on the winning car. An early sight of one of the new, now more modified 914/6s for IMSA GTU. As we see, the new regulations allowed the bodywork to be more radical, along with the tyres. (MK BO)

255

Porsche The Racing 914s

The Walt Maas 914/6; the car was to see race action in 1971, '72, '76, '77, '78, '79, '83, '84 and '85 with various owners, having been one of the early 914/6s supplied to Art Bunker. (MK BO)

Walt Maas' mighty 914/6, which started life as Porsche 914/6 914 143 0332. Now, with an ample dose of steroids applied, it was fast and efficient, coming 7th overall and 1st in GTU at Laguna Seca, just two laps down on the GTO overall winner. (MK BO)

At the beginning of May 1976 we see the first appearance of another one of the early, more modified cars, that of Walt Maas. This was the 914/6 GT post-factory kitted chassis 043 0332, a car that first went to Art Bunker back in 1970, then on to Daniel Muñiz in 1972; it would also have a long life after Maas.

Maas was nearing the end of an interesting racing career and found himself without a ride in 1976. He acquired a basket case! It is reported that the 914 was completely rebuilt by members of the Porsche Club America and Walt's team crew, Jerry Woods and John Clever. Walt Maas, in an interview ten years later, said: "I thought at the time that the 914/6 could be competitive with the Datsuns that were dominating the GTU class." Walt was well qualified to think this, having won the GTU Championship in 1974 with a Datsun 240Z. Maas went on to say: "In the early 1970s, the 914 had been raced in the US and Europe with a fair amount of success. Our Porsche 914 had been built up for racing at Sebring. It was in fairly good condition, but with no engine. We gutted it, put in a new roll cage, got an engine and modified it, and once the aerodynamics were sorted we had a state-of-the-art race car. We won first time out!"

Garretson Enterprises was the base for the work. The car was acquired in early 1976 and had two engines: one a 2464cc short-stroke with Porsche 906 internals, and the other a 2494cc long-stroke with RSR internals. Carburetion was by 46 IDA Webers. The first outing would be at Sears Point for a test day on 27 March. A second test at Willow Springs sorted out some teething troubles from Sears Point, and at a final test session at Laguna Seca ahead of the Camel GT Road Race, the Monterey Triple Crown Championship, the large rear spoiler was added. Maas found he was

256

What came next USA and Europe 1976-present

The No 87 car of Jim Cook. Improved since Sebring, now finishing 11th overall, 3rd in GTU, at Laguna Seca. (MK BO)

lapping under the lap record for GTU at this track. Carlsen Porsche+Audi came on board with sponsorship, and the all-amateur team was ready. The result was emphatic: 7th overall, 1st in GTU. Maas was to prove a formidable competitor in the months to come. The No 87 car, also an early one, and said to be 914/6 914 043 1325, entered by Altec Lansing for Jim Cook, would finish 11th overall and 3rd in GTU.

A week later on 9 May, Walt Maas, Jim Cook, John Hotchkis and Jim Gaeta were out again in the Ontario 100 Miles. The previously useful No 51 car of Hotchkis could only finish 24th, with Gaeta a dnf. Maas was first in GTU once more, coming home 8th overall behind the bigger-capacity GTOs, though only one lap down at the Ontario Motor Speedway, California, after 34 laps of the 2.9-mile road course, a total distance of 98.6 miles.

Frank Harmstad, in a 914/6, was running at the SCCA Trans Am race at Pocono the same day. He took 1st in GTU, behind some 20 others in the GTO class. Walt Maas again: "I began to realize we had the possibility of winning the championship. But we didn't have the financial means – that was our next goal."

Walt Maas again had a good run at Lime Rock on 31 May, 6th overall and 2nd in GTU, the 240Z of Frisselle beating him to the top

Paddock work: here we see the extent of the modifications to these now super-powerful GTU cars. (BM)

spot in GTU. Maas was again 2nd in GTU (7th overall) at Mid-Ohio on 6 June, once more with Jim Cook, who finished 3rd in GTU, 15th overall, hard on his heels.

At Sears Point for the Coca-Cola Bottler's weekend, the Sears Point 100 Miles on 25 July, Walt Maas returned to his winning ways, taking GTU honours again and 7th overall behind the bigger GTOs. Three other 914/6s were dnfs.

Porsche The Racing 914s

Walt Maas was proving the one to beat in GTU, as the fight was growing between the 914/6 and the Brad Frisselle Datsun 240Z. Walt Maas had won the GTU Championship in 1974 in a Datsun 240Z. (MK BO)

Second in the GTU Championship at the first attempt: an impressive performance by Walt Maas in the very rapid 914/6, seen here ahead of the Corvette of Dick Raymond at Sears Point. The strong GTU class had around 20 competitors at each round in 1976. In 1977 Maas would go one place better. (MK BO)

What came next USA and Europe 1976-present

A nice try, but no luck for the Robert Kirby/John Hotchkis Sr/Dennis Aase 914/6 at Daytona, 1977. (MK BO)

Maas cleaned up again in GTU at the Laguna Seca 100 Miles on 3 October, 9th overall behind the GTOs. He finished the season, after six races, with four victories and two 2nds, giving him 2nd in the IMSA GTU Championship to Brad Frisselle and that pesky Datsun 240Z! Maas was the only one to be pulling off regular class victories in a 914. However, John Hulen, Ron Coupland and Rich Mandella were still performing, and in addition Frank Harmstad got a decent result with two Trans Am class wins at the SCCA Pocono rounds of that championship in May and June. Jim Cook took a 2nd to Walt Maas at Laguna Seca.

Race programme-wise, the 1977 season would, for the most part, be a repeat of 1976. Porsche was dominant in Europe with the latest 911, the 935. In the USA, most of the earlier 911-mounted competitors who had tried the 914 now returned to the 911 in its 935 version. However, for the 914/6 model, 1977 in the USA was the time for it to win its second championship in GTU, the last being Gregg/Haywood in 1971. Starting with Daytona, now linked in a friendly way to the Le Mans organization outside the clutches of the FIA, both races would run Group 4 GT cars and Group 5 Silhouettes. Only the No 51 914/6 of Robert Kirby/John Hotchkis/Dennis Aase was involved. However, after qualifying their 914 GT 38th on the grid, they went out with engine failure after 47 laps.

On 19 March, the still deteriorating Sebring circuit was host to the next race, strictly an IMSA class race and without some of the star international cars of previous years. A wide range in types of 911s was entered; Carrera RSRs and 934s dominated, with only the No 51 car (914/6 GT) once more coming closest to finishing of the four 914s running in the IMSA GTU class, but obliged to retire

A dnf at Sebring for the Spirit Racing Henn/Sahlman/Cook 914/6. (MK BO)

Porsche The Racing 914s

The WQXI Road Atlanta 100 IMSA GT race: 16th overall, 3rd in GTU for John Hulen/Ron Coupland. (FL)

on lap 164 – a race best forgotten on the 914 front. However, this was not the case on the US national scene, where, on 17 April, at the WQXI radio station-sponsored Road Atlanta 100 IMSA GT race, John Hulen/Ron Coupland, in their No 85 914/6 modified car, finished 16th overall, picking up 3rd in GTU.

Walt Maas was back with determination for 1977, and his No 45 914/6 GT, suitably improved from 1976, was to win the championship this time. Walt Maas: "We had more horsepower, which was important." The GT class (GTO-GTU) was still a popular series, and it is recorded that nearly half a million fans would see the 16 races that made up the season. Interestingly, it would be the last season in this era when a normally-aspirated car would win the championship – and it was a 914.

At Laguna Seca for the Monterey Triple Crown meeting on 1 May, Maas laid down the gauntlet, coming 11th overall and 1st in GTU, beating many of the GTO cars in this Camel GT and IMSA GT Championship round 4. The race also saw the first win for the new Porsche 934 Turbo of former drag race driver Danny Ongais, running in GTO. In fact, these cars took 2nd, 3rd and 10th, too, amongst the Chevrolet Monzas. Walt Maas came home 11th overall but, more importantly, won the GTU class.

On 15 May, Walt Maas did it again at the Mid-America 100 Mile race: 8th overall this time, behind the GTOs with drivers of the calibre of Hurley Haywood, John Paul and Al Holbert, who took victory in a Chevrolet Monza ahead of him. Two GTU race wins out of two efforts in the bag.

GTU class win number three came at Lime Rock on 30 May. Al Holbert took overall victory again, but Walt Maas was in 12th, ahead of 11 theoretically faster GTO entries in the 34-car field. He got pipped at Mid-Ohio on June 5, though: 2nd in GTU. Sam Posey in the Datsun 240Z took 11th overall after a race-long fight with Maas and won GTU, while Walt came in 12th overall. David Hobbs, in a GTO-class BMW, took victory from Al Holbert in the Chevy Monza. Maas was back on it, though, at the Brainerd 100 Miles, coming 6th overall, 1st GTU. Walt Maas: "On the track, Sam and I were awfully close. We were always pretty even."

What came next USA and Europe 1976-present

Walt Maas goes shoulder-to-shoulder with the 91 Corvette of Gene Bothello. 2.5L beats V8: Bothello finished 13th, Maas 11th overall and 1st in GTU. (MK BO)

Mid-America in Wentzville, Missouri, 15 May: Walt Maas wins the GTU class in the 100-mile race, finishing 8th overall. The 914 had never placed lower than 4th since the start in 1976, frequently beating much faster machinery, but it would be a tough fight in 1977 with Sam Posey's Datsun 240Z. (MK BO)

The Datsun 240Z factory-supported professional team, with driver Sam Posey, would give Walt Maas a hard time during the 1977 season. (FL)

261

But of course Sam Posey's car was a factory-backed entry. Walt Maas: "We couldn't afford a lot of things, even though we had more money than in 1976. But the Porsche was extremely reliable. We finished every race we started. We never dnf'd. The upshot of it was we could live within our means and were still competitive against the factory teams."

The Pepsi Cola Grand Prix weekend Camel GT round 8 race would go to Danny Ongais from Hurley Haywood in the Bob Hagestad-entered Porsche 934; Al Holbert was 2nd. Walt Maas' 6th overall put him ahead of all but five of the GTOs (all over-2.5L cars). It's worth mentioning here, though I doubt he was happy about it, that John Hulen was having a continued run of bad luck, dnf-ing at Sebring, Mid-America and Mid-Ohio. Only at the Daytona 250 miles did he get a result, coming 9th in GTU.

24 July was the date of the Hallett Motor Racing Circuits Camel GT Challenge round 10. Maas had given the previous round at Daytona (the Paul Revere 250) a miss in the 914, running instead in a 911 with Bob Hindson; they dnf'd.

Hallett, a new track 35 miles west of Tulsa, was hosting its first meeting of professional racing. The GTU class had its own race. Twenty-five cars lined up on a very hot day – over 100°F (37.7°C). The race turned into a three-car battle for the top spot over 45 laps. Starting from P3 on the grid, Walt Maas pulled off an overall victory for the Garretson-sponsored 914.

At Sears Point in Mid-Oklahoma on 31 July in another GTU-only race, Maas was beaten to 3rd, his second lowest point of the season! It had happened due to a coming together with Sam Posey in the last corner, the altercation allowing Dennis Aase to get by in his 911 Porsche to take the victory from Sam Posey in the Datsun 240Z. They finished on the same lap, all three running to the line together, with just fractions of seconds in it. 14 August saw Maas remedy the situation when, at Pocono, a 9th overall in the mixed GTO/GTU race of 33 starters was good enough to whip a few more GTOs and take 1st in GTU. Sam Posey in the Datsun was hard on his rear bumper in 10th.

Two weeks later, on 28 August, it was again the Sam and Walt Show at the Mid-Ohio 3 Hours, but here Posey had his engine let go

A busy pit stop on the championship trail. The mighty, though some might say now antiquated, 914/6 of Walt Maas cleaned up in the IMSA GTU class for 1977. (BO)

and Maas took another 1st in GTU from the field of 45 cars that ran in this round 12 of the Camel GT series. This time, Maas even beat Al Holbert, when Holbert suffered a minor exhaust problem. Robert Kirby/John Hotchkis/Dennis Aase (4th in GTU) were also present in the No 51 914/6. John Hulen/Ron Coupland in the No 85 car dnf'd yet again.

Maas slipped up at Road Atlanta on 5 September with a 4th overall and 4th in GTU when he took a hit in the rear from Dave White, braking too late in his 911 and damaging his exhaust. However, normal service was resumed on 9 October, when it was the top spot in GTU again at the Laguna Seca 100 Miles (Shasta Monterey Grand Prix), where he finished in 12th place, but ahead of eighteen GTOs in the 43-car field.

It was anyone's guess as to who would win that year's GTU championship: Posey or Maas. Walt Maas: "It wasn't certain until the last race. At the time, (the championship) had been back and forth all season." Maas said he had thought his win in 1974 with the Datsun had been a fluke, but it was no fluke this time. Walt Maas: "It was tremendous winning the championship. Right from the beginning of the season we were all goal-orientated toward winning that championship. We did it." The Monterey Grand Prix had again been

What came next USA and Europe 1976-present

a rip-roaring race, with Walt Maas taking victory by dint of better use of his skills in moving through the slower back-marker traffic. This class win was sufficient for him to clinch the 1977 IMSA GTU Championship ahead of Sam Posey.

With over two years of racing, racking up twelve wins, three 2nds, one 3rd and one 4th, the Maas-driven car was probably the most successful 914/6 in the history of the model in that period. Walt Maas is recorded as saying: "After 16 years of racing, that's my last race. Winning a national championship with the pros with an under-financed operation against a factory team is very satisfying. The big thing for me was beating Sam Posey this season for the championship. For me, personally, this is a tremendous accomplishment. It's a good way to go out. I'll never forget, nor be able to repay, the loyalty of my crew and my wife, and the encouragement of the fans."

Into retirement, Walt Maas moved the car on to Bruce Sanders, who ran it in 1979. In 1983, it would find its way to Will Swope. Jerry Woods, who was to become Garretson's number one engine builder, and was Walt Maas' engineer, would join Kremer Brothers Racing in Germany in 1987. In 1977, Woods was named mechanic of the year. For the other teams running the 914, it was an inauspicious time for the top five positions; a look at the stats in chapter 10 will reveal all.

1978 started just as badly as 1977 for John Hulen at the Daytona 24 Hours: the engine failed on the first lap. Walt Maas had retired, and of the four cars entered it was the No 62 William Koll-entered 914/6, driven by Koll himself together with David Hamren/Dennis Sherman, which performed best, finishing 10th overall and 3rd in GTU. The Daytona race was round 1 of the World Challenge for Endurance Drivers.

The No 62 car was running one of the new ANDIAL engines that were to become famous in the years ahead. Alwin Springer was the key engine man at ANDIAL. Dieter Inzenhofer – the 'DI' in ANDIAL – had met Springer along with Arnold Wagner at Vasek Polak's Porsche dealership in Manhattan Beach, California, in the

Bill Koll/David Hamren/Dennis Sherman finished 10th overall and 3rd in GTU at Daytona. Note: this car has an ANDIAL-prepared engine. (DM)

Founding members of ANDIAL, the company set up in 1975: (l-r) the late Arnold Wagner, Alwin Springer and Dieter Inzenhofer, in front of the ANDIAL shop during the 1990s. (©PNA)

late 1960s. In 1975 ANDIAL was born to service and build Porsche engines. They were to evolve into one of America's most successful and respected independent authorities on Porsche performance tuning, starting with the six-cylinder units in the 911s and 914s of the late 1970s.

At Sebring, round 2 of the World Challenge for Endurance Drivers, John Hulen/Ron Coupland/Nick Engels would get the No 85 car to the finish at last. Porsche 935s and 911s dominated the first seven places at the finish of the Sebring 12 Hours. These two races – the Daytona 24 Hours and the Sebring 12 Hours – would continue to see 914s in the line-up in GTU.

On 2 April, there was also an additional race in the USA for the Drivers' Championship World Challenge: the Talladega 6 Hours. Bill Koll/David Hamren would put in a fine performance to come home 11th overall and 4th in GTU behind three Porsche 911Ss. Peter Gregg/Brad Frisselle took overall victory in the Porsche 935 entered by Brumos, carrying the famous No 59 on the side.

30 April would see the Laguna Seca GT races, with both the 100 Miles for the GTO class and a race for GTUs only. Rod Harrison would show again here, having finished 4th in GTU in October 1977. This time he would go one better in the Porsche 914/6 914 143 0178, finishing 3rd overall and thus 3rd in GTU behind the 240Z

A finish at last: John Hulen/Ron Coupland/Nick Engels got the No 85 car to the finish at Sebring, taking 23rd overall, 9th IMSA GTU, a good result after the traumas of 1977. The car is seen here ahead of the Kirby/Hotchkis/Aase 911. (MK BO)

264

What came next USA and Europe 1976-present

The Watkins Glen 6 Hours was run to SCCA Trans Am regulations. A 914/6 was entered – a sky-blue example with Dan Slodowick/Cliff McCandless behind the wheel – but did not qualify. They had tried to run at the Sebring 12 Hours, but did not start due to engine problems.

At Mid-Ohio on 27 August, the results show that John Hulen/ Ron Coupland took 4th in GTU in the 250-mile race, but that would be the last top-six finish of 1978 for the 914/6s.

The 1979 season started with the Daytona 24 Hours, as usual, but the two 914/6 entries failed to finish. 1979 would also see the emergence of a few new names, almost a new era of drivers: Wayne Baker and Tom Winters, names for the future, were driving at the Sebring 12 Hours with Robert Kirby in the No 51 914/6. Seventy-two cars lined up. Interestingly, with most of the previously-raced 914s running in GTU being six-cylinder cars, with just a sprinkling of four-cylinder cars, we now begin to see the four-cylinder VW unit being developed beyond the wildest dreams of anyone back in Germany. Let's hear from Wayne Baker, no stranger to racing Porsches: "It goes back to 1974, when I started my business here in San Diego and a customer had a 2L 914/4. The owner and I entered it into Porsche time trials locally, and then in 1975 I took a 914/4 car, stripped it down to end up at around 1400lb, and put in a 2.5L carburetted four-cylinder. You can get 2.5 out of the VW 2L unit quite easily. We competed with that and won what they called Group X for the unlimited class for that type of time trial. I sold it on

Laguna Seca 1978: Rod Harrison would show again here, having finished 4th in GTU in October 1977. This time he would go one better in the Porsche 914/6 143 0178, finishing 3rd overall. (BM)

of Frank Leary and the now 260Z of Sam Posey. For the record, Bob Zulkowski in the Metalcraft-entered 914/6 finished 11th overall, and Bill Koll 12th. Rod Harrison also finished in the top five at the Hallett GTU race on 7 May, taking 4th place. On June 18 at Brainerd, Bill Koll took 3rd place in GTU.

Bill Koll – suited, booted, helmeted, net up – ready to go at Hallet on 7 May 1978. (BM)

At the Daytona 24 Hours 1979, Southard/Koch/Roe ran for 385 laps before a problem intervened and they recorded a dnf. (MK BO)

and in 1976-77, through '78, I entered a 914 2L in the SCCA classes. Basically it had 175bhp on Solex carburettors, due to the rules, in the 'D' class Production.

"In 1977 we won the Southern Pacific Championship here in Southern California. I wanted to get into IMSA, so at the end of 1978 we decided to do IMSA in 1979 – I say 'we,' because I owned an engine with Robert Kirby, who also owned the chassis, and the third man was Tom Winters. He brought some cash and we put all this together. I took an open trailer and motorhome, and we drove down to Sebring with Robert. So there we are practising on the Friday, the day before the 12-hour race. Robert had had a few class wins in GTO class, so he was qualifying the car. But one lap he never

What came next USA and Europe 1976-present

came around; he had hit a bump. [Author's note: remember, Sebring was not in the best state of repair at that time.] Well, he was up in the air and crashed down on landing, bottomed the suspension, broke the engine and transaxle mounts, etc. We did a lot of work for customers and a load of these enthusiasts had come along to see us in their 914s. They found out what had happened and started taking parts off their own cars! We took the parts and over that night until 10am the next morning, the Saturday of the race, we managed to put it all back together. Robert and Tom didn't want to drive it, and told me to drive it! So I drove it. We started dead last, because we didn't qualify, but they allowed us to run. After two hours, I came in to get fuel and got out, and the other two said no, stay in there, so I ran another two hours. Well eventually, because of the rules, I had to come in. Robert and Tom each did stints and as things went pretty well, excepting a few little glitches which we fixed, we kept it moving and in the end we finished 4th in GTU!"

Also at that 1979 Sebring 12 Hours, in 22nd place, was the Bill Koll/Jim Cook/Dennis Aase 914/6, the No 62 car, and in 23rd a Canadian team with a 914/6, David Deacon/Regan Riley/Hank Franczak, with No 93 on the side. Four more 914s failed to finish.

At Road Atlanta in an all-GTU race, the highest placed would be Bill Koll in the No 62 car. Then, at the Riverside 6 Hours, Koll got on the GTU podium in 3rd place, finishing 13th overall.

1979 would be a busy year for the 914s, a resurgence of the now outdated chassis which nevertheless seemed popular. Chassis raced in the Group 4 period and earlier IMSA GTU days were changing hands as new teams appeared, with the cars now much modified from the originals. The records show 65 entries on 25 different tracks. Four-cylinder cars were receiving close attention, probably due to the rapidity of Wayne Baker's car. More would appear trackside in the years ahead. However, the IMSA GTU season closed with the 914 having only been in the top three on three occasions; 15 races counted. Datsun 240/260/280Zs took nine victories in total, the Mazda RX7 and Porsche 911 shared three wins apiece. The 914 was being outpaced, and the last GTU victory had been Walt Maas back in 1977 at the Laguna Seca 100 Miles.

Since 1978 and through to 1981, we see that Porsche, always at the front end of the field, proved to be as dominant in the post-prototype era as it had been before it; now it was the 935 in the Group 5 Special production. The Silhouette class was cleaning up in Europe and the USA, where the GTX class cars followed loosely the Group 5 spec from Europe. There were, too, several specials that started life as 934s – or even 911s – thus taking the term 'Silhouette' literally. In IMSA GTU, the Datsuns and remaining 911s proved to be very potent and, even with the recent IMSA regulation

Bill Koll in the well-developed 914/6 was a regular podium finisher in the IMSA GTU class throughout 1979. He would race the car at Daytona 1980 from 48th on the grid to 5th overall and 1st in GTU, before moving the car on. (BM)

changes that brought some wild 914s out on the track, it looked like the 914 was now out of its depth in the GTU class, no matter what the power unit. But there was a flash of light at the 1980 Daytona 24 Hours.

No one was looking, or really interested. Three 914s started (four were entered, but the No 12 car of Smith/Johnson/Schoepflin did not start due to clutch failure). It was thought that Wayne Baker/Dan Gilliland/Geoff Scott's 914/4 might do something, as Baker had proved he was capable of some effective performances with the VW-engine car. The No 83 914/6 built by the Zotz garage, with Harro Zitza/Doug Zitza/John Belperche aboard, went out after just

Wayne Baker's personalized Autohaus Porsche four-cylinder 914, a neat, tidy example of the modified cars of the period. At the Daytona 24 Hours it would go 486 laps before it had to be parked up. He lent it to Jeff Scott with Paul and Margie Smith-Haas to drive in the Riverside 6 Hours. (BM)

267

Westwood, September 1980: Scott Taylor (11), who would finish 13th overall, mixing it with the 83 Corvette of Herb Forest and 69 of Canadian Gary Pullyblank. (BM)

44 laps. The No 57 car of Wayne Baker ran well in the early part of the race but succumbed on lap 486. Not so the No 62 914/6, which was pounding round, ticking off the competition one by one as it marched up the field to 5th overall and 1st in GTU. It was the final time for the No 62 car – what a way to bow out!

Wayne Baker was, and still is, in the business of racing cars, and he was to let the No 57 car out to Jeff Scott after using it himself at Sebring and Road Atlanta. Scott used it at the Riverside 5 Hours with Paul and Margie Smith-Haas. The best result for the car in 1980 was a 9th in GTU at Riverside.

We mustn't forget that the SCCA was running the Trans Am class throughout this period from the mid-1970s, and the 914s would mix it with some pretty fancy Trans Am cars. Here we see the No 11 car of Scott Taylor, who would finish 13th overall, mixing it with the No 83 Corvette of Herb Forest (9th overall) and No 69 Corvette of Canadian Gary Pullyblank, 8th overall, at Westwood in 1980.

14 races had made up the IMSA GTU Championship in 1980, and apart from the class victory at Daytona it was left to Baker to take the fight to the Datsuns and Mazdas that would dominate. Baker had built a new car and, running with No 2 on the side, he came home 3rd overall at Road Atlanta in an all-GTU race behind the inevitable (by now) Mazda RX7 and a 911. It showed promise for 1981.

Wayne Baker told the author: "After Road Atlanta, sometime in 1980 – I don't remember exactly – I spoke to the tech people at IMSA about the car. They said if I would build as a manufacturer, as opposed to a privateer, they would accept anything I needed to be competitive with the 914/4 in GTU class, so that was the green light. One of the key things they required was that when you looked through the window at the floor, it had to be to their stock standard. So what we did, we took 4in out of the car from the top to the bottom, so proportionally when you looked through the window it looked stock, but what I had to do was sit on the floor myself, and my head was touching the hood [roof]. By the time we got that done, the car weighed only 1600lb. Engine-wise, the key for reliability is for the cylinder heads to last; they were always cracking or coming loose and we were just working on them constantly. To keep the heads on the cylinders, they [IMSA] allowed us to put six bolts per head, so the engine would stay together. Push rods were a problem, but we were able to make it so they would survive up to 8000rpm. Basically, we would shift it at 7000rpm for reliability, and we would drive it about 10-12 hours before racing, then it became reliable. It was still the Volkswagen-type engine, type 4. Originally they put them in VW vans. They put it in a 914/4 in 1969. Anyway, by that time we had a chassis that would out-handle anybody in a turn. Where the sill boxes are that we step over to get in, those were all open and air was sucked through them, coming out at the grill where the engine is. This system turned out to give me more grip in the turns. They also allowed us a very small spoiler in the back. In 1981 I did a complete series; I think we finished 4th overall in GTU, but reliability was a really big problem. I had a lot of good starts from the front, and four or five that were on GTU pole. I had problems with leaks more than anything else; we eventually solved it, and by that time we were at the end of the events for that year!"

At Daytona in 1981 the best performance for a 914/6 came from the No 45 car entered by Autosport Technology and driven by Marion Speer/Dwight Mitchell/Ray Ratcliff; 13th overall on 581 laps put them 7th in the GTU class. Ahead of them was a 911 that was 3rd overall and then five Mazda RX7s! Three more 914s started, but failed to finish.

After the Daytona 24 Hours in 1981, the results for the 914 model were hardly inspiring, with many dnfs. Until, that is, at Road Atlanta on 12 April, when Wayne Baker came home 8th overall in the No 22 car. Reliability was still a problem, but then at Laguna Seca on 3 May, Baker finished 5th overall, leading home the GTU contingent for another class victory for the 914/4. At Mid-Ohio on 31 May, Baker's No 22 car only managed 14th, but at the Brainerd 200 Miles on 14 June, he moved up again to 8th overall.

Wayne Baker again: "At the Datsun Camel Sears Point race in 1981 (26 July), we beat everyone with the four-cylinder – Mazda RX7s, 911s, Datsun 280Zs. I think we were on pole, too. [Author's

What came next USA and Europe 1976-present

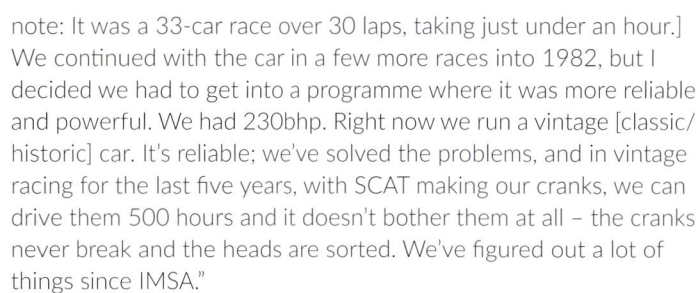

note: It was a 33-car race over 30 laps, taking just under an hour.] We continued with the car in a few more races into 1982, but I decided we had to get into a programme where it was more reliable and powerful. We had 230bhp. Right now we run a vintage [classic/historic] car. It's reliable; we've solved the problems, and in vintage racing for the last five years, with SCAT making our cranks, we can drive them 500 hours and it doesn't bother them at all – the cranks never break and the heads are sorted. We've figured out a lot of things since IMSA."

The No 45 car, chassis 043 0593, first seen at the hands of Bill Koll in 1978, as we know had a successful career before being moved on to take in a whole season of IMSA GTU with Ray Ratcliff, achieving a best result in GTU of 8th at Portland on 2 August. Also in evidence at this time was the No 57 car of Jeff Scott at the Portland GI Joe's Datsun Grand Prix meeting 2 August 1981; this was the

Daytona 1981: Marion Speer/Dwight Mitchell/Ray Ratcliff, 13th overall on 581 laps and 7th in GTU. (BM)

The Datsun Camel Sears Point race in 1981: Wayne Baker en route to overall GTU victory. This time the car stayed together for a great result. (BM)

A change of rear spoiler for No 45 (chassis 043 0593), here driven by Dwight Mitchell/Ray Ratcliff/Bill Cooper at Sears Point and Portland races. (BM)

A colourful, if not so quick, 914/6: the former Bill Polich chassis 043 0529, now in the hands of John Longmire, Sears Point 1981. (BM)

The No 57 914/4 Robert Kirby car, driven by Jeff Scott, seen here at the Portland GI Joe's Datsun Grand Prix meeting, 2 August 1981. (BM)

269

Porsche The Racing 914s

earlier Robert Kirby-owned 914/4, now tuned by Wayne Baker. Jeff would finish 3rd of the 914s and 11th overall in this event, while Wayne Baker finished 3rd overall in the No 22 car. Wayne Baker says: "Yes, I took care of Jeff's car, and we ran quite a few things together. His wife was also a driver; we did a few races with her, too, so we had a good run – a lot of work, a lot of fun.

"In my opinion [the 914] is the best mid-engine car around. Every time Porsche makes a mid-engine car they're superior for the track and absolutely a delight to drive when you get them sorted; you just relax and it works. Of course, to get a lot of power, as I said earlier, we have to do a lot of things. We fitted a dry-sump system where on the originals they had an oil tank on the left side, but on the race car we had a tank on the right – very tall, it carried about 16 quarts – to feed the dry-sump set-up. Now the other thing is, to run with a pump on there, you couldn't get a fan on it because it sticks out 2in beyond the body that holds the fan, the housing, so we put two electric fans inside the car next to me in the passenger side. It was electrically cooled; the alternator was charged by the axle on a pulley to run the generator above it attached to the top of the transmission.

"On a track that's short or medium, you're very competitive. When you go to a long track like Road America or Daytona, in 1980 when we originally had a 914 which was basically stock, it was not very competitive; for example, at Daytona the first year we only got up to 140mph. When we got the bodywork on the new car, we shortened it, reshaped it, made every bit of wind-cheating we could

16 August 1981: Wayne Baker/Bob Overby at the Mosport 6 Hours. They managed 95 laps before the car had to be parked up. (RK)

What came next USA and Europe 1976-present

on the nose and getting air off the back, so it would do 168mph at Daytona, but by then the competitors who were still running in GTU were coming up against the 911, which could do 175mph. You just couldn't compete, though as I said, on the shorter tracks we were extremely competitive because with the weight-to-power ratio the acceleration was very good.

"It's still the case today; we have customers who run 914s in vintage racing. Today, of course, all the bodywork – the fenders, the hood, the top, the doors, everything – is in glass fibre and the body weighs just 76lb! In the wind, you could see the body on the hood sort of collapse," Wayne laughs, "so we put a bracket underneath it so it wouldn't collapse. It's glass fibre too. Made by hand, it was pretty thin. Then came carbon fibre. For vintage racing you have to weigh 1800lb, so you don't have to worry about the weight. I got ours down to 1780lb, easy."

On 28 August at the Elkhart Lake 500 Miles, Wayne Baker/Bob Overby had a better time, finishing 11th overall and 3rd in GTU, so on the podium again. But looking at the records, we can see that this was probably the last time through to the end of our particular study period that a 914 would see a podium finish in the early 1980s.

In 1980, Doc Bundy, driving for the Al Holbert Race Team, won the Production 'D' championship with the new and first water-cooled and front-engine car from Porsche – the 924. But another driver had been making steady headway over the previous years, and had now reached the upper echelons of SCCA racing: Dave Finch.

The Doc Bundy 924 Production 'D' race car, the top chassis of 1980, and the first front-engine and water-cooled car from Porsche. (©P)

271

Porsche The Racing 914s

It turned out that the new 924 was to have a long future. In 1981 at the Road Atlanta Finals, Doc Bundy was on pole in the pouring rain, with 914 racer Dave Finch alongside. Dave was no slouch, having started racing and tuning 914s in the mid-1970s. He was getting good results in the SCCA series, but at Atlanta it all went wrong. Dave Finch told the author: "Doc Bundy was on pole, me second and Tom Brennan on third. It was pouring with rain. The water was so deep in my lane that the car just turned sideways and I bounced off of Doc and ended up off the side of the track, stopped in about a foot of water. The year before, I was leading when after three laps the engine broke. That 914 for 'D' Production was 2L and similar to the 'E' and 'F' engines, except that it used a stock crank (regulation at the time), which was a problem. It cost me the SCCA National Championship that year. Doc Bundy won with the 924."

1981 Road Atlanta Finals – oops! Too much right foot, a deep puddle, and Doc Bundy receives a visit from Dave Finch. (DF)

What came next USA and Europe 1976-present

As we begin to draw our story to a close, we will look at some other 914s that raced in the period of the 1980s. Doug Zitza of Zotz Racing, still operational today, raced a 914 with enclosed lights at the Daytona 24 Hours of 1982. Wayne Baker took his regular car, now named the Araki after the engineering company Wayne was involved with, who were doing a top job engineering components. So good, in fact, that at the IMSA GTU race at Laguna Seca on 2 May 1982, Wayne Baker put the four-cylinder car on pole, ahead of 36 other competitors, including many Datsun 280Zs, 911 Porsches and a plethora of Mazda RX7s. At the start he stormed away, but it was a short-lived lead as reliability was a problem, and the No 22 went out after 15 laps. On 23 May he was out again, and once more put the No 22 car with its four-cylinder trick VW engine on pole. Twenty-three entries again, bursting with what should have been faster machinery. However, once again it

The Zotz Racing 914 at Daytona – a neat arrangement for the lights, similar to the 924 Carrera GTS that had come on the scene the year before. (NV)

Fast but fragile: the Wayne Baker four-cylinder 914 took pole at Laguna Seca and at Mid-Ohio, but dnfs spoilt the party. (DW)

273

Porsche The Racing 914s

was a dnf for Baker's 914 – fast but fragile. A week later, at the Lime Rock 1-Hour Coca-Cola 100, he did manage to finish, but only in 14th.

In SCCA, Dave Finch was still a force to be reckoned with – seen left at the finals at Atlanta in 1982.

Dave has this to say about the yellow car: "Brumos was my original Porsche dealer connection to my 944 'C' Production/GT2 project, and we raced the 914 in 'C' Production waiting for the 944 project to materialize. I was good friends with Harro Zitza, the senior partner of Zotz. The 'C' Production 914 engine was a 2.5L six-cylinder that we prepped with high-compression pistons, race cams, head work and Weber carbs. My 914/4 engine for 'E' and 'F' Production was a fully race-prepared 1.8L. It had a dry-sump oil system, custom crank and rods, custom aluminium cylinders, high-compression pistons, custom cam with roller rocker arms and highly modified oil-cooled cylinder heads with titanium valves. We also used highly modified Solex 40mm carbs."

SCCA 'C' Production: Finch driving to 5th place in the 1982 championship finals. Dave had campaigned the car since the mid 1970s. (DF)

The No 22 silver car is Bob Kirby driving to the 1984 SCCA 'E' Production National Championship in the Dave Finch Raetech 914/4. (DF)

What came next USA and Europe 1976-present

We now complete our study of the racing 914s. I hope that for you, the reader, this has been an enjoyable drive through the years of the 914. However, the story is not quite over. In the USA and Europe, the 914 would appear on race tracks and rallies in many guises over the years that followed, right up to the present day. So to finish off we will take a pictorial look at a variety, though by no means anywhere near all, of the racing 914s.

The GI Joe's Portland 3 Hours, 31 July 1983, with Will Swope in car 66. In 1983, Swope had taken over the former Walt Maas car, running it through 1983-85. (BM)

Seen at the Riverside 6 Hours 1984: Maurice Chasse/Robert Kirby would come home 17th overall in a GTU 914/6 car entered by Chasse. (BM)

275

Watkins Glen 500 Miles in 1986: Hendricks/Jones finished 16th overall. (RK)

What came next USA and Europe 1976-present

The SCCA series is not to be overlooked, and here we see Handley's No 78 car at the 1996 Mid-Ohio 'E' Production race. This is an interesting machine which, according to Porsche Central region key man, Steve Limbert, was, when in its original form, one of the very first 914s in 1970 to tour the USA as a demonstration car, a driver training school car and, as we see here, still a race car. (NV)

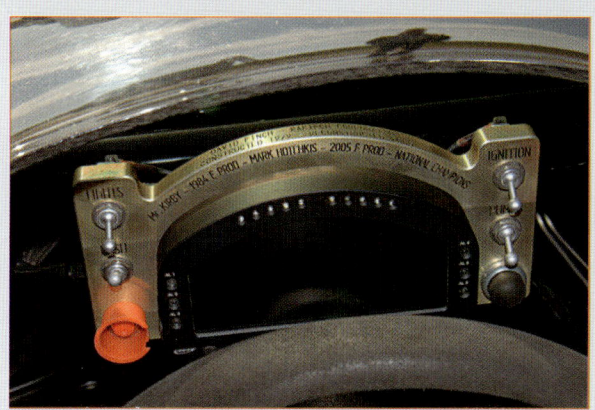

Many of the tuners from the 1970s and 1980s were still producing winners well into the millennium – Wayne Baker and Dave Finch's Raetech concerns, to name but two. Both helped with some of the details in this work. Mark Hotchkis (son of John) was driving the No 22 914 in the 2005 SCCA Class 'F' Production championships, as shown in this testament on the car to its pedigree. (DF)

Mark Hotchkis driving the Kirby Racing/Raetech 'F' Production 914 to the 2005 SCCA 'F' Production National Championship. A car and a team with history. (DF)

277

Porsche The Racing 914s

It was not only in the USA but also in Europe, including the UK, that the 914 was to see a continued racing life. James Calvert of Stateside Tuning in the UK says: "We had been tuning Beetles for years along with 356 Porsches, and in the early 90s we put together a 914, a superlight car with a 2L that we took out to 2.4L and found 200bhp. They wouldn't let us run it in the Porsche series, but the HSCC (Historic Sports Car Club) said we could run in their series. So, in 1995 we started out. It was a great car: we could beat 911s, Morgans, Jensens, etc. The car was featured in a number of magazines, and we raced that car through to 2005, racing and rallying it on tarmac rallies."

Variety was the name of the game: James Calvert's 200+bhp 914/4 in the late 1990s. (JC)

Flat-out on a stage rally in the UK: Richard Morgan in his well-used 914/6. He is still competing today, in hillclimbs. (RM)

Wayne Eason runs his former Ian McMath Porsche 914/6 in a hillclimb in the UK in 2009. This activity demonstrates the longevity of the model and the variety of competition, even in recent times. (AR)

What came next USA and Europe 1976-present

In the year 2000, a re-run of the London-Sydney Marathon saw Steve Pickering from South Africa enter with a 914/6. This gruelling event saw 100 competitors tackle thousands of miles of tough terrain through Europe and Turkey in the first 14 days, then move on by transport to northern Thailand, followed by driving south through Malaysia for 12 days before being flown to Australia for the last eight days of the rally. Of the 100 starters who left London, 78 reached Sydney, with Stig Blomqvist and Ben Rainsford scoring victory ahead of Michèle Mouton in a Porsche 911. And Steve? Yes, he finished, in 71st place, and what an adventure!

Still racing, at the time of writing, is the original chassis 914 043 0306 914/6 GT: the former Edgar Dören racer in action in Sweden, here with Nicke Nilsson at the wheel on the Knutstorp Ring in Skåne, Sweden, in 2011. (NN)

The Tour Auto in France is one of the major historic events. Held annually and starting in Paris, it takes in race tracks, hillclimbs and long road sections. Here, in the 2013 edition, we see a 914/6 shadowed by a GTO Ferrari and a 906 Porsche. Past champion drivers are often seen on this event, where they demonstrate that the cars are definitely the stars. (PC)

279

Porsche The Racing 914s

This is the car of Glenn Stazak in the USA, a former Ralph Meaney four-cylinder car, built originally into the No 28 car that Meaney ran at Sebring in 1971. It was modified in 1983 to run in the IMSA series. Stazak acquired the car and regularly races it, as in this image from Blackhawk Farms Raceway, October 2010. (GS)

Last and by no means least, we can't leave our story without a mention of Glenn Stazak, who has done valuable work discovering the whereabouts of numerous 914 racers in the USA, and even races one, too, as we see here in an image from 2015.

It is absolutely certain, therefore, from what you have seen here, that the car that was deemed not a 'proper' Porsche, and was thought to have been forgotten by many, is alive and well, its history and pedigree unquestioned. The future for this car of the 1970s is guaranteed. Love it or hate it, you can be sure that on the race tracks of the world we will still be seeing the racing 914s.

Not quite 'the end.'

10

Race records
Europe – North America
– rallying – hillclimbs

Europe
Race records of the Porsche 914 four- and six-cylinder, compiled from numerous sources – see acknowledgements in introductory pages
This list contains selected results of the more notable meetings of interest – it is not definitive.

EC = European Sports Prototype Championships
NRF = Not running at finish
NC = Not Classified
G Nat = German National level race
N Nat = Netherlands National and local International race
A Nat = Austrian National race
Int = International

ov = Overall race postion
GT = Grand Touring
GTP = Grand Touring Prototype
? = uncertain of accuracy
gr = Grid position

In general non-finishers are not listed, unless of particular significance
Note: every effort has been made to ensure correctness, but it is possible that some minor errors may be present.
Note: Not every 914/6 GT is identified as such, other than the factory cars. Some 400 GT aftermarket kits to convert the production 914/6 were supplied, therefore all the cars are generally referred to as 914/6

Date	Car	Event	#	Drivers	Result	Notes	Entrant if known
March	914/6 GT	Targa Florio Int		Various for test	Testing, did not race	Chassis 914 043 0705	
March	914/6 GT	Targa Florio Int		Various for test	Testing, did not race	914 043 0709	
12/04/70	914/6 GT	Hockenheim GT (G Nat)	136		9th ov	First event 914/6 GT kitted car	Autohaus Max Moritz
12/04/70	914/6 GT	Hockenheim AVD Jim Clark	136	Sauter	9th GT2	Possibly 043 0691	
19/04/70	914/6 GT	Nürburgring 300km (G Nat)	35	Nolte W	7th GT2	914 043 0462	Willi Nolte

281

Porsche The Racing 914s

Date	Car	Event	#	Drivers	Result	Notes	Entrant if known
26/04/70	914/6 GT	Montlhéry Coupes Vitesse (F Nat)	28	Leinenweber	4th ov	Not known if GT kitted	Porsche Racing team Pirmasens
03/05/70	914/6 GT	DARM Kaufbeuren GT2 (G Nat)	150	Gotz	8th ov	Privately built with factory GT kit	Autohaus Rolf Gotz
03/05/70	914/6 GT	DARM Kaufbeuren GT2 (G Nat)	152	Hopp	3rd GT2	Privately built with factory GT kit	Ingo Hopp
17/05/70	914/6	DARM Zolder (N Nat)	32	Hopp	6th ov	Privately built with factory GT kit	Ingo Hopp
31/05/70	914/6	Bremgarten IntKaiser/Steckkönig		Denu	3rd GT over 1300	Privately built with factory GT kit	Autohaus Rolf Gotz
31/05/70	914/6 GT	Nürburgring 1000km Int	93		20th ov, 3rd GT2, gr 42	International track debut 043 0258	Hahn Motorfahrzeuge
31/05/70	914/6 GT	Nürburgring 1000km Int	88	Huhn/Schwarz	19th ov, 2nd GT2, gr 36	International track debut 043 1415	Hahn Motorfahrzeuge
31/05/70	914/6 GT	Nürburgring 1000km Int	101	Nolte A/Christmann	21st ov, 4th GT2, gr 45	043 0462 built with factory GT kit	Hulpert Porsche
31/05/70	914/6 GT	Nürburgring 1000km Int	96	Quist/Krumm	23rd ov, 5th GT2, gr 41	International track debut 043 0691	Max Moritz
07/06/70	914/6 GT	Anderstorp (EC) Int	31	Hansen	7th ov, 1st in Gr 4 race 1 & 2	European Sports Proto and GT Championship	Lief Hansen
13-14/6/70	914/6 GT	Le Mans 24 Hours Int	40	Ballot-Léna/Chasseuil	6th ov, 1st GT2, gr 45	043 1020	Sonauto
14/06/70	914/6 GT	DARM Hockenheim (D Nat)	53	Seiler	5th ov, 4th GT2	043 0181	Hart Ski Racing Team
14/06/70	914/6	DARM Hockenheim (D Nat)	56	Hopp	? 6th GT2	Privately built with factory GT kit	Ingo Hopp
14/06/70	914/6	DARM Hockenheim (D Nat)	60	Kaiser	7th ov, 2nd GT2	043 0258	Hahn Motorfahrzeuge
14/06/70	914/6	DARM Hockenheim (D Nat)	61	Schwarz	8th ov, 3rd GT2	043 1415	Scuderia Lufthansa
20-21/06/70	914/6	Int AvD-Rennen Mainz-Finthen	146	Kaiser	2nd Prod GT & Spec GT up-to-2L	043 0258	Hahn Motorfahrzeuge
20-21/06/70	914/6	Int AvD-Rennen Mainz-Finthen	148	Quist	3rd Prod GT & Special GT up-to-2L	043 0691	Autohaus Max Moritz
05/07/70	914/6 GT	Hockenheim (EC) Int	37	Seiler	9th ov in Gr 4 race 2 NC final	043 0181	Hart Ski Racing Team
05/07/70	914/6	Hockenheim (EC) Int	38	Schlup	13th ov		Ecurie Biennoise
05/07/70	914/6	Hockenheim GT (G Nat)	18	Quist	4th ov, 1st GT2	043 0691	Autohaus Max Moritz
05/07/70	914/6	Hockenheim GT (G Nat)	23	Schwarz	24th	043 1415	Scuderia Lufthansa
05/07/70	914/6	Hockenheim GT (G Nat)	31	Denu	15th	Privately built with factory GT kit	Autohaus Rolf Gotz
05/07/70	914/6	Hockenheim GT (G Nat)	33	Kaiser	8th ov, 2nd GT2	043 0258	Hahn Motorfahrzeuge
19/07/70	914/6	Mugello (EC) Int	119	Schulp/Sartori	? 10th GT2		Ecurie Biennoise
19/07/70	914/6	Mugello (EC) Int	121	Fabri	? 9th GT2		
19/07/70	914/6	Mugello (EC) Int	123	Zanini	? 5th GT2		
19/07/70	914/6	DARM Ulm Laupheim (G Nat)		Kaiser	2nd ov	043 0258	Hahn Motorfahrzeuge
19/07/70	914/6	DARM Ulm Laupheim (G Nat)		Krumm	1st ov	043 0691	Autohaus Max Moritz
19/07/70	914/6	DARM Ulm Laupheim (G Nat)	297	Seiler	3rd ov	043 0181	Hart Ski Racing Team
25-26/07/70	914/6	AvD/ISCC-Flugplatzrennen Sembach	216	Dorner	1st Special GT up-to-2L		Escuderia Lufthansa
25-26/07/70	914/6	AvD/ISCC-Flugplatzrennen Sembach	219	Hopp	2nd Special GT up-to-2L	Privately built with factory GT kit	Ingo Hopp

Race records Europe – North America – rallying – hillclimbs

Date	Car	Event	#	Drivers	Result	Notes	Entrant if known
25-26/07/70	914/6	AvD/ISCC-Flugplatzrennen Sembach	222	Nolte	3rd Special GT up-to-2L	Hülpert Porsche	
26/07/70	914/6	Niederstetten (G Nat)		Krumm	2nd ov	043 0691	Autohaus Max Moritz
26/07/70	914/6	Niederstetten (G Nat)		Kaiser	1st ov	043 0258	Hahn Motorfahrzeuge
09/08/70	914/6	DMV Hessen Hockenheim	21	Dietrich Krumm	1st gr4 2L	043 0691	Autohaus Max Moritz
09/08/70	914/6	DMV Hessen Hockenheim	18	Robert Huhn	2nd Gr 4 2L	043 1415	Scuderia Lufthansa
09/08/70	914/6	DMV Hessen Hockenheim	19	Peter Kaiser	4th Gr 4 2L	043 0258	Hahn Motorfahrzeuge
09/08/70	914/6	DMV Hessen Hockenheim	17	Ingo Hopp	6th Gr 4 2L	Privately built with factory GT kit	Ingo Hopp
09/08/70	914/6	DMV Hessen Hockenheim	23	Bob Stoddard	10th Gr 4 2L		AvD Pirmasens Porsche Racing Team
19-23/08/70	914/6 GT	Marathon de la Route Int	1	Larrousse/Haldi/Marko	1st ov	043 2541	Porsche Factory team
19-23/08/70	914/6 GT	Marathon de la Route Int	2	Ballot-Léna/Steckkönig/Koob	3rd ov	043 2542	Porsche Factory team
19-23/08/70	914/6 GT	Marathon de la Route Int	3	Waldegård/Anderson A/Chasseuil	2nd ov	043 2543	Porsche Factory team
06/09/70	914/6 / GT	Nürburgring 500km (EC) Int	61	Egerland	27th ov	043 0983, former works car	Gotthard Egerland
06/09/70	914/6	Nürburgring 500km (EC) Int	62	Huhn	45th	043 1415	Scuderia Lufthansa
06/09/70		Monza Coppa Europa	61	Seiler	3rd ov, 2nd in class	043 0181	
13/09/70	914/6	Hockenheim GT (G Nat)	87	Quist	2nd ov, 1st GT2		Autohaus Max Moritz
13/09/70	914/6	Hockenheim GT (G Nat)	89	Steckkönig	4th ov, 2nd GT2		Paul Ernst Strähle
13/09/70	914/6	Hockenheim GT (G Nat)	80	Goring	8th ov, 3rd GT2		Hahn Motorfahrzeuge
19-27/09/70	914/6 GT	Tour de France Auto Int	120	Ballot-Léna/Morenas	6th ov	043 1020, 105 BC 92	Sonauto
19-27/09/70	914/6 GT	Tour de France Auto Int	121	Ballas/Imbert	8th ov	043 0457, 100 SW 38	Sonauto
27/09/70	914/6	Kinnekulle Ring, Goetene, Sweden	4	Leif Hansen	2nd GT up to 3L	Pole in class and fastest lap in class	
04/10/70	914/6	Mendig (T+2.0/GT)	63	Ingo Hopp	4th GT2	Privately built with factory GT kit	Ingo Hopp
11/10/70	914/6 GT	Zeltweg 1000km Int	51	Steckkönig/vonHohenzollern	12th ov, 1st GT2, gr 23		Paul Ernst Strähle
11/10/70	914/6 GT	Zeltweg 1000km Int	49	Seiler/Ettmueller/Pesch	14th ov, 2nd GT2, gr 25		Paul Ernst Strähle
11/10/70	914/6 GT	Zeltweg 1000km Int	41	Garant/Masoneri	18th ov, 3rd GT2, gr 31		Wicky Racing Team
11/10/70	914/6 GT	Zeltweg 1000km Int	53	Liotte/Ruspa	15th ov, 1st GT2.5, gr 28		Jolly Club
18/10/70	914/6	Paris 1000km Montlhéry Int	34	Pravedoni/Franey	22nd, gr 28		Fabrizio Pravedoni
18/10/70	914/6	DARM Nürburgring (GT/T+2)	142	Nolte	5th ov, 1st GT2	043 0462	Alexander Nolte
18/10/70	914/6	DARM Nürburgring (GT/T+2)	141	Thomas Kruger	4th GT2		Thomas Kruger
18/10/70	914/6	DARM Nürburgring (GT/T+2)	138	Gotthard Egerland	5th GT2	043 0983	Gotthard Egerland
18/10/70	914/6	DARM Nürburgring (GT/T+2)	137	Horst Godel	DNF		Braun Sixtant Racing Team
25/10/70	914/6	Neubiberg (GT+1.6)	238	Quist	1st GT2		Autohaus Max Moritz
25/10/70	914/6	Neubiberg (GT+1.6)	242	Steckkönig	3rd GT2		Strähle KG
01/11/70	914/6	Jarama 6 Hours Int	40	Juncadella/Fernández	11th ov, 1st GT2, gr 4	043 1569 Fitted with injection	Escudería Montjuich
29/11/70	914/6	Hockenheim Finale (G Nat)	34	Neureuther	6th ov	043 0734	Hermann Neureuther
29/11/70	914/6	Hockenheim Finale (G Nat)		Goring	1st ov		Rolf Goring/Hahn Motorfahrzeuge
29/11/70	914/6	Hockenheim Finale (G Nat)		Krumm	4th		Autohaus Max Moritz

Porsche The Racing 914s

Date	Car	Event	#	Drivers	Result	Notes	Entrant if known
29/11/70	914/6	Hockenheim Finale (G Nat)		Stoddard	5th		Robert Stoddard
28/03/71	914/6	DARM Zolder GT+1.6	283	Werner Kastner	3rd GT2		Werner Kastner
28/03/71	914/6	DARM Zolder GT+1.6	284	Friedhelm Theissen	2nd GT2	043 0653	Porsche Kremer Racing Team
28/03/71	914/6	DARM Zolder GT+1.6	288	Horst Godel	8th GT2		Braun Sixtant Racing Team
04/04/71	914/6	Hockenheim (G Nat)	39	Stoddard	10th ov, 5th GT2		Robert Stoddard
04/04/71	914/6	Hockenheim (G Nat)	35	Steckkönig	6th ov, 2nd GT2	043 0163	Strähle KG
04/04/71	914/6	Hockenheim (G Nat)	37	Schwarz	12th ov, 7th GT2	043 1415	Scuderia Lufthansa
04/04/71	914/6	Hockenheim (G Nat)	38	Godel	11th ov, 6th GT2		Sixtant Racing Team
11/04/71	914/6	Zolder non-championship race		Hans-Christian Jürgensen	1st GT2		Hans-Christian Jürgensen
11/04/71	914/6	Zolder non-championship race		Horst Godel	2nd GT2		Sixtant Racing Team
11/04/71	914/6	Zolder non-championship race		Bert Lips	4th GT2		Bert Lips
18/04/71	914/6	Le Mans 3 Hours	88	Haldi/Chenevière	11th ov, 3rd GT2, gr 17		Porsche Club Romand
25/04/71	914/6 GT	Monza 1000km	58	Seiler/Ettmueller	13th ov, 1st GT2, gr 18	043 0181	Tartaruga
25/04/71	914/6	Sembach (GT) non-champ race	358	Gustav Schlup	12th GT2		Ecurie Biennoise
25/04/71	914/6	Sembach (GT) non-champ race	359	"Peter Zbinden"	8th GT2		Scuderia Basilea
25/04/71	914/6	Sembach (GT) non-champ race	365	Walter Bauer	5th GT2		Max Moritz Racing Team
25/04/71	914/6	Sembach (GT) non-champ race	366	Rudolf Sauter	1st GT2		Max Moritz Racing Team
25/04/71	914/6	Sembach (GT) non-champ race	368	Alexander Nolte	6th GT2	043 0462	Alexander Nolte
25/04/71	914/6	Sembach (GT) non-champ race	373	Horst Godel	14th GT2		Braun Sixtant Racing Team
25/04/71	914/6	Sembach (GT) non-champ race		Hermann Dorner	7th GT2		MHSTC
09/05/71	914/6 GT	Spa 1000 km Int	49	Quist/Krumm	9th ov, 1st GT2, gr 21	143 0178	Max Moritz
09/05/71	914/6 GT	Spa 1000 km Int	51	Sage/Keller	Disqualified lap 38, gr 26	received outside assistance	Porsche Club Romand
09/05/71	914/6	DARM Fassberg (GT) non-champ race	130	Friedhelm Theissen	1st GT2	043 0653	
09/05/71	914/6	DARM Fassberg (GT) non-champ race	133	Hans Joachim Bartsch	3rd GT2		Hans Joachim Bartsch
09/05/71	914/6	DARM Fassberg (GT) non-champ race	136	Hermann Dorner	4th GT2	043 1415	Hermann Dorner
09/05/71	914/6	DARM Fassberg (GT) non-champ race	137	Werner Kastner	2nd GT2	043 1034	Werner Kastner
16/05/71	914/6 GT	Targa Florio Int	56	Kauhsen/Steckkönig/von Hohenzollern	13th ov, 3rd GT2, gr 31	143 2542	Paul Ernst Strähle
16/05/71	914/6	Kaufbeuren ADC Championship		Gerhard Fetzer	1st GT2		
16/05/71	914/6	Kaufbeuren ADC Championship		Horst Godel	3rd GT2		
22-23/05/71	914/6	Bremgarten Int		Zbinden	1st GT 1600+		
22-23/05/71	914/6	Bremgarten Int		Paul Keller	6th GT 1600+		
22-23/05/71	914/6	Bremgarten Int		Walter Bauer	7th GT 1600+		Autohaus Max Moritz
22-23/05/71	914/6	Bremgarten Int		Horst Godel	8th GT 1600+		Braun Sixtant Racing Team
23/05/71	914/6	Nürburgring 750m GT (G Nat)		Simonis/Hoier	2nd GT		
23/05/71	914/6	Nürburgring 750m GT (G Nat)		Schimpf/Mathiess	3rd GT		Eckhard Schimpf
30/05/71	914/6	DARM Neuhausen (GT2)	71	Theissen	2nd	914 043 0653	Porsche Kremer Racing Team
30/05/71	914/6	DARM Neuhausen (GT2)	80	"Impakt"	3rd		Ecurie Biennoise
30/05/71	914/6	Salzburgring GT (A Nat)		Neureuther	1st ov	043 0734	Hermann Neureuther
30/05/71	914/6	Nürburgring 1000km	94	Quist/Krumm	14th ov, 1st GT2, gr 36	143 0178	Max Moritz

Race records Europe – North America – rallying – hillclimbs

Date	Car	Event	#	Drivers	Result	Notes	Entrant if known
30/05/71	914/6	Nürburgring 1000km	95	Stecköning/Schmid	15th ov, 2nd GT2, gr 41	143 2542	Paul Ernst Strähle
30/05/71	914/6	Nürburgring 1000km	93	Simonis/Hoier	18th ov, 3rd GT2, gr 42	043 0185	Automobilclub Rübenach
30/05/71	914/6	Nürburgring 1000km	96	Rieder/Scheeren	19th ov, 4th GT2, gr 33		Kremer Brothers
30/05/71	914/6	Nürburgring 1000km	108	Nolte/Christmann	NRF, gr 24	043 0462	Alexander Nolte
30/05/71	914/6	Zolder (GT)		Hans-Christian Jürgensen	3rd GT2		Hans-Christian Jürgensen
12-13/06/71	914/6 GT	Le Mans 24 Hours	69	Quist/Krumm	Dnf lap 37 gearbox, gr 37	143 0178	Max Moritz
12-13/06/71	914/6 GT	Le Mans 24 Hours	46	Sage/Keller	Dnf lap 44 oil pressure, gr 44		Porsche Club Romand
20/06/71	914/6	DARM Mainz-Finthen (G Nat) GT	194	Theissen	1st ov	043 0653	Porsche Kremer Racing
20/06/71	914/6	DARM Mainz-Finthen (G Nat) GT	198	Martin	5th ov		Michael Martin
20/06/71	914/6	Bavaria Salzburg (SRP1.15+GT)	135	Neureuther	1st GT2	043 0734	Team Matter – Uberrollbugel
27/06/71	914/6 GT	Österreichring 1000km Int	37	Stecköning/Schmid/Bauer	9th ov, 1st GT2, gr 23	143 2542	Paul Ernst Strähle
04/07/71	914/6	AVU Int DMV		Hans-Christian Jürgensen	1st GT2		Hans-Christian Jürgensen
04/07/71	914/6	AVU Int DMV		Eckhard Schimpf	3rd GT2		Jägermeister Racing Team
04/07/71	914/6	Hockenheim GT (G Nat)	20	Stecköning	11th ov, 4th GT2		Strähle KG
04/07/71	914/6	Hockenheim GT (G Nat)	23	Godel	13th ov, 6th GT2		Sixtant Racing Team
04/07/71	914/6	Hockenheim GT (G Nat)	22	Quist	8th ov, 1st GT2	143 0178	Autohaus Max Moritz
04/07/71	914/6	Hockenheim GT (G Nat)	19	Maraggia	16th ov, 9th GT2		Apag Racing
04/07/71	914/6	Hockenheim GT (G Nat)	17	Seiler	10th ov, 3rd GT2	043 0181	Squadra Tartaruga
04/07/71	914/6	Hockenheim GT (G Nat)	15	Kaiser	9th ov, 2nd GT2	143 0306	Heinz Blind
04/07/71	914/6	Vila Real (Portugal)	25	Miguel Correia	15th ov, 28 laps		
11/07/71	914/6	DARM Norisring (GT+1.6)	21	Theissen	4th GT2	43 0653	
11/07/71	914/6	DARM Norisring (GT+1.6)	22	Seiler	15 laps, 1st GT2	043 0181	Ernst Seiler
11/07/71	914/6	DARM Norisring (GT+1.6)	23	Kaiser	5th GT2	043 03 06	Heinz Blind
11/07/71	914/6	DARM Norisring (GT+1.6)	24	Dorner	15 laps, 2nd GT2	0431415	Sports Touring Club Mannheim
11/07/71	914/6	DARM Norisring (GT+1.6)	25	Godel	8th GT2		Sixtant Racing Team
11/07/71	914/6	DARM Norisring (GT+1.6)	27	Bauer	15 laps, 3rd GT2		Strähle KG
11/07/71	914/6	DARM Norisring (GT+1.6)	28	Neureuther	9th GT2	043 0734	Team Matter
11/07/71	914/6	DARM Norisring (GT+1.6)	29	Hans-Heinrich Timm	6th GT2		Renngemeinschaft Ford-Timm-Racing
18/07/71	914/6	Diepholz Flugplatzrennen	231	Hans-Christian Jürgensen	4th GT 1300, 1st GT2		Hans-Christian Jürgensen
18/07/71	914/6	Diepholz Flugplatzrennen	228	Friedhelm Theissen	3rd GT2		Auto Kremer Racing Team
18/07/71	914/6	Diepholz Flugplatzrennen	230	Willi Nolte	4th GT2	043 0462	Willi Nolte
18/07/71	914/6	Diepholz Flugplatzrennen	221	Heinz Blind	6h GT2	143 03 06	Sports Car Club of Stuttgart
18/07/71	914/6	Diepholz Flugplatzrennen	232	Bartsch	7th GT2		Hans-Joachim Bartsch
24-25/07/71	914/6	Hessen DMV Hockenheim (GT+1.3)	16	Fetzer	4th GT2		Autohaus Max Moritz
24-25/07/71	914/6	Hessen DMV Hockenheim (GT+1.3)	13	Doherty	5th GT2		Mannheim-Heidelberg Sportstouring-Club
24-25/07/71	914/6	Hessen DMV Hockenheim (GT+1.3)	12	Blind	6th GT2		Sports Car Club of Stuttgart
01/08/71	914/6	Salzburgring ACS Std1		Seiler	2nd ov	043 0181	
15/08/71	914/6	Niederstetten (GT2)	121	Doherty	1st ov		Mannheim-Heidelberg Sportstouring-Club
15/08/71	914/6	Wunstorf (GT2)	126	Jürgensen	Pole + 1st ov, 1st GT2		Hans-Christian Jürgensen
15/08/71	914/6	Wunstorf (GT2)	127	Timm	4th ov, 4th GT2, gr 3		Hans-Heinrich Timm
15/08/71	914/6	Wunstorf (GT2)	128	Willi Nolte	5th GT2 or DNA?		Willi Nolte

285

Porsche The Racing 914s

Date	Car	Event	#	Drivers	Result	Notes	Entrant if known
22/08/71	914/6	Kassel Calden Flugplatz ADAC Int	376	Christmann	1st ov, 1st GT2	043 0462	Werner Christmann
22/08/71	914/6	Kassel Calden Flugplatz ADAC Int	371	Hans-Christian Jürgensen	4th ov, 4th GT2		Hans-Christian Jürgensen
22/08/71	914/6	Kassel Calden Flugplatz ADAC Int	372	Timm	5th ov, 5th GT2		Hans-Heinrich Timm
22/08/71	914/6	Kassel Calden Flugplatz ADAC Int	374	Fetzer	8th ov, 8th GT2	043 2075	Autohaus Max Moritz
22/08/71	914/6	Kassel Calden Flugplatz ADAC Int	377	Theissen	3rd ov, 3rd GT2	043 0653	Auto Kremer Racing Team
22/08/71	914/6	Kassel Calden Flugplatz ADAC Int	378	Michael Martin	7th ov, 8th GT2		Michael Martin
29/08/71	914/6	Mendig (GT+1.3)	56	Bauer	9th GT2	043 2075	Autohaus Max Moritz
29/08/71	914/6	Mendig (GT+1.3)	61	Hans-Christian Jürgensen	5th ov, 3rd GT2		Hans-Christian Jürgensen
29/08/71	914/6	Mendig (GT+1.3)	63	Timm	4th GT2		Hans-Heinrich Timm
29/08/71	914/6	Mendig (GT+1.3)	65	Christmann	4th ov, 2nd GT2		Willi Nolte
29/08/71	914/6	Mendig (GT+1.3)	69	Lips	6th GT2	043 1034	Kremer Racing
05/09/71	914/6 GT	Nürburgring 500 km (EC) Int	80	Quist	18th ov, 19 laps, 2nd GT2	143 0178	Autohaus Max Moritz
05/09/71	914/6	Nürburgring 500 km (EC) Int	65	Kremer/Neuhaus	20th ov, 19 laps, 3rd GT2	043 0653	Porsche Kremer Racing
05/09/71	914/6	Nürburgring 500 km (EC) Int	82	Christmann/Nolte	Dnf	043 0462	EFG Dortmund
11/09/71	914/6	DARM Hockenheim (GT/T2)	52	Seiler	2nd ov, 1st GT2, 1st GT	043 0181	Ernst Seiler
11/09/71	914/6	DARM Hockenheim (GT/T2)	53	Theissen	5th GT2		Auto Kremer Racing Team
11/09/71	914/6	DARM Hockenheim (GT/T2)	54	Fetzer	4th GT2		Autohaus Max Moritz
11/09/71	914/6	DARM Hockenheim (GT/T2)	55	Dietrich Krumm	4th ov, 3rd GT2		Autohaus Max Moritz
11-12/09/71	914/6	Geilenkirchen ADAC	2	Hans-Christian Jürgensen	1st GT2		Hans-Christian Jürgensen
11-12/09/71	914/6	Geilenkirchen ADAC	2	Bert Lips	3rd GT2		Auto Kremer Racing Team
11-12/09/71	914/6	Geilenkirchen ADAC	2	Edgar Dören	4th GT2		Edgar Dören
19/09/71	914/6	Dalsland Ring Final Sweden	2	Bengt Ekberg	2nd GT up to 3L		Valvoline Circle of Racing
19/09/71	914/6	Mainz Finthen (T+2.5/GT+1.6)	216	Hans-Christian Jürgensen	3rd GT2		Hans-Christian Jürgensen
19/09/71	914/6	Mainz Finthen (T+2.5/GT+1.6)	219	Hans-Heinrich Timm	6th GT2		Hans-Heinrich Timm
19/09/71	914/6	Mainz Finthen (T+2.5/GT+1.6)		Stephen Behr	1st GT2		
19/09/71	914/6	Mainz Finthen (T+2.5/GT+1.6)		Bert Lips	7th GT2		Auto Kremer Racing Team
19/09/71	914/6	Mainz Finthen (T+2.5/GT+1.6)	210	Johann Foster	8th GT2		
17/10/71?	914/6	Nürburgring GT+T ADAC	16	Edgar Dören	2nd GT2		Edgar Dören
17/10/71?	914/6	Nürburgring GT+T ADAC	17	Hans Joachim Bartsch	4th GT2		Hans-Joachim Bartsch
07/11/71	914/6	Jarama 2 Hours (EC)	57	Bernard Chenevière	9th ov, 3rd GT2, gr 11		Porsche Club Romand
07/11/71	914/6	Karlsruhe Hockenheim (GT2)		Fetzer	1st ov		Autohaus Max Moritz
07/11/71	914/6	Karlsruhe Hockenheim (GT2)		Egerland	4th ov		Kamei Racing Team
07/11/71	914/6	Karlsruhe Hockenheim (GT2)		Bartsch	5th ov		Hans-Joachim Bartsch
07/11/71	914/6	Karlsruhe Hockenheim (GT2)	273	Neureuther	9th ov		Team-Matter-Uberrolbügel
07/11/71	914/6	Karlsruhe Hockenheim (GT2)		Jim Doherty	11th ov		MHSTC
13/11/71	914/6	Hockenheim (GT2)		Egerland	3rd ov		Kamei Racing Team
13/11/71	914/6	Hockenheim (GT2)		Walter Bauer	4th ov		Autohaus Max Moritz
28/11/71	914/6	Hockenheim Finale		Walter Bauer	5th LG3		Autohaus Max Moritz
03/04/72	914/6	Nürburgring 300km (G Nat)	155	Nolte	14th, 5th GT2	043 0462	Willi Nolte
03/04/72	914/6	Nürburgring 300km (G Nat)	156	Edgar Dören	16th, 6th GT2		Edgar Dören
03/04/72	914/6	Nürburgring 300km (G Nat)	158	Sasse	7th GT2		Horst Sasse
09/04/72	914/6	DARM Zolder (G Nat + N Nat)	294	Nolte	4th GT2	043 0462	Willi Nolte
09/04/72	914/6	DARM Zolder (G Nat + N Nat)	295	Hans-Christian Jürgensen	2nd ov, 1st GT2		Hans-Christian Jürgensen

Race records Europe – North America – rallying – hillclimbs

Date	Car	Event	#	Drivers	Result	Notes	Entrant if known
09/04/72	914/6	DARM Zolder (G Nat + N Nat)		Klauke	3rd GT2		
15-16/04/72	914/6	Hockenheim Jim Clark	27	Günther Schwarz	5th TC/GT over 1300, 2nd GT2/4 2L		MHSTC
15-16/04/72	914/6	Hockenheim Jim Clark	33	Walter Bauer	8th TC/GT over 1300, 5th GT2/4 2L		Autohaus Max Moritz
15-16/04/72	914/6	Hockenheim Jim Clark	32	Roland Bauer	11th TC/GT over 1300, 8th GT2/4 2L		Autohaus Max Moritz
30/04/72	914/6	DARM Sembach (G Nat)		Singenberger	11th ov		
30/04/72	914/6	DARM Sembach (G Nat)		Jürgensen	3rd ov and GT2		Hans-Christian Jürgensen
30/04/72	914/6	DARM Sembach (G Nat)		Doherty	4th ov and GT2		MHSTC
13/05/72	914/6	Hockenheim GT	168	Fetzer	4th GT2	143 0178	Max Moritz GmbH
13/05/72	914/6	Hockenheim GT	174	Walter Bauer	9th GT2	043 2075	Walter Bauer
21/05/72	914/6	DARM Zolder (N Nat + G Nat)		Hans-Christian Jürgensen	1st ov		Hans-Christian Jürgensen
21/05/72	914/6	DARM Zolder (N Nat + G Nat)		Edgar Dören	2nd		Edgar Dören
21/05/72	914/6	DARM Zolder (N Nat + G Nat)		Sasse	7th		Horst Sasse
21/05/72	914/6	Targa Florio Int	35	Schmid/Floridia	9th ov, 2nd GT2		Paul-Ernst Strähle
28/05/72	914/6	Nürburgring 1000km Int	81	Simonis/Hoier	29th, 4th GT2, gr 49		Walter Simonis
11/06/72	914/6	DARM Hockenheim (GT)	62	Jochen Engel	3rd GT2		STC Mannheim-Heidelberg
11/06/72	914/6	DARM Hockenheim (GT)	72	Roland Bauer	9th GT2		Roland Bauer
18/06/72	914/6	Euro GT Zandvoort	12	Theo Kinsbergen	13th ov, 4th GT2, gr 16		Stichting Team Radio Veronica
18/06/72	914/6	DRM Mainz-Finthen	75	Gerhard Fetzer	3rd GT2		Autohaus Max Moritz GmbH
18/06/72	914/6	DRM Mainz-Finthen	77	Eckhard Schimpf	4th GT2		Jägermeister Racing Team
18/06/72	914/6	Sassotetto hillclimb, Sarnaro It		Francesco Miglionini	8th GTS, 4th in class		
24/06/72	914/6	Hohenloher ADAC Niederstetten		Jim Doherty	4th GT2		Mannheim-Heidelberg Sport-Touring-Club
24/06/72	914/6	Hohenloher ADAC Niederstetten		Walter Bauer	8th GT2		Autohaus Max Moritz
25/06/72	914/6	Niederstettern (GT)		Jim Doherty	4th GT2		MHSTC
25/06/72	914/6	Niederstettern (GT)		Walter Bauer	8th GT2		Autohaus Max Moritz GmbH
02/07/72	914/6	Bavaria Salzburgring (GT)		Jochen Engel	4th GT2		MHSTC
02/07/72	914/6	Bavaria Salzburgring (GT)		Dieter Schmid	5th GT2		Strähle KG
16/07/72	914/6	Diepholz (T/GT2)		Eckart Gutowski	2nd ov		Eckhart Gutowski
16/07/72	914/6	DRM Diepholz		Doherty	4th ov, 4th Div II	043 1415	MHSTC
16/07/72	914/6	Salzburgring (GT)		Roland Bauer	1st GT2		
29/07/72	914/6	Nürburgring Euro GT (G Nat Int)	25	Canonica	16th ov, 5th GT2		Porsche Club Romand
29/07/72	914/6	Nürburgring Euro GT (G Nat Int)	27	Schimpf	15th ov, 4th GT2		Jägermeister Racing Team
29/07/72	914/6	Nürburgring Euro GT (G Nat Int)	30	Doherty	14th ov, 3rd GT2		MHSTC
06/08/72	914/6	DARM Norisring (GT+1.6)		Hermann Dorner	2nd GT2		MHSTC
06/08/72	914/6	DARM Norisring (GT+1.6)		Karl-Heinz Gerner	4th GT2		Porsche Club Nurnberg
13/08/72	914/6	Wunstorf GT (G Nat)		Gutowski	2nd ov, 2nd GT2	043 0462	Eckhart Gutowski
13/08/72	914/6	Wunstorf GT (G Nat)		Hans-Christian Jürgensen	1st ov, 1st GT2		Hans-Christian Jürgensen
13/08/72	914/6	Wunstorf GT (G Nat)		Engel	3rd ov, 3rd GT2	043 1415	MHSTC
13/08/72	914/6	Wunstorf GT (G Nat)		Bauer	4th ov, 4th GT2	043 0163	Strähle KG
13/08/72	914/6	DARM Zandvoort (G Nat + N Nat)		Edgar Dören	2nd		Edgar Dören
13/08/72	914/6	Nürburgring (GT/T+2.0)	45	Horst Sasse	2nd GT2		MCS Langenfeld

Porsche The Racing 914s

Date	Car	Event	#	Drivers	Result	Notes	Entrant if known
20/08/72	914/6	DARM Kassel-Calden (G Nat)	88	Hans-Christian Jürgensen	8th		Hans-Christian Jürgensen
20/08/72	914/6	Karlsruhe Hockenheim (GT)		Walter Bauer	3rd GT2		Autohaus Max Moritz GmbH
20/08/72	914/6	Karlsruhe Hockenheim (GT)		Dieter Weber	4th GT2		Dieter Weber
27/08/72	914/6	Euro GT Hockenheim	48	Gerhard Fetzer	11th ov, 3rd GT2	043 2075	Autohaus Max Moritz
27/08/72	914/6	Vila do Conde	121	Miguel Correia	4th ov, gr 6	43 0418	
03/09/72	914/6	Nürburgring 500km	66	Jean Canonica	Raced, result unknown		Club Porsche Romand
10/09/72	914/6	500km Watkins Glen	58	Rebaque/Rojas	10th ov		Peter Gregg
10/09/72	914/6	Mainz-Finthen (GT)	58	Dieter Kilb	6th GT2		Autohaus Kaufmann OHG
10/09/72	914/6	Mainz-Finthen (GT)	60	Hans-Christian Jürgensen	7th GT2		Hans-Christian Jürgensen
10/09/72	914/6	Mainz-Finthen (GT)	63	Walter Bauer	2nd GT2		Autohaus Max Moritz
10/09/72	914/6	Monza Euro GT Int		Seiler	17th, gr 17	043 0181	Squadra Tartaruga
10/09/72	914/6	Monza Euro GT Int	64	Monticone/Fossati	DNS		Scuderia Brescia Corse
16/09/72	914/6	Jyllandsringen (D Nat)		Hans-Christian Jürgensen	2nd		Hans-Christian Jürgensen
17/09/72	914/6	Zolder GT		Edgar Dören	4th GT2		Edgar Dören
24/09/72	914/6	Estoril GT/S (P Nat)	44	Correia	3rd, gr 6		
24/09/72	914/6	Hugelheim Hockenheim (GT)		Walter Bauer	DNF		Autohaus Max Moritz
01/10/72	914/6	Zolder 60 Miles		Edgar Dören	3rd GT2		Edgar Dören
01/10/72	914/6	Zolder 60 Miles		Hans-Christian Jürgensen	1st GT2		Hans-Christian Jürgensen
08/10/72	914/6	DRM Sauerland		Eckart Gutowski	8th Div II		Eckard Gutowski
05/11/72	914/6	Jarama 2 Hours (EC)		Canonica	10th ov	023 0032	Bricolens Interacing
12/11/72	914/6	Estoril Euro GT Int	81	Canonica	7th ov, 3rd GT2, gr 13	023 0032	Bricolens Interacing
12/11/72	914/6	Estoril Euro GT Int	82	Correia	NC, gr 17	43 0418	
03/12/72	914/6	Hockenheim Finale (GT/T)	22	Hans-Christian Jürgensen	23rd		Hans-Christian Jürgensen
03/12/72	914/6	Hockenheim Finale (GT/T)	27	Karl-Heinz Schrey	17th		Karl-Heinz Schrey
03/12/72	914/6	Hockenheim Finale (GT/T)	40	Hermann Neureuther	Disqualified	043 0734	Hermann Neureuther
03/12/72	914/6	Hockenheim Finale (S/GT)	38	Jochen Engel	6th ov, 5th LG3		Jochen Engel
25/03/73	914/6	DARM Zolder (GT+1.6)	228	Edgar Dören	2nd GT2	043 0165	Bergischer Motor Club
25/03/73	914/6	DARM Zolder (GT+1.6)	238	Peter Karl Nowak	5th GT2		Braun Sixtant Racing Team
25/03/73	914/6	DARM Zolder (GT+1.6)	239	Lothar Ohren	3rd GT2		Rheydter Club fur Motorsport
25/03/73	914/6	DARM Zolder (GT+1.6)	?	Werner Christmann	6th GT2		Werner Christmann
31/03/73	914/6	DARM Nürburgring (GT)	143	Edgar Dören	11th ov, 4th GT2, 4th Class 3	043 0165	Bergischer Motor Club eV im ADAC
31/03/73	914/6	DARM Nürburgring (GT)	149	Jochen Engel	13th ov, 6th GT2, 6th Class 3	043 1415	Mannheim Heidelberger Sports TC
31/03/73	914/6	DARM Nürburgring (GT)	154	Lothar Ohren	21st ov, 8th GT2, 8th Class 3	043 0251 ?	Same chassis # as supplied to Porsche-USA car
31/03/73	914/6	DARM Nürburgring (GT)	155	Werner Christmann	6th ov, 1st GT2, 1st Class 3	143 0306	Werner Christmann
01/04/73	914/6	Europ Champ (GT) Nürburgring Int	154	Ohren	17th, 6th GT2		Lothar Ohren
01/04/73	914/6	Europ Champ (GT) Nürburgring Int	143	Edgar Dören	8th, 3rd GT2		Bergischer Motor Club
08/04/73	914/6	Zolder GT (G Nat)		Schrey	1st		Karl-Heinz Schrey
22/04/73	914/6	DARM Zolder GT		Edgar Dören	3rd GT2		Bergischer Motor Club
22/04/73	914/6	DARM Zolder GT		Werner Christmann	2nd GT2		Werner Christmann
07-08/04/73	914/6	Hockenheim Jim Clark	127	"Ronald Knudel"	1st GT2		HMSTC
07-08/04/73	914/6	Hockenheim Jim Clark	130	Peter Karl Nowak	5th GT2		Peter Karl Nowak
07-08/04/73	914/6	Hockenheim Jim Clark	125	Hans-Christian Jürgensen	DNF		Hans-Christian Jürgensen

Race records Europe – North America – rallying – hillclimbs

Date	Car	Event	#	Drivers	Result	Notes	Entrant if known
08/04/73	914/6	Zolder (GT/T)		Karl-Heinz Schrey	1st		Karl-Heinz Schrey
15/04/73	914/6	Zolder 60 Miles		Hans-Christian Jürgensen	1st GT2		Hans-Christian Jürgensen
22/04/73	914/6	DARM Zolder (GT)		Edgar Dören	3rd GT2	43 0165	
22/04/73	914/6	DARM Zolder (GT)		Werner Christmann	2nd GT2		Werner Christmann
06/05/73	914/6	AvD/ISCC Sembach	482	Edgar Dören	3rd GT		Bergischer Motor Club
06/05/73	914/6	AvD/ISCC Sembach	451	Peter Karl Nowak	5th GT		Braun Sixtant Racing Team
06/05/73	914/6	AvD/ISCC Sembach	458	Robert Frostrom	6th GT		
13/05/73	914/6	Targa Florio	123	Nieri/Fabri	36th 8 laps, 4th GT2, gr 47		Carlo Fabri
13/05/73	914/6	Targa Florio	127	Mannino/de Gregorio	21st 9 laps, 2nd GT2, gr 55		Giuseppe de Gregorio
13/05/73	914/6	Avus (GT)		Dieter Bohnhorst	3rd	043 1034	Dieter Bohnhorst
19-20/05/73	914/6	Hockenheim 100 Miles		Horst Godel	2nd Gr 3&4 2L		Sixtant Racing Team
19-20/05/73	914/6	Hockenheim 100 Miles		Hans Stähli	3rd Gr 3&4 2L		Braun Sixtant Racing Team
19-20/05/73	914/6	Hockenheim 100 Miles		Lothar Ohren	6th Gr 3&4 2L		Lothar Ohren
19-20/05/73	914/6	Hockenheim 100 Miles		Eckhard Schimpf	7th Gr 3&4 2L		Jägermeister Racing Team
19-20/05/73	914/6	Hockenheim 100 Miles		Robert Frostrom	8th Gr 3&4 2L		
20/05/73	914/6	DARM Salzburgring		Edgar Dören	2nd GT2	043 0165	Bergischer Motor Club
02/06/73	914/6	Imola Euro GT Int	67	Carlo Fabri ("Cam")	20th ov, 6th GT2		
03/06/73	914/6	Nivelles (GT)		Lothar Ohren	2nd GT2		Lothar Ohren
10/06/73	914/6	Zolder GT (G Nat)		Edgar Dören	2nd GT2	043 0165	Bergischer Motor Club
10/06/73	914/6	Misano		Carlo Fabbri ("Cam")	2nd in class		
17/06/73	914/6	Zolder (GT)		Werner Christmann	1st Div 2		Werner Christmann
17/06/73	914/6	DMV Rhein Pokal Int Hockenheim		Frostrom	2nd GT2		
17/06/73	914/6	DMV Rhein Pokal Int Hockenheim		Peter Karl Nowak	4th GT2		
27/06/73	914/6	Hockenheim (GT)		Alfred Kunze	started, result unknown		
27/06/73	914/6	Hockenheim (GT)		Robert Frostrom	2nd GT2		
27/06/73	914/6	Hockenheim (GT)		Peter Karl Nowak	4th GT2		
01/07/73	914/6	Avus (GT)		Hans-Christian Jürgensen	1st GT2		Hans-Christian Jürgensen
01/07/73	914/6	Avus (GT)		Eckhard Schimpf	2nd GT2		Eckhard Schimpf
07-08/07/73	914/6	DARM Niederstetten		Walter Bauer	2nd GT2		Autohaus Max Moritz
07-08/07/73	914/6	DARM Niederstetten		Edgar Dören	1st GT2	043 0165	Bergischer Motor Club
07-08/07/73	914/6	DARM Niederstetten		"Rudolf Knudel"	4th GT2		MHSTC
07-08/07/73	914/6	DARM Niederstetten		Hans Stähli	1st GT2 Swiss class		
15/07/73	914/6	DRM Diepholz (G Nat)		Christmann	5th Div IIgr 7	143 0306	Werner Christmann
15/07/73	914/6	DRM Diepholz (GT)		Christmann	1st GT2, gr 1	143 0 06	Werner Christmann
15/07/73	914/6	DRM Diepholz (GT)		Eckhard Schimpf	2nd GT2	143 0178	Jägermeister Racing Team
15/07/73	914/6	DRM Diepholz (GT)		Franz Konrad	3rd GT2	043 0462	Franz Konrad
15/07/73	914/6	DARM Hockenheim		Edgar Dören	4th GT2	043 0165	Bergischer Motor Club
15/07/73	914/6	DARM Hockenheim		Albrecht Schütz	1st GT2		Autohaus Max Moritz
15/07/73	914/6	DARM Hockenheim		"Rudolf Knudel"	5th GT2		MHSTC
22/07/73	914/6	Hockenheim GT (G Nat)	326	Albrecht Schütz	1st ov		Autohaus Max Moritz
22/07/73	914/6	Hockenheim GT (G Nat)	327	Hans Stähli	4th		Formel Rennsport Club
22/07/73	914/6	Hockenheim GT (G Nat)	328	Nowak	5th		Braun Sixtant Racing Team
05/08/73	914/6	DARM Nürburgring (G Nat)	39	Schimpf	13th	143 0178	Jägermeister Racing Team

Porsche The Racing 914s

Date	Car	Event	#	Drivers	Result	Notes	Entrant if known
05/08/73	914/6	DARM Nürburgring (G Nat)	40	Hans Stähli	18th		Formel Rennsport Club
12/08/73	914/6	Hessen Hockenheim (GT)		Peter Karl Nowak	3rd GT2		Sixtant Racing Team
12/08/73	914/6	Hessen Hockenheim (GT)		Walter Bauer	1st GT2		Autohaus Max Moritz
26/08/73	914/6	Hockenheim Euro GT Int	73	Hans Stähli	18th ov, 2nd GT2	043 2075	Autohaus Max Moritz
26/08/73	914/6	Hockenheim Euro GT Int	74	Hans Stähli	21st ov, 4th GT2		FRC
26/08/73	914/6	Hockenheim Swiss AC Trophy		Bauer	1st Swiss GT		Autohaus Max Moritz
26/08/73	914/6	Hockenheim Swiss AC Trophy		"Ronald Knudel"	2nd Swiss GT		MHSTC
26/08/73	914/6	Hockenheim Swiss AC Trophy		Hans Stähli	3rd Swiss GT		FRC
01-02/09/73	914/6	Nürburgring 500km		Christmann	13th ov, 1st Gr 4 Race 1 and 2	1403 06	Hubert Engbert Olde
02/09/73	914/6	6H Monza		Zanini/Zanini	Raced, result unknown gr 30		
09/09/73	914/6	Mainz-Finthen (GT)	177	Peter Karl Nowak	5th GT2, 5th Gr4 2L		Sixtant Racing Team
09/09/73	914/6	Mainz-Finthen (GT)	180	Walter Bauer	1st GT2, 1st Gr 4 2L		Autohaus Max Moritz GmbH
09/09/73	914/6	Mainz-Finthen (GT)	181	"Ronald Knudel"	2nd GT2, 2nd Gr 4 2L		MHSTC
09/09/73	914/6	Mainz-Finthen (GT)	256	Hubert Flickmann	4th GT2, 4th Gr 4 2L		Huber Flickmann
16/09/73	914/6	Ulm GT2 (G Nat)	311	Steckkönig	2nd ov	043 0163	Günter Steckkönig
16/09/73	914/6	Ulm GT2 (G Nat)		Albrecht Schütz	1st ov	043 2075	Autohaus Max Moritz
16/09/73	914/6	Ulm GT2 (G Nat)		"Knudel"	4th ov	043 1415	MHSTC
23/09/73	914/6	Misano Trofeo Città dei Mille		Carlo Fabbri ("Cam")	2nd in class		
30/09/73	914/6	Dueren/Nordheim Zolder		Werner Christmann	1st GT2		Werner Christmann
30/09/73	914/6	Dueren/Nordheim Zolder		Edgar Dören	2nd GT2	043 0165	Bergischer Motor Club
21/10/73	914/6	Zolder GT (G Nat + N Nat)		"Knudel"	4th		MHSTC
21/10/73	914/6	Zolder GT (G Nat + N Nat)		Edgar Dören	3rd ov		Bergischer Motor Club
11/11/73	914/6	Hockenheim (GT)		Peter Karl Nowak	5th GT2		Sixtant Racing Team
11/11/73	914/6	Hockenheim (GT)		Walter Bauer	2nd GT2		Autohaus Max Moritz
24/03/74	914/6	DARM Zolder GT/T+2		Albrecht Schütz	2nd GT2		Autohaus Max Moritz
24/03/74	914/6	DARM Zolder GT/T+2		Edgar Dören	1st GT2		
24/03/74	914/6	DARM Zolder GT/T+2		Peter Karl Nowak	3rd GT2		
07/04/74	914/6	DARM Hockenheim (G Nat)	135	Albrecht Schütz	1st ov		Autohaus Max Moritz
07/04/74	914/6	DARM Hockenheim (G Nat)	136	Ehlert	4th ov	043 0734	Peter Ehlert
07/04/74	914/6	DARM Hockenheim (G Nat)	137	Nowak	6th ov		Sixtant Racing Team
07/04/74	914/6	DARM Hockenheim (G Nat)	138	Edgar Dören	2nd ov	043 0165	Bergischer Motor Club
28/04/74	914/6	DARM Nürburgring (G Nat)	90	Siegle	8th ov	043 0734	Wilhelm-Horst Siegle
28/04/74	914/6	DARM Nürburgring (G Nat)	94	Edgar Dören	5th ov	043 0165	Bergischer Motor Club
04-05/05/74	914/6	Hockenheim 100 Miles		Siegle	1st Gr 4 2L	043 0734	Wilhelm-Horst Siegle
04-05/05/74	914/6	Hockenheim 100 Miles		Ronald Arzdorf	2nd Gr 4 2L		
04-05/05/74	914/6	Hockenheim 100 Miles		Peter Karl Nowak	3rd Gr 4 2L		Braun Sixtant Racing Team
05/05/74	914/6	Neubiberg Flugplatzrennen	242	Dieter Ankele	4th GT2	0432075	Autohaus Max Moritz
05/05/74	914/6	Neubiberg Flugplatzrennen	241	Manfred Laub	1st GT2	043 0178	Autohaus Max Moritz
12/05/74	914/6	Zandvoort Junior Trophy	311	Hubert Schlieckmann	1st GT2		Hubert Schlieckmann
05/05/74	914/6	100 Mile Hockenheim (GT)		Ronald Arzdorf	2nd GT2		Ronald Arzdorf
12/05/74	914/6	DARM Sembach	315	Wilhelm Siegle	4th GT2	043 0734	Wilhelm-Horst Siegle
12/05/74	914/6	DARM Sembach		Peter Karl Nowak	6th GT2		Sixtant Racing Team
12/05/74	914/6	DARM Sembach		Herbert Mohr	2nd GT2		Autohaus Max Moritz

Race records Europe –North America – rallying – hillclimbs

Date	Car	Event	#	Drivers	Result	Notes	Entrant if known
12/05/74	914/6	DARM Sembach		Edgar Dören	1st GT2		Edgar Dören
12/05/74	914/6	DARM Sembach		Jochen Engel	5th GT2		MHSTC
12/05/74	914/6	DARM Sembach		Albrecht Schütz	3rd GT2		Autohaus Max Moritz
26/05/74	914/6	Zolder		Edgar Dören	1st GT2		Bergischer Motor Club
26/05/74	914/6	Zolder		Dieter Ankele	2nd GT2		Autohaus Max Moritz
02/06/74	914/6	DARM Mainz Finthen (G Nat)	116	Laub	8th	143 0178	Autohaus Max Moritz
02/06/74	914/6	DARM Mainz Finthen (G Nat)	123	"Knudel"	12th ov	0431415	MHSTC
02/06/74	914/6	DARM Mainz Finthen (G Nat)		Nowak	15th ov		Sixtant Racing Team
02/06/74	914/6	DARM Mainz Finthen (G Nat)		Edgar Dören	10th ov	043 0165	Bergischer Motor Club
02/06/74	914/6	DARM Mainz Finthen (Int)		Edgar Dören	10th Div II	043 0165	Bergischer Motor Club
02/06/74	914/6	DARM Mainz Finthen (Int)		"Ronald Knudel"	1st Gr 1-3, 12th Div II		MHSTC
02/06/74	914/6	DARM Mainz Finthen (Int)		Peter Karl Nowak	4th ov, 15th Div II		Sixtant Racing Team
02/06/74	914/6	DARM Mainz Finthen (Int)		Manfred Laub	8th Div II		Autohaus Max Moritz
09/06/74	914/6	Targa Florio	48	Fabri/Micangeli	19th ov, 1st GT2 gr 35		
09/06/74	914/6	DARM Wunstorf		Peter Karl Nowak	5th GT2		Sixtant Racing Team
09/06/74	914/6	DARM Wunstorf		Hubert Schlieckmann	7th GT2		Hubert Schlieckmann
09/06/74	914/6	DARM Wunstorf		Edgar Dören	1st GT2		Bergischer Motor Club
09/06/74	??	DARM Wunstorf		Dieter Bohnhorst	2nd GT2		Jägermeister Racing Team
09/06/74	914/6	DARM Hockenheim (G Nat)	72	Laub	6th ov	143 0178	Autohaus Max Moritz
17/06/74	914/6	Nürburgring 300km	52	Jochen Engel	4th GT2		Mannheim-Heidelberg Sport-Touring-Club
17/06/74	914/6	Nürburgring 300km	54	Edgar Dören	1st GT2	043 0165	Bergischer Motor Club eV
17/06/74	914/6	Nürburgring 300km	55	Wilhelm Siegle	2nd GT2		Wilhelm-Horst Siegle
17/06/74	914/6	Nürburgring 300km	56	Albrecht Schütz	3rd GT2		Autohaus Max Moritz
30/06/74	914/6	DARM Avus (G Nat)	164	Edgar Dören	4th ov		Bergischer Motor Club
30/06/74	914/6	DARM Avus (G Nat)	166	Franz Konrad	DNF		Franz Konrad
30/06/74	914/6	DARM Avus (G Nat)	166	Dieter Kossack	6th		Dieter Kossack
30/06/74	914/6	DARM Avus (G Nat)	171	Albrecht Schütz	1st ov		Autohaus Max Moritz
30/06/74	914/6	DARM Avus (G Nat)	172	Mohr	2nd ov		Autohaus Max Moritz
30/06/74	914/6	DARM Avus (G Nat)	173	Bohnhorst	3rd ov		Jägermeister Racing Team
14/07/74	914/6	Euro GT Hockenheim	28	Dieter Ankele	23rd ov, 22nd GT3		Autohaus Max Moritz
21/07/74	914/6	Hockenheim GT (G Nat)	387	Lampert	4th ov		SAR
21/07/74	914/6	Hockenheim GT (G Nat)	389	Nowak	3rd ov		Sixtant Racing Team
21/07/74	914/6	Hockenheim GT (G Nat)	390	Laub	1st ov		Autohaus Max Moritz
21/07/74	914/6	Hockenheim GT (G Nat)	391	Ankele	2nd ov		Autohaus Max Moritz
21/07/74	914/6	Hockenheim GT (G Nat)	392	Siegle	5th ov	043 0734	Wilhelm-Horst Siegle
21/07/74	914/6	Diepholz (GT2/T1.6)	240	Franz Konrad	1st GT2	043 0462	Franz Konrad
04/08/74	914/6	DRM Nürburgring European	252	Edgar Dören	1st GT2, 7th Div II		Bergischer Motor Club
08/08/74	914/6	DRM Nürburgring (G Nat)	252	Edgar Dören	7th ov	043 0165	Bergischer Motor Club
11/08/74	914/6	Hessen Hockenheim (GT)	14	Wilhelm Siegle	3rd GT2	043 0734	Wilhelm Siegle
11/08/74	914/6	Hessen Hockenheim (GT)		Hubert Schlieckmann	4th GT2		Hubert Schlieckmann
11/08/74	914/6	Hessen Hockenheim (GT)		Dieter Ankele	2nd GT2		Autohaus Max Moritz
11/08/74	914/6	Hessen Hockenheim (GT)		Manfred Laub	1st GT2		Autohaus Max Moritz

Porsche The Racing 914s

Date	Car	Event	#	Drivers	Result	Notes	Entrant if known
11/08/74	914/6	Hessen Hockenheim (GT)		Peter Karl Nowak	5th GT2		Sixtant Racing Team
11/08/74	914/6	Hessen Hockenheim (GT)		Klaus Erle	6th GT2		Klaus Erle
18/08/74	914/6	Coppa Florio race 1		Fabri	11th, 9th Gr 4		
18/08/74	914/6	Coppa Florio race 2		Fabri	13th, 11th Gr 4		
18/08/74	914/6	DARM Kassel-Calden	41	Edgar Dören	1st ov, 1st GT2		Bergischer Motor Club
18/08/74	914/6	DARM Kassel-Calden	45	Manfred Laub	2nd ov, 2nd GT2		Autohaus Max Moritz/VW-Porsche Sportwagenzentrum
18/08/74	914/6	DARM Kassel-Calden	42	Albrecht Schütz	3rd ov, 3rd GT2		Autohaus Max Moritz/VW-Porsche Sportwagenzentrum
18/08/74	914/6	DARM Kassel-Calden	47	Franz Konrad	4th ov, 4th GT2		Franz Konrad
18/08/74	914/6	DARM Kassel-Calden	43	Peter Karl Nowak	5th ov, GT2		Sixtant Racing Team
25/08/74	914/6	Hockenheim GT CH		Dieter Ankele	1st GT2		Autohaus MaxMoritz
25/08/74	914/6	Hockenheim GT CH		Albrecht Schütz	3rd GT2		
25/08/74	914/6	DRM Hockenheim	82	Dieter Ankele	7th Div II	043 2075	Autohaus Max Moritz
25/08/74	914/6	DRM Hockenheim	76	Hans Stähli	12 Div II		Formel Rennsport Club Zurich
25/08/74	914/6	NTK Zandvoort	18	Edgar Dören	9th ov , 4th Div II	043 0165	Bergischer Motor Club
25/08/74	914/6	DARM Zandvoort (G Nat + N Nat)		Edgar Dören	1st ov		Bergischer Motor Club
25/08/74	914/6	DARM Zandvoort (G Nat + N Nat)		Konrad	3rd ov	043 0462	Franz Konrad
25/08/74	914/6	DARM Zandvoort (G Nat + N Nat)		Schlieckmann	8th ov		Hubert Schlieckmann
01/09/74	914/6	Monza 6 Hours	48	Fabri/Mola	1st GT2	"CAM"	
01/09/74	914/6	Monza 6 Hours	51	Citterio/del Curto	4th GT2		Scuderia Città del Mille
01/09/74	914/6	Monza 6 Hours	49	Pianta/Zanini	?		Elvio Maria Zanini
01/09/74	914/6	Monza 6 Hours	52	Rebai/Rebai	?		Scuderia Città del Mille
01/09/74	914/6	DARM Mainz-Finthen (GT)	140	Edgar Dören	2nd GT2		Bergischer Motor Club
01/09/74	914/6	DARM Mainz-Finthen (GT)	141	Albrecht Schütz	4th GT2		Autohaus Max Moritz
01/09/74	914/6	DARM Mainz-Finthen (GT)	142	Hans Christian Jürgensen	6th GT2		Hans-Christian Jürgensen
01/09/74	914/6	DARM Mainz-Finthen (GT)	144	Peter Karl Nowak	8th GT2		Sixtant Racing Team
01/09/74	914/6	DARM Mainz-Finthen (GT)	146	Wilhelm Siegle	3rd GT2		Wilhelm-Horst Siegle
01/09/74	914/6	DARM Mainz-Finthen (GT)	147	Klaus Erie	10th GT2		Klaus Erle
01/09/74	914/6	DARM Mainz-Finthen (GT)	150	Dieter Weber	7th GT2		Scuderia Lindau/Bodensee
01/09/74	914/6	DARM Mainz-Finthen (GT)	151	Werner Christmann	1st GT2		Werner Christmann
14/09/74	914/6	Mainz Hockenheim GT		Klaus Erie	2nd ov, 2nd G+1.6		Klaus Erle
14/09/74	914/6	Mainz Hockenheim GT		Peter Karl Nowak	3rd ov, 3rd GT+1.6		Sixtant Racing Team
15/09/74	914/6	DRM Norisring (Int)	61	Manfred Laub	5thgr 9	143 0178	Autohaus Max Moritz
15/09/74	914/6	Zolder ADAC (G Nat)	239	Hans-Christian Jürgensen	1st in GT2		Hans-Christian Jürgensen
15/09/74	914/6	Zolder ADAC (G Nat)	240	Schlieckmann	2nd GT2		Hubert Schlieckmann
15/09/74	914/6	Ulm GT		Rene Lampert	4th GT2		
15/09/74	914/6	Ulm GT		Albrecht Schütz	2nd GT2		Autohaus Max Moritz
15/09/74	914/6	Ulm GT		Hans Stähli	3rd GT2		
29/09/74	914/6	DRM Hockenheim	61	Albrecht Schütz	7th Div II	143 0178	Autohaus Max Moritz
29/09/74	914/6	DRM Hockenheim	69	Wilhelm Siegle	8th Div II	043 0734	Wilhelm-Horst Siegle
29/09/74	914/6	DRM Hockenheim		Dieter Franke	10th Div II		
29/09/74	914/6	DRM Hockenheim	66	Klaus Erie	16th Div II	143 0100	Klaus Erle
06/10/74	914/6	Zolder		Dieter Ankele	3rd GT2		Dieter Ankele

Race records Europe – North America – rallying – hillclimbs

Date	Car	Event	#	Drivers	Result	Notes	Entrant if known
06/10/74	914/6	Zolder		Hubert Schlieckmann	2nd GT2		Autohaus Max Moritz
06/10/74	914/6	Zolder		Edgar Dören	1st GT2		Bergischer Motor Club
10/11/74	914/6	Hockenheim		Dieter Ankele	1st GT2		Autohaus Max Moritz
10/11/74	914/6	Hockenheim	335	Wilhelm Siegle	2nd GT2	043 0734	Wilhelm-Horst Siegle
10/11/74	914/6	Hockenheim		Hans-Christian Jürgensen	3rd GT2		Hans-Christian Jürgensen
10/11/74	914/6	Hockenheim		Peter Karl Nowak	4th GT2		Sixtant Racing Team
01/12/74	914/6	Hockenheim Finale (Race K)	21	Wilhelm Siegle	4th	043 0734	Wilhelm-Horst Siegle
01/12/74	914/6	Hockenheim Finale (Race G)		Dieter Ankele	5th LG2		Autohaus Max Moritz
01/12/74	914/6	Hockenheim Finale (Race G)		Manfred Laub	3rd LG2		Autohaus Max Moritz
22/02/75	914/6	Preis der Stadt Stuttgart		Hans-Christian Jürgensen	2nd GT+1.6		Hans-Christian Jürgensen
23/03/75	914/6	DARM Zolder (GT)	332	Edgar Dören	1st GT2	043 0165	Bergischer Motor Club
23/03/75	914/6	DARM Zolder (GT)	337	Hans-Christian Jürgensen	3rd GT2		Hans-Christian Jürgensen
23/03/75	914/6	DARM Zolder (GT)	340	Peter Karl Nowak	6th GT2		Peter-Karl Nowak
23/03/75	914/6	DARM Zolder (GT)	343	Alberto Zirkel	5th GT2		Bergischer Motor Club
30/03/75	914/6	Nürburgring GT (G Nat)	86	Ankele	6th Div II	043 2075	Autohaus Max Moritz
30/03/75	914/6	Nürburgring GT (G Nat)	87	Edgar Dören	4th Div II	043 0165	Bergischer Motor Club
30/03/75	914/6	Nürburgring GT (G Nat)	90	Rolf Färber	11th Div II	043 0185	Rolf Färber
31/03/75	914/6	Nürburgring Goodyear Pokal Int	87	Edgar Dören	5th Div II	043 0165	Bergischer Motor Club
31/03/75	914/6	Nürburgring Goodyear Pokal Int	86	Dieter Ankele	6th Div II	043 2075	Autohaus Max Moritz
31/03/75	914/6	Nürburgring Goodyear Pokal Int	91	Horst Oberhemm	14th Div II, gr 11		BMC Wuppertal
13/04/75	914/6	DARM Hockenheim (GT2/T2)	68	Edgar Dören	3rd ov, 1st GT2		Bergischer Motor Club
13/04/75	914/6	DARM Hockenheim (GT2/T2)	61	Manfred Laub	2nd GT2		Autohaus Max Moritz
13/04/75	914/6	DARM Hockenheim (GT2/T2)	62	Albrecht Schütz	3rd GT2		Autohaus Max Moritz
13/04/75	914/6	DARM Hockenheim (GT2/T2)	65	Peter Karl Nowak	6th GT2		Peter Karl Novak
13/04/75	914/6	DARM Hockenheim (GT2/T2)	71	Alberto Zirkel	5th GT2		Bergischer Motor Club
13/04/75	914/6	DARM Hockenheim (GT2/T2)	66	Wilhelm Siegle	DNQ		Wilhelm-Horst Siegle
13/04/75	914/6	DARM Hockenheim (G Nat)	68	Edgar Dören	3rd ov	043 0165	Bergischer Motor Club
27/04/75	914/6	DRM Nürburgring (G Nat)	54	Ankele	9th ov	0432075	Autohaus Max Moritz
27/04/75	914/6	DRM Nürburgring (G Nat)	65	Edgar Dören	4th	043 0165	Bergischer Motor Club
27/04/75	914/6	DRM Nürburgring (G Nat)	72	Nowak	16th		Peter-Karl Nowak
04/05/75	914/6	DARM Sembach (GT)		Alberto Zirkel	7th GT2		Bergischer Motor Club
04/05/75	914/6	DARM Sembach (GT)		Peter Karl Novak	8th GT2		Peter Karl Nowak
04/05/75	914/6	DARM Sembach (GT)		Hans-Christian Jürgensen	4th GT2		Hans-Christian Jürgensen
04/05/75	914/6	DARM Sembach (GT)		Manfred Laub	2nd GT2		Autohaus Max Moritz
04/05/75	914/6	DARM Sembach (GT)		Edgar Dören	1st GT2		Bergischer Motor Club
04/05/75	914/6	DARM Sembach (GT)		Wilhelm Siegle	3rd GT2	043 0734	Wilhelm Siegle
04/05/75	914/6	DARM Sembach (GT)		Albrecht Schutz	5th GT2		Autohaus Max Moritz
11/05/75	914/6	Saarlouis (GT)		Peter Karl Novak	3rd GT2		Peter Karl Nowak
18/05/75	914/6	DARM Salzburgring	11	Albrecht Schütz	2nd GT2		Autohaus Max Moritz
18/05/75	914/6	DARM Salzburgring		Klaus Erie	3rd GT2		Klaus Erle
18/05/75	914/6	DARM Salzburgring		Edgar Dören	1st GT2	043 0165	Bergischer Motor Club
24-25/05/75	914/6	Hockenheim 100 Miles		Siegle	1st Gr 3/4 2L	043 0734	Wilhelm Siegle
24-25/05/75	914/6	Hockenheim 100 Miles		Ankele	2nd Gr 3/4 2L		Autohaus Max Moritz

293

Porsche The Racing 914s

Date	Car	Event	#	Drivers	Result	Notes	Entrant if known
30/05/75	914/6	Nürburgring GT (G Nat)	90	Rolf Färber	11th Div II		Hans-Christian Jürgensen
08/06/75	914/6	DRM Hockenheim	82	Ankele	8th ov, 7th Div II	043 2075	Autohaus Max Moritz
15/06/75	914/6	DRM Mainz-Finthen	114	Dieter Ankele	7th Div II gr 10	043 2075	Autohaus Max Moritz
15/06/75	914/6	DRM Mainz-Finthen	115	Manfred Laub	14th Div II, gr 11	143 0178	Autohaus Max Moritz
15/06/75	914/6	DRM Mainz-Finthen	124	Ulrich Mönninghoff	9th Div II gr 24	143 03 06	Hubert Engbert Olde
22/06/75	914/6	Avus (G Nat)		Oberhemm	8th, 2nd GT2		Bergischer Motor Club
22/06/75	914/6	Avus (G Nat)		Edgar Dören	4th GT2	043 0165 cooling fan	Bergischer Motor Club
22/06/75	914/6	Avus (G Nat)		Hans-Christian Jürgensen	1st GT2		Hans-Christian Jürgensen
22/06/75	914/6	Avus (G Nat)		Klaus Erie	3rd GT2		Klaus Erle
29/06/75	914/6	DRM Norisring	70	Dieter Ankele	5th Div I, gr 14	043 2075	Autohaus Max Moritz
29/06/75	914/6	DRM Norisring		Edgar Dören	DNFgr 11		Bergischer Motor Club
06/07/75	914/6	Karlsruhe Hockenheim (GT)		Wilhelm Siegle	1st GT2	043 0734	William H Siegle
06/07/75	914/6	Karlsruhe Hockenheim (GT)		"Klaus"	6th GT2		VSA Munich
06/07/75	914/6	Karlsruhe Hockenheim (GT)		Peter Karl Novak	5th GT2		Peter Karl Nowak
20/07/75	914/6	DRM Diepholz	57	Dieter Ankele	8th Div II gr 13	0432075	Autohaus Max Moritz
20/07/75	914/6	DRM Diepholz		Hans-Christian Jürgensen	DNF		Jürgensen Racing Team
20/07/75	914/6	Diepholz GT	237	Ulrich Mönninghoff	3rd GT2		Ulrich Mönninghoff
20/07/75	914/6	Diepholz GT		Hans-Christian Jürgensen	1st GT2		Hans-Christian Jürgensen
20/07/75	914/6	DARM Hockenheim (T1.6/GT)	311	Edgar Dören	1st GT2	043 0165	Bergischer Motor Club
20/07/75	914/6	DARM Hockenheim (T1.6/GT)	315	Peter Karl Novak	6th GT2		Peter Karl Nowak
20/07/75	914/6	DARM Hockenheim (T1.6/GT)	316	Klaus Erie	3rd GT2	143 0100	Klaus Erie
27/07/75	914/6	Wunstorf GT (G Nat)	303	Hans-Christian Jürgensen	1st		Hans-Christian Jürgensen
27/07/75	914/6	Wunstorf GT (G Nat)	305	Nowak	2nd		Peter-Karl Nowak
03/08/75	914/6	DRM Nürburgring (G Nat)	214	Ankele	12th	043 2075	Autohaus Max Moritz
03/08/75	914/6	DRM Nürburgring (G Nat)	228	Laub	14th	043 0178	Autohaus Max Moritz
17/08/75	914/6	DRM Kassel Calden (G Nat)	8	Ankele	5th Div II	043 2075	Autohaus Max Moritz
17/08/75	914/6	DRM Kassel Calden (G Nat)	16	Nowak	7th Div II		Peter-Karl Nowak
17/08/75	914/6	DRM Kassel Calden (G Nat)	24	Ulrich Mönninghoff	9th Div II	143 0306	Ulrich Mönninghoff
23/08/75	914/6	Zandvoort (GT/T)	27	Hans-Christian Jürgensen	1st GT2		Hans-Christian Jürgensen
24/08/75	914/6	DARM Mainz-Finthen (G Nat)		Laub	2nd ov, 1st GT2, 1st GT	043 0178	Autohaus Max Moritz
24/08/75	914/6	DARM Mainz-Finthen (G Nat)		Edgar Dören	3rd ov, 2nd GT2	043 0165	Bergischer Motor Club
24/08/75	914/6	DARM Mainz-Finthen (G Nat)	22	Wilhelm Siegle	3rd GT2		Wilhelm Siegle
24/08/75	914/6	DARM Mainz-Finthen (G Nat)		Albrecht Schütz	4th GT2		Autohaus Max Moritz
31/08/75	914/6	DRM Hockenheim (G Nat)	46	Laub	1st GT2	043 0178	Autohaus Max Moritz
31/08/75	914/6	DRM Hockenheim (G Nat)	314	Ankele	9th ov	043 2075	Autohaus Max Moritz
31/08/75	914/6	DRM Hockenheim (G Nat)	315	Siegle	10th ov	043 0734	Wilhelm-Horst Siegle
31/08/75	914/6	DRM Hockenheim (G Nat)	316	Erle	12th ov	143 0100	Klaus Erie
06/09/75	914/6	Hockenheim GT		Nowak	2nd		Peter-Karl Nowak
14/09/75	914/6	DARM Ulm-Mengen (G Nat)		(G Nat)Linning	14th		Bergischer Motor Club
14/09/75	914/6	DARM Ulm-Mengen (G Nat)		Laub	1st	043 0178	Autohaus Max Moritz
14/09/75	914/6	DARM Ulm-Mengen (G Nat)		Erle	4th ov		Klaus Erle
14/09/75	914/6	DARM Ulm-Mengen (G Nat)		Albrecht Schütz	3rd ov		Autohaus Max Moritz

Race records Europe –North America – rallying – hillclimbs

Date	Car	Event	#	Drivers	Result	Notes	Entrant if known
14/09/75	914/6	DARM Ulm-Mengen (G Nat)		Edgar Dören	2nd ov	043 0165	Bergischer Motor Club
14/09/75	914/6	DARM Ulm-Mengen (G Nat		Nowak	6th ov		Peter-Karl Nowak
28/09/75	914/6	Monza 6 Hours Int	51	)Pegger/Stähli	13th, gr 31		Emillio Pegger
28/09/75	914/6	Monza 6 Hours Int	54	Ghinzani/del Curto	11th, gr 21		Scuderia Città del Mille
28/09/75	914/6	DRM Hockenheim (G Nat)	107	Edgar Dören	10th ov, Div II	043 0165	Bergischer Motor Club
28/09/75	914/6	DRM Hockenheim (G Nat)	116	Nowak	14th ov, 14th Div II		Peter-Karl Nowak
28/09/75	914/6	Hockenheim GT (G Nat)	4	Laub	1st	043 0178	Autohaus Max Moritz
19/10/75	914/6	Zolder GT (G Nat + N Nat)	84	Edgar Dören	6th ov	043 0165	Bergischer Motor Club
19/10/75	914/6	Zolder GT (G Nat + N Nat)	86	Erle	9th ov	143 0100	Klaus Erle
19/10/75	914/6	Zolder GT (G Nat + N Nat)	87	Linning	14th ov		Rolf Linning
09/11/75	914/6	Hockenheim GT		Laub	1st GT2		Autohaus Max Moritz
09/11/75	914/6	Hockenheim GT		Ankele	2nd GT2		Autohaus Max Moritz
30/11/75	914/6	Vallelunga		Redolfi	2nd GT2		
30/11/75	914/6	Vallelunga		Carminati	1st GT2		
30/11/75	914/6	Hockenheim Finale (G Nat)		Laub	1st Race N LG4	043 0178	Autohaus Max Moritz
30/11/75	914/6	Hockenheim Finale Race		Gunther Luttecke	10th LG1		Günther Luttecke
21/03/76	914/6	DARM Zolder (G Nat + N Nat)		MAnkele	20th		Hans Gunther Agosti
21/03/76	914/6	DARM Zolder (G Nat + N Nat)		Hans-Christian Jürgensen	3rd		Hans-Christian Jürgensen
21/03/76	914/6	DARM Zolder (G Nat + N Nat)		Erle	12th		Hans-Christian Jürgensen
21/03/76	914/6	DARM Zolder (G Nat + N Nat)		Holtmanns	18th		Kannacher GT Racing
21/03/76	914/6	DARM Zolder (G Nat + N Nat)		Nowak	14th		Peter Karl Nowak
03/04/76	914/6	DRM Nürburgring	37	Erle	10th 2L		Klaus Erle
03/04/76	914/6	DRM Nürburgring	45	Agosti	9th 2L		Bergischer Motor Club
03/04/76	914/6	DRM Nürburgring	49	Nowak	11th 2L		Peter Karl Nowak
03/04/76	914/6	DRM Nürburgring	50	Ankele	2nd 2L		Autohaus Max Moritz
11/04/76	914/6	DARM Hockenheim	901	Hans-Günther Agosti	9th 2L		BMC Wuppertal
11/04/76	914/6	DARM Hockenheim	903	Klaus Erie	10th 2L		Klaus Erle
11/04/76	914/6	DARM Hockenheim	904	Peter Karl Novak	12th 2L		Peter Karl Nowak
19/04/75	914/6	Magione Ital champ		Rebai	2nd ov, 2nd gr 5 3L		
25/04/76	914/6	Sylt (T/GT2)		Jurgen Holtmanns	6th		Kannacher GT Racing
25/04/76	914/6	DARM Sembach		Dieter Ankele	6th 2L		Autohaus Max Moritz
23/05/76	914/6	DARM Avus (G Nat)	60	Ankele	3rd	043 2075	Autohaus Max Moritz
09/05/76	914/6	Varano		Ronconi	5th ov, gr 4		
23/05/76	914/6	DRM Mainz-Finthen	52	Peter Karl Novak	8th Div II gr 14		Peter Karl Nowak
23/05/76	914/6	DARM Avus (G Nat)	60	Ankele	3rd	043 2075	Autohaus Max Moritz
20/06/76	914/6	DRM Hockenheim		Peter Karl Novak	16th Div II, gr 22		Team Baracuda Tauchsport
27/06/76	914/6	DARM Zolder (T/GT2)		Agosti	7th ov GTU		Bergischer Motor Club
04/07/76	914/6	DARM Salzburgring (GT/Gr 5N)	9	Klaus Erie	3rd 2L		Klaus Erle
04/07/76	914/6	DARM Salzburgring (GT/Gr 5N)	27	Agosti	6th 2L		Hans-G Agosti
04/07/76	914/6	Karlsruhe Hockenheim (T/GT)	188	Wilhelm Siegle	1st GT2	043 0734	Wilhelm-Horst Siegle
04/07/76	914 4	Karlsruhe Hockenheim (T/GT)		Gunter Oberhauser	1st Gr 3 2L		MSC Stuttgart
15/08/76	914/6	Zolder (T/GT)	74	Hans-Christian Jürgensen	4th 2L		Hans-Christian Jürgensen
15/08/76	914/6	DARM Zandvoort(T/GT)	278	Klaus Erie	6th 2L		Klaus Erle

295

Porsche The Racing 914s

Date	Car	Event	#	Drivers	Result	Notes	Entrant if known
22/08/76	914/6	DRM Kassel Calden	59	Peter Karl Novak	6th, gr 12		Team Barakuda Tauchsport/Peter Nowak Tuning
29/08/76	914/6	DRM Hockenheim (G Nat)	176	Erle	11th	143 0100	Klaus Erle
05/09/76	914/6	Diepholz GT2		Kopatz	6th ov		
12/09/76	914/6	DRM Nürburgring Supersprint	51	Peter Karl Novak	13th ov, gr 18		Team Barakuda-Tauchsport/Peter Nowak Tuning
12/09/76	914/6	DARM Ulm (T/GT2)		Klaus Erie	3rd		Valvoline Deutschland
26/09/76	914/6	DRM Hockenheim (G Nat)	66	Nowak	15th, gr 19		Team Barakuda-Tauchsport
26/09/76	914/6	DRM Hockenheim (G Nat)	67	Siegle	13th, gr 17	043 0734	Wilhelm-Horst Siegle
26/09/76	914/6	DRM Hockenheim (G Nat)	68	Erle	11th ov, gr 16	143 0100	Valvoline Deutschland
10/10/76	914/6	Nurburging (T/GT)	22	Peter Karl Novak	22nd ov, 4th 2L		Team Barakuda-Tauchsport/Peter Nowak Tuning Hochst
17/10/76	914/6	Zolder (T/GT+1.6))	42	Agosti	11th		BMC Wuppertal
17/10/76	914/6	Zolder (T/GT2)	42	Agosti	6th		BMC Wuppertal
23/10/76	914/6	Nürburgring Neuss		Agosti	4th 2L		Hans Gunther Agosti
24/10/76	914/6	Mainz Finthen (T/GT2)	15	Klaus Erie	10th		Valvoline Deutschland
24/10/76	914/6	Mainz Finthen (T/GT2)	22	Wilhelm Siegle	2nd	043 0734	Wilhelm Siegle
24/10/76	914/6	Mainz Finthen (T/GT2)	28	Peter Karl Novak	5th		Team Barakuda Tauchsport
31/10/76	914/6	Euro GT Hockenheim Int	31	Siegle	16th	043 0734	Wilhelm-Horst Siegle
31/10/76	914/6	Hockenheim (T/GT)	448	Siegle	3rd 2L		Wilhelm Siegle
31/10/76	914/6	Hockenheim (T/GT)	449	Peter Karl Novak	9th 2L		Team Barakuda Tauchsport
07/11/76	914/6	Hockenheim		Peter Karl Novak	1st GT2		Team Barakuda Tauchsport/Peter Nowak Tuning
26/02/77	914/6	Hockenheim (GT/Gr5)		Gunter Oberhauser	2nd Gr 3 2L		Günther Oberhauser
26/02/77	914/6	Hockenheim (GT/Gr5)		Dieter Ankele	4th GT3		Autohaus Max Moritz
13/03/77	914/6	DRM Zolder (G Nat)	33	Agosti	12th, gr 19	043 0165	Bergischer Motor Club
17/04/77	914/6	DARM Hockenheim Jim Clark	472	Agosti	2nd GT2, 4th Div 3000		BMC Wuppertal-Cronenberg
17/04/77	914/6	DARM Hockenheim Jim Clark	473	Ankele	1st Gr 2, 3rd Div 3L		Autohaus Max Moritz
01/05/77	914/6	DRM ADAC Eifelrennen (G Nat)	41	Ankele	11th ov in Div 2 race, gr 19	043 2075	Autohaus Max Moritz
01/05/77	914/6	DRM ADAC Eifelrennen (G Nat)	33	Agosti	14th, gr 21	043 0165	Bergischer Motor Club
08/05/77	914/6	DARM Saarlouis		Agosti	1st ov, 1st GT3		Bergischer Motor Club
15/05/77	914/6	DARM Hockenheim		Ankele	7th GT3		Autohaus Max Moritz
15/05/77	914/6	DARM Hockenheim		Agosti	6th GT3		Bergischer Motor Club
15/05/77	914/6	Zandvoort Junior Trophy	115	Knuth Mentel	1st Gr 4/5 2L		Knuth Mentel
19/05/77	914/6	Diepholz		Heinz Kopatz	5th Gr 4-5+1.3		Heinz Kopatz
29/05/77	914/6	1000km Nürburgring	67	Capra/Rebai/"Archimede"	DNQ		Scuderia Città dei Mille
12/06/77	914/6	DARM Wunstorf	413	Helge Probst	5th GT3		Helge Probst
26/06/77	914/6	DARM Zolder		Ankele	4th GT3		Autohaus Max Moritz
26/06/77	914/6	DARM ZolderAgosti		Agosti	3rd GT3		Bergischer Motor Club
03/07/77	914/6	Nürburgring Neuss			1st T/GT2		Bergischer Motor Club
16/07/77	914/6	Varano Gr 4		Aldo Raggi	6th ov, 1st GT2		
17/07/77	914/6	Nürburgring Bayerkreuz		Helge Probst	4th T/GT2		Helge Probst
24/07/77	914/6	Diepholz (Gr 2/4/5)	254	Agosti	7th 2L		Bergischer Motor Club
07/08/77	914/6	DARM Mainz-Finthen	14	Agosti	4th ov, 4th GT3		Bergischer Motor Club

Race records Europe – North America – rallying – hillclimbs

Date	Car	Event	#	Drivers	Result	Notes	Entrant if known
14/08/77	914/6	Zandvoort		Agosti	1st Gr 4/5 2L		Hans-G Agosti
14/08/77	914/6	Zandvoort		Ursula Hubert	2nd Gr 4/5 2L		Ursula Hubert
21/08/77	914/6	DARM Kassel-Calden	111	Agosti	3rd GT3		Bergischer Motor Club
21/08/77	914/6	DARM Kassel-Calden	112	Kopatz	4th GT3		Heinz Kopatz
28/08/77	914/6	Nürburgring T/GT		Agosti	3rd ov, 3rd GT2		Bergischer Motor Club
28/08/77	914/6	Nürburgring T/GT	66	Knuth Mentel	8th ov, 8th GT2		Knuth Mentel
18/09/77	914/6	Pergusa Gr 4 Coppa Città di Enna		Raggi	1st Gr 4 2L		
16/10/77	914/6	DARM Zolder (G Nat + N Nat)	29	Probst	8th ov, 3rd GT2		Helge Probst
16/10/77	914/6	DARM Zolder (G Nat + N Nat)	30	Agosti	6th ov, 2nd GT2		BMC Wupperta

North America

Note: as this chart is for the North American races the dates are shown in the American format, not the European style. The chart is compiled from numerous records – see acknowledgements in the opening pages. The period covered is from 1970 to 1983.
Note – Every effort has been made to ensure correctness but it is possible that some minor errors may be present.
This list contains selected results of the more notable meetings of interest, it is not definitive.

Int = International
US Nat = USA National or regional level race
Can Nat = Canadian National race, with some International entries
ov = Overall race position
Non finishers are not listed
NRF = Not running at finish
NC = Not classified

GTP = Grand Touring Prototype
gr = grid position
Prod C+D = Production cars modified
GT = Grand Touring
GTO = Grand Touring Omologato
GTU = GT cars under 2L

Date	Car	Event	#	Drivers	Result	Notes	Entrant if known
06/14/70	914/6	Mosport (C Nat)	10	Hochreuter	9th		Knob Hill Service Station
07/11/70	914/6	Watkins Glen 6 HoursInt	94	Meaney/Behr	NC 181 laps, gr 19	043 663	Ralph Meaney
09/07/70	914/6	SCCA Bonneville (US Nat)		Johnson	2nd ov	C+D Production	
09/07/70	914/6	SCCA Bonneville (US Nat)		Forbes-Robinson	1st ov	C+D Production	Ginther Racing
09/13/70	914/6	SCCA Portland (US Nat)	2	Forbes-Robinson	1st ov	C+D Production	Ginther Racing
09/19/70	914/6	Ontario SCCA Nat (CD+DP+EP	2	Forbes-Robinson	3rd ov, 3rd CP		Richie Ginther Racing Inc
09/20/70	914/6	Grattan SCCA Nat (CD+DP+BS)		Chuck Dietrich	1st		
09/20/70	914/6	Grattan SCCA Nat (CD+DP+BS)		Bill Stroh	2nd		
09/20/70	914/6	SCCA Nat Mid-America		Bob Hindson	1st CP		Bunker-Hindson
09/27/70	914/6	Phoenix SCCA Nat Prod C+D		Forbes-Robinson	2nd		
11/29/70	914/6	Road Atlanta SCCA C Prod US Nat	55	Gregg	8th ov		
11/29/70	914/6	Road Atlanta SCCA C Prod US Nat	1	Johnson	5th ov		
11/29/70	914/6	Road Atlanta SCCA C Prod US Nat	2	Forbes-Robinson	4th ov		
11/29/70	914/6	Road Atlanta SCCA C Prod US Nat	43	Noah	7th ov		
11/29/70	914/6	Road Atlanta SCCA C Prod US Nat	42	Hindson	9th ov		
11/29/70	914/6 GT	Road Atlanta SCCA C Prod US Nat	16	Stroh	10th ov		
1/30-31/71	914/6 GT	Daytona 24 HoursInt	5	Duval/Nicholas/Bailey	7th ov, 1st GT2.5, gr 28	043 1017	Sun Oil

Porsche The Racing 914s

Date	Car	Event	#	Drivers	Result	Notes	Entrant if known
1/30-31/71	914/6 GT	Daytona 24 Hours Int	19	Behr/Buffum/Kremer E	8th ov, 2nd GT2.5, gr 32	043 0691	Ralph Meaney
03/20/71	914/6 GT	Sebring 12 Hours Int	59	Gregg/Haywood	14th ov, 2nd GT2.5, gr 28	043 0705	Brumos Porsche
03/20/71	914/6 GT	Sebring 12 Hours Int	28	Meaney/Wright/Laucks	NRF gearbox lap 187, gr 30	043 0663	Ralph Meaney
03/20/71	914/6 GT	Sebring 12 Hours Int	5	Duval/Nicholas/Bailey	17th ov, 4th GT2.5, gr 39	043 1017	Jacques Duval
03/20/71	914/6	Sebring 12 Hours Int	29	Behr/Conrad/Buffum	NC lap 112, gr 31	043 0691	Ralph Meaney
04/18/71	914/6	Virginia 300 Miles IMSA (US Nat)	29	Meaney/Behr	3rd ov, 2nd GTU	043 0691	Ralph Meaney
04/18/71	914/6	Virginia 300 Miles IMSA (US Nat)	59	Gregg/Haywood	1st ov, gr 2	043 03 15	Brumos Porsche
05/15/71	914/6	Talladega 200 Miles IMSA (US Nat)	59	Gregg/Haywood	2nd ov, 1st GTU	043 03 15	Brumos Porsche
05/15/71	914/6	Talladega 200 Miles IMSA (US Nat)	19	Bytzek	5th ov, 4th GTU	043 0033	
05/23/71	914/6	Charlotte 3 Hours (US Nat)	59	Gregg/Haywood	2nd ov	043 0315	Brumos Porsche
05/23/71	914/6	Charlotte 3 Hours (US Nat)	29	Behr	5th ov	043 0691	Ralph Meaney
05/31/71	914/6	Mont Tremblant, Canada	9	Klaus Bytzek/Harry Bytzek	Qualified 2nd	Part of Eastern Canadian Endurance Championship	
06/27/71	914/6	Bridgehampton 3 Hours (US Nat)	59	Gregg/Haywood	1st ov	043 03 15	Brumos Porsche
06/27/71	914/6	Bridgehampton 3 Hours (US Nat)	58	Theodoracopulos/Gregg	3rd ov		Brumos Porsche
06/27/71	914/6 GT	Bridgehampton 3 Hours (US Nat)	19	Bytzek H/Bytzek K	4th ov	043 0033	
07/24/71	914/6	Watkins Glen 6 Hours	59	Gregg/Haywood	6th ov, 1st GTU2.5, gr 19		Brumos Porsche
08/01/71	914/6	Paul Whiteman Trophy Daytona	171	David McClain	19th ov, lap 15, 5th CP		
08/21/71	914/6	Mosport Park	9	Klaus Bytzek/Harry Bytzek	2nd (2nd ov in championship)	Part of Eastern Canadian Endurance Championship	
09/19/71	914/6	Summit Point 250 Miles (US Nat)	59	Gregg/Haywood	1st ov, gr 4	043 03 15	Brumos Porsche
09/19/71	914/6	Summit Point 250 Miles (US Nat)	12	Meaney/Perry	28th		Ralph Meaney
09/19/71	914/6	Summit Point 250 Miles (US Nat)	19	Harry Bytzek	5th, gr 55	43 0033	
12/04/71	914/6	Texas 200 Miles (US Nat)	9	Bytzek H/Bytzek K	7th		
12/04/71	914/6	Texas 200 Miles (US Nat)	44	Durant	4th		
02/06/72	914/6 GT	Midnight Challenge Daytona	81	Daniel Muñiz	1st Class 4		
02/06/72	914/6 GT	Daytona 6 Hours Int	81	Muñiz/Novoa	13th ov, 3rd GT2.5, gr 56	143 0332	Daniel Muñiz
02/06/72	914/6 GT	Daytona 6 Hours Int	72	McDonald/Everett	NC lap 131, gr 33		Lee McDonald/Algar Porsche Audi
02/06/72	914/6 GT	Daytona 6 Hours Int	58	Rebaque/Rojas	Dnf lap 70, gr 41		Brumos Porsche
03/25/72	914/6 GT	Sebring 12 Hours Int	78	Muñiz/Novoa/Luis	9th ov, 2nd GT2.5, gr 50	143 0332	Daniel Muñiz
03/25/72	914/6	Sebring 12 Hours Int	27	Kirby/Hotchkis/Cuddy	15th ov, 6th GT2, gr 29		Bozani Porsche
03/25/72	914/6 GT	Sebring 12 Hours Int	58	Rebaque/Rojas	NC lap 152, gr 46		Brumos Porsche
03/25/72	914/6 GT	Sebring 12 Hours Int	68	Stoddard/Hines/Harmstad	NC lap 146, gr 35		Hines-Stoddard
03/25/72	914/6 GT	Sebring 12 Hours Int	19	McClain/White	Dnf lap 51 engine, gr 49	043 1262	David H McClain
03/25/72	914/6	Sebring 12 Hours Int	70	McDonald/Everett	Dnf lap 22 oil leak, gr 38		Lee McDonald
04/01/72	914/6	Daytona 3 Hours Int	19	McClain/White	9th	043 1262	David H McClain
04/01/72	914/6	Daytona 3 Hours Int	58	Rebaque/Rojas	8th		Bozzani Porsche
04/16/72	914/6	Virginia 250 Miles (US Nat)	78	Muñiz/van Beuren Jr	3rd ov, GTU race		
05/26/71	914/6	SCCA National Lime Rock		Holbert	2nd CP		
05/29/72	914/6	Lime Rock 200 Miles (US Nat)	70	McDonald	11th ov, 8th GTU		Lee McDonald
07/09/72	914/6	Mid Ohio 6 Hours (US Nat)	70	McDonald/Bytzek	18th		ALGAR Ent
07/17/72	914/6	SCCA National Bridgehampton		Al Holbert	3rd CP		

Race records Europe – North America – rallying – hillclimbs

Date	Car	Event	#	Drivers	Result	Notes	Entrant if known
11/19/72	914/6	Daytona 250 Miles (US Nat)	67	MCclain/White	18th ov, 8th GTU		David McClain
11/27/72	914/6	Road Atlanta Finale (US Nat)		Holbert	4th		Holbert Porsche
11/27/72	914/6	Road Atlanta Finale (US Nat)		Harmstad	9th	043 1177	Competition Motors
11/27/72	914/6	Road Atlanta Finale (US Nat)		Countryman	12th		7 Up Carousel
03/24/73	914/6	Sebring 12 Hours	67	McClain/White/Floyd	23rd, 8th IMSA GT2, gr 40	043 1262	David H McClain
07/28/73	914/4	Road America Trans Am (US Nat)	86	Parish/Hulen	25th ov		C P Racing
10/07/73	914/6	Westwood 7 Hours	25	Barron/Webb	6th		Performance Unlimited
10/14/73	914/6	Indianapolis 3 Hours (US Nat)	84	Hulen/Parish/Coupland	19th ov		Donald Parish
11/04/73	914/6	US Champions Road Atlanta 'C' Prod	67	Frank Harmstad	6th	043 1177	Rapid Transit Systems
05/19/74	914/6	Ontario 4 Hours (US Nat)	9	Gupton/Mandella	17th ov, 6th GTU		Rich Mandella
06/30/74	914/6	Mid Ohio 5 Hours (US Nat)	85	Hulen/Coupland	27th ov		John E Hulen
07/04/74	914/6	Daytona 250 Miles (US Nat)	55	Cutler/Campbell	21st		
07/04/74	914/6	Daytona 250 Miles (US Nat)	67	McClain/White	41st		David McClain
08/10/74	914/6	Talladega 200 Miles	67	McClain/White	15th ov		David McClain
08/18/74	914/6	Charlotte 300 Miles	85	Hulen/Coupland/Causey	12th ov GTU		John E Hulen
08/25/74	914/6	SCCA Regional Virginia	95?	Robert Frostrom	1st BSR		
09/02/74	914/6	Lime Rock 1	67	David McClain	28th ov, 10th GTU	914043 1262, decider for Lime Rock 2 grid	David McClain
09/02/74	914/6	Lime Rock 2	85	John Hulen	27th ov, 9th GTU		John E Hulen
09/02/74	914/6	Lime Rock 2	67	Dave White	33rd ov, 13th GT	043 1262	David McClain
10/12/74	914/6	SCCA Regional Virginia	95	Robert Frostrom	2nd ov, 1st BSR		
10/13/74	914/6	Virginia Enduro	95	Robert Frostrom	2nd ov, 1st BSR		
10/20/74	914/6	Mexico 1000km Int	2	Forbes-Robinson/Davis/Brown	28th, gr 22		
10/20/74	914/6	Mexico 1000km Int	12	Pereyda/Arenas/Izquierdo	14th ov, gr 29		
10/20/74	914/6	Mexico 1000km Int	21	Tabe/de Velazco	21st, gr 32		
11/03/74	914/6	US Champions Road Atlanta 'C' Prod	69	Frank Harmstad	8th	043 1177	Competition Motors
11/03/74	914/6	US Champions Road Atlanta 'C' Prod	88	Dan Gilliland	12th		Gilliland Transfer Co
12/01/74	914/6	Daytona 250 Miles	67	McClain/White	17th ov, 5th GTU	043 1262	David McClain
12/01/74	914/6	Daytona 250 Miles	22	Bill Polich	36th ov, 11th GTU	43 0529	
02/1-2/75	914/6	Daytona 24 Hours Int	85	Hulen/Coupland/Engels	18th ov, 5th GTU, 4th GT, gr 37		John E Hulen
03/20/75	914/6	Sebring 12 Hours qualifying race	85	Hulen	7th ov, 1st IMSA GT2.5	5-lap qualifier	John E Hulen
03/21/75	914/6	Sebring 12 Hours Int	914	Bundy/Schmid	NC lap 151, gr 71		Al Holbert Racing
04/20/75	914/6	Road Atlanta 100 Miles race 1 (US Nat)		Coupland	21st ov, 5th GTU, gr 40		John E Hulen
04/20/75	914/6	Road Atlanta 100 Miles race 2 (US Nat)		Hulen	22nd ov, 6th GTU, gr 21		John E Hulen
04/27/75	914/6	Laguna Seca 100 Miles (US Nat)		Kirby	21st ov		
04/27/75	914/6	Laguna Seca 100 Miles (US Nat)		Hotchkis	22 ov		
04/27/75	914/6	Laguna Seca 100 Miles (US Nat)		Polich	23rd ov	914 043 0529	
05/10/75	914/6	Riverside 6 Hours Int	51	Kirby/Jones	40th ov, 15th GTU, gr 39	fuel pump	Max Dial
05/10/75	914/6	Riverside 6 Hours Int	80	Polich/Basurto	17th ov, 4th GTU, gr 27	043 0529	Montgomery Real Estate

299

Porsche The Racing 914s

Date	Car	Event	#	Drivers	Result	Notes	Entrant if known
05/10/75	914/6	Riverside 6 Hours Int	96	Mandella/Thomas	37th ov, 13th GTU, suspension, gr 33		
05/26/75	914/6	100 Mile Lime Rock Race 2	51?	John Hotchkis	16th, 58 laps, 2nd GTU, gr 26		
06/14/75	914/6	Mosport 100 Miles (Can Nat)	51	Kirby/Hotchkis	16th ov, gr 15		Kirby Hitchcock
07/04/75	914/6	Daytona 250 Miles (US Nat)		Panaccione	42nd		
07/20/75	914/6	Mid America 100 Miles (US Nat)		Jones	14th, 2nd GTU		
08/09/75	914/6	Talladega 1 Hour (US Nat)		Hulen	18th ov, 24 laps, 4th GTU		John E Hulen
08/24/75	914/6	Mid Ohio 6 Hours (US Nat)	51?	Hotchkis/Kirby	34th ov, 12th GTU		
08/24/75	914/6	Mid Ohio 6 Hours (US Nat)	51?	Hulen/Coupland	27th ov, 10th GTU		
01/31-01/02/76	914/6	Daytona 24 Hours	51	Jones/Kirby/Hotchkis	13th ov, 3rd IMSA GTU, gr 42		Max Dial
01/31-01/02/76	914/6	Daytona 24 Hours	54	Job/Southard/Sahlman	23rd ov, 9th IMSA GTU, gr 66		Spirit Racing
03/20/76	914/6	Sebring 12 Hours Int	51	Jones/Kirby/Hotchkis	14th ov, 4th GTU, gr 51		Max Dial Porsche
03/20/76	914/6	Sebring 12 Hours Int	54	Sahlman/Southard/Job	32nd ov, 14th GTU, gr 77		Spirit Racing
03/20/76	914/6	Sebring 12 Hours Int	87	Thomas/Cook	22nd ov, 7th GTU, gr 26		R Mandella
04/11/76	914/6	Road Atlanta 100 Miles	58	Adrian Gang	20th ov, 4th GTU, gr 31		
05/02/76	914/6	Laguna Seca 100 Miles (US Nat)	45	Maas	7th ov, 1st GTU, gr 8		Carlsen Porsche Audi
05/02/76	914/6	Laguna Seca 100 Miles (US Nat)	51	Kirby	23rd ov, 7th GTU, gr 38		Max Dial Porsche Audi
05/02/76	914/6	Laguna Seca 100 Miles (US Nat)	87	Cook	11th ov, 3rd GTU, gr 14	043 1325	Altec Lansing
05/02/76	914/6	Laguna Seca 100 Miles (US Nat)	58	Gang	22nd ov, 6th GTU, gr 30		Edelweiss Porschaus
05/09/76	914/6	Ontario 100 Miles Int	45	Walt Maas	8th ov, 1st GTU, gr 18		Carlsen Porsche Audi
05/09/76	914/6	Ontario 100 Miles Int	87	Jim Cook	9th ov, 2nd GTU, gr 16	043 1325	Altec Lansing
05/09/76	914/6	Ontario 100 Miles Int	51	John Hotchkis	24th ov, 9th GTU, gr 26		Max Dial Porsche/Audi
05/09/76	914/6	Ontario 100 Miles Int	54	Jim Gaeta	37th ov, 14th GTU, gr 25		Altec/Lansing
05/09/76	914/6	Trans-Am Pocono	69	Frank Harmstad	21st ov, 1st GTU, gr 7		
05/31/76	914/6	Lime Rock 100 Miles	45	Walt Maas	6th ov, 2nd GTU, gr 7		Carlsen Porsche Audi
06/06/76	914/6	Mid Ohio 100 Miles	85	John Hulen	23rd ov, 9th GTU, gr 46		John Hulen
06/06/76	914/6	Mid Ohio 100 Miles	45	Walt Maas	7th ov, 2nd GTU, gr 9		Carlsen Porsche Audi
06/06/76	914/6	Mid Ohio 100 Miles	15	Jim Cook	15th ov, 3rd GTU, gr 11		
06/25/76	914/6	Trans-Am Pocono	69	Frank Harmstad	21st ov, 1st GTU, gr 27		
07/25/76	914/6	Sears Point 100 Miles (US Nat)	45	Maas	7th ov, 1st, GTU, gr 18		Carlsen Porsche Audi
08/07/76	914/6	Talladega 120 Miles (US Nat)	54	Sahlman	11th ov, 4th GTU, gr 22		
08/07/76	914/6	Talladega 120 Miles (US Nat)		Coupland	DNF lap 18, 7th GTU, gr 25		
08/15/76	914/6	Pocono 100 Miles (US Nat)	51	Hotchkis	17th ov, 7th GTU, gr 25		
08/15/76	914/6	Pocono 100 Miles (US Nat)		Mandella	18th ov, 8th GTU, gr 22		
09/19/76	914/6	Road Atlanta 500Km (US Nat)	85	Hulen/Coupland	20th ov, 6th GTU, gr 25		
10/03/76	914/6	Laguna Seca 100 Miles (US Nat)	45	Maas	9th ov, 1st GTU, gr 13		Carlsen Porsche Audi
10/03/76	914/6	Laguna Seca 100 Miles (US Nat)	58	Gang	26th ov, 6th GTU, gr 38		Edelweiss Porschaus
10/03/76	914/6	Laguna Seca 100 Miles (US Nat)	87	Cook	14th ov, 2nd GTU, gr 23		Altec Lansing
10/31/76	914/6	US Champions Road Atlanta	69	Frank Harmstad	6th		Competition Motors
04/17/77	914/6	Road Atlanta 100 Miles (US Nat)	85	Hulen/Coupland	16th ov, 3rd GTU, gr 37		John E Hulen
05/01/77	914/6	Laguna Seca 100 Miles (US Nat)	45	Maas	11th ov, 1st GTU, gr 19		Walt Maas
05/15/77	914/6	Mid-America 100 Miles (US Nat)	45	Maas	8th ov, 1st GTU, gr 13		Walt Maas

Race records Europe – North America – rallying – hillclimbs

Date	Car	Event	#	Drivers	Result	Notes	Entrant if known
05/30/77	914/6	Lime Rock 100 Miles (US Nat)	45	Maas	12th ov, 1st GTU, gr 14		
06/05/77	914/6	Mid Ohio 100 Miles (US Nat)	45	Maas	12th, 2nd GTU, gr 9		
06/19/77	914/6	Brainerd 100 Miles (US Nat)	45	Maas	6th ov, 1st GTU, gr 12		
07/04/77	914/6	Daytona 250 Miles Paul Revere	85	Hulen/Coupland	24th ov, 9th GTU, gr 33		John Hulen
07/31/77	914/6	Sears Point IMSA GTU (US Nat)	45	Mass	3rd ov, 3rd GTU, gr 3		
07/31/77	914/6	Sears Point IMSA GTU (US Nat)	82	Harrison	10th ov, 10th GTU, gr 13		
08/14/77	914/6	Pocono 100 Miles (US Nat)	45	Maas	9th ov, 1st GTU, gr 16		
08/28/77	914/6	Mid-Ohio 3 Hours (US Nat)	45	Maas	13th ov, 1st GTU, gr 8		
08/28/77	914/6	Mid-Ohio 3 Hours (US Nat)	51	Kirby/Hotchkis/Aase	18th ov, 4th GTU, gr 30		Kirby Hitchcock
09/03/77	914/6	Road America Trans Am Race I	70	Dick Salem	29th ov, 21st TA-I, gr 39		
09/04/77	914/6	Road America Trans Am Race II	70	Dick Salem	24th ov, 8th TA-II, gr 29		
09/05/77	914/6	Road Atlanta GTU (US Nat)	45	Maas	4th ov, 4th GTU, gr 3		Walt Maas
09/05/77	914/6	Road Atlanta GTU (US Nat)	69	Harmstad	12th ov, 12th GTU, gr 9		
10/09/77	914/6	Laguna Seca 100 Miles (US Nat)	45	Maas	12th ov, 1st GTU, gr 21		Walt Maas
10/09/77	914/6	Laguna Seca 100 Miles (US Nat)	58	Gang	26th ov, 6th GTU, gr 32		
10/09/77	914/6	Laguna Seca 100 Miles (US Nat)	82	Harrison	22nd ov, 4th GTU, gr 27		
11/27/77	914/6	Daytona 250 Miles (US Nat)	20	DiLella/Cueto	27th ov, 10th GTU, gr 60		Vince DiLella
03/18/78	914/6	Sebring 12 Hours	62	Koll/Hamren/Sherman	10th ov, 3rd IMSA GTU, gr 53		William Koll
03/18/78	914/6	Sebring 12 Hours	85	Hulen/Coupland/Engels	23rd ov, 9th IMSA GTU, gr 40		John E Hulen
04/02/78	914/6	Talladega 6 Hours	62	Koll/Hamren	11th ov, 4th IMSA GTU, gr 32		William Koll
04/30/78	914/6	Laguna Seca IMS GTU (US Nat)	82	Harrison	3rd ov, 3rd GTU, gr 6	143 0178	
04/30/78	914/6	Laguna Seca IMS GTU (US Nat)	62	Koll	12th, gr 12	043 0593	William Koll
05/07/78	914/6	Hallett GTU (US Nat)	82	Harrison	4th, gr 10	143 0178	
05/21/78	914/6	Sears Point Trans Am	23	Zulkowski	8th ov, 4th TA-I, gr 8		
05/29/78	914/6	Lime Rock GTU (US Nat)	62	Koll	4th, gr 6	043 0593	William Koll
06/11/78	914/6	Portland Trans Am (US Nat)	51	Taylor	17th ov, 11th TA-I, gr 39		
06/18/78	914/6	Brainerd 100 Miles (US Nat)	62	Koll	18th ov, 3rd GTU, gr 22	043 0593	William Koll
07/04/78	914/6	Daytona 250 Miles (US Nat)	62	Koll	22nd ov, 8th GTU, gr 48	043 0593	William Koll
07/04/78	914/6	Daytona 250 Miles (US Nat)	85	Hulen/Coupland	28th ov, 13th GTU, gr 42		John Hulen
07/30/78	914/6	Sears Point GTU (US Nat)	03	Sanders	15th, gr 15		Bruce Sanders
07/30/78	914/6	Sears Point GTU (US Nat)	13	Overstreet	22nd, gr 18		Overstreet Racing
07/30/78	914/6	Sears Point GTU (US Nat)	23	Zulkowski	28th, gr 20		Metalcraft Racing
07/30/78	914/6	Sears Point GTU (US Nat)	82	Harrison	6th ov, gr 7		
08/13/78	914/6	Brainerd Trans Am	10	Salem	26th ov, 10th TA-II, gr 35		
08/27/78	914/6	Mid Ohio 250 Miles (US Nat)	85	Hulen/Coupland	18th ov, 4th GTU, gr 48		John E Hulen
09/04/78	914/6	Road America Trans Am (US Nat)	0	Salem	18th ov, 9th TA-II, gr 37		
09/04/78	914/6	Road Atlanta GTU (US Nat)	9	Harmstad	10th, 8th GTU, gr 28	043 1177	Frank Harmstad
09/04/78	914/6	Road Atlanta GTU (US Nat)	85	Hulen/Coupland	16th ov, 14th GTU, gr 22		John E Hulen
10/08/78	914/6	Laguna Seca Trans Am (US Nat)	16	Overstreet	25th ov, 9th TA-II, gr 39		Overstreet Racing
10/08/78	914/4	Laguna Seca Trans Am (US Nat)	23	Zulkowski	DNF lap 33 turbo failure, gr 24		Metalcraft Racing
11/26/78	914/4	Daytona 250 Mile Finale	21	DiLella/Cueto	44th ov, 10th GTU, gr 67	471291225	DiLella Racing
03/17/79	914/6	Sebring 12 Hours Int	51	Kirby/Baker/Winters	20th ov, 4th IMSA GTU, gr 61		Personalized Porsche
03/17/79	914/6	Sebring 12 Hours Int	62	Koll/Cook/Aase	22nd ov, 6th IMSA GTU, gr 20	043 0593	William Koll

301

Porsche The Racing 914s

Date	Car	Event	#	Drivers	Result	Notes	Entrant if known
03/17/79	914/6	Sebring 12 Hours Int	93	Deacon/Riley/Franczak	23rd ov, 7th IMSA GTU, gr 60		David Deacon
04/08/79	914/6	Road Atlanta GTU (US Nat)	16	Overstreet	14th, gr 17		Overstreet Racing
04/08/79	914/6	Road Atlanta GTU (US Nat)	62	Koll	11th, gr 7	043 0593	William Koll
04/08/79	914/6	Road Atlanta GTU (US Nat)	82	Brewster	15th, gr 20		Schneider Autohaus
04/08/79	914/6	Road Atlanta GTU (US Nat)	85	Coupland	12th, gr 11		Ron Coupland
04/22/79	914/6	Riverside 6 Hours Int	62	Koll/Bean	13th ov, 3rd IMSA GTU, gr 31	043 0593	William Koll
04/22/79	914/4	Riverside 6 Hours Int	O6	Overstreet/Mitchell	20th ov, 7th IMSA GTU, gr 33		Darrel Overstreet
04/22/79	914/6	Riverside 6 Hours Int	52	Baker/Winters	NC lap 123, gr 50		Personalized Autohaus
04/29/79	914/4	Laguna Seca GTU (US Nat)	16	Overstreet	10th, gr 9		Overstreet Racing
04/29/79	914/6	Laguna Seca GTU (US Nat)	52	Baker	15th, gr 13		Personalized Autohaus
04/29/79	914/6	Laguna Seca GTU (US Nat)	62	Koll	9th, gr 15	043 0593	William Koll
04/29/79	914/6	Laguna Seca GTU (US Nat)	82	Harrison	11th, gr 11		Schneider AutoHaus
05/06/79		Mexico Trans Am Int	25	Zulkowski	8th ov, 4th Cat I		Metalcraft Racing
05/13/79	914/6	Hallett GTU (US Nat)	62	Koll	6th, gr 8	043 0593	William Koll
05/13/79	914/6	Hallett GTU (US Nat)	82	Harrison	4th		Schneider AutoHaus
05/13/79	914/4	Hallett GTU (US Nat)	85	Coupland	8th, gr 7		
05/28/79	914/6	Lime Rock GTU (US Nat)	52	Baker	11th, gr 8		Personalized Autohaus
05/28/79	914/6	Lime Rock GTU (US Nat)	62	Koll	6th, gr 7	043 0593	William Koll
06/03/79	914/6	Westwood Trans Am (US Nat)	56	Sanders	13th ov, 7th Cat I, gr 19		Bruce Sanders
06/03/79	914/6	Westwood Trans Am (US Nat)	111	Scott Taylor	14th ov, 8th Cat I, gr 22		
06/10/79	914/6	Portland Trans Am (US Nat)	23	Zulkowski	6th ov, 3rd Cat I, gr 18		Metalcraft Racing
06/10/79	914/6	Portland Trans Am (US Nat)	56	Sanders	11th ov, 7th Cat I, gr 21		Bruce Sanders
06/17/79	914/6	Brainerd 100 Miles (US Nat)	62	Koll	22nd ov, 2nd GTU, gr 16	043 0593	William Koll
07/04/79	914/6	Daytona 250 Miles (US Nat)	62	Koll/Cook	16th ov, 5th GTU, gr 31	043 0593	William Koll
07/15/79	914/6	Mid Ohio 250 Miles (US Nat)	40	Southard/Roe	17th ov, 5th GTU, gr 27		Performance Specialists
07/15/79	914/6	Mid Ohio 250 Miles (US Nat)	85	Hulen/Coupland	24th ov, 8th GTU		John E Hulen
07/15/79	914/6	Mid Ohio 250 Miles (US Nat)	95	Riley/Deacon	25th ov, 8th GTU		
07/21/79	914/6	Road America Trans Am (US Nat)	23	Zulkowski	20th, gr 27		Metalcraft Racing
07/29/79	914/6	Sears Point IMSA GTU (US Nat)	3	Bottom	12th ov, gr 18		
07/29/79	914/6	Sears Point IMSA GTU (US Nat)	16	Overstreet	9th ov, gr 17		Darrel Overstreet
08/05/79	914/6	GI Joe's Portland GTU (US Nat)	56	Sanders	11th, gr 11		
08/05/79	914/6	GI Joe's Portland GTU (US Nat)	62	Koll	9th ov, gr 10	043 0593	William Koll
08/05/79	914/6	GI Joe's Portland GTU (US Nat)	58	Gang	12th, gr 14		
08/19/79	914/6	Mosport Trans Am (Can Nat)	98	Deacon	14th ov, 9th Cat I, gr 21		Dave Deacon
09/02/79	914/6	Road America 500 Miles	40	Southard/Roe	21st ov, 7th GTU, gr 39		Performance Specialists
09/02/79	914/6	Road America 500 Miles	62	Koll/Cook	13th ov, 4th GTU, gr 24	043 0593	William Koll
09/02/79	914/6	Elkart Lake 500 Miles (US Nat)	62	Koll/Cook	13th ov, 4th IMSA GTU, gr 24	043 0593	William Koll
09/02/79	914/6	Elkart Lake 500 Miles (US Nat)	40	Southard/Roe	21st ov, 7th IMSA GTU, gr 39		Performance Specialists
09/02/79	914/4	Elkart Lake 500 Miles (US Nat)	85	Hulen/Coupland	NRF 89 laps, gr 34		John E Hulen
09/02/79	914/6	Elkart Lake 500 Miles (US Nat)	52	Baker/Haas/Smith Haas (Mrs)	NC 85 laps, gr 40		Wayne Baker
09/23/79	914/6	Road Atlanta GTU (US Nat)	62	Koll	8th, gr 7	043 0593	William Koll
09/23/79	914/4	Road Atlanta GTU (US Nat)	85	Hulen			John E Hulen

Race records Europe – North America – rallying – hillclimbs

Date	Car	Event	#	Drivers	Result	Notes	Entrant if known
02/03-04/80	914/6	Daytona 24 Hours Int	57	Baker/Gilliland/Scott	NC 486 laps, gr 67		Wayne Baker
02/03-04/80	914/6	Daytona 24 Hours Int	62	Koll/Cook/La Cava	5th ov, 1st IMSA GTU, gr 48	043 0593	William Koll
03/22/80	914/4	Sebring 12 Hours	22	Hirsch/Brezinka/Aschenbrenner	20th ov, 6th IMSA GTU, gr 71		R&H Racing
03/22/80	914/4	Sebring 12 Hours	57	Baker/Gilliland/Scott	NC 163 laps, gr 64		Personalized Autohaus
04/13/80	914/6	Road Atlanta GTU (US Nat)	57	Baker	12th ov, gr 14		Personalized Autohaus
04/26/80	914/4	Riverside 10-lap qualifying race	45	Ratcliff/Koll	9th ov		R F Ratcliff
04/26/80	914/6	Riverside 10-lap qualifying race	57	Haas/Scott/Smith/Haas (Mrs)	8th ov		Personalized Porsche
04/27/80	914/6	Riverside 5 Hours (US Nat)	28	Zulkowski/Brisken/Johnson	NC 67 laps 67, gr 57		Metalcraft Racing
04/27/80	914/4	Riverside 5 Hours (US Nat)	45	Ratcliff/Koll/Speer	21st ov, 6th IMSA GTU, gr 49		Ray Ratcliff
04/27/80	914/6	Riverside 5 Hours (US Nat)	57	Haas/Scott/Smith/Haas (Mrs)	26th ov, 9th IMSA GTU, gr 48		Personalized Porsche
05/04/80	914/4	Laguna Seca GTU (US Nat)	57	Baker	9th ov, gr 10		Personalized Autohaus
07/27/80	914/4	Golden State IMSA GTU (US Nat)	57	Scott	14th ov, gr 15		
08/03/80	914/6	Portland GTU (US Nat)	57	Scott	11th, gr 14		
08/31/80	914/6	Road America 500 Miles	52	Baker/Scott	28th ov, 11th GTU, gr 34		Personalized Autohaus
09/07/80	914/4	Westwood Trans Am (US Nat)	11	Taylor	13th ov, gr 19		Lewis Apparel
09/21/80	914/6	Road Atlanta GTU (US Nat)	2	Baker	3rd, gr 3		Personalized Autohaus
09/21/80	914/6	Road Atlanta GTU (US Nat)	69	Harmstad	7th, gr 5		Frank Harmstad
10/25/80	914/6	Riverside Trans Am (US Nat)	23	Zulkowski	23rd, gr 24		Metalcraft Racing
11/30/80	914/6	Daytona 250 Miles (US Nat)	O4	DiLella/Cueto	26th ov, 9th GTU, gr 69		DiLella Racing
01/31-02/01/81	914/6	Daytona 24 Hours Int	45	Speer (Ms)/Mitchell/Ratcliff	13th ov, 7th IMSA GTU, gr 58		Autosport Technology
03/21/81	914/4 Araki	Sebring 12 Hours Int	45	Mitchell/Ratcliff/Cooper	NRF lap 189 gearbox, gr 32		Autosport Technology
04/12/81	914/6	Road Atlanta GTU (US Nat)	22	Baker	6th		Personalized Autohaus
04/25/81	914/6	Riverside 10-lap qualifier	57	Overby	20th ov		Personalized Autohaus
04/26/81	914/6	Riverside 6 Hours (US Nat)	22	Baker/Overby/Scott	28th ov, 7th IMSA GTU, gr 64		Personalized Autohaus
04/26/81	914/4 Araki	Riverside 6 Hours (US Nat)	45	Mitchell/Ratcliff/Cooper	NC lap 132, gr 30		Autosport Technology
05/03/81	914/6	Laguna Seca GTU (US Nat)	22	Baker	5th ov, 1st IMSA GTU, gr 48		Personalized Autohaus
05/03/81	914/4 Araki	Laguna Seca GTU (US Nat)	3	Longmire	18th		Jon Longmire
05/31/81	914/4 Araki	Mid Ohio 200 Miles (US Nat)	22	Baker	14th		Personalized Autohaus
06/14/81	914/6	Brainerd 200Km (US Nat)	22	Baker	8th		Personalized Autohaus
07/26/81	914/4 Araki	Sears Point IMSA GTU (US Nat)	45	Ratcliffe	11th ov, gr 21		Autosport Technology
07/26/81	914/4 Araki	Sears Point IMSA GTU (US Nat)	22	Baker	1st		Personalized Autohaus
08/02/81	914/6	Portland IMSA GTU (US Nat)	22	Baker	3rd		Personalized Autohaus
08/02/81	914/6	Portland IMSA GTU (US Nat)	45	Mitchell/Ratcliff/Cooper	8th ov, gr 7		Autosport Technology
08/02/81	914/6	Portland IMSA GTU (US Nat)	57	Scott	11th, gr 16		
08/16/81	914/6	Mosport 6 Hours (Can Nat)	27	Aschenbrenner/Tescher	17th ov, 3rd IMSA GTU, gr 32		Alps Restoration
08/16/81	914/4 Araki	Mosport 6 Hours (Can Nat)	57	Overby/Baker	NC lap 139, gr 26		Personalized Autohaus
08/16/81	915 4 Araki	Mosport 6 Hours (Can Nat)	22	Baker/Overby	Dnf lap 95, gr 20		Personalized Autohaus
08/23/81	914/4 Araki	Elkhart Lake 500 Miles (US Nat)	22	Baker/Overby	11th ov, 3rd IMSA GTU, gr 27		Personalized Autohaus
09/27/81	914/6	Pocono 500 Miles (US Nat)	22	Baker/Overby	15th ov, gr 19		Personalized Autohaus
03/20/82	914/6	Sebring 12 Hours Int	O7	Buckley/Aschenbrennet/Rutherford	NC lap 142, gr 67		Road Runner

Porsche The Racing 914s

Date	Car	Event	#	Drivers	Result	Notes	Entrant if known
04/25/82	914/6	Riverside 6 Hours Int	45	Hefner/Cooper/Luckman	16th ov, gr 34		Garretson Development
04/25/82	914/4 Araki	Riverside 6 Hours Int	58	Gang/Middlebrook	21st		Edelweiss Porschaus
05/02/82	914/4 Araki	Laguna Seca GTU (US Nat)	22	Baker	31st		Personalized Autohaus
05/23/82	914/4 Araki	Mid Ohio IMSA GTU (US Nat)	22	Baker	Dnf, gr Pole		Personalized Autohaus
05/31/82	914/6	Lime Rock GTU (US Nat)	22	Baker	14th		Personalized Autohaus
09/05/82	914/6	Mid Ohio 6 Hours (US Nat)	26	Selby/Roe	17th, gr 33		Roe/Selby Racing
06/19/83	914/6	Mid Ohio 6 Hours (US Nat)	23	Selby/Roe	16th, gr 37		Selby-Roe
06/20/82	914/4 Araki	Summit Point GTU (US Nat)	14	Apgar	15th		Apgar
06/20/82	914/6	Summit Point GTU (US Nat)	22	Baker	19th		Personalized Autohaus
08/14/83	914/6	Mosport 6 Hours (Can Nat)	77	Resnick/Barnabe/Zwiren	17th ov, gr 27		
08/22/82	914/6	Road America 500 Miles (US Nat)	26	Selby/Roe	20th		Selby-Roe Racing
09/05/82	914/6	Mid Ohio 6 Hours (US Nat)	26	Selby/Roe	17th		Selby-Roe Racing
09/26/82	914/6	Pocono 500 Miles (US Nat)	6	Apgar/Jones	21st		Apgar
05/30/83	914/6	Lime Rock 3 Hours (US Nat)	77	Resnick/Barnabe	17th		
05/30/83	914/6	Lime Rock 3 Hours (US Nat)	94	Apgar/Jones	24th		Bruce Jones
06/19/83	914/6	Mid Ohio 6 Hours (US Nat)	23	Selby/Roe	16th		Selby-Roe Racing
08/14/83	914/6	Mosport 6 Hours (Can Nat)	23	Selby/Roe	8th		Selby-Roe Racing
08/14/83	914/6	Mosport 6 Hours (Can Nat)	77	Resnick/Barnabe/Zwiren	17th		Porsche Auto Recyclers
08/14/83	914/6	Mosport 6 Hours (Can Nat)	94	Apgar/Jones	24th		Bruce Jones
08/21/83	914/6	Road America 500 Mile (US Nat)	23	Selby/Roe	14th		Selby-Roe Racing
09/11/83	914/6	Pocono 500 Miles (US Nat)	3	Graves/Graves	17th		RAG Enterprises
09/11/83		Pocono 500 Miles (US Nat)	94	Apgar/Jones	21st		Bruce Jones

Rally

Here we see the records of the 914 story from the point of view of rallying and rally cross.
The chart is not definitive and shows only selected events. There were many local club events – too numerous to list.

dnf = did not finish
ov = overall
NC = not classified, though probably finished
Mostly these records are from those of the old ONS in Germany
In general, only cars in the top six are listed, except where it is of interest to show a lower position

Date	Car	Event	#	Drivers	Result	Notes	Entrant if known
06-08/02/70	914/4	Bayerische Winter-Rallye Marktredwitz		Wineberger/Trübsbach	5th Special GT unlimited		
04/04/70	VW/P 914	ADAC-Rallye Ulm Int		Wineberger/Trübsbach	1st GT up to 1L		
04/04/70	VW/P 914	ADAC-Rallye Ulm Int		Sauter/Lobert	NC		
11-12/04/70	914/6	Rallye Trifels Int		Wineberger/Trübsbach	3rd Special GT up-to-2L		
11-12/04/70	914	Rallye Trifels Int		Herrmann/Helduser	NC		
6-10/05/70	914/6	Austrian Alpenfahrt	1	Schlindler/Hrushka	Dnf		Bosch Racing Team Vienna
6-100/5/70	914/6	Austrian Alpenfahrt	2	Janger/Wessiak	Dnf	S28-061	Bosch Racing team Vienna

304

Race records Europe – North America – rallying – hillclimbs

Date	Car	Event	#	Drivers	Result	Notes	Entrant if known
09-10/05/70	914/6	Rudolf-Diesel-Rallye		Wineberger/Trübsbach	1st Special GT up-to-2L		Scuderia München
22-24/05/70	914	Int Rallye Wiesbaden – Deutschland-Rallye		Rossner/Kreuzer	4th Special GT up-to-2L		
22-24/05/70	VW/P914/6	Int Rallye Wiesbaden – Deutschland-Rallye		Feiler/Niedermeier	6th Special GT up-to-2L		V10 Kleber Team
22-24/05/70	VW/P 914	Int Rallye Wiesbaden – Deutschland-Rallye		Müller/Säckel	3rd Prod GT up to 2500		
22-24/05/70	VW/P914/4	Int Rallye Wiesbaden – Deutschland-Rallye		Herrmann/Druba	Accident		
23-24/05/70	VW 914	ADAC-Hunnenring-Rallye		Jegen	Accident		
28-30/05/70	914/6	Bodensee-Neusiedlersee Rally	8	Schindler/Hruschka	3rd Ov	S29.917	European Rally Championship
28-30/05/70	914	Bodensee-Neusiedlersee Rally	9	Müller/Säckl	1st production class	GL.DK914	European Rally Championship
30-31/05/70	914/6	ADAC-Junioren-Trophy Zandvoort		Hopp	3rd Special GT over 1600		
04-05/06/70	VW/P914/6	ADAC-Nordgau-Rallye Amberg		Feiler/Niedermeier	1st Special GT over 1600		
04-05/06/70	VW/P914/6	ADAC-Nordgau-Rallye Amberg		Wineberger/Trübsbach	3rd Special GT over 1600		Scuderia München
04-05/06/70	VW/P914/6	ADAC-Nordgau-Rallye Amberg		Wesol/Hartsch	5th Special GT over 1600		
06/06/70	VW/P914/6	Aalener ADAC-Zuverlässigkeitsfahrt		Nickel/Brücker	2nd Prod GT & Special GT up-to-2L		
06-07/06/70	VW/P914/6	Int ADAC-Süd-Rallye 24 Fränkische Zuverl-Fahrt		Wineberger/Trübsbach	2nd Special GT 1300-2000		Scuderia München
06-07/06/70	VW/P914/6	Int ADAC-Süd-Rallye 24 Fränkische Zuverl-Fahrt		Hermann/Schiller	1st Prod GT 1300-2000		Scuderia München
27-28/06/70	VW/P914/6	ADAC-Zuverl-Fahrt 'Rund um den Meissner'		Wesol/Hartsch	2nd Prod GT over 1600		
04-05/07/70	VW/P914/6	ADAC-Nordgau-Rallye Amberg		Wineberger/Trübsbach	1st Prod GT & Special GT over 1600		
04-05/07/70	VW/P914/6	ADAC-Nordgau-Rallye Amberg		Feiler/Niedermeier	4th Prod GT & Special GT over 1600		
04-05/07/70	VW/P914/6	ADAC-Nordgau-Rallye Amberg		Wesol/Hartsch	3rd Prod GT & Special GT over 1600		
05/07/70	VW/P914/6	Marburger ADAC-Auto-Slalom		Binder	4th Prod GT & Special GT up-to-2L		
06/07/70	VW/P914/6	Sauerländische ADAC-Seen-Rallye		Allemeyer	6th Prod GT & Special GT unlimited		
11-12/07/70	VW/P914/6	Nordbayerische ADAC-Grenzlandfahrt		Hartsch/Wesol	1st Special GT up-to-2L		
11-12/07/70	VW/P914/6	Nordbayerische ADAC-Grenzlandfahrt		Rossner/Kreuzer	3rd Special GT up-to-2L		
17/07/70	VW/P914/6	ADAC-Rallye 'Preis des Schlossstadt Bensberg'		Küper/Lobschart	5th Prod GT & Special GT over 1600		
18/07/70	VW/P914/6	ADAC-Leistungsprüfung '3000 Kurven Nürburgring'		Bremmekamp/Dederichs	2nd Special GT unlimited		
18/07/70	VW/P914/6	ADAC-Leistungsprüfung '3000 Kurven Nürburgring'		Christen/Dederichs	4th Special GT unlimited		
25/07/70	VW/P914/6	Rheingauer ADAC-Zuverl-Fahrt '8H Nürburgring'		Müller/Hess	Accident		
29/07-01/08/70	914/6	Danube Elan – Elf Rally	2	Schindler/Hruschka	2nd ov		
29/07-01/08/70	914/6	Danube Elan – Elf Rally	1	Poeltinger/Hartinger	7th ov		
25-26/07/70	VW/P914/6	ADAC-Niederrhein-Rallye		Ressing/Bald	4th Special GT unlimited		
25-26/07/70	VW/P914/6	ADAC-Niederrhein-Rallye		Allemeier/Plöger	Accident		
08-09/08/70	VW/P914/6	ADAC-Rallye Wolfsburg		Hartsch/Wesol	1st Prod GT & Special GT over 1300		

305

Porsche The Racing 914s

Date	Car	Event	#	Drivers	Result	Notes	Entrant if known
08-09/08/70	VW/P914/6	ADAC-Rallye Wolfsburg		Ressing/Balk	3rd Prod GT & Special GT over 1300		
28-30/08/70	VW/P914/6	Int ADAC-Rallye Avus Berlin		Wesol/Hartsch	3rd Prod GT up-to-2L		
28-30/08/70	VW/P914/6	Int ADAC-Rallye Avus Berlin		Wineberger/Trübsbach	Accident		Scuderia München
29/08/70	VW/P914/6	DMV-Leistungsprüfung Nürburgring 'Um die Chevron Trophy'		Küper/Christen	1st Prod GT over 1300		
26-27/09/70	914	ADAC-Zuverl-Fahrt 'Mittelholstein'		Wesol/Hartsch	1st Prod GT unlimited		
16-18/10/70	914/6	Rallye der 1000 Minuten	5	Poeltinger/Hartinger	9th ov		Bosch Racing Team
10-11/10/70	VW/P914/6	AvD-Rallye Hamburg		Hartsch/Wesel	1st Special GT over 1600		
17-18/10/70	VW/P914/6	AvD-Klingenrallye		Küper/Nottebaum	4th Prod GT & Special GT unlimited		
17-18/10/70	VW/P914/6	AvD-Klingenrallye		Brink/Schilling	Accident		
17-18/10/70	VW/P 914	ADAC-Rallye Lufthansa		Hechenberger/Maier	6th Special GT unlimited		
31/10/70	VW/P914/4	AvD-MAC-Gleichmässigkeitsprüfung 'Rund ums Karussell'		Römer/Kichniawy	2nd Prod GT up-to-2L		
28-29/11/70	VW/P914/6	ADAC-Rallye Kohle und Stahl		Ruess/Küper	3rd Prod GT & Special GT over 1300		
28-29/11/70	914/6	Critérium des Cévennes	87?	Ballot-Léna/Morenas	9th ov, 3rd GT	105 BC 92	Sonauto
14-15/11/70	914/6	Rallye Barcelona-Andorra	4	JM Fernández/Cortel	5th ov, 4th Gr 4		Escudería Montjuich
13-18/11/70	914/6 GT	RAC Rally Great Britain	37	Haldi/Chappuis	12 ov, 3rd Gr 6	S-X 7495, 914 043 1732	
30/01/71	914/6	ADAC-Winter-Rallye Nürburgring		Simonis/Diedrich	4th Prod GT & Special GT unlimited		
23-29/01/71	914/6 GT	Monte Carlo Rally Int	7	Waldegård/Thorzelius H	3rd ov		
23-29/01/71	914/6 GT	Monte Carlo Rally Int	69	Gudladt	dnf		
23-29/01/71	914/6 GT	Monte Carlo Rally Int	1	Larrousse-/Perramond	dnf		
23-29/01/71	914/6	Monte Carlo Rally Int	17	A Andersson/B Thorzelius	Retired – gearbox		
23-29/01/71	914/6	Monte Carlo Rally Int	118	Fernández/Fernández	dnf accident		
05-07/02/71	914/6	Int Bayerische ADAC-Winter-Rallye Marktredwitz		Feiler/Niedermeyer	18th ov, 1st Special GT up-to-2L		
05-07/02/71	914/6	Int Bayerische ADAC-Winter-Rallye Marktredwitz		Löw/Löw	4th Special GT up-to-2L		
05-07/02/71	914/6	Routes du Nord Nat		Bedet/Ronet	3rd		
05-07/02/71	914/6	Routes du Nord Nat		Letesse/Danger	9th		
13/02/71	914/6	Rallye Costa Brava	8	Fernández	dnf		
27-28/02/71	914/6	Rallye de la Lana	2	JM Fernández/Cortel	1st ov	VD 5248	Escudería Montjuich
05-07/03/71	914/6	Rallye Lyon-Charbonnières-Stuttgart-Solitude	12	Gudladt/Schummelfeder	26th ov		
27-28/02/71	914/6	ADAC-Rallye Ostwestfalen Gütersloh		Brink/Wiese	1st Prod & Special GT unlimited		
06-07/03/71	914/4	ADAC Vehrter Nachtfahrt – Burgmann Rallye		von Hartz/Fürstenau	2nd Prod & Special GT unlimited		
06-07/03/71	914/6	ADAC-Rallye Marienberg, Würzburg		Franke/Eirich	5th Special GT up-to-2L		
20/03/71	914	Rally Anoia		JM Fernández/Cortel	1st ov, 1st Gr 4		Escudería Montjuich
20-21/03/71	914/6	Int Rallye Trifels		Gudladt/Schümmelfeder	2nd Special GT up to and over-2L		MSC Stuttgart
20-21/03/71	914/6	Ravensberger ADAC-Nachtzuverlässigkeitsfahrt		Brink/Wiese	1st Special GT & GT over-2L		

Race records Europe – North America – rallying – hillclimbs

Date	Car	Event	#	Drivers	Result	Notes	Entrant if known
26-28/03/71	914/4	Int ADAC-Rallye Hanseatic, Hamburg		von Hartz/Seyfferth	2nd Prod & Special GT unlimited		
27/03/71	914/6	ADAC-Rallye Hameln		Ellermann/Tacke	2nd Prod & Special GT unlimited		
03/04/71	914/6	Nordwestfälische ADAC-Zuverl Dortmund		Küper/Lobschat	1st Special GT up to 1300		Scuderia Blau-Weiss Bochum
03-04/04/71	914/6	Unterfränkische ADAC-Zuverl Alzenau		Franke/Schäfer	3rd Special GT 850 to over-2L		
17-18/04/71	914/6	Int ADAC-Rallye Ulm		Graepel/Karl	2nd Special GT up-to-2L		
20/04/71	914/4	AvD-AMSC-Rallye Nürburgring		Römer/?	2nd Prod & Special GT unlimited		
20/04/71	914/4	AvD-AMSC-Rallye Nürburgring		Kilb/Ziegler	2nd Prod & Special GT unlimited		
24/04/71	914/6	ADAC-Barbarossa-Rallye Nürburgring des MSC Sinzig eV		Küper/Christen	2nd Prod GT over 1300		
24-25/04/71	914/6	ADAC-Rallye Gifhorn		von Hartz/Seyfferth	2nd Prod & Special GT unlimited		
29/04-02/05/71	914/6	Int ADAC-Rallye Nordland and Deutsche ADAC-Journalisten-Rallye		Gudladt/Schümmelfeder	3rd Special GT unlimited		Auto- und Motorsportclub Karlsruhe
08/05/71	VW/P 914	ADAC-Barock-Rallye Ludwigsburg		Nickel	2nd Prod & Special GT up-to-2L		MSC Bad Canstatt
04-06/06/71	914	Rallye d'Antibes (Rallye des Roses)	27	Calais/Jullian	9th		
15-16/05/71	914/6	ADAC-Rallye Harz-Solling		von Hartz/Martin	1st Prod & Special GT unlimited		
05-06/06/71	914/6	Int ADAC-Süd-Rallye Nürnberg		Franke/Eirich	4th Special GT over 1300		
12-13/06/71	914/4	ADAC-Rallye 'Rund um Wolfenbüttel'		von Hartz/Seyffert	1st Special GT up to 1600		
19/06/71	914/6	Tag der Hohenloher ADAC-Sonderprüfung		Nickel/Brücker	2nd Prod & Special GT up-to-2L		MSC Bad Canstatt
19/06/71	914/6	Tag der Hohenloher ADAC-Sonderprüfung		Altenheimer/Gwinner	5th Prod & Special GT up-to-2L		MSC Bad Canstatt
19-20/06/71	VW 914/6	ADAC-Rallye Mayen-Nürburgring		Römer/Dimmendal	3rd Prod GT up to and over-2L		
19-20/06/71	914/6	ADAC-Rallye Mayen-Nürburgring		Simonis/Diedrich	2nd Special GT unlimited		
03-04/07/71	914/6	Rallye del Cid Int		Gargallo/Ramon	3rd ov		
03-04/07/71	914/6	ADAC-Rallye Ennepe		Küper/Lobschatz	2nd Prod & Special GT up to 1600		Scuderia Blau-Weiss
24-25/07/71	914/6	ADAC-Rallye Wolfsburg		Eberhard/Schöne	4th Prod & Special GT over 1600		
25/07/71	914/6	Rallye de Benicàssim	6	Fernández/Cortel	1st ov, 1st Gr 4		
13-14/08/71	914/6	Rallye Rías Baixas	6	Gargallo/Guerrero	7th		
21/08/71	914	Rally Osona	1	JM Fernández/Cortel	1st ov, 1st Gr 4		Escudería Montjuich
04/09/71	914/6	Vuelta a Andalucía	3	Fernández/Cortel	1st ov, 1st Gr 4	VD 35227	
18-19/09/71	914/6	DMV-Rallye Wuppertal		Küper/Christen	6th Prod & Special GT over 1300		Scuderia Blau-Weiss
21-23/9/71	914/6	Int Sherry Rally	4	Gargallo-Ramón	1st ov	857 Z 2756	
09/10/71	914	ADAC-Maifeld-Rallye Nürburgring		Simonis/Hoier	1st Prod & Special GT unlimited		
17-18/10/71	914/6	Rallye Torre del Oro	1?	Gargallo	1st		
17-18/10/71	VW/P914/6	AvD-Klingenrallye		Küper/Nottebaum	4th Prod & Special GT unlimited		
23/10/71	VW 914/4	DMV-Rallye 'Kaiser Karl' Aachen, Nürburgring		Römer	2nd Prod GT over 1300		
23/10/71	VW 914/4	DMV-Rallye 'Kaiser Karl' Aachen, Nürburgring		Kilb/Götting	5th Special GT over 1300		ADAC-Ortsclub Hofheim
30-31/10/71	VW 914/4	Sauerländische ADAC-Seen-Rallye, Castrol GTX Cup		Eisenhuth/Benthaus	1st Prod & Special GT unlimited		

Porsche The Racing 914s

Date	Car	Event	#	Drivers	Result	Notes	Entrant if known
30-31/10/71	VW 914/4	Sauerländische ADAC-Seen-Rallye, Castrol GTX Cup		Küper/Müller	NC		
13-14/11/71	914/6	Rally Int Firestone Macizo Cantabro		Gargallo/Ramón	4th ov		
20/11/71	914/6	Rally Barcelona-Andorra	2	JM Fernández/Cortel	dnf – accident	VD 35227	
7-8/12/71	914/6	Rallye Costa del Sol		Gallardo/Guerrero	3rd		
15-16/01/72	VW 914/4	Hessisch-Waldeckische-ADAC-Berglandfahrt – Continental Rallye		Eisenhuth/Flieger	1st Prod & Special GT all classes		
22/01/72	914/6	AvD-RSCG-Rallye Gross-Gerau 'Eis & Schnee'		Eisenhuth/Benthaus	2nd Prod & Special GT over 1300		
29-30/01/72	914/6	ADAC-Franken-Winter-Rallye Hersbruck 'Zur Olympiade 1972'		Franke/Eirich	3rd Prod & Special GT unlimited		
05/02/72	914/6	ADAC-Winterfahrt Hessen		Graepel/Karl	3rd Prod & Special GT unlimited		
19/02/72	914/6	ADAC-Rallye Ostwestfalen, Gütersloh		Eisenhuth/Benthaus	2nd Prod & Special GT unlimited		
26-27/02/72	914/6	Rheinisch-Bergische ADAC-Winter-Rallye		Eisenhuth/Benthaus	4th Prod & Special GT over 1600		
11-12/03/72	914/6	ADAC-Rallye Marienberg, Würzburg		Franke/Claussen	4th Prod & Special GT over 1600		
18-19/03/72	914/6	ADAC-Rallye Nürnberg		Franke/Claussen	5th Prod & Special GT over 1600		
25-26/03/72	VW 914/4	DMV-Münsterland-Rallye 'Autol-Desolite-Rallye'		Eisenhuth/Benthaus	1st Prod & Special GT up-to-2L		
26/03/72	914/6	ADAC-MTZ-Auto-Slalom Königstein		Kilb	3rd Prod & Special GT up-to-2L		
26/03/72	914/6	DMV-Bergpreis Zotzenbach/Odw Veith-Pirelli Prize		Neureuther	1st Prod & Special GT up-to-2L		
26/03/72	914/6	DMV-Bergpreis Zotzenbach/Odw Veith-Pirelli Prize		Egerland	3rd Prod & Special GT up-to-2L		Kamei RT Wolfsburg
11/04/72	914/6	Rallye Torre del Oro		Gargallo/Guerrero	1st		
14-16/04/72	914/6	Int Aschaffenburger ADAC-Edelweiss-Rallye		Franke/Claussen	5th Prod & Special GT unlimited		
22/04/72	914/6	ADAC-Barbarossa-Rallye Nürburgring des MSC Sinzig		Löw/Löw	NC		
22-23/04/72	VW 914/4	ADAC-Werraland-Rallye, Bad Sooden-Allendorf		Gallo/Walter	1st Prod GT unlimited		
25/05/72		ADAC-Werraland-Rallye, Bad Sooden-Allendorf		Roche/Rey	24th ov, 4th Gr 4		
21/05/72	914/6	Int ADAC Rallye-Cross Niederelbe		Bohnhorst	1st Prod & Special GT unlimited		
03-04/06/72	914/6	Int ADAC-Süd-Rallye (Fränkische ADAC-Zuverl-Fahrt)		Franke/Eirich	4th Prod & Special GT unlimited		
03-04/06/72	VW 914/4	ADAC-Niederrhein-Rallye, Wesel		Eisenhuth/Benthaus	1st Prod & Special GT unlimited		
18/06/72	914/6	ADAC-Eifelfaht 'Rund um Mayen'		Sasse/Westermann	4th Erinnerung, Prod & Special GT over 1300		
23-25/06/72	914/6	Int ADAC-Rallye Stuttgart-Strassburg-Stuttgart		Graepel/Karl	1st Prod & Special GT up-to-2L		
13-19/08/72	914/6	Olympia-Rallye 1972		Franke/Eirich	4th Special GT up to 2000		
26-27/08/72	914/6	AvD/SGZ-Rallye Schwalm		Eisenhuth/Benthaus	1st Special GT unlimited		
26-27/08/72	914/6	ADAC-Rallye Ennepe '1200km-Bilstein-Trophäe'		Sasse/Dören	2nd Prod & Special GT over 1300		MSC Langenfeld
02/09/72	914/6	ADAC-Rallye Nordbaden, Karlsruhe		Hechenberger/Laub	4th Prod & Special GT over 1600		Reifag RT, Darmstadt
08/09/72	914/6	Avd/STH-Hunsrück-Rallye		Eisenhuth/Benthaus	2nd Prod & Special GT over 1600		
09-10/09/72	914/6	ADAC-Saarland-Rallye Dillingen		Bisenius/Becker	3rd Prod & Special GT unlimited		
16/09/72	914/6	DMV-Rallye 'Kaiser Karl' Aachen, Nürburgring		Sasse/Westermann	6th & Erinnerung Special GT over 1300		RG MSC Langenfeld
27-29/10/72	914/6	RACE Rally Spain		Gargallo/Ramón	4th ov		
03/12/72	914	Rally Isla de Tenerife		Mansito/JM Rodríguez	4th ov		
14-15/04/73	VW 914/4	ADAC-Rallye Gifhorn		Menzel/König	2nd Prod & Special GT unlimited		

Race records Europe – North America – rallying – hillclimbs

Date	Car	Event	#	Drivers	Result	Notes	Entrant if known
31/05-02/06/73	VW 914/4	Int Semperit-Rallye, Austria		Leistner/Scholz	2nd Prod GT over 1600		
16-17/06/73	914/6	ADAC-Rallye der 30,000 Sekunden, Fallersleben		Schmolke/Harms	4th Prod & Special GT unlimited		
07-08/07/73	914/6	ADAC-Peiner Stahl-Rallye		Schmolke/Harms	1st Prod & Special GT unlimited		
15-16/09/73	914/6	ADAC-Saarlandrallye		Becker/Becker	6th Prod & Special GT unlimited		
13-14/10/73	VW 914/4	Int AvD-Rallye Hubertus Bremen		Eckhoff/Budde	3rd Prod & Special GT up-to-2L		
01/06/74	914/6	ADAC-Rallye 'Dammer Berge'		Schwager/Broock	2nd Prod & Special GT up-to-2L		
29/06/74	914/6	ADAC-Rallye Königsbrunn		Göbel/Schmid	2nd Prod GT unlimited		
05-06/04/75	VW 914/4	ADAC/MSGB-Rallye Berlin		Kossack/Pürschel	1st Gr 3 up-to-2L		
19/04/75	914/6	ADAC-Neckar-Rallye, Ludwigsburg		Barthel/Barthel	3rd Gr 3-4 up-to-2L		
20/04/75	914/6	Int ADAC-Rallye-Cross Niederelbe, Hamburg		Smet, E	5th Special Rallye-Cross up-to-2L		
20/04/75	914/6	Int ADAC-Rallye-Cross Niederelbe, Hamburg		Smet, G	10h Special Rallye-Cross up-to-2L		
31/05-01/06/75	914/6	Int ADAC-Rallye-Cross 'Hessen', Stadt Allendorf		Smet, E	13th Gr Special Rallye Cross		
21/06/75	VW 914/4	ADAC-Cheruskerfahrt, Detmold		Sierges/Nölke	2nd Gr 3 up to and over-2L		
21/06/75	VW 914/4	ADAC-Cheruskerfahrt, Detmold		Tschorn/Dütz	3rd Gr 3 up to and over-2L		MSC Gütersloh
24/08/75	914/6	Int ADAC-Rallye-Cross Niederelbe, Estering		Smet, G	9th Special Rally Cross unlimited, joint 10th ov		
25-26/10/75	914/6	ADAC/RCK-Rallye Zenith Time, Hannover		Tschorn/Hinrichs	2nd Gr 3-4 unlimited		
08-09/11/75	914/6	ADAC-Ostsee-Nordseefahrt – Nordmark-Rallye		Tschorn/Hinrichs	2nd Gr 3-4 unlimited		
10/04/76	914/6	ADAC-Vogelsberg-Rallye		Seemann/Böttner	3rd Gr 3-4 up-to-2L		
16/05/76	914/6	Int ADAC-Rallye-Cross 'Hessen'		Ankele	3rd Gr C: 2, 4 & 5 Nat up-to-2L		Max Moritz
12/06/75	914/6	ADAC-Ahr-Eifel-Rallye, Nürburgring		Silbernagel/Senger	2nd Gr 2 & 5 Nat up-to-2L		
14-15/08/76	914/6	ADAC-Bayerwald-Rallye		Möller/Wimmer	16th Gr 1 & 3 up-to-2L		
09/10/76	914/6	ADAC-Rallye Schleswig-Holstein		Müller/Reimers	3rd Gr 3-4 up-to-2L		Pepsi-Cola-MC, Offenbach
30/04-01/05/77	914	Dreux Bois-Guyon (Rally Cross)		Guy Deladrière	5th Class 2		
14-15/05/77	914/6	Quenne-Auxerre (Rally Cross)		Guy Deladrière	5th Class 2		
06-07/05/78	914/6	Int ADAC-Rallye-Cross Estering		Philipsen	4th Gr 3-4 unlimited		

Hillclimbs

Records of hillclimbing in Europe, compiled from the archives of the then ONS organization.
Note: this list is not definitive, but demonstrates the capability of the 914 in this discipline of motorsport.
ov = overall
Only top six are recorded here, unless the entry is of significant interest.

Date	Car	Event	#	Driver	Result (podium positions in bold)	Entrant
19/04/70	914/6	Int ADAC-Bruckberg-Bergrennen		Neureuther	1st Special GT up-to-2L	
25-26/04/70	914/6	Int ADAC-Bergrennen Riedenburg		Neureuther	2nd Prod GT & Special GT up-to-2L	
02-03/05/70	914/6	ADAC-Frankenwald-Bergrennen		Schlienz	1st Prod GT & Special GT up-to-2L	
03/05/70	914/4	ADAC-Schlossberg-Rennen Gernsbach		Sauter	2nd Prod GT over 1300	Autohaus Max Moritz
17/05/70	914/6	Int ADAC-Nibelungen-Bergrennen		Greger	1st Prod GT & Special GT up-to-2L	
17/05/70	914/6	Int ADAC-Nibelungen-Bergrennen		Neureuther	3rd Prod GT & Special GT up-to-2L	
24/05/70	914/6	Montseny hillclimb		Greger	9th ov, 2nd Gr 4	
21/06/70	914/6	Mont Ventoux hillclimb		Greger	9th ov, 1st Gr 4	

Porsche The Racing 914s

Date	Car	Event	#	Driver	Result (podium positions in bold)	Entrant
21/06/70	914/6	Mont Ventoux hillclimb		Henri Balas	17th ov, 5th Gr 4	
05/07/70	914/6	Trento Bondone hillclimb		Greger	3rd Gr 4	
05/07/70	914/6	Trento Bondone hillclimb		Rondanini	4th Gr 4	
06-07/06/70	914/6	Int AvD-Alpen-Bergpreis Berchtesgaden		Neureuther	1st Special GT up-to-2L	
07/06/70	914	Bergrennen Wissembourg		Leinenweber	1st Gr 4	
15/07/70	914/6	Cesana/Sestrieres hillclimb	328	Greger	3rd Gr 4	
26/07/70	914/6	Freiburg-Schauinsland		Greger	3rd Gr 4	
30/08/70	914	Gubbio-Madonna delle Cima (I)		Valle	4th over-2L	
11/10/70	914/6 GT	Subida a Pont de Vilumaria (Spain)		Fernández	2nd ov, 1st Gr 4	
18/10/70	914/6	Subida a la Rabassada	78	Fernández	9th ov, 1st Gr 4	
27-28/03/71	914/4	DMV-Bergpreis Zotzenbach/Odw		Medler	2nd Prod GT over 1300	
27-28/03/71	914/6	DMV-Bergpreis Zotzenbach/Odw		Neureuther	1st Special GT up-to-2L	
28/03/71	914	Hillclimb Montserrat		Fernández	6th ov	
03-04/04/71	914	Hillclimb Montjuich Castle		Fernández	1st ov	
11/04/71	914/6	S C Sant Bartomeu del Grau	80	Fernández	8th ov, 2nd Gr 4	
12/04/71	914/6	Subida a Lurdes	48	Fernández	1st ov, 1st Gr 4	
01-02/05/71	914/6	Heilbronner ADAC-Bergpreis		Sauter	1st Prod & Special GT up-to-2L	Autohaus Max Moritz
01-02/05/71	914/6	Heilbronner ADAC-Bergpreis		Bauer	3rd Prod & Special GT up-to-2L	Autohaus Max Moritz
01/05/70	914/6	Subida a la Mata	36	Fernández	2nd ov, 2nd Gr 4	
02/05/71	914/6	Int ADAC-Nibelungen-Bergrennen, Passau		Neureuther	1st Prod & Special GT over 1600	
07-08/05/71	914/6	Int ADAC-Wallberg-Rennen München		Neureuther	2nd Prod & Special GT up-to-2L	
22-23/05/71	914/6	Int ADAC-Wasgau-Bergpreis		Kilb	2nd Special GT 1600-2000	
05-06/06/71	914/6	Int AvD-Alpen-Bergpreis Berchtesgarden		Neureuther	3rd Prod & Special GT over 1600	
05-06/06/71	914/6	Int AvD-Alpen-Bergpreis Berchtesgarden		Federhofer	2nd sports cars up-to-2L	
20/06/71	914/6	Sassotetto hillclimb, Sarnaro It		Francesco Miglionini	6th Gr 4, 2nd in class	
11/07/71	914/6	Gironella-Casserras hillclimb	69	Fernández	1st ov, 1st Gr 4	
17-18/07/71	914/6	AvD/ATCW-Bergpeis d Oberpfalz, Weiden		Neureuther	1st Special GT up-to-2L	
01/08/71	914/6	Bien Aparecida hillclimb		Gargallo	5th ov	
08/08/71	914/6	Mont Dore hillclimb		Monticone	18th ov, 4th Gr 4	
07-08/08/71	914/6	ADAC-Rheingau-Bergrennen, Lorch		Godel	1st Prod & Special GT up-to-2L	
13-15/08/71	914/6	Int ADAC-Rusel-Bergrennen		Neureuther	1st Prod & Special GT up-to-2L	Team Matter Überollbügel Karlsdorf
15/08/71	914/6	ADAC-Hunsrück-Bergrennen, Veldenz		Kilb	2nd Prod GT up-to-2L	ADAC-Ortsclub Hofheim
21-22/08/71	914/6	Trierer AvD/RTT-Bergrennen		Bisenius	5th Prod & Special GT over 1300	EMSC Bitburg
21-22/08/71	914/4	ADAC-Ratisbona-Bergrennen, Kelheim		Koch	1st Prod GT up-to-2L	
21-22/08/71	914/4	AvD-MSCR-Heidelstein-Bergrennen		Medler	2nd Prod GT up-to-2L	
28/08/71	914/6	Subida Tarrasa-Rellinas	36	Fernández	1st ov, 1st Gr 4	
29/08/71	914/6	Ollon-Villars hillclimb		Quist	25th ov, 3rd Gr 4	
29/08/71	914/6	Ollon-Villars hillclimb		Chenevière	30th ov, 6th Gr 4	
29/08/71	914/6	Ollon-Villars hillclimb		Peter Zbinden	34th ov, 8th Gr 4	
04-05/09/71	914/6	ADAC-Weser-Bergpreis Höxter		Egerland	1st Special GT up-to-2L	Kamei RT Wolfsburg

Race records Europe – North America – rallying – hillclimbs

Date	Car	Event	#	Driver	Result (podium positions in bold)	Entrant
04-05/09/71	914/6	ADAC-Weser-Bergpreis Höxter		Lips	3rd Special GT up-to-2L	
04-05/09/71	914/6	Int Windhausener ADAC-Bergpreis, Burg-Falkenstein Trophy		Bisenius	2nd Special GT up-to-2L	
25-26/09/71	914/6	Int ADAC-Auerbergrennen		Neureuther	1st Prod & Special GT up-to-2L	
17/11/71	914/6	Subida a Port de Vilumara		Fernández	4th ov, 1st Gr 4	
02/01/72	914	Tolmezzo-Verzegnis (It) (Hill)	?164	Trenti	1st Gr 2 cl 3 (up-to-2L)	
08-09/04/72	914/6	DMV-Dünsberg-Bergrennen, Rodheim-Bieber		Schimpf	2nd Prod & Special GT up-to-2L	Jägermeister RT
22-23/04/72	914/6	Int DMV-Krähberg-Rennen, Erbach, Veith-Pirelli Prize		Neureuther	1st Prod & Special GT up-to-2L	
23/04/72	914/6	ADAC-Bergrennen Teutoburger Wald, Detmold		Gutowsky	1st Special GT up-to-2L	
23/04/72	914/6	ADAC-Bergrennen Teutoburger Wald, Detmold		Bohnhorst	4th Special GT up-to-2L	Jägermeister RT
29-30/04/72	914/6	Heilbronner ADAC-Bergpreis		Bauer	2nd Prod & Special GT over-2L	Autohaus Max Moritz
30/04/72	914/6	ADAC-Nibelungen-Bergrennen, Obernzell		Neureuther	1st Prod & Special GT over 1600	
13-14/05/72	914/6	Int ADAC/PMSC-Harz-Bergpreis		Gutowski	1st Prod & Special GT up to and over-2L	
13-14/05/72	914/6	Int ADAC/PMSC-Harz-Bergpreis		Bohnhorst	3rd Prod & Special GT up to and over-2L	
13-14/05/72	914/6	Int ADAC-Eurohill-Bergrennen, Nürnberg		Löw	3rd Prod & Special GT over 1600	
13-14/05/72	914/6	Int ADAC-Eurohill-Bergrennen, Nürnberg		Neureuther	2nd sports cars over 1600	
14/05/72	914/6	ADAC-Barock-Bergpreis Ludwigsburg		Kreutz	2nd Prod & Special GT up-to-2L	
21-22/05/72	914/6	Wittlicher ADAC-Bergpreis 'Um das Piesporter Goldtröpfchen		Gotowski	2nd Prod & Special GT up to 2000	
27-28/05/72	914/6	AvD/GAMSC-Bergrennen Sulzthal		Neureuther	1st Prod & Special GT up to 2000	
10-11/06/72	914/6	Int ADAC-Bergrennen Rotenburg/Fulda		Egerland	1st Prod & Special GT up to 1300	
10-11/06/72	914/6	Int ADAC-Bergrennen Rotenburg/Fulda		Gutowski	2nd Prod & Special GT up to 1300	Kamei RT Wolfsburg
10-11/06/72	914/6	Int ADAC-Bergrennen Rotenburg/Fulda		Neureuther	3rd Prod & Special GT up to 1300	
10-11/06/72	914/6	ADAC-Rheinhessen-Bergrennen "Teufelsrutsch", Alzey		Kreutz	3rd Prod & Special GT up-to-2L	MC Stuttgart
17-18/06/72	914/6	ADAC-Jura-Bergrennen, Neumarkt/Opf		Neureuther	2nd Prod & Special GT over 1600	
25/06/72	914/6	Algar hillclimb Spain		Jungk	7th ov	
08-09/07/72	914/6	AvD/ATCW-Bergpreis der Oberpfalz		Neureuther	1st Prod & Special GT up-to-2L	
09/07/72	914/6	Cesana-Sestriere hillclimb It		Carlo Fabbri ("Cam")	5th in class	
09/07/72	914/6	Cesana-Sestriere hillclimb It		Bohnhorst	22nd ov, 6th in class	
23/07/72	914/6	Ascoli hillclimb It		Miglionini	5th GT Special, 2nd in class	
23/07/72	914/6	Preis von Tirol		Schmid	1st Special GT up-to-2L	
23/07/72	914/6	Preis von Tirol		Greger	2nd Special GT up-to-2L	
29-30/07/72	914/6	ADAC-Ellerberg-Rennen, Bamberg		Neureuther	1st Prod & Special GT over 1600	
29-30/07/72	914/6	Int Osnabrücker ADAC-Bergrennen		Gotowski	1st Prod & Special GT up-to-2L	
29-30/07/72	914/6	Int Osnabrücker ADAC-Bergrennen		Egerland	2nd Prod & Special GT up-to-2L	Kamei RT Wolfsburg
12-13/08/72	914/6	AvD/GAMSC-Bergrennen Unterfranken		Neureuther	1st Prod & Special GT up-to-2L	
26-27/08/72	914/6	Amberger NAVC-Bergpreis 72		Neureuther	1st Prod & Special GT up-to-2L	
26-27/08/72	914/6	Malegno-Ossimo-Borno (I) Hill		Monticone	9th ov, 1st up-to-2L	
02-03/09/72	914/6	ADAC-Weser-Bergpreis Höxter		Gotowski	1st Special GT over 1300	
02-03/09/72	914/6	Int ADAC-Bergrenne Happurg		Egerland	1st Prod & Special GT up-to-2L	Kamei RT Wolfsburg
16-17/09/72	914	Griesbacher ADAC-Bergrennen, Simbach		Neureuther	1st Prod & Special GT up-to-2L	
17/09/72	914/6	Int ADAC-Bergrennen "Kalter Wangen"		Kreutz	3rd Prod & Special GT over 1300	

311

Porsche The Racing 914s

Date	Car	Event	#	Driver	Result (podium positions in bold)	Entrant
30/09-01/10/72	914/6	ADAC-Auerbergrennen		Neureuther	1st Prod & Special GT up-to-2L	
07-08/10/72	914/6	Int ADAC-Bergpreis Steibis des MSG Oberstaufen		Neureuther	2nd Prod & Special GT up-to-2L	
14-15/10/72	914/6	AvD/HMSC-Taunus-Bergprüfung Lorch		Egerland	1st Prod & Special GT over 1600	
14-15/10/72	914/6	Int ADAC-Augusta-Bergrennen		Neureuther	1st Prod & Special GT up-to-2L	
15/10/72	VW 914/4	ADAC-Bergrennen "Haldenhof", Stockach		Weber	3rd Prod & Special GT over 1300	
11/02/73	914/6	Hillclimb Coll de Rates		"Crady" Gemar	2nd ov	
05/03/73	914/6	Hillclimb Pererio		"Crady" Gemar	1st ov	
17-18/03/73	914	Hillclimb Mountains of Malaga		"Crady" Gemar	5th ov	
21-22/04/73	914/6	ADAC-Frankenwald-Bergrennen Stadtsteinach		Weber	3rd Prod & Special GT over 1500	Scud Lindau, Bodensee
28-29/04/73	VW 914/4	ADAC-Bergrennen Teutoburger Wald, Detmold		Eichler	2nd Prod GT up-to-2L (1st place not awarded)	
28-29/04/73	914/6	ADAC-Bergrennen Teutoburger Wald, Detmold		Schimpf	1st Special GT up-to-2L	Jägermeister RT Braunschweig
05-06/05/73	914/6	Int Heilbronner ADAC-Bergpreis		Bauer	2nd Prod & Special GT up-to-2L	
11-12/05/73	914/6	Int ADAC-Wallbergrennen, Rottach-Egern		Egerland	2nd Prod & Special GT up-to-2L	
11-12/05/73	914/6	Int ADAC-Wallbergrennen, Rottach-Egern		Weber	4th Prod & Special GT up-to-2L	Scud Lindau, Bodensee
19-20/05/73	914/6	Int ADAC-Eurohill-Bergrennen "um den KAMA-Preis", Nürnberg		Koch	5th Prod & Special GT over 1600	
26-27/05/73	914/6	Int ADAC-Nibelungen-Bergrennen, Obernzell-Passau		Weber	1st Prod & Special GT up-to-2L	Scud Lindau, Bodensee
03/06/73	914/6	Hillclimb Berchtesgaden/Rossfeld	52	Egerland	7th GT	
02-03/06/73	914/6	ADAC-Bergpreis Ulm		Weber	2nd Prod & Special GT up-to-2L	Scud Lindau, Bodensee
02-03/06/73	914/6	Int AvD-Alpenbergpreis Berchtesgaden		Egerland	6th Prod & Special GT over 1600	
10-11/06/73	914/6	Wolsfelder AvD/EMSC-Bergrennen, Bitburg		Bisenius	5th Prod & Special GT over 1300	
17/06/73	914/6	Hillclimb Urbasa		"Crady" Gemar	5th ov	
14-15/07/73	VW 914/4	AvD/ATCW-Bergpreis der Oberpfalz, Weiden		Koch	1st Prod GT unlimited	
20/07/73	914/6	Morcuera hillclimb		"Crady" Gemar	3rd ov	
11-12/08/73	914/6	Int ADAC-Altmühlstal-Bergrennen, Nürnberg		"Crady" Gemar	2nd Prod & Special GT up-to-2L	
11-12/08/73	914/6	Int ADAC-Altmühlstal-Bergrennen, Nürnberg		Koch	4th Prod & Special GT up-to-2L	
18-19/08/73	914/6	AvD-MSCR-Heidelstein-Bergrennen, Bad Neustadt		Egerland	3rd Prod & Special GT up to and over-2L	
18-19/08/73	914/6	ADAC-Wallonen-Bergrennen Otterberg		Schimpf	1st Special GT up-to-2L	Jägermeister RT
25-26/08/73	914/6	Int ADAC-Ratisbona-Bergrennen, Kelheim		Egerland	1st Prod & Special GT up-to-2L	
25-26/08/73	914/6	ADAC-Weser-Bergpreis Höxter, Bielefeld		Eichler	1st Prod GT over 1600	
25-26/08/73	914/6	ADAC-Weser-Bergpreis Höxter, Bielefeld		Schimpf	1st Special GT over 1600	Jägermeister RT
01-02/09/73	914/6	Int ADAC-Bergrennen Happurg		Egerland	1st Prod & Special GT up-to-2L	
01-02/09/73	914/6	Int ADAC-Bergrennen Happurg		Weber	3rd Prod & Special GT up-to-2L	Scud Lindau, Bodensee
22-23/09/73	914/6	Int ADAC-Bergpreis Schwäbisch Alb-Neuffen		Schütz	3rd Prod & Special GT up-to-2L	Autohaus Max Moritz
22-23/09/73	914/6	Int ADAC-Bergpreis Schwäbisch Alb-Neuffen		Weber	4th Prod & Special GT up-to-2L	Scud Lindau, Bodensee
22-23/09/73	914/6	Int ADAC-Bergpreis Schwäbisch Alb-Neuffen		Kirschner	5th Prod & Special GT up-to-2L	SFC Württ, Gerlingen

Race records Europe – North America – rallying – hillclimbs

Date	Car	Event	#	Driver	Result (podium positions in bold)	Entrant
13-14/10/73	914/6	Trierer AvD/RTT-Bergrennen		Schimpf	1st Prod & Special GT up-to-2L	Jägermeister RT
13-14/10/73	914/6	Trierer AvD/RTT-Bergrennen		Bisenius	2nd Prod & Special GT up to2L	
27-28/04/74	914/6	Heilbronner ADAC-Bergpreis		Egerland	1st Prod & Special GT up-to-2L	
27-28/04/74	914/6	Heilbronner ADAC-Bergpreis		Weber	3rd Prod & Special GT up-to-2L	Scud Lindau, Bodensee
11-12/05/74	914/6	Int ADAC-Wasgau-Bergpreis – Wasgau-Bergprüfung		Weber	3rd Prod & Special GT unlimited	Scud Lindau, Bodensee
02-03/06/74	914/6	Wolsfelder AvD/EMSC-Bergrennen		Weber	3rd Prod & Special GT over 1300	Scud Lindau, Bodensee
02-03/06/74	914/6	Wolsfelder AvD/EMSC-Bergrennen		Bisenius	5th Prod & Special GT over 1300	
08-09/06/74	914/6	ADAC-Bergpreis Ulm		Weber	2nd Special GT over-2L	Scud Lindau, Bodensee
08-09/06/74	914/6	Int ADAC-Bergrennen Rotenburg/Fulda		Münzer	4th Prod & Special GT over 1600	
13/06/74	914/6	ADAC-Edelstein-Bergrennen, Idar-Oberstein		Weber	2nd Prod & Special GT up-to-2L	Scud Lindau, Bodensee
15-16/06/74	914/6	Int ADAC-Jura-Bergrennen Neumarkt		Weber	3rd Prod & Special GT up-to-2L	Scud Lindau, Bodensee
23/06/74	914/6	ADAC-Rusel-Bergrennen Deggendorf		Weber	1st Special GT up-to-2L	Scud Lindau, Bodensee
21/07/74	914/6	ADAC-Ellerberg-Rennen, Bamberg		Weber	1st Prod & Special GT over 1600	Scud Lindau, Bodensee
03-04/08/74	914/6	Int Osnabrücker ADAC-Bergpreis		Conrad	3rd Prod & Special GT over 1600	
10-11/08/74	914/6	Int ADAC-Eurohill-Bergrennen "um den KAMA-Preis", Nürnburg		Weber	3rd Prod & Special GT over 1600	
10-11/08/74	914/6	Int ADAC-Eurohill-Bergrennen "um den KAMA-Preis", Nürnburg		Koch	5th Prod & Special GT over 1600	
31/08-01/09/74	914/6	Int ADAC-Weser-Bergpreis Höxter, Bielefeld		Bohnhorst	4th Special GT over 1600	Jägermeister RT
07-08/09/74	914/6	ADAC-Augusta-Bergrennen, Augsburg		Weber	1st Special GT up-to-2L	Scud Lindau, Bodensee
21-22/09/74	914/6	Int ADAC-Bergpreis Schwäb Alb-Neuffen		Siegle	2nd Special GT over-2L	
21-22/09/74	914/6	Int ADAC-Bergpreis Schwäb Alb-Neuffen		Schütz	3rd Special GT over-2L	Autohaus Max Moritz
21-22/09/74	914/6	Int ADAC-Bergpreis Schwäb Alb-Neuffen		Laub	4th Special GT over-2L	Autohaus Max Moritz
21-22/09/74	914/6	Int ADAC-Bergpreis Schwäb Alb-Neuffen		Weber	5th Special GT over-2L	Scud Lindau, Bodensee
29/09/74	914/6	ADAC Auerberg-Bergrennen, Kaufbeuren		Weber	1st Prod & Special GT up-to-2L	Scud Lindau, Bodensee
05-06/10/74	914/6	Int ADAC-Sauerland-Bergpreis, Gevelinghausen		Lüttecke	4th Prod & Special GT up-to-2L	
15-16/03/75	914/6	ADAC-Rheingold-Bergrennen, Simmern		Färber	2nd Gr 4 unlimited	
19-20/04/75	914/6	Int DMV-Krähbergrennen "um den Veith-Pirelli-Preis"		Weber	4th Gr 3-4 up-to-2L	
26-27/04/75	VW 914/4	ADAC-Bergrennen Teutoburger Wald, Detmold		Koch	1st Gr 3 up-to-2L	
26-27/04/75	914/6	Hilbronner ADAC-Bergpreis		Egerland	3rd Gr 4 up-to-2L	
03-04/05/75	914/6	AvD/HMSC-Taunus-Bergprüfung Lorch		Weber	1st Gr 3-4 up-to-2L	Scud Lindau, Bodensee
18-19/05/75	914/6	Wolsfelder AvD/EMSC-Bergrennen		Bisenius	2nd Gr 3-4 over 1600	
23-24/05/75	914/6	ADAC-Wallberg-Rennen, Rottach-Egern		Weber	2nd Gr 3-4 up-to-2L	Scud Lindau, Bodensee
25/05/75	914/6	ADAC-Bergrennen Nürburgring "Preis der Stadt Wuppertal"		Färber	3rd Gr 3-4 up-to-2L	
29/05/75	914/6	ADAC-Edelstein-Bergrennen Idar-Oberstein		Siegle	1st Gr 4 up-to-2L	
29/05/75	914/6	ADAC-Edelstein-Bergrennen Idar-Oberstein		Färber	3rd Gr 4 up-to-2L	
14-15/06/75	914/6	Int ADAC Wasgau-Bergpreis, Wasgau-Bergprüfung		Weber	2nd Gr 4 up-to-2L	Scud Lindau, Bodensee
05-06/07/75	914/6	AvD/ATCW-Bergpreis der Oberpfalz, Weiden		Weber	1st Gr 3-4 up to and over-2L	Scud Lindau, Bodensee
26-27/07/75	914/6	Int ADAC-Bayerwald-Bergrennen, Rötz		Weber	2nd Gr 3-4 up-to-2L	Scud Lindau, Bodensee
27/07/75	914/6	DMV-Risselberg-Bergrennen, Niederstadtfeld		Bisenius	4th Gr 3-4 up to 2500	
16-17/08/75	914/6	Int ADAC-Eurohill-Bergrennen "Um den KAMA-Preis", Nürnburg		Weber	2nd Gr 3-4 up to and over 1600	Scud Lindau, Bodensee
16-17/08/75	914/6	Int ADAC-Eurohill-Bergrennen "Um den KAMA-Preis", Nürnburg		"Klaus"	3rd Gr 3-4 up to and over 1600	VSA Munich
23-24/08/75	914/6	AvD/MSCR-Hauenstein-Bergrennen Bad Neustadt		Weber	3rd Gr 3-4 up to 1600	Scud Lindau, Bodensee
23-24/08/75	914/6	ADAC-Augusta-Bergrennen Augsburg		"Klaus"	1st Gr 4 up-to-2L	VSA Munich

Porsche The Racing 914s

Date	Car	Event	#	Driver	Result (podium positions in bold)	Entrant
30-31/08/75	914/6	Int ADAC-Bergrennen Happurg		Weber	2nd Gr 3-4 up to and over-2L	Scud Lindau, Bodensee
30-31/08/75	914/6	Int ADAC-Bergrennen Happurg		"Klaus"	4th Gr 3-4 up to and over-2L	VSA Munich
07/09/75	914/6	Int ADAC-Ratisbona-Bergrennen, Kelheim		Weber	1st Gr 3-4 up-to-2L	Scud Lindau, Bodensee
07/09/75	914/6	Int ADAC-Ratisbona-Bergrennen, Kelheim		Koch	4th Gr 3-4 up-to-2L	
13-14/09/75	914/6	Amberger AvD/NAVC-Bergpreis		Weber	1st Gr 3-4 up-to-2L	Scud Lindau, Bodensee
20-21/09/75	914/6	Int ADAC-Bergpreis Schwäb Alb-Neuffen		Weber	1st Gr 3-4 up-to-2L	Scud Lindau, Bodensee
20-21/09/75	914/6	Int ADAC-Bergpreis Schwäb Alb-Neuffen		Siegle	4th Gr 3-4 up-to-2L	
20-21/09/75	VW 914/4	Int ADAC-Bergpreis Schwäb Alb-Neuffen		Schütz	6th Gr 3-4 up-to-2L	Autohaus Max Moritz
17-18/04/76	914/6	Dürener ADAC-Bergrennen Vossenack		Agosti	1st Gr 2 & 5 Nat up-to-2L	Bergischer MC, Wuppertal
17-18/04/76	914/6	Dürener ADAC-Bergrennen Vossenack		Hebben	1st Gr 4 over 1600	Valvoline Deutschland
24-25/04/76	914/6	ADAC-Bruckberg-Bergrennen Marktl/In		"Klaus"	3rd Gr 5 Int over-2L	VSA Munich
15-16/05/76	914/6	ADAC-Schwanbergrennen		"Klaus"	2nd Gr 5 Int over-2L	VSA Munich
22/05/76	914/6	ADAC-Pokal-Bergrennen "um den Bergischen Schmied"		Agosti	3rd Gr 2 and 5 nat up-to-2L	Bergischer MC, Wuppertal
06-07/06/76	914/6	Int Wolsfelder AvD/EMSC-Bergrennen		Hebben	4th Gr 2, 4 & 5 Nat up-to-2L	Valvoline Deutschland
06-07/06/76	914/6	Int Wolsfelder AvD/EMSC-Bergrennen		Bisenius	4th Gr 2, 4 & 5 Nat over2L	
13/06/76	914/6	Int ADAC-Bergrennen Rotenburg/Fulda		Münzer	6th Gr 3 up to and over-2L	
13/06/76	VW 914/4	ADAC-Rusel-Bergrennen, Deggendorf		Möller	3rd Gr 3 up-to-2L	
13/06/76	914/6	ADAC-Rusel-Bergrennen, Deggendorf		"Klaus"	2nd Gr 5 Int over-2L	VSA Munich
13/06/76	914/6	ADAC-Weseler-Rhein-Lippe-Bergpreis		Agosti	4th Gr 2, 4 & 5 Nat up-to-2L	Bergischer MC, Wuppertal
19-20/06/76	914/6	ADAC-Donnersbergpreis		Weber	3rd Gr 2, 4 & 5 Nat up-to-2L	Scud Lindau, Bodensee
10-11/07/76	914/6	DMV/PMC-Bergrennen Aachen		Hebben	4th Gr 2, 4 & 5 Nat up-to-2L	Valvoline Deutschland
10-11/07/76	914/6	DMV/PMC-Bergrennen Aachen		Agosti	5th Gr 2, 4 & 5 Nat up-to-2L	Bergischer MC, Wuppertal
17-18/07/76	914/6	ADAC-Teufelskopf-Bergrennen		Weber	2nd Gr 2, 4 & 5 Nat up-to-2L	
25/07/76	914/6	DMV-Risselberg-Rennen		Hebben	1st Gr 3-4 over 1600	Valvoline Deutschland
21-22/08/76	914/6	AvD/MSCR-Hauenstein-Bergrennen		Stürtz	3rd Gr C: Gr 2, 4 & 5 Nat over-2L	VSA Munich
28-29/08/76	914/6	Int ADAC-Weser-Bergpreis Höxter		Agosti	2nd Gr 5 Int up-to-2L	Bergischer MC, Wuppertal
05/09/76	914/6	ADAC-Radschläger-Bergpreis, Düsseldorf		Agosti	5th Gr 2, 4 & 5 Nat up-to-2L	Bergischer MC, Wuppertal
05/09/76	914/6	Int ADAC-Bergrennen Happurg am See		"Klaus"	1st Gr 5 over-2L	
24-26/09/76	914/6	Int ADAC-Auerbergrennen		"Klaus"	3rd Gr 5 Int over-2L	VSA Munich
03/10/76	914/6	ADAC-Samerberg-Bergrennen		"Klaus"	3rd Gr 5 Int over-2L	VSA Munich
23/10/76	914/6	Wuppertaler ADAC-Bergpreis		Agosti	2nd Gr 2, 4 & 5 nat up to 1300	Bergischer MC, Wuppertal
11-12/06/77	914/6	Int ADAC-Bergpreis Berchtesgaden		"Klaus"	3rd Gr 5 up to 3L	VSA Munich
12/06/77	914/6	Hillclimb Berchtesgaden/Rossfeld	278	"Klaus"	3rd Gr 5	
27/08/77	914/6	Int ADAC-Ratisbona-Bergrennen		"Klaus"	1st Gr 5 over-2L	VSA Munich
24-25/09/77	914/6	Int ADAC-Auerbergrennen		"Klaus"	3rd Gr 5 over-2L	VSA Munich
01-02/10/77	914/6	Int ADAC-Samerberg-Bergrennen		"Klaus"	1st Gr 5 over-2L	VSA Munich

Also from Roy Smith and Veloce –

AMÉDÉE GORDINI
– a true racing legend

Roy Smith

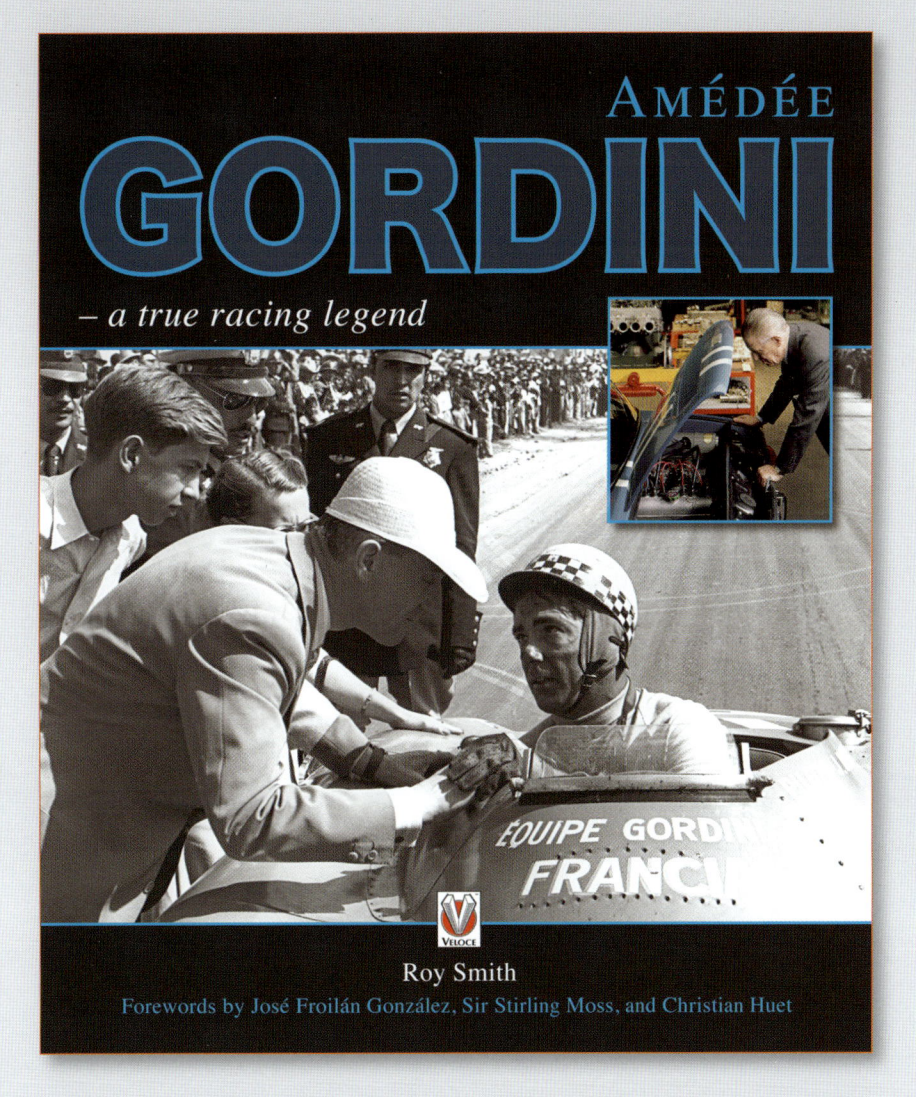

Forewords by José Froilán González, Sir Stirling Moss, and Christian Huet

This is the story of a man, a team, and their life and times, as well as a complete record of all their achievements and failures. It logs the financial and personal cost of racing in the prewar and postwar periods. It tells of how the mighty car company Renault became involved with them in the late 1950s, and how Amedee Gordini became known throughout the world as one of the greatest engine tuners of his time.

ISBN: 978-1-845843-17-5
Hardback • 25x20.7cm • 288 pages • 410 colour and b&w pictures
£55* UK/$89.95* USA

For more info on Veloce titles, visit our website at www.veloce.co.uk • email: info@veloce.co.uk • Tel: +44(0)1305 260068
* prices subject to change, p&p extra

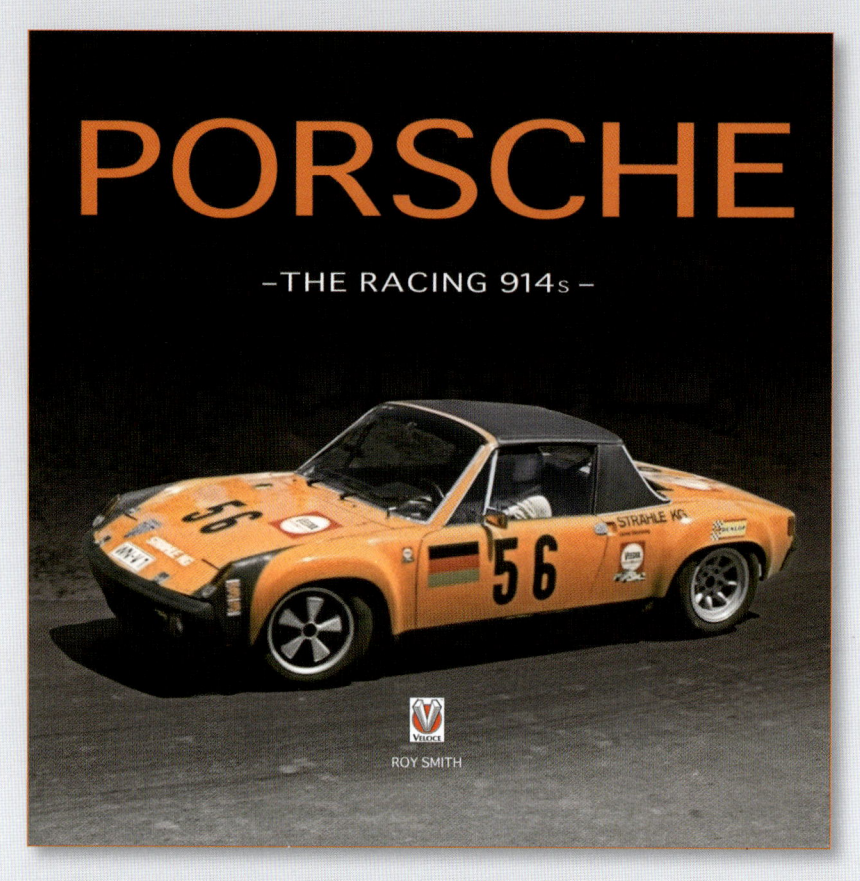

PORSCHE
– THE RACING 914s –

ROY SMITH

New paperback edition!

There are still those who see the Porsche 914 model as a 'funny little car,' compared to the immortal 911. Granted, in its day, professional rally drivers were not keen on the 914: they were nervous driving it at the limit. Yet the records show that 914s were driven to at least 41 class wins, and at least 71 positions on the other two steps of the podium in Regional, National, and International Rallies. Racing on the circuits of Europe, 914s came home first in their class, and even took overall victory many times. In the USA, in IMSA GTU championship, in nationals, and internationals, it was the same story – and that's not counting the multitude of SCCA regional races. The 914 first raced in 1970 ... the last? Who knows: even now they're still used in the USA's SCCA GT classes.

ISBN: 978-1-787119-34-5
Paperback • 22.5x22.5cm • 320 pages • 452 colour and b&w pictures
£50* UK/$80* USA

For more info on Veloce titles, visit our website at www.veloce.co.uk • email: info@veloce.co.uk • Tel: +44(0)1305 260068
* prices subject to change, p&p extra

Porsche 914 & 914-6
THE DEFINITIVE HISTORY OF THE ROAD & COMPETITION CARS

Brian Long

Back in print!
The Porsche 914's early history was blighted by political problems with VW's new management. However, by the end of production, almost 119,000 examples had been sold. This book records the full international story of the mid-engined 914, from concept through to the final production car.

ISBN: 978-1-845849-78-8
Paperback • 25x20.7cm • 208 pages • 610 colour and b&w pictures
£37.5* UK/$65* USA

For more info on Veloce titles, visit our website at www.veloce.co.uk • email: info@veloce.co.uk • Tel: +44(0)1305 260068
* prices subject to change, p&p extra

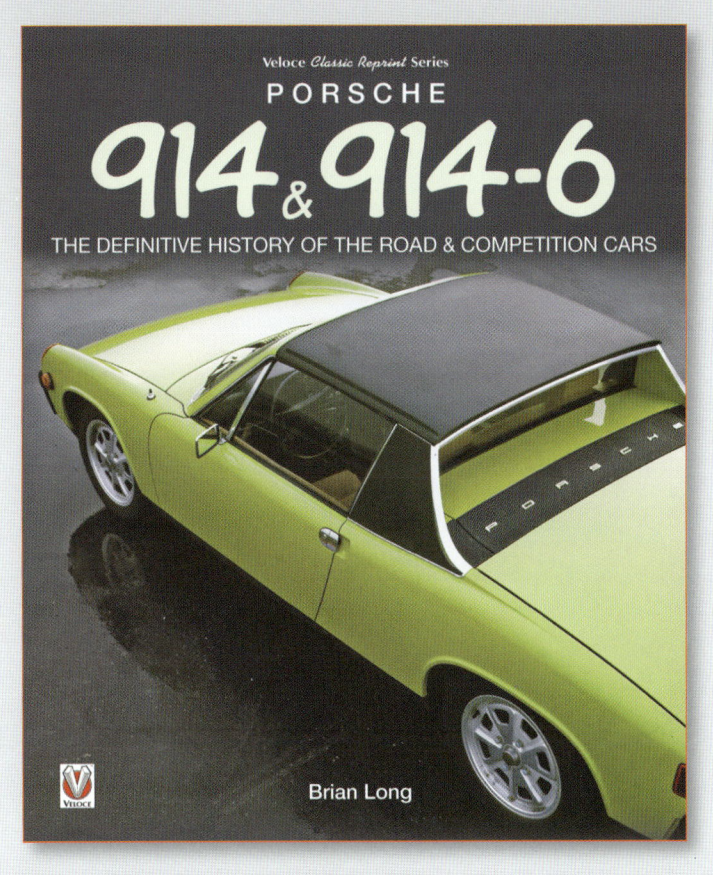

Also from Veloce –

The full history of Porsche's racing cars from 2006 onwards, this is the third book in the series, bringing the story to the end of 2023. Illustrated throughout with contemporary photography sourced from the factory, this book serves as the perfect record of Porsche's motorsport exploits from 2006 onwards. Written by an acknowledged Porsche expert, with the full co-operation of the factory.

ISBN: 978-1-787117-94-5
Hardback • 25x25cm • 256 pages • 475 pictures
£75*/$90* USA

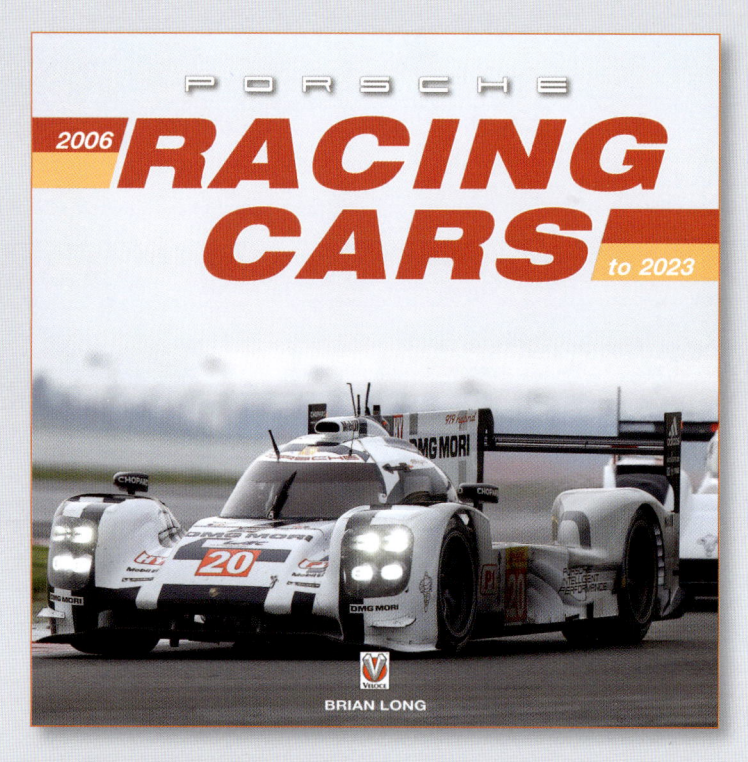

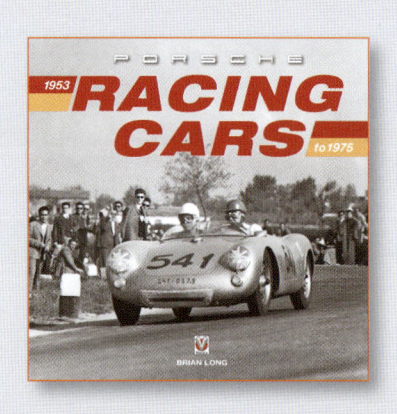

Follows Porsche's year-by-year progress in top flight racing, this volume starts with the story of the giant-killing 550 Spyders of 1953 vintage, and takes the reader, car-by-car, through all of the subsequent racing models.

ISBN: 978-1-787111-57-8
eBook • Flowing layout • 441 pictures • Base price £14.99

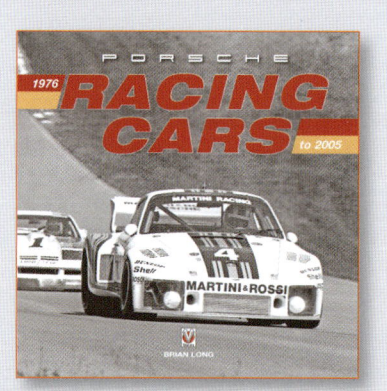

Beginning with the story of the pure racers of 1976 vintage, this volume takes the reader, car-by-car, through all of the subsequent racing models, including the glorious 956 and 962, up to 2005.

ISBN: 978-1-787115-08-8
eBook • Flowing layout • 629 pictures • Base price £29.99

For more info on Veloce titles, visit our website at www.veloce.co.uk • email: info@veloce.co.uk • Tel: +44(0)1305 260068
* prices subject to change, p&p extra

Index

Aase, Denis 235, 259, 267
Altmann 204
Andersson, Åke 59, 83, 90, 92, 143, 182, 187, 191, 196, 197, 202
Andersson, Ove 203, 204
ANDIAL 263, 264
Andretti, Mario 222
Andruet, Jean-Claude 203, 205
Attwood, Richard 55, 61, 73, 77
Austrian Alpenfahrt Rally 183
Austro-Daimler 13
Auto Union 15, 31

Bailey, Jim 235
Baker, Wayne 265, 267-271, 273
Ballot-Léna, Claude 73, 74, 83, 87, 90, 97, 191
Barret, Robert 183
Barth, Jürgen 41, 47, 61, 83, 158, 159, 196, 214, 215
Bauer, Walter 165
Behr, Stephen 220
Bell, Derek 114, 125, 172
Benz, K 13
Bishop, John 225, 248
Bonhorst, Dieter 161, 163, 170, 176
Bosch 44, 45, 182-184, 188
Bott, Helmut 55, 113, 140, 141, 178, 214
Bozzani 241, 242
Bratenstein, Rainer 41, 56, 61, 82, 143, 178-180
Brock, Peter 217
Broughton, Harold 217, 248
Brumos 52, 61, 83, 101, 216, 228, 230, 238, 247
Bundy, Doc 251, 252, 271, 272
Bunker, Art 216-end
Bytzek, Harry 232, 233, 234, 237

Calvert, James 278
Canonica, Jean 161-163
Carrera Panamericana 27
Chasseuil, Guy 73, 74, 83, 90
Cheinisse, Jacques 188
Chenevière, Bernard 76, 111, 117
Christmann, Werner 68, 167, 170-172, 176, 177
Cisitalia 19
Clark, Jim 107, 156, 157
Col des Rates 166
Cook, Jim 235, 257, 259
Cortel, Alfredo 185, 206, 207, 211
Coupland, Ron 251-253, 259, 264, 265

Crayford Auto Developments 51

Daimler-Benz 31
Daytona 24 Hours 216
de Tomaso 31
Denu, Gerhard 65, 80
Deugra 144, 145
Dören, Edgar 156, 157, 159, 164, 166, 168, 170, 173-176
Dunlop 182, 193, 194, 198
Dusio, Pierre 19
Duval, Jacques 83, 225, 227-230, 236

Eason, Wayne 278
Ecclestone, Bernie 149, 152-154
Egerland, Gotthard 95, 158
Elan-Elf-Danube Rally 184
Elford, Vic 46, 61, 74, 81, 95, 111, 114, 115, 117, 158, 172, 198
Engel, Jochen 163, 165, 167
Escudería GES 166
Escudería Montjuich 96, 99, 185, 206
Escudería Orense 212, 213
Estoril 165

Fabri, Carlo 81, 161, 170, 174
Fernández, JM 95, 98, 99, 105, 106, 108, 109, 132, 137, 185-187, 190, 197, 198, 206-209, 211
Ferrari 31
Finch, Dave 271, 272, 274, 277
Fitzpatrick, John 156
Flegl, Helmut 36
Floridia, Armando 158
Forbes-Robinson, Elliott 217, 218, 221, 234
France, Bill 225, 228
Frankenberg, Richard von 26
Freiburg-Schauinsland 155
Frère, Paul 26
Fröhlich, K 19
Fuhrmann, Dr Ernst *throughout*

Ganley, Howden 155
Gargallo, Julio 100, 132, 166, 173, 207, 208, 209, 211, 212, 214
Gemar, JBM ('Crady') 166, 207, 214
Ghia 34
Giménez, Ruiz 211
Ginther, Richie 216-end

Glöckler, Helm 25
Glöckler, W 24-26, 31, 55
Godel, Horst 108, 121, 130, 133, 170
Götz, Rolf 65, 80
Greger, Sepp 65, 79, 80, 104
Gregg, Peter 61, 83, 100, 216, 218, 220, 222, 223, 225, 226, 228-232, 234-238, 240, 244, 245, 248
Gudladt 204
Gugelot 32

Hahn 67, 79, 81, 100, 116, 132
Haldi, Claude 111, 189, 190
Hansen, Leif 71, 96
Hanstein, Huschke von 24, 26, 56, 147, 159
Harrison, Rod 265
Haywood, Hurley 52, 220, 225, 226, 228, 230, 231, 234-237, 240, 244, 245, 247, 248
Hendrix 276
Hensler, Paul 35, 143
Herrmann, Hans 27, 45, 55, 73, 77
Hilburger, Werner 85
Hindson, Bob 216-end
Hirst, Major Ivan 28
Hitler, A 15, 17
Hockenheim Circuit 129
Hoffman, Max 24
Holbert, Al 220, 223, 238, 253, 254
Holbert, Bob 220, 223
Holpert Porsche 65, 68
Hopp, Ingo 79, 81
Hoppen, Jo 216, 223, 225
Hotchkis, John 220, 241, 251-253, 255, 257, 259, 262
Hruschka, Gustav 182, 183
Hulen, John 249-253, 260, 262-264

Jägermeister 159, 160-162, 176, 212
Janger, Günther 182, 183
Jenkinson, Denis 28
Johnson, Alan 218-220, 225, 237
Jones, Len 251-253, 255, 276
Jürgensen, Hans-Christian 134, 156, 157, 163, 165, 168, 176

Kaiser, Peter 67, 79, 81, 107, 232
Karmann Karosserie 29, 30, 31, 34, 35, 38, 39, 83
Karosseriebau Weinsberg 178
Kastner, Kas 217
KDF Wagen 18

Porsche The Racing 914s

Keyser, Michael 158, 159, 237, 244
Kilb, Dieter 164
Kinnunen, Leo 61, 68, 81, 155
Kinsbergen, Theo 160
Kirby, Robert 241, 251, 252, 255, 259, 262, 265, 266, 274, 275
Klauser, Hans 18
Klie, Heinrich 32
Koll, Bill 263, 265, 267, 269
Komenda, E 13, 17, 19
Konrad, Franz 71
Kremer 88, 89, 97, 105, 117, 121, 122, 134, 135, 226, 263
Krumm, Dieter 81, 102, 115, 116, 122, 123, 125-128
Krupp-Widia 193
Kussmaul, Roland 83, 91, 92, 95, 191, 202, 214

Lamborghini 31
Larrousse, Gérard 73, 83, 114, 115, 117, 174, 188, 190, 192, 197, 199-201
Le Mans 24 Hours 124
Ledwinka, Hans 13
Linge, Herbert 18, 19, 28, 36, 77, 78, 82 *throughout chapter 5*, 180
Lotus 31
Lotz, Kurt 35037, 39, 52
Ludvigsen, Karl 13, 18, 51

Maas, Walt 234, 244, 256-260, 262, 263
MAP 21, 23
Marathon de la Route 82, 83, 94, 100, 104
Matra 31
Max Moritz 63, 64, 67, 71, 80, 100-102, 116, 123, 124, 126, 127, 129, 134, 137, 159, 160, 162, 165, 171, 173, 174, 177, 226, 227
Maxted Page & Prill 154
McQueen, Steve 77, 78, 218
Meaney, Ralph 101, 220, 226-230, 232, 233, 237, 280
Merzario, Arturo 158, 169, 172
Mille Miglia 27, 28
Minter, Milt 217
Mitchell, Dwight 269
Mont Ventoux 155
Monte Carlo Rally 55, 56, 95, 104, 180, 181, 200, 201, 205
Monza 95, 112, 113, 152
Morgan, Richard 278
Moss, Stirling 28
Mugello 81
Müller, Herbert 120, 146, 147, 169, 170
Müller, Peter-Max 24
Muñiz, Daniel 240, 244, 248, 249

Näher, Walter 56, 61, 82
Neubauer, Alfred 28
Neureuther, Christian 163
Newman, Paul 222
Nicolas, Jean-Pierre 190
Noah, Kendal 216, 223
Nolte, Willi 68, 134, 156, 177
Nordhoff, Heinz 28, 29, 31, 32, 34
Norisring 131-133
NSU 15

Ollons-Villars hillclimb 134, 155
ONS (Oberste Nationale Sportkommission), 59, 118, 119, 143, 145, 148, 150, 152, 153

Opel 28

Porsche Panorama magazine *throughout*
Parish, Don 249, 250
Perón, President 19
Perramond, Jean-Claude 196, 197
Peterson, Ronnie 153
Pickering, Steve 279
Piëch, Dr Anton 19
Piëch, Ferdinand 49, 55, 83, 140, 178
Pininfarina 31
Polensky, Helmut 28
Porsche Club of America 217-end
Porsche Club Romand 115, 123, 126, 148, 162, 165
Porsche, Dr Ferdinand *throughout*
Porsche, F A ('Butzi') 32
Porsche, 'Ferry' *throughout*
Porsche+Audi 216-end
Posey, Sam 261, 262, 265

Quist, Gert 71, 79, 96, 115, 116, 122, 125-128, 159

Rabe, Karl 13, 17
RAC Rally 188
Rallycross 214
Ramelow, Hermann 25
Rebaque, Hector 228, 235, 238-240, 242-246
Recaro 151, 154
Redman, Brian 61, 68, 76, 97
Reimspiess, F 17
Renault 21, 31
Reutter 19, 30, 150
Reverter, Estanislao 208, 211-213
Rindt, Jochen 95
Rodríguez, Pedro 61, 68, 131
Rojas, Guillermo 228, 235, 238-240, 242-246
Rosenberger, Adolf 15
Rossfeld 155
Rumpler, Dr E 11, 13

Sage, John 115, 116, 123, 124, 126
SCCA (Sports Car Club of America), 216-end
Schimpf, Eckhard 121, 128, 159, 161-163, 212
Schindler, Carl Christian 182-184
Schmidt, Dieter 158
Schmücker, Toni 53
Schulp, Gustav 79
Schwarz, Günther 79, 80, 110
Scott, Jeff 268, 269
Sebring 55, 60, 216
Seiler, Ernst 79, 81, 95-98, 105, 111, 129, 131, 133, 135-137
Sestrieres 161
Sherry Rally 208, 213
Siffert, Jo 45, 61, 67, 68, 76, 97, 114, 125, 131
Simonis, Walter 58, 89, 116, 117, 121, 122, 159
Sixtant Racing 108
Sonauto 23, 73, 75, 96, 128, 191
Spa 112
Staudenmaier, Mr 40
Stazak, Glenn 280
Steckkönig, Günter 61, 67, 69, 83, 87, 88, 90, 96-98, 107, 108, 117, 118, 120, 121, 127-129, 132, 155, 178, 182
Steinemann, Rico 60, 83, 88, 187, 218
Stewart, Jackie 128, 150
Stoddard, Robert 81, 101, 109

Stone, David 190, 203
Storez 28
Strähler 67, 100, 116, 118, 122, 132, 137, 158
Stuck, Hans 15
Sunoco 227
Swope, Will 275

Targa Florio 60, 81, 112-114, 117, 157, 168, 170
Thérier, Jean-Luc 203
Thomas, John 235
Thomas, JP 183
Thorszelius, Bö 196, 197, 202
Thorszelius, Hans 197
Tour de Corse 60
Tour de France Auto 60, 96, 97
Tramont, Bernard 208
Tropfenwagen 11, 14, 15
Trübsbach 183, 184
Type 114 19, 21, 22
Type 356 19-21
Type 369 25
Type 502 25
Type 547 26
Type 550 26-29, 55
Type 64 21
Type 718 28, 29, 55
Type 901 28, 31
Type 904 28, 55
Type 906 28, 55
Type 907 55
Type 908 55
Type 911 28, 31
Type 912 31
Type 917 55
Type VW 411 31
Type VW 728 31

Unser, Al 222
Unser, Bobby 221, 222

Vaccarella, Nino 81, 117, 158
Veuillet, A 23
Vögelsang 24
Volkswagen *throughout*

Walb, W 16
Waldegård, Björn 58, 59, 61, 71, 83, 90, 154, 180-182, 191-194, 196, 197, 199-201, 204, 205
Ward, Roger 222
Watkins, Professor Sid 150, 153
Weinberger 183, 184
Weissach *throughout*
Werlin, J 17
Wessiak, Walter 182, 183
White, Dave 250
Williams, Jonathan 77, 78
Winters, Tom 265, 266
Woods, Jerry 263
Wyre, John (Gulf) 110, 112-114, 117, 131, 137, 220

Zbinden, Peter 121
Zitza, Harro 267, 274
Zolder 156
Zotz Garage 267, 273